Praise for the previous edition of

100 Best Cruise Vacations

"During my 15 years of covering the cruise industry, I have met no one more knowledgeable about the cruise ships and vacations at sea than Theodore W. Scull. His latest book, 100 Best Cruise Vacations, seems destined to be both the perfect companion for armchair travelers dreaming of a cruise and the ideal guidebook for active cruisers planning their next voyage. Ted's 'Top 100' include my favorite cruises, and likely will include yours, too."

—Charles Doherty
Managing Editor, Cruise Travel magazine

"From historic tall ships to river cruisers, Ted Scull tells you where to find the unique cruises that make lifelong memories. His research and presentation are first-rate."

—Steve Blount
Editorial Director, World Publications,
Caribbean Travel & Life

Help Us Keep This Guide Up to Date

Every effort has been made by the author and editors to make this guide as accurate and useful as possible. However, many things can change after a guide is published— phone numbers change, itineraries vary, ships come under new management, etc.

We would love to hear from you concerning your experiences with this guide and how you feel it could be made better and be kept up to date. While we may not be able to respond to all comments and suggestions, we'll take them to heart and we'll also make certain to share them with the author. Please send your comments and suggestions to the following address:

The Globe Pequot Press
Reader Response/Editorial Department
P.O. Box 480
Guilford, CT 06437

Or you may e-mail us at:

editorial@globe-pequot.com

Thanks for your input, and happy travels!

100 BEST CRUISE VACATIONS

SECOND EDITION

The Top Cruises
throughout the World for
All Interests and Budgets

THEODORE W. SCULL

The
Globe
Pequot
Press

GUILFORD, CONNECTICUT

Cover design: Saralyn D'Amato
Cover photos: Gary Hotheimer/Index Stock Imagery; Thomas del Amo
Text design: Nancy Freeborn
Page layout: Deborsh Nicolais

Library of Congress Cataloging-in-Publication Data

Scull, Theodore W., 1941-
    100 best cruise vacations : the top cruises throughout the world for all interests and budgets / Theodore W. Scull.-- 2nd ed.
        p. cm. — (100 best resorts series)
    ISBN 0-7627-0981-2
        1. Ocean travel--Guidebooks. 2. Cruise ships--Guidebooks. I. Title: One hundred best cruise vacations. II. Title.

G550 .S38 2001
910'.2'02--dc21   2001033986

Printed in Korea
Second Edition/First Printing

The schedules and rates listed in this guidebook were confirmed at press time. We recommend, however, that you call before traveling to obtain current information.

To my dear wife, Suellyn,
who has also taken a cotton to cruising.

—TWS

AUTHOR'S THANKS

This book is now in its second edition, and revising, deleting, and adding to the entries was a daunting, if highly pleasurable task, but one that could not have been accomplished without the help of friends and fellow cruisers who suggested and wrote up their favorite experiences.

Ben Lyons, an officer in the U.S. merchant marine, wrote six chapters, four of which are new to the book, for the *Queen Elizabeth 2* transatlantic, *Regal Empress, Disney Wonder, Voyager of the Seas, Crown Odyssey,* and *Olympia Voyager.* We shared several of these trips and some others, including the *Marco Polo* along the west coast of South America.

David Price, a Glaswegian I encountered aboard the five-masted *Royal Clipper,* contributed the transatlantic portion after I disembarked in Malaga. Art Ferguson, whom I met aboard the old *Oriana,* wrote up the chapter on cruising to Antarctica, the Falklands, and South Georgia aboard the *Caledonian Star* (now *Endeavour*). Brad Hatry, a fellow New Yorker and ship aficionado, supplied the chapter on the *Valtur Prima* cruise to Havana, and Dick Faber gave me some additional insights into this legal way to travel to Cuba. Esty Foster, a former boss, supplied his Nile cruise on *Hapi I,* and it appealed to me so much that my wife, Suellyn, and I made the same cruise a year later. Vincent Messina, a friend since 1965, has now taken two more world cruise segments on the *Rotterdam VI.* Bill Mayes, European ferry traveler and generous B&B provider in England, helped update the chapter on sailing between Copenhagen and Oslo aboard the *Crown of Scandinavia.*

Cruise writer Heidi Sarna, a great buddy, again contributed invaluable help from her numerous shipboard experiences and equally important, a timely sense of humor when needed via e-mail between the East Side and West Side of Manhattan.

My brother Sandy and I left our wives at home to cruise the Columbia and Snake Rivers aboard the *Columbia Queen.* Finally, my dear wife, Suellyn, accompanied me on about half these cruises and larked out on her own aboard the *Legend of the Seas* to visit the old country, Australia. In addition, she has given me great moral support over the months of rewriting. Lastly, thanks to Jan Cronan at The Globe Pequot Press for editing this second edition.

CONTENTS

ATLANTIC OCEAN

BERMUDA

TRANSATLANTIC CROSSINGS

THE BAHAMAS AND CARIBBEAN ISLANDS

THE BAHAMAS

CARIBBEAN ISLANDS

LATIN AMERICA

PACIFIC OCEAN

EUROPE

AFRICA, THE MIDDLE EAST, AND THE INDIAN OCEAN

AFRICA

THE MIDDLE EAST

THE INDIAN OCEAN

SOUTHEAST ASIA AND THE FAR EAST

SOUTHEAST ASIA

THE FAR EAST

POLAR REGIONS

ARCTIC

INTRODUCTION

The popularity of cruise vacations has increased more than 300 percent in the last ten years. By the end of 2000, seven million Americans—up from a little more than five million in 1998—had embarked. Cruises are increasingly seen as affordable, great fun, romantic, and a relaxing, hassle-free way to visit many parts of the world. To both meet and fuel the demand for cruise vacations, more than three dozen large cruise liners are on order for completion between 2002 and 2004, joining the several hundred oceangoing ships that currently sail the high seas. Additional fleets of coastal and inland-waterway vessels, with many more under construction, explore inshore waters, rivers, and canals.

A traveler's cruising options have become mind-boggling, with so many different lines and respective reputations. The multitudinous decisions to be made include the specific type of cruise, itinerary, optimum ship size, whether it's a brand-new one or a classic liner, how much to spend on a cabin (and if to pay extra for a private veranda), the best time to go, and the relative personal importance attached to food, service, entertainment, and activities. Who are the other passengers going to be, mostly Americans? Or will there be persons of several nationalities aboard? What's the age range? And is this a cruise for children?

100 Best Cruise Vacations will help sort out the options by selecting the top ships, taking into account a fair balance between a ship's particular ambience, standards, and itineraries. Some of my choices will be obvious and others may seem quirky or head scratchers.

Oceangoing ships come in sizes from 137,000 gross tons down to a little more than 2,000 tons, with passenger lists from less than one hundred to more than three thousand. The very largest may qualify as destinations themselves, where the itinerary is secondary to the rich shipboard experience, whereas others may offer a new port every day. Some people like lots of time at sea, so perhaps a voyage with ports spaced out every few days or a transocean crossing will fill the bill.

Enrichment cruises accompanied by top lecturers in a variety of fields may take in the great sites of the ancient world, while expedition-style voyages explore remote regions with a team of naturalists to lead passengers ashore. Some of the latter take you to places that may be hard, even impossible, to get to any other way, such as remote sections of Australia's Great Barrier Reef, the Galápagos Islands, Chilean fjords, Cuba, the Canadian Arctic, and the white continent of Antarctica. Voyaging under sail through the Greek islands and along the Turkish coast or among the Caribbean's Leeward and Windward Islands may seem a romantic concept, and terrific choices are happily expanding. If you like water sports, some ships fold out their own marinas, with all sorts of boating, snorkeling, and diving equipment available for use.

To celebrate Americana, listen to great jazz and big-band sounds, and dine on Southern and Cajun cuisine, board a stern-wheeler for a river cruise in the antebellum South, along the Upper Mississippi, or the Ohio up past Cincinnati. European river journeys ply the Rhine, Moselle, and Danube to visit timeless medieval towns, hunting castles, and great Romanesque and Gothic cathedrals; and exotic inland trips penetrate deep into the Amazon Basin or into the heart of China. The pokiest cruises are aboard luxury barges, where the distance covered takes second place to savoring the passing countryside, biking into a nearby village, and sharing wonderful food and wines with a passenger complement of two dozen or fewer.

A cruise can be as short as an overnight crossing between the Scandinavian capitals, but more typically lasts a week to ten days. Vacationers with time and money can sail for several weeks around the bottom of South America or along the African coast, or go all the way, taking three to four months to circumnavigate the globe. Anyone remotely interested in taking a cruise vacation, or looking for something different, will find several that should appeal.

In this book, the cruise vacations are grouped into logical geographical regions beginning in North America and then casting a wider net overseas.

Defining the Best

What is terrific to one person may not appeal to someone else, and I am sure there will be lots of agreement and disagreement about the ships and the cruise itineraries I have chosen. Right up front, each cruise is entirely my own selection. After spending three and one half years at sea since I made my first crossing to Europe as a teenager aboard the dear-departed French Line, I have come to thrive on the increasing diversity of available cruise experiences. I can be equally happy crossing the Atlantic, cruising around Britain, navigating Alaska's Inside Passage, exploring the Upper Amazon, or transiting the Panama Canal. For me the cover has long since blown off such clichés that cruises attract only old people, are nonstop drinking parties, or that they are stuffy, regimented, dull, crowded, and claustrophobic.

The best cruise vacation might imply the most expensive, and although some of the highest-rated boutique ships can cost upward of $500 to $1,000 a day per person, this need not be the case at all, because there are excellent cruises at a third of that price and great values for even less. You will find itineraries at all fare levels.

The best cruises may involve the tangible and intangible features of a particular ship. The biggest ships on the high seas have always had a following, and I have picked those that truly excel in design and layout, have a pleasing or delightfully offbeat decor, provide lots of things to do aboard all day and well into the night, and have sound reputations for serving, feeding, and handling a small city of passengers and crew. If a midsize ship is more appealing, I have chosen these on the same but scaled-down basis. Remember, this is a selective guide, not inclusive of every best cruise vacation on the high seas, so if your favorite is not listed here, you already know about it.

Many of the finest ships, in terms of food and service, have passenger capacities that range from one hundred to about four hundred, and some cruisers choose the ship first, then one of several itineraries, and return again and again to the same ship or sistership.

The itinerary may be paramount. For the popular Panama Canal cruise, I offer several choices with different Caribbean and Pacific ports and a variety of onboard lifestyles and prices. Alaska and the Mediterranean also offer several alternatives.

Not all cruises should stand alone as the total travel experience, so for the Yangzte, the Inside Passage of Alaska, and others, I have suggested land extensions.

I happen to be partial to older liners, and, in some cases, knowledgeable cruisers will wonder why I have included an over-the-hill ship, but she may offer something unique, giving readers the chance to sample what sea travel used to be like, before it's too late.

The Itinerary

Some Caribbean ships may cruise year-round to the same set of ports, whereas others move seasonally to the Mediterranean or Alaska from late spring to early fall. I might suggest a ship for one itinerary and then make reference to another region where the same ship or a fleet mate cruises. Several top ships may get more than one full entry, as they cruise in many different parts of the world during one calendar year. A few ships may not repeat itineraries from one year to the next, and a set of ports for one Mediterranean or South American cruise might change the following year. While this muddies the waters, if the ship seems attractive to you, there will likely be some draw for a different itinerary. Cruise lines typically announce their schedules a year in advance, but then a ship gets sold or transferred elsewhere and another ship comes on line to take its place. Cruising is always in a state of flux, so please don't expect to be able to exactly duplicate every cruise vacation listed here. Rather use this book, literally, as a guide to what's out there—then get the latest news from your travel agent, the Internet, or the cruise line.

Specialized destinations, such as the Galápagos and the Yangzte, sometimes include two ships making more or less the same cruise, and although their relative merits will be treated separately, the itineraries will be combined to save reading unnecessary repetition.

Every chapter will have a reference section that lists the following useful information:

Address/Phone: This listing includes the line's name and address, phone numbers, fax number, e-mail addresses, and Web sites, when available. Some lines do not take direct bookings because they sell cabins only through travel agents or tour companies, so the phone numbers may be for information and brochures only. Cruise-line Web sites vary from excellent to you-wonder-why-they-bother, because the information is so thin or out of date.

The Ship: The vital statistics are the year of build, rebuilding, and previous names, if any; gross tonnage and length to give an indication of size; and draft (how deep in the water the ship sits), with a larger figure generally indicating more stability in heavy seas when matched with tonnage. Coastal ships and riverboats naturally have shallow drafts, so an exact figure is not always important, but it is likely to be 8 feet or less.

Passengers: This figure is usually for double occupancy, two to a cabin, whereas the maximum capacity may be higher as some cabins have third and fourth beds, perhaps a sofa bed or upper foldaway berths. The average age and nationality of one's fellow passengers are key points of information. Generally, the shorter the cruise, the younger the passenger, and average age increases markedly when the cruise begins to exceed a week. You can enrich the experience by sailing with Europeans or South Americans, or you may prefer to keep it simple and travel with passengers from your own country.

Dress: As most people increasingly seem to balk at getting dressed up, it is important to note what a line suggests for a particular evening, hoping that most passengers will comply to maintain the ambience. A little dressing up is part of the cruise experience for special occasions. I have used male evening dress codes, as they tend to be less understood and they can act also as a guide for women. "Formal" here means a tuxedo, dinner jacket, or a dark suit for men; "informal" means jacket with or without a tie; and "casual" means collared shirt and long pants. Daytime wear is even more casual. For women formal would be a gown or cocktail dress; informal, a dress or pants suit; and casual, a skirt or pants. You will not find me using terms such as "casually elegant" and telling people no T-shirts or tank tops in the dining room. If this is your style when the suggested dress at dinner is otherwise, you're on your own.

Officers/Crew: Some ships trade on the nationality of their officers and crew, so here we find out who's in charge and who does the serving.

Cabins: In addition to the accommodation information in the text, the number of cabins is listed, plus the number that are outside (with portholes or windows) and the availability of verandas, those private cabin balconies that let you step outside, found on many of the newer and largest ships. Few ships have dedicated single cabins, but if they do, this information is listed.

Fare: The $ signs are designed to give approximations for comparative purposes and are cruise brochure rates per person, double occupancy, per day for a standard outside cabin: $ = $100–150; $$ = $150–250; $$$ = $250–400; $$$$ = $400–$600; $$$$$ = $600 upward.

Cruise-line fares are all over the map, even with the same ship on different itineraries. It's really no different from the yield management of the airlines. An empty cabin is lost revenue not only for its fare, but also for what passengers will spend for shore excursions, drinks, shopping, gambling, spa treatments, and so on. Except for some small expedition ships and riverboats, the brochure rate is usually only the

starting point for determining what you will ultimately pay. Nearly all lines have early booking discounts and may offer deals for departures selling poorly, which could occur months out or announced just before sailing. There are many ways to find the best-value fare, and it may be through a travel agent, a cruise-only specialist, a newspaper ad, the Internet, or directly from the line.

What's included: The $ to $$$$$ is based on what's normally included. A separate listing for what's not included specifies the extras. Most fares are cruise only, but increasingly the port charges are bundled into the fare. When they appear as a separate line item, they may add $100 to $200 to a typical seven-day cruise. Airfare to and from the ship is usually not included, but the line may have special add-on rates that are less than you can get on your own. Remember, if the line books the air travel, they can route you any way they want, but they are more likely to help you catch up to the ship if the flights are delayed or cancelled than if you have made your own arrangements, including the use of frequent-flyer mileage. Some expedition cruises include shore excursions in the cruise fare, but most lines do not. A few upscale lines offer complimentary wine with meals, and fewer still include drinks and stocked minibars. For most lines tipping is your responsibility, but they will also almost always tell you what's expected, usually about $10 to $13 per day per person. The bottom line is to see what's included and what's not—the $ to $$$$$ may be skewed upward for a few lines, because so much is already built into the fare.

Highlights: A summary of what makes this ship and/or cruise worth writing home about.

Other itineraries: If you like what you read but want to take a particular ship somewhere else, you will find references to other itineraries.

Ships Have Personalities

Some ships come from the same mold, but as they mature, they begin to show distinctive characteristics and differences from those of their fleet mates. Hundreds of passengers and crew help make a ship a living, breathing, seagoing community. A few ships have souls, and this special aspect will usually come across whether you are looking for it or not. All ships have personalities, and the best ones are happy ships, important not only to you as a paying passenger but also to the officers and crew who live aboard for months on end. Their time onboard may eventually add up to years, more than they spend ashore.

I hope you find your ship. I have, and it is present in these pages in great variety.

NORTH AMERICA

CUNARD LINE'S *QUEEN ELIZABETH 2*
A Canada and New England Getaway

The venerable Cunard Line has an impressively long history dating back to 1840, and today the company is part of the Carnival Corporation, the world's largest and most successful cruise company. The *Queen Elizabeth 2*, or simply the *QE2*, has entered her fourth decade of cruise service. She underwent a major refit of virtually all the soft furnishings at the end of 1999 and seems to get better with age.

The cabin category determines the restaurant, with the grills reserved for passengers in suites and deluxe staterooms. The top-of-the-line Queen's Grill offers table-side cooking and carving as well as an exclusive bar for use by all three grill rooms. Many veteran passengers prefer the more intimate one-hundred-seat Princess Grill and the newer, nearly identical Britannia Grill. The food in the grills is as good as its gets on the high seas. The one-sitting, high-ceiling Caronia restaurant has been attractively redecorated into an English-style hotel dining room, and the Mauretania restaurant, for the lowest priced cabins, offers two sittings. The Lido, with its own serving galley, is an informal spot for breakfast, luncheon, dinner, and late-night buffets.

The Grand Lounge is a sophisticated room for entertainment, whereas the Queen's Room hosts a formal afternoon tea and after-dinner dancing, including dance hosts. Real-ale and international beer drinkers will enjoy the Golden Lion Pub. The late-night crowd, including officers and staff, is drawn to the Yacht Club, where a band and pianist perform before and after dinner. The nautically themed Chart Room sees a harpist or pianist using the piano that at one time resided on the *Queen Mary*.

The two-level cinema qualifies as one of the largest afloat, and in addition to screening films, it offers excellent lectures by experts on subjects ranging from finance to filmmaking. The professionally staffed, two-room library is a wonder, offering maritime books, videos and posters for sale, and a quiet room for reading. The state-of-the-art computer education center offers daily classes and lots of free time to practice. In addition, the shopping arcade includes big-name boutiques and a Cunard signature store.

Deep down in the hull, the spa boasts some of the most elaborate fitness facilities afloat, including a room-size hot tub. Pools are inside and out, the latter with two whirlpools. Boat Deck is populated by joggers in the early hours and by walkers the rest of the day.

Choosing the right stateroom and corresponding restaurant is daunting. Cabins come in dozens of configurations, from small inside cabins with upper and lower berths to suites with balconies and every imaginable amenity. The palatial, paneled original cabins boast elliptical windows, walk-in closets, bars, refriger-

If sailing to Europe aboard this great liner is not your cup of tea, then consider the QE2's six-night cruise that embarks in Quebec City and calls at Halifax, Bar Harbor, Boston, and Newport, disembarking in New York. Regardless of what cabin level you book, you get the virtual run of the ship and all its activities and entertainment.

ators, and large baths with tubs. Cabins that fetch the lowest fares have been finally refurbished and offer a good value considering the ship is otherwise wide open, apart from the Queen's Grill Lounge. No other vessel can quite match the *QE2's* distinctive high-quality feel.

The Itinerary

The *Queen Elizabeth 2* will have completed a seven-night transatlantic crossing from Southampton and Cherbourg prior to sailing from **Quebec City** for New York, so many passengers will already be aboard. Leaving the French-flavored city behind, the liner sails down the ever-widening **St. Lawrence,** which to the Quebecois becomes *la mer* (the sea) well before the river empties into the Gulf of St. Lawrence and the Atlantic Ocean.

Following two nights and a day at sea, the *QE2* calls in at **Halifax,** Nova Scotia, from where Samuel Cunard hailed and originated his transatlantic passenger and mail service. This old stone city has much to see on foot—from high up at the Citadel, overlooking the huge harbor basin, to the Historic Properties down along the waterfront, which includes an excellent indoor-outdoor maritime museum, including a *Titanic*-related collection. Pier 21, adjacent to the cruise berth, is Canada's equivalent of New York's Ellis Island immigration museum, and the top attractions are personal video and audio accounts from arriving passengers.

Next, an overnight sail to **Bar Harbor,** Maine, allows for a glimpse into this upscale summer resort and the great view from Cadillac Mountain in Acadia National Park. By the following morning, the *QE2* is threading her way through **Boston's Harbor Islands.** Logan Airport suspends its flights while the ship slides past the end of the runway to dock within reasonable walking distance or a short taxi ride from downtown Bean Town, its waterfront, trendy Quincy Market, leafy Boston Common, historic Beacon Hill, and shopping and restaurants at Back Bay. The last call at **Newport,** Rhode Island, even grander than Bar Harbor, shows off huge "summer cottages" side by side along Bellevue Avenue. You can visit several on tours or enjoy their views free of charge from the Cliff Walk, a public footpath that runs for several miles above the sea.

From Newport, it's an overnight sail to **New York.** At dawn the ship passes beneath the Verrazano-Narrows Bridge into upper New York Bay, sliding by the Statue of Liberty, Ellis Island, and Manhattan's majestic skyline on the way to its West Side berth.

Cunard's *Queen Elizabeth 2*

Address/Phone: Cunard Line, 6100 Blue Lagoon Drive, Suite 400, Miami, FL 33126; (305) 463-3000 or (800) 7–CUNNARD; fax: (305) 463–3010; www.cunardline.com

The Ship: *Queen Elizabeth 2* was built in 1969, has a gross tonnage of 70,327, a length of 963 feet, and a deep draft of 33 feet.

Passengers: 1,740; Americans, British, and Europeans; all ages, especially in the summer school holiday months

Dress: Formal, informal, and casual nights

Officers/Crew: British officers; international staff

Cabins: 925, sold in twenty-one wide-ranging categories, 689 outside, 150 singles, and 30 with verandas. Cabin determines restaurant allocation.

Fare: $$$

What's included: Cruise and port charges

What's not included: Airfare, drinks, tips

Highlights: Lots of shipboard activities and entertainment and the chance to sail on the best-known ship in the world

Other itineraries: In addition to the six-night Canada–New England cruise in late September, the *QE2* makes six-night crossings between New York and Southampton, England, and occasionally other ports, from April to December; cruises from New York to the Caribbean and from Southampton, England, to Northern Europe, Iberia, the Mediterranean, and South Africa. The annual world cruise departs New York and Florida in early January, calling at about three dozen ports, traveling out via the Panama Canal and home via Suez or South Africa.

Queen Elizabeth 2

REGAL CRUISES' *REGAL EMPRESS*

New England and Canada on a Budget

Regal Cruises is a one-ship company that has operated the *Regal Empress* since 1993. Built in 1953 she is one of the few well-preserved remainders from the transatlantic era, and her wood paneling, gleaming brass, and well-proportioned profile show off her pedigree. The company is best known for offering a tremendous bargain, with food and service well above what you pay for, while cruising a mix of unusual as well as standard itineraries.

The *Regal Empress* attracts two very different types of passengers. One half of the ship brings back memories of Atlantic crossings in the ocean liner golden age. The other half is strictly a budget cruise ship, with unimaginative decor, flowing drinks, and loud music out by the pool. Passengers will naturally congregate with like-minded others, with the traditionalists reveling in the ship's promenade deck and the library while the mostly younger crowd parties by the pool. Even though the number of party-goers diminishes on longer itineraries, the low rates still attract a certain number who want a lively and loud time.

The *Regal Empress* is a comfortable ship, accommodating a maximum of 1,068 passengers. There is a refreshing quality to the ship's size. She does not overwhelm you, and one does not have to walk a quarter mile to get a drink, but the ship feels large enough to be substantial and offers varied activities. Built for the Atlantic run, she is well suited for the sometimes

cooler northern climes. There is an enclosed promenade deck as well as some cozy lounges.

The best part of the ship is her intimate library, done in an Edwardian style with heavy, dark wood paneling. This room is a real time capsule with old writing desks from the days before e-mail.

The ship's restaurant, in a lighter wood paneling and etched glass, is low down in the hull, but is still pleasant and airy. An original mural of New York City, the ship's western embarkation port in the 1950s, still graces one end of the room. Service is helpful if not always fine tuned. An excellent pizzeria at the stern produces pies throughout the day.

The last space that still retains some original character is the Commodore Club, a small bar forward of the nightclub. On either side of the room, there are two sunken wells that can seat eight people perfect for pre- or post-dinner drinks.

The rest of the ship is fairly dull, however, with a standard one-story converted show lounge, a large casino, and a two-story cinema-cum-nightclub. Entertainment can be a bit bawdy and crude, although again it is tempered down on the longer itineraries.

Cabins come in a variety of shapes and sizes, so choosing your specific cabin can be important. There are a few Category 11 cabins with bunk beds and portholes yet are priced cheaper than just about all of

Appealing to both classic ship traditionalists and the younger, party-all-night revelers, the veteran **Regal Empress** *leads very much a split life. The ship's wood-paneled library and dining room are some of the best examples from the transatlantic era, while the Margarita Madness parties out on deck are some of the liveliest you will find. With its exceptionally low fares, this ship offers a great value while cruising to some historic and scenic ports in the Northeast.*

the inside cabins. While the nicer cabins are attractive and spacious, many of the budget cabins are fairly small and lack the old-school charm found in other cabins. As part of the company's ongoing improvements, however, every cabin now has a TV and a safe.

Regal should be lauded for the continual upgrading during almost yearly refits. Recently, an Internet cafe was installed onboard, and some cabins were even given verandas. Despite being a small cruise line, Regal operates it in a professional manner.

The Itinerary

The *Regal Empress* summers in **New York** and is the only ship sailing regularly to these ports during the season. The excitement begins moments after sailing, as you slip quietly past the World Trade Center and the Statue of Liberty and enjoy your first sunset at sea.

The next morning the ship anchors off **Newport,** Rhode Island, for six hours. You can explore the elegant "summer cottages" along the Cliff Walk or stroll downtown Newport, a major East Coast sailing center. After setting sail in the early afternoon, you have almost twenty-four hours at sea to relax and enjoy the classic features of the ship before you arrive in **Saint John,** New Brunswick, Canada's first incorporated city. Passengers can see the famous reversing tidal bore in the Bay of Fundy, kayak along the scenic coast, or simply take a walking tour of this historic city.

If you wake up in time the next morning, you will be greeted by a passage through the Casco Bay Islands and a sail past Portland Head Lighthouse to dock along **Portland**'s waterfront. When in Maine, most passengers seek out a lobster lunch at one of the many restaurants lining the harbor. Guided tours take you on drives along the scenic coast and include a stop in the famous town of **Kennebunkport.**

The next day is spent anchored off **Martha's Vineyard,** an upscale summer resort island south of Cape Cod. There is plenty to do, including a visit to the gingerbread Victorian community of **Oak Bluffs.** There are tranquil walks along the beaches, or you can take one of the low-cost shuttle buses to **Edgartown** for its pleasing New England architecture and short ferry ride to **Chappaquiddick Island.** Despite the crowds of summer, there are still places on the island that feel removed from the rest of the world.

After one last evening at sea, you awake to find the skyscrapers of **New York** appearing over the horizon.

Regal Cruises *Regal Empress*

Address/Phone: Regal Cruises, 300 Regal Cruises Way, Palmetto, FL 34220; (941) 721–7300 or (800) 270–7245; fax: (941) 723–0900; e-mail: info@regalcruises.com; www.regalcruises.com

The Ship: *Regal Empress* was built in 1953 as the *Olympia*, then sailed as the *Caribe I*. It has a gross tonnage of 21,909, a length of 612 feet, and a draft of 28 feet.

Passengers: 914; mostly Americans of all ages

Dress: Casual, with a jacket for the formal night

Officers/Crew: International

Cabins: 457, of which 228 are outside and 8 have verandas

Fare: $

What's included: Cruise fare only

What's not included: Airfare, port charges, tips, drinks, shore excursions

Highlights: An exceptional value on a well-maintained ship to some delightful ports

Other itineraries: In addition to this five-day New England and Canada cruise that operates between June and September, the *Regal Empress* offers a series of mostly two-night cruises to nowhere almost every weekend and in the fall usually does a longer itinerary to Quebec and Newfoundland. During the winter, she is based out of Port Manatee, Florida, calling at a variety of Central American and Caribbean ports. She also makes occasional trips from other ports, including Charleston, Norfolk, and Philadelphia.

SCOTIA PRINCE CRUISES' *SCOTIA PRINCE*
An Overnight Ferry Cruise: Maine to Nova Scotia

Scotia Prince Cruises has operated this service since 1970, using a succession of ships until 1982, when the present *Scotia Prince* arrived. Built in 1972 and enlarged in 1986, the stabilized eight-deck ship can take up to 1,500 cabin and deck passengers.

The public rooms include the forward Dolphin Lounge, used as the principal entertainment venue, a bar with TV sports channels, and a quiet nonsmoking lounge. In addition, there is a popular casino with blackjack, roulette, and slot machines, as well as a duty-free shop offering liquor, perfumes, and jewelry. For late-evening diners on the 8:00 P.M. night sailing from Portland, there's a full buffet from 7:30 P.M., but give yourself a Down East treat and enjoy a sit-down dinner served in the Princess Dining Room. The à la carte menu features broiled or steamed lobster, plucked alive from the tank, prime rib special with shrimp cocktail, grilled haddock, succulent steaks, and vegetarian dishes. Prices, including wines, are reasonable, and service is attentive.

On the day crossing from Yarmouth, the dining room offers an à la carte lunch menu, and from 3:30 to 6:30 P.M. the Bountiful Buffet includes salads, hot dishes, and a carvery with roast turkey and roast beef. A prix-fixe menu includes two starters, four entrees including lobster and prime rib, and two desserts. A kid's menu is also available, and a coffee shop serves hot meals including breakfast.

Accommodations range from suites with sitting rooms to simple two-, four-, and even six-berth family arrangements that comprise 199 upgrade cabins with private facilities and 115 standard cabins without shower but with at least a washbasin and sometimes a toilet. Although there is no pool for this cool-weather crossing, the ample deck space can be enjoyed on the Yarmouth to Portland day crossing.

The Scotia Prince qualifies as the only ferry liner on the East Coast that offers anything close to cruise ships standards on its nightly runs, May through October, from Portland, Maine, to Yarmouth, Nova Scotia. For East Coasters the service offers a quick getaway, and for those on a driving vacation, the ship provides the shortest route from New England to parts of the maritime provinces.

Scotia Prince Cruises'
Scotia Prince

Address/Phone: Scotia Prince Cruises, P.O. Box 4216, Portland, ME 04101-0416; (207) 775–5616 or (800) 341–7540; fax: (207) 773–7403; www.scotiaprince.com

The Ship: *Scotia Prince*, first built in 1972 as the *Stena Olympica*, then enlarged in 1986, has a gross tonnage of 11,968, a length of 470 feet, and is stabilized.

Passengers: 1,052 in berths and up to 1,500 on day crossings

Dress: Casual at all times

Officers/Crew: International

Cabins: 324; simply furnished, insides and outsides, some with upper and lower berths; most with shower and toilet, some standard cabins without

Fare: $ (day) $$ (with cabin)

What's included: Cruise only, including port charges unless buying one of the many packages, including the twenty-two-hour minicruise

What's not included: Transportation to the ship, tips, meals, drinks

Highlights: A chance to sample a European-style overnight ferry cruise; lobster dinner

Itineraries: Daily crossings (some no-sailing dates in the early and late season) depart Portland, Maine, at 9:00 P.M., and Yarmouth, Nova Scotia, at 10:00 A.M. between May and October.

The Itinerary

There are lots of creative ways to use this service with or without a car. The shortest is a twenty-three-hour round-trip, overnight from Portland to Yarmouth, with a sixty-minute stopover and an eleven-hour daylight return. Departing **Portland** in the summer and on the way back, you will see the pretty Casco Bay Islands and Portland Head lighthouse. Approaching the rocky Nova Scotia coastline, an impressive solitary lighthouse marks the narrow entrance to **Yarmouth**'s inner harbor.

Entertainment aboard includes Broadway, country, and rock and roll singers and dancers and a six-piece band that stages a show at 10:00 P.M. on the night crossing and 4:30 P.M. on the day return. Other daytime activities include a feature film, karaoke, bingo, horse racing, trivia quiz, and country line-dancing lessons. During the summer vacation period, kids can enjoy supervised activities such as face painting, a scavenger hunt, arts and crafts, and cartoons and videos.

You may also choose to stay at a nearby Yarmouth hotel for a couple of days and, of course, take along your car for a driving tour through Nova Scotia to Prince Edward Island or by two major ferry routes to Newfoundland. While cruise ferries abound in Europe, the *Scotia Prince* is the only game on the U.S. East Coast. For some vacationers, the crossing is an all-night party, while for others, it is a comfortable way to avoid many driving miles.

HOLLAND AMERICA LINE'S
RYNDAM AND *STATENDAM*
Alaska's Glacier Discovery Cruises and Alaska/Yukon Land Tours

Holland America Line dates back to 1873, operating transatlantic passenger service for the first hundred years. Now owned by the Carnival Corporation, Holland America runs one of the largest and most modern fleets, combining classical interiors with up-to-date amenities.

The *Statendam,* the first in the new series, and the *Ryndam,* the third, both offer ten decks of accommodations for 1,266 passengers. The Crow's Nest on Sports Deck is a delightful sightseeing lounge during the day and an intimate nightclub in the evening. The Lido Deck offers health and fitness facilities and a large pool area that can be covered by a retractable dome during Alaska's cooler weather.

The buffet restaurant amidships is designed to keep the queues short and provides a great selection at both breakfast and lunch. The aft dining room's two-level space offers decent food in a beautiful setting, with such regional specialties as baked Alaska cod fillet, steamed king crab legs, and sesame-roasted king salmon fillet. The show lounge has both balcony and orchestra levels for cruise-ship-style extravaganzas. The Ocean Bar, a Holland America Line trademark, is the social center for drinks and dancing, while the Explorer's Lounge provides a similar, though quieter, venue. Both ships have attractive, understated three-story atriums that lead to the Java Café and the Wajang theater as well as to the lower level of the show room forward and the dining room aft.

The 633 cabins and suites range from 187-square-foot inside cabins to four-room penthouse suites measuring 1,126 square feet. Avoid cabins above the theater if you retire early. Both ships have lots of open deck space for viewing the scenery, and the Lower Promenade is fully teaked for the constitutional walkers.

The Cruise Itinerary

Holland America offers more than one hundred departures each season, and presented here will be a one-week northbound cruise embarking at **Vancouver.**

Following two nights and a day cruising between Vancouver Island and the mountainous British Columbia coast, the *Ryndam* or *Statendam* will call at **Ketchikan,** where the active might kayak the fishing harbor's waterfront or take a drive out to see the world's largest collection of totems depicting legends of Native Alaskans. Next, at **Juneau,** you can see the Mendenhall Glacier from the road or a small plane, or by helicopter that lands on the glacier. The capital is worth a look on foot as is the still-raucous Red Dog Saloon, Alaska's most famous entertainment bar. Pay a visit to the museum for exhibits on the state's history, wildlife, and Native culture, or ride the Mount Roberts Tram for a 2,000-foot-high view.

Holland America sends most of its big-ship fleet north to Alaska in the late spring on round-trip Inside Passage cruises from Vancouver and on one-way voyages between Vancouver and Seward in South Central Alaska. The latter will be described here along with the terrific choice of land options aboard vista-dome railroad cars, lounge-equipped coaches, and flights deep into the interior, adding immeasurably to the cruise experience.

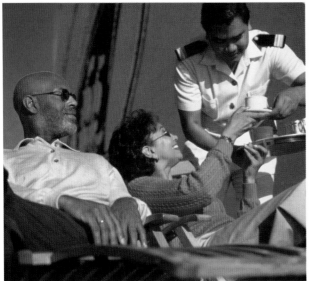

At **Sitka,** passengers go ashore by tender, arriving within walking distance of many attractions. The New Archangel Dancers perform a show worth seeing in the Centennial Hall, which also houses the visitor center. Nearby stands St. Michael's Russian Orthodox Cathedral, rebuilt after a fire in 1966. At the edge of town, the Sitka National Memorial Park has the most finely carved totems in the state.

Sailing across the Gulf of Alaska with the Wrangell–St. Elias National Park forming a backdrop, the ship turns to cruise up to the **Hubbard Glacier.** Enter **Prince William Sound** for a morning call at **Valdez,** known as the Switzerland of Alaska because of its magnificent setting. The southern terminus of the 800-mile Trans-Alaska pipeline can be visited by tour, and rafting and sea-kayaking trips are also available. The afternoon is spent cruising **College Fjord,** with sixteen glaciers named after eastern colleges and universities, before sailing overnight to **Seward** for disembarkation.

The Land Itineraries

Holland America Westours provides nearly three dozen escorted pre- and post-cruise options. The following eight-day tour includes the most popular destinations, but there are shorter and less expensive offerings.

The tour begins with a scenic drive across the **Kenai Peninsula** to **Anchorage** for the night, followed by a rail cruise, including a full meal, aboard the **McKinley Explorer** dome cars, which seat sixty-six in a lounge and at tables. Overnight at a lodge on the Nenana River is followed by a drive into **Denali National Park** to look for caribou and grizzly bears beneath 20,320-foot Mount McKinley (Denali). Rejoin the McKinley Explorer for the rail trip to **Fairbanks.**

From Fairbanks there's a short river cruise, then a drive along the Alaska Highway to **Tok** for an overnight. The next day, a 102-mile **Yukon River** cruise from Eagle travels to the preserved former boomtown of **Dawson City.**

The Alaska-Yukon Explorer coaches, equipped with a lounge and galley, travel to the **Yukon Wildlife Preserve** for sightings of moose, musk oxen, caribou, and Dall sheep. Both Dawson City and **Whitehorse** provide spirited Follies-style entertainment. From Whitehorse, drive to the summit of the White Pass to join the **White Pass and Yukon Railroad** for a vintage train ride spiraling down along the Trail of '98 to **Skagway,** the main port of entry for the gold prospectors. The last stage is a daylight cruise along the Lynn Canal, a natural waterway leading to **Juneau** and flights south to the Lower 48.

Holland America Line's *Ryndam* and *Statendam*

Address/Phone: Holland America Line, 300 Elliott Avenue West, Seattle, WA 98119; (800) 426–0327; brochures: (800) 626–9900; fax: (206) 281–7110; www.hollandamerica.com

The Ship: *Statendam* was built in 1992 and the *Ryndam* in 1994, and they share a gross tonnage of 55,451, a length of 719 feet and a draft of 25 feet.

Passengers: 1,266; mostly Americans, age fifty-five and up

Dress: Formal, informal, and casual nights

Officers/Crew: Dutch officers; Indonesian and Filipino crew

Cabins: 633; 502 outside and 150 with verandas

Fare: $$$

What's included: Cruise only unless a fly-cruise-land package is purchased, basic tips

What's not included: Airfare, port charges, shore excursions, drinks, extra tips

Highlights: Most attractive ships on which to spend time at sea; lots to do on shore excursions during the cruise and on land tours in Alaska

Other itineraries: In addition to this seven-night Glacier Discovery cruise, which operates between early May and mid-September, there are seven-night Inside Passage cruises round-trip from Vancouver. The *Statendam* cruises to Hawaii, and both ships sail through the Panama Canal to the Caribbean. Holland America's large fleet pretty much covers the globe, including the *Amsterdam*'s and *Rotterdam*'s round-the-world cruises.

PRINCESS CRUISES' *SEA PRINCESS, DAWN PRINCESS, OCEAN PRINCESS,* AND *SUN PRINCESS*

Big-Ship Cruising and Touring the Inside Passage, Gulf of Alaska, and National Parks

Princess Cruises, based in Los Angeles, is owned by P&O of London, one of the world's largest shipping lines. Here the *Sea Princess* is the featured ship, but sisters *Dawn Princess*, *Ocean Princess*, and *Sea Princess* are so similar in design, layout, and services that they may be considered interchangeable. Completed in 1995, the *Sea Princess* is 77,000 gross register tons and has ten principal passenger decks. The four-story Grand Plaza is the main social center, with public spaces, shops, cafes, and the two dining rooms radiating from it. The marble foyer offers connecting circular staircases, glass elevators, and a stained-glass dome.

The two attractively decorated main restaurants, using wood-grain paneling and etched glass, are located aft, one atop the other, with the tables arranged in small groupings on different levels to avoid a large-room feeling. The menus are typically varied and the quality and presentation average. The twenty-four-hour Horizon Court (the cruise industry's first) has a bistro menu for dinner, a bar, dance floor, and sweeping panoramic views over the bow. A pizzeria serves excellent, freshly prepared varieties, and there's a steak house, a caviar and wine bar, a hamburger grill, and a patisserie for pastries and special coffees. Two show rooms offer lavish productions in a Broadway-style theater and in smaller-setting cabarets. All shows are repeated for both sittings in both dining rooms. Dining options include open sittings.

There are pools in three locations, five whirlpools, and a huge amount of outside deck space with bars nearby. A paddle-tennis court located by the ship's funnel can be used for basketball and volleyball. Other amenities are a two-level spa with pool and whirlpools, a movie theater, a disco, a casino, a library, a card room, a beauty salon, and children and teenage rooms.

Two thirds of the cabins are outside, and about 70 percent of these have private verandas. Standard features include queen-size or twin beds, decent storage space, phones, TVs bringing in CNN and ESPN, refrigerators, safes, and bathrooms with showers.

The Cruise Itinerary

Northbound the *Sea Princess* sails from **Vancouver** out under the Lion's Gate suspension bridge. Threading through the fast-flowing Seymour Narrows, the ship encounters Pacific swells for several hours before returning to the protection provided by the Queen Charlotte Islands.

Ketchikan, reached on the second morning, was Alaska's salmon capital and is now oriented to tourism,

Princess Cruises sends six of its big liners to Alaska from the middle of May to late September. The four largest sisters, Sea, Dawn, Ocean, *and* Sun Princesses, *offer similar one-week itineraries northbound and southbound between Vancouver and Seward via the Inside Passage and across the Gulf of Alaska, including three port calls and Glacier Bay cruising. All cruises are one-way and can be combined with a variety of land packages that feature lodge stays near Mount McKinley (Denali) and on the Kenai Peninsula as well as rides on the dome-equipped Midnight Sun Express.*

especially along the once-bawdy Creek Street and at the two splendid totem pole parks. The active might canoe on a lake or go mountain biking or fly fishing. **Juneau,** the state capital, provides a walkable visit, although expect steep streets and steps, as the city is set against a mountainside. The state museum is a good bet, and tours that drive and fly out to the **Mendenhall Glacier** include a guided alpine walk and sea kayaking in nearby Auke Bay. Departing late evening, the ship sails overnight to **Skagway,** a town that trades entirely on its historic link with the Klondike Gold Rush. The best excursion is on the White Pass and Yukon's vintage train that climbs out of Skagway to the top of the White Pass.

For many people **Glacier Bay** is the high point of the cruise, where the *Sea Princess* enters at about dawn to cruise amid floating ice. Mount Logan can be seen rising nearly 20,000 feet as the *Sea Princess* crosses the **Gulf of Alaska.** Twenty-four hours later, the ship passes through **Prince William Sound** to reach **College Fjord,** where sixteen long glacial tongues slide into the sea. The cruise ends at **Seward,** where you can fly home or stay to enjoy one of the land extensions.

The Land Itineraries

Three- to nine-night land tours are very popular before or after the week's cruise. They comprise several mix-and-match ingredients, lodge and hotel stays, train rides, river excursions, rafting, fishing, hiking, and flightseeing. Most tours begin with a drive from Seward through the Kenai Mountains to **Anchorage,** Alaska's largest city, for the night.

The **Midnight Sun Express**, using Princess Tours rail cars, provides a scenic daylight ride to **Denali National Park.** The bi-level dome cars offer lounge seating with bar service beneath glass windows on the upper level and a dining room and open platforms below. **Mount McKinley** (Denali), North America's highest peak at more than 20,000 feet, is the centerpiece of the park where Princess operates two wilderness lodges. Tours may continue by Midnight Sun Express to **Fairbanks** for gold-mine tours, a paddlewheel excursion, visits to an Athabascan Indian village, and a flight to **Fort Yukon** above the Arctic Circle.

The **Kenai Peninsula** extension provides stays at the wilderness lodge and sport-fishing trips, rafting through the Kenai Canyon, naturalist hikes, horseback riding, and a wildlife cruise. Additional tours penetrate into the more remote regions of Alaska into the Yukon Territory. Many land itineraries can be taken without the cruise through Princess Tours (800–835–8907).

Princess Cruises' *Sea Princess*, *Dawn Princess*, *Ocean Princess*, and *Sun Princess*

Address/Phone: Princess Cruises, 24305 Town Center Drive, Santa Clarita, CA 91355; (661) 753–0000 or (800) 774–6237; brochures: (888) 478–6732; fax: (661) 259–3108; www.princesscruises.com

The Ship: *Sea Princess* was built in 1998, *Sun Princess* in 1995, *Dawn Princess* in 1997, and *Ocean Princess* in 2000. They share a gross tonnage of 77,000, a length of 856 feet, and a draft of 26 feet.

Passengers: 1,950; mostly Americans, all ages in summer, but mainly forty-five and up

Dress: Formal, informal, and casual

Officers/Crew: British and Italian officers; international crew

Cabins: Sun (975); Dawn, Ocean, and Sea (1,050); with more than 400 veranda cabins

Fare: $$$

What's included: Cruise only

What's not included: Airfare, port charges, shore excursions, drinks, tips

Highlights: Spectacular glacier and mountain scenery, creative optional tour programs

Other itineraries: In addition to these seven-day cruises between Vancouver and Seward, which operate from the middle of May to late September, Princess offers many other Alaskan, Caribbean, Bermuda, and European itineraries, and elsewhere.

NORWEGIAN CRUISE LINE'S *NORWEGIAN SKY*
Freestyle Cruising from Seattle to Alaska

Like its namesake, the *Sky* is a bright and sun-filled ship with an abundance of floor-to-ceiling windows. Surrounding the central atrium on several levels, you will find a bar, a pianist, and clusters of chairs creating relaxing pockets. All total, there are nearly a dozen watering holes, including a dark and cozy cigar club with the most comfortable thick leather chairs and couches imaginable, Gatsby's wine bar, a sports bar, Checkers nightclub/disco, two large poolside bars, and a coffee bar connected to the Internet cafe.

For kids, the *Sky*'s huge children's area includes a sprawling playroom with high ceilings, a teen center with a large movie screen, a pair of foosball games, and a video arcade. For the active adult, the well-stocked gym may be on the small side for a ship of this size, but, like the large adjacent aerobics room, it has floor-to-ceiling windows that make workouts a pleasure and a convenient location abutting the main pool deck. Nearby, the attractive spa and beauty salon are ocean-view too, with lovely gilded Buddha statuary dotting the area. Out on deck, there are a four hot tubs clustered between a pair of pools. There's a fifth hot tub and kids' wading pool sequestered at the aft end of the Sports Deck above. Here you will also find the combo basketball/volleyball court, a pair of golf driving nets, and shuffleboard.

The *Sky*'s cabins are pretty, done up in wood tones and pastels, but they're small and there's scant stowage for your clothes. All cabins, even suites, have only a two-panel closet and a small bureau with four slim drawers. The 252 suites with balconies measure 202 square feet, including the veranda, and the vast majority of standard outside and inside cabins measure about 150 square feet (compared to Carnival's standard 188 square feet). All cabins have a small sitting area, a mini-fridge (not stocked), a hair dryer, robes, TVs, and a desk and chair. Bathrooms are compact, with tubular shower stalls and slivers of shelving. A note of interest: The ship was originally designed for Costa Cruises with large cabin portholes and no balconies, but after the shipyard went bust, NCL took it over and worked around the existing portholes and added balconies, resulting in an odd door-and-porthole combination.

But what really stands out is the line's "freestyle cruising" concept, where you choose what to wear and where and when to dine. In all five dining venues, dinner is served anytime between 5:30 P.M. and midnight, and you can wear what you want. In the French-inspired Le Bistro, the most elegant and cozy venue on the ship, try the warm goat cheese spinach salad and sautéed salmon in sorrel sauce.

*The **Norwegian Sky** marked Norwegian Cruise Line's entry into the modern megaship world, and the Sky comes loaded with today's must-have features, from cabin balconies to an Internet cafe, a cigar bar, and, most importantly, a fabulous dining program boasting five restaurants, all of which operate under a casual open-seating policy that allows you to dine anytime between 5:30 and midnight.*

The Portofino Grill serves buffet-style at breakfast and lunch and a sit-down, reservations-only dinner, in an intimate setting with tables for two or four. In the evenings, the grill is transformed into a cozy, dimly lit Northern Italian restaurant with antipasti choices of marinated salmon rings or bresaola carpaccio with parmesan cheese and mushrooms.

Elegant suites are cloaked in shades of deep gold, beige, and burnt orange. Nearly ninety percent have private balconies, the highest number for any ship until the 100 percent suite *Seven Seas Mariner* arrived in 2001. The standard suites are a roomy 301 square feet, including a 55-square-foot balcony; and the eighteen top suites range from 448 square feet to 1,067 square feet, not including balconies. In addition to palatial marble-covered bathrooms, every abode has a wide walk-in closet, a tall built-in dresser, a safe, terry robes, a TV/VCR, and a minibar stocked with two complimentary bottles of wine or spirits. Twenty-four-hour room service includes a full-course dinner served in the sitting area or out on the private balcony facing the sea.

The Itinerary

The most numerous Alaskan itineraries offered are one-week round-trips from **Vancouver.** The voyage north follows the **Inside Passage** between Vancouver Island and the British Columbia coast, with two nights and a day en route to a side trip into **Misty Fjords National Park,** a narrow steep-sided waterway that the largest ships do not penetrate. Later that day, the first port call at **Ketchikan** offers the standard totem park and town tour or a nature hike through a coastal rain forest. At **Juneau,** water choices include an ocean kayak trip, a twelve-person traditional Native American canoe ride into **Mendenhall Lake,** and gentle white-water rafting near the glacier.

At the north end of the Lynn Canal, the **Skagway** tours offer a bike ride to Dyea, now a partial ghost town, and a trip on the **White Pass and Yukon Route** rail line to the top of the pass and back. At the edge of the Pacific Ocean, **Sitka,** once the Russian American capital, reveals its colorful past on a town center walking tour or more energetically on a bicycle ride along a winding path between mountains and sea.

Northward into the Gulf of Alaska, the *Navigator* sails up to **Hubbard Glacier,** located in the shadow of the **Wrangell-St. Elias** mountain range, to listen for the crack of calving ice. Later in the morning, the ship crosses the gulf to dock at **Seward,** where there is a choice of land extensions to **Denali National Park.**

Radisson Seven Seas Cruises' *Seven Seas Navigator*

Address/Phone: Radisson Seven Seas Cruises, 600 Corporate Drive, Suite 410, Fort Lauderdale, FL 33334; (954) 776–6123 or (800) 285–1835; brochures: (800) 477–7500; fax: (954) 772–3763; www.rssc.com

The Ship: *Seven Seas Navigator* was completed in 1999. It has a gross tonnage of 33,000, a length of 560 feet, and a draft of 21 feet.

Passengers: 490; mostly Americans age forty-five and up

Dress: Formal, informal, and casual nights

Officers/Crew: European officers; largely European crew

Cabins: 245; all outside and 215 with balconies

Fare: $$$$

What's included: Cruise fare, gratuities, wines with dinner, soft drinks and juices, stocked minibar

What's not included: Port charges, airfare, alcoholic drinks

Highlights: Spacious ship with nearly all balconies, top European service

Other itineraries: In addition to this seven-day Alaska cruise that operates between May and September, the *Seven Seas Navigator* and *Seven Seas Mariner*, *Radisson Diamond*, *Song of Flower*, *Paul Gauguin*, and chartered *Hanseatic* cruise the entire world.

CRUISE WEST'S *SPIRIT OF ENDEAVOUR*

Small-Ship Cruising Alaska's Inside Passage

Cruise West, in business since 1973, is the best known of the Alaska-going small-ship companies. The cruise line offers intimate encounters along southeastern Alaska's Panhandle with a casual, folksy atmosphere aboard seven ships. One of the largest and most sophisticated is the 102-passenger *Spirit of Endeavour*.

Oak and teak are used throughout this light and airy ship. The all-purpose lounge, bathed in windows, is where guests congregate, socialize, and listen to presentations by naturalists, park rangers, and the cruise director on the landscape, geology, and local culture. In keeping with the informal atmosphere, the speakers mingle with passengers to answer questions and share experiences.

The dining room serves up simple, hearty American fare in one open-seating arrangement. Young crew members earn an "A" in enthusiasm and a "B" on the finer points of dining-room service, contributing to CW's laid-back, summer-camp feel. After dinner there may be a lecture about the next day's attractions, a crew talent show, or a reading by a volunteer guest. Videos and books are also available for borrowing.

All cabins are outside, most with picture windows for superb views, and Upper Deck cabins open to the side promenade. The TVs are closed circuit for viewing videos. Outside decks are ample fore, aft, and topside, and most passengers spend much of the day bundled up in jackets, windbreakers, and hats to ward off the often damp, drizzly weather. It's commonplace for the captain to speed up, slow down, backtrack, or do whatever it takes to spot wildlife such as humpback whales, orcas, seals, bald eagles, and porpoises. Spot a brown bear, and you are in luck.

The Itinerary

The *Spirit of Endeavour*'s eight-night itinerary, including a hotel night in Juneau, operates northbound and southbound between Seattle and Juneau. Sailing northbound from **Seattle,** the ship spends the first two days cruising the **Strait of Georgia** between the British Columbia mainland and Vancouver Island, sharing the waterway with rafts of logs being pushed by tugs. The waterway opens up into **Queen Charlotte Sound,** where the ship may roll to Pacific swells, and then it's back in the protection of the **Inside Passage** approaching the Alaskan Panhandle. Part of the third day is spent cruising through the eerily quiet canals of the **Misty Fjords National Monument,** a vast area of primeval wilderness, steep-sided fjords, and waterways. The nimble *Endeavour* can maneuver right up to 3,000-foot-high granite walls and catch the spray from the cascading waterfalls.

Ketchikan, originally a Tlingit Indian fishing camp, retains its rugged feeling. Take a tour and benefit from the narration or hire a taxi to avoid the crowds and see the totems at the Saxman Indian Village, a few miles south of town, or at Totem Bight State Park, about 10 miles away. From Creek Street, a boardwalk-cum-street

From the decks of the 102-passenger **Spirit of Endeavour,** *the fjords, glaciers, and wildlife of Alaska's Inside Passage are so close that you can practically reach out and touch them. That's the beauty of exploring in a small ship, akin to the experience of adventurous pioneers who preceded you foraging through the great unknown.*

of charming shops, take the funicular up to Westmark Lodge for spectacular views of the harbor. For something really different, fishing excursions take four to six passengers on working, commercial trawlers to watch, pitch in, and enjoy the catch—yummy steamed shrimp and crabs in warm butter accompanied by homemade wine. **Tracy Arm** is considered to be the most beautiful spot in Alaska and features some of the most dramatic topography, with sheer rock walls soaring 3,000 feet, and it's 22 miles inland to the twin Sawyer Glaciers at the far end.

Sitka is Russian Alaska, and it was here in 1867, at what is now the 105-acre Sitka National Historical Park, that the transfer of land that became the state of Alaska to the United States took place. It's a nice walk from the ship to see the park's enormous, telephone-pole-straight spruce, hemlock, and cedar trees, dripping with rainfall, and its collection of towering totem poles carved by local artisans.

Only a small ship can negotiate the twists and turns of Peril Strait to reach **Glacier Bay National Park,** the best-known destination of most itineraries. Here, more than a dozen tidewater glaciers rise as high as 7,000 feet above the bay. Glacial activity in this area has been phenomenal, in the past 200 years exposing nearly 60 miles of fjords, inlets, and islands as the area's glacial ice has melted and retreated. It's easy to feel as though you've been swept back in time, way back to a prehistoric place. There is pin-drop silence, periodically broken by the sound of calving glaciers crashing into the sea while the *Endeavour* slowly glides through the still, glasslike water like some child's toy boat set in a huge pond.

Juneau, Alaska's capital and third-largest city, is set against a sheer mountain wall, easily demonstrating why there is no road to the outside world. Steep streets promise a good workout, and a nice waterfront area hosts plenty of shops selling local handicrafts and souvenirs. Alaska State Museum, easily walkable from town, is a worthwhile visit for great exhibits on how the Alaskan natives lived, dressed, hunted, and used the sea for fishing.

Cruise West's
Spirit of Endeavour

Address/Phone: Cruise West, 2401 4th Avenue, Suite 700, Seattle, WA 98121; (800) 426–7702; fax: (206) 441–4757; e-mail: info@cruisewest.com; www.cruisewest.com

The Ship: *Spirit of Endeavour* was built in 1983 as the *Newport Clipper* and has a length of 217 feet and a shallow draft.

Passengers: 102; mostly Americans and Canadians in their forties to seventies

Dress: Casual morning, noon, and night

Officers/Crew: American

Cabins: 51, all outside, most with windows and most with twin beds, some at right angles

Fare: $$

What's included: Cruise fare and port charges

What's not included: Airfare, shore excursions, drinks, tips

Highlights: Glorious mountains, fjords, and glaciers, seen close up; intimate atmosphere

Other itineraries: In addition to this seven-day cruise between Seattle and Juneau, which operates between May and September, there are many additional variations along Alaska's Inside Passage, in South Central Alaska, overland extensions, and cruises along the Columbia and Snake Rivers, in California Wine Country, and the Sea of Cortez.

ALASKA'S GLACIER BAY TOURS & CRUISES' *WILDERNESS ADVENTURER*
Alaskan Wilderness Cruise

Alaska's Glacier Bay Tours & Cruises is a small-ship line owned by an Alaska Native corporation based in Juneau. On its Alaska sailings the line actively emphasizes its Native American ownership by stressing understanding of the natural environment and respect for local culture. Any presentation of famous Tlingit legends is understated and may happen or not, depending on the natural turn of events.

The *Wilderness Adventurer* first sailed as American Canadian Caribbean Line's *Caribbean Prince,* and like other ships built by ACCL owner Luther Blount, it serves as a vehicle to take you to some extraordinary places. Cabins are simple places to sleep, with minimal storage and very basic bathrooms with a sink, toilet, and hand-held shower. The dining room and lounge/bar are interconnecting. Meals are served in one open seating, with a set menu at breakfast and lunch and two entree options for dinner. The food is generally tasty and plentiful, with fresh seafood a highlight. Evenings are social, and, in good weather, passengers gather on the top deck for drinks, snacks, and sharing the scenery or a surprise sighting of a playful pod of porpoises. A friendly informality develops among passengers, naturalists, and crew. With a shallow draft and a patented bow ramp, the *Wilderness Adventurer* lands passengers directly on the shore. The fleet of stable, two-person sea kayaks, launched from a stern platform, allow passengers to maneuver close to points of interest with guidance from accompanying naturalists.

Here is a true Alaskan wilderness cruise—the only city on the itinerary is Juneau, at embarkation and then a week later at disembarkation. The program concentrates on spotting wildlife in the air, on the sea, and ashore, spending a full day in Glacier Bay and actively participating in the adventure on hikes and in kayaks. The casual no-frills atmosphere of the sixty-eight-passenger **Wilderness Adventurer** *is geared to the out-of-doors.*

The Itinerary

The versatile *Wilderness Adventurer* cruises less traveled waterways and stops at islands that are not otherwise visited, though one can expect to see the big cruise ships at Juneau and in Glacier Bay. Excursions are freely structured, and the exact route and landings will be determined by the captain, the availability of wildlife, and the interest of passengers.

The trip sets off from **Juneau,** the state capital, to follow the Gastineau Channel, and by the second day, you are cruising in the West Arm of **Glacier Bay** among chunks of blue-tinted icebergs floating alongside the ship as it gingerly approaches the massive glacier's edge. The *Wilderness Adventurer* seems tiny and insignificant compared to the majestic and pristine scenery all around. You should see whales, sea lions, seals, and lots of nesting birds. A stop is made at the company-owned **Glacier Bay Lodge** for a walk in the forest.

Chichagof Island provides the first opportunity to try out the two-person kayaks and explore the shoreline while the ship remains at anchor. Eagles will soar overhead, and if you are lucky, you may see black and brown bears and their cubs ambling along the shore. **Point Adolphus** and **Icy Strait** attract humpback whales and sea otters looking for shellfish. The **Chatham Strait** between Admiralty, Baranof, and Chichagof islands, known as the ABC islands, flows through the heart of the seventeen-million-acre **Tongass National Forest.** Admiralty has the world's highest concentration of brown bears, and there are opportunities to explore the coves and islets in kayaks and take a guided walk ashore through spruce and hemlock forests.

Tracy Arm Fjord is a narrow waterway with massive cliff faces soaring several thousand feet and cascading waterfalls to approach to feel the spray. At the fjord's far end, **South Sawyer Glacier** may calve ice as the ship nears; then, in nearby **Endicott Arm,** there's a last chance to go sea kayaking among good-sized bergs before the cruise ends at Juneau.

Alaska's Glacier Bay Tours & Cruises' *Wilderness Adventurer*

Address/Phone: Alaska's Glacier Bay Tours & Cruises, 226 Second Avenue West, Seattle, WA 98119; (206) 623–2417 or (800) 451–5952; fax: (206) 623–7809; e-mail: gbinfo@cruisetours.com; www.glacierbaytours.com

The Ship: *Wilderness Adventurer* was built in 1984 as the *Caribbean Prince* and has a gross tonnage of 89, a length of 157 feet, and a draft of 6.5 feet.

Passengers: 68; mostly Americans, ages forty and up, interested in the outdoors and active

Dress: Casual at all times

Officers/Crew: American

Cabins: 30 of 34 cabins are outside, small and spartan; no verandas.

Fare: $$

What's included: Cruise, port charges, excursions, transfers, and use of kayaks and snorkeling equipment

What's not included: Airfare, tips, drinks

Highlights: A fantastic opportunity to get close to nature, glaciers, and wildlife

Other itineraries: In addition to this seven-day cruise, which operates from May through September, the company has three other small ships with different Alaskan itineraries, including land tours, whereas the *Wilderness Adventurer* also sails the Sea of Cortez, January through April, under the associated Voyager Cruise Line banner.

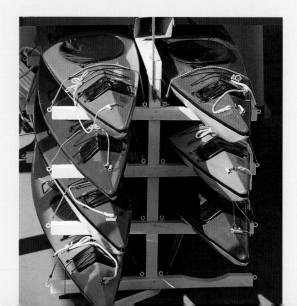

ALASKA MARINE HIGHWAY'S *COLUMBIA, MATANUSKA, TAKU,* AND *KENNICOTT*

The Inside Passage: On Your Own

The Alaska Marine Highway, with its present fleet of nine blue-and-white ferries, was established in 1963 to serve Alaskan Panhandle communities, including the state capital of Juneau, that have no road access to the outside world. Three principal services are of interest for cruise passengers: They begin at Bellingham, Washington, just north of Seattle; at Prince Rupert, British Columbia; and at Juneau, the state capital. You may make one-way or round-trip voyages on all of them.

The *Columbia, Matanuska, Taku,* and *Kennicott,* all named after Alaskan glaciers, share many of the same offerings such as a forward observation lounge, a cocktail bar, and hot and cold meal cafeteria-style dining with big window viewing. The food, pay-as-you-go, is good American fare, and entrees include Alaskan salmon and halibut, chicken teriyaki, and New York strip steaks. The *Columbia* also has a dining room. The top-deck, heated solarium gives protection and warmth and has seating facing aft. The ship provides films, informal on-deck talks, and an easy social atmosphere in which to meet Alaska residents, other cruisers, backpackers, motorists, and commercial drivers.

The cabins, sold as a unit, are plainly furnished and comprise two-, three-, and four-berth insides and outsides incorporating private showers and with configurations and capacities unique to each vessel. Cabins book up fast for the summer months, and the ships carry deck passengers who find space to sleep in the lounges and the solarium. If making stopovers, some of the connecting daylight passages do not require a cabin.

As the ferries serve a basic transportation function, all carry cars, recreational vehicles, and trucks that are driven on and off during port calls. These occur at all hours of the day and night but stops are short in duration, from one to four hours, so elaborate excursions require a stopover. The scenery en route is never-ending beauty, and some passengers find it satisfying to simply make a round trip.

The Itineraries

Bellingham to Skagway: Taken as a continuous round-trip voyage, the weekly trip departs **Bellingham,** Washington, located north of Seattle, on a Friday evening aboard either the 500-passenger *Matanuska* in

There are basically three ways to see the forty-ninth state: aboard a large cruise liner taking 1,000 to 2,000 passengers, a small expedition-style ship averaging about 100 passengers, or the Alaska Marine Highway system's network of cruise ferries. These state-owned ships, sailing on regular schedules, transport Alaskan residents and visitors between Washington State, British Columbia, and ports along the Inside Passage and in South Central Alaska. You can make a round-trip or stopover, then continue on a later sailing, and customize the itinerary using connecting BC Ferries, BC Rail, Via Rail, and the Alaska Railroad.

the off-season, or the 625-passenger *Columbia* in summer, generally June through September.

The initial two nights and a day are spent cruising north along the British Columbia coast. Vancouver Island, off to port, provides protection from the Pacific swells for much of the way. The scenery is mountainous, forested, and deeply incised with bays and narrow arms of the sea penetrating far inland. The narrow passage through the fast-flowing, and once dangerous, **Seymour Narrows** is particularly dramatic. Most commercial traffic travels on barges and ferries, and in summer you also encounter some of the two dozen cruise ships that ply the **Inside Passage.**

The ferry's first call is at **Ketchikan,** Alaska. As this is a purposeful ship, it remains long enough to load and unload passengers, vehicles, and cargo, giving through passengers time for a quick visit to the town center. **Wrangell** and **Petersburg** come later that same day, and only Marine Highway vessels and small cruise ships treat passengers to the **Wrangell Narrows** passage, where seventy channel markings require several hours of constant course changes. **Juneau's Auk Bay** terminal is reached on Monday morning, and persons wishing to see something of the capital, excellent state museum, and Mendenhall glacier should disembark for a day or two, then continue northward on the daily summer ship to Haines (5.5 hours) and Skagway (6.5 hours).

Passengers remaining aboard are rewarded with a beautiful daylight sail up the Lynn Canal, flanked by high mountain peaks and an occasional glacier, to call at **Haines,** where many vehicles leave for the trip through the Yukon Territory to Alaska over the Haines and Alaska highways. An hour later the ship docks at **Skagway,** the most northerly Inside Passage port, remaining three hours before returning south. Consider leaving the vessel here, to explore the restored gold rush entry point for prospectors bound overland to the Klondike from 1898 onward. A road runs inland to Whitehorse, Yukon Territory's capital, and the **White Pass and Yukon Route** operates excursion trains alongside the old Chilkat Trail, which the railroad replaced, to the top of the White Pass and back.

The southbound Marine Highway ferry will leave Skagway early Monday evening, call briefly at Haines, sail overnight to Juneau, then negotiate the twisting Peril Strait route (too narrow for the big cruise ships) to **Sitka.** The island town was Russian Alaska's capital until the United States took possession in 1867. Sights are St. Michael's Russian Orthodox Cathedral and a rain-forest walk through the Sitka National Historical Park to see the great collection of tall totems and an early nineteenth-century fort. The ship retraces the route south, calling on Wednesday at Petersburg, Wrangell, and Ketchikan, then spends two nights and a day cruising through Queen Charlotte Sound and Strait of Georgia for an early Friday morning arrival back at Bellingham, Washington.

Prince Rupert to Juneau: Ferry service sails north to Alaskan Panhandle ports from **Prince Rupert,** two to six times a week, increasing from one- to the three-ship maximum strength in summer. If you're not driving, there are two creative ways to reach Prince Rupert, one by rail and one by sea. BC Rail operates a daylight train from North Vancouver over a spectacular route through the mountains, high ranch country, and along steep canyons to Prince George, where following a night in a hotel, Via Rail's domeliner the Skeena provides a second all-day scenic mountain, lake, and valley ride west to Prince Rupert for the Alaska ferry north. From Vancouver and Victoria on Vancouver Island, bus connections to Port Hardy, near the top of the island, connect to the BC Ferries *Queen of the North* for a highly scenic ferry cruise to Prince Rupert.

Some Marine Highway ferries departing Prince Rupert call at **Ketchikan,** pass through the Wrangell Narrows, then stop at **Wrangell** and **Petersburg,** turning around at **Juneau** for a twenty-seven-hour one-way transit. Sailings to Juneau take two nights and a day if the route diverts via Sitka. Once a week this latter route is extended to **Haines** and **Sitka** aboard the seagoing *Kennicott.* All ships return to Prince Rupert via the same set of ports, so it is relatively easy to transfer between ships, but remember, cabin space for the overnight portions is at a premium in the summer months.

Prince Rupert to Juneau, Valdez, and Seward: In 1998 Alaska Marine Highway took delivery of its seagoing ferry *Kennicott,* a deep draft vessel, whereas the rest of the Inside Passage fleet have flat bottoms and shallow drafts. The *Kennicott* is designed to handle the rough waters sometimes encountered when crossing the Gulf of Alaska. For the first time in about a half century, it is now possible to sail from the Lower 48 and Inside Passage ports to South Central Alaska with onward road and rail connections to Anchorage, Denali National Park, and Fairbanks, avoiding the long Alaska Highway route.

While the *Kennicott* leaves from Prince Rupert for the direct sailing, persons coming from Bellingham can transfer to it at **Ketchikan** or **Juneau.** The *Kennicott* then sails directly to **Valdez,** in Prince William Sound, a thirty-seven-hour passage, or onto **Seward** in two nights and a day, or about fifty hours. Valdez is connected by road to the interior, and Seward has both road and Alaska Railroad links. Transit time from Prince Rupert to Seward is four nights and three days. For the return trip the *Kennicott* sails from Seward and Valdez to Juneau, Ketchikan, and Prince Rupert, the full elapsed time taking three nights and three days.

Alaska Marine Highway's *Columbia, Matanuska, Taku,* and *Kennicott*

Address/Phone: Alaska Marine Highway, 1591 Glacier Avenue (P.O. Box 25535), Juneau, AK 99801; (907) 465–3941/42 or (800) 642–0066; fax: (907) 277–4829; www.state.ak.us or www.north-to-alaska.com for Alaska and British Columbia information.

The Ships: *Taku*, built in 1963, length 352 feet; *Matanuska*, built in 1963, then enlarged, length 408 feet; *Columbia*, built in 1974, length 418 feet; *Kennicott*, built in 1998, length 380 feet. The first three have shallow drafts, and the Kennicott is deep draft.

Passengers: Total capacity including berths and deck: *Taku* 450, *Matanuska* 500, *Columbia* 625, *Kennicott* 748; all ages and mostly North Americans

Dress: Casual at all times

Officers/Crew: Alaskan

Cabins: Number of berths: *Taku* 106, *Matanuska* 247, *Columbia* 311, *Kennicott* 320, all in two- to four-berth cabins sold as units

Fare: $

What's included: Fare, port charges, and cabin (if purchased)

What's not included: Transportation to and from ports, meals, drinks, excursions

Highlights: Great scenery; social life aboard ferries; ease of stopovers, variety of routes

Other itineraries: Alaska Marine Highway also operates several smaller ferries, without cabins, to a half dozen other ports in the Alaska Panhandle. Ferries with and without cabins operate between South Central and Southwest Alaska. The 68 passenger *Tustumena*, (two- and four-berth cabins) makes monthly, five-day round-trips from Kodiak Island to the Aleutian Islands a seagoing adventure with potentially some of the roughest sea conditions in the world.

BC FERRIES' *QUEEN OF THE NORTH* AND *QUEEN OF PRINCE RUPERT*

The Canadian Inside Passage and Queen Charlotte Islands

BC Ferries, a British Columbia provincial company, operates a forty-vessel fleet providing the missing links in the BC highway system. The routes are complex, so a good map will help when planning itineraries around the two featured ships with cabin accommodations.

The *Queen of the North*, reflecting her Scandinavian origins, is newer, larger, and sleeker than the simpler but no less comfortable Canadian-built *Queen of Prince Rupert*. In the main summer season, the *Queen of the North* holds down the scenic daylight run between Port Hardy at the northern tip of Vancouver Island and Prince Rupert, while the *Queen of Prince Rupert* sails between Prince Rupert and Skidegate on Queen Charlotte Island.

Both ships have a lounge, a licensed bar, and cafeteria, and the *Queen of the North* has, in addition, an elaborate prix-fixe buffet for breakfast, lunch, and dinner. These meals may be prepaid at the time of booking, resulting in savings and convenience when making the two-day round-trip. The deck space is well-designed for viewing, and both ships have video arcades for children. On the *Queen of the North*'s daylight sailings, entertainment includes films, live music, and informal talks by naturalists and creative artists.

Simple double and quad cabins have lower berths that become sofas during the day, and the uppers fold away. All inside and outside cabins have washbasins and toilets, and those above the vehicle deck have showers, too. The least expensive cabins below the car deck will be claustrophobic for some. On the *Queen of the North*'s fifteen-hour daylight sailings, cabins may be booked for the day, or if making a round-trip, they may be occupied that turnaround night. If you are joining at either port early in the morning, you must stay ashore the night before sailing. In the off-season the Port Hardy–Prince Rupert route changes to a longer twenty-two-hour run making one to three intermediate calls en route. The *Queen of Prince Rupert* may be substituted when the other ship is undergoing drydocking.

The Itineraries

Port Hardy to Prince Rupert: Port Hardy is an obscure little place that really only exists for the ferry. To connect to the sailings without a car, there is regular bus service from Victoria with pickup stops along the way, which take most of the day, and another equally long ride from Vancouver using the ferry to Nanaimo to reach Vancouver Island. A creative way is to take Vancouver Island's railway, which operates 1950s diesel-powered railcars from Victoria to Courtney, about halfway to Port Hardy, then switch to the bus. Motels in Port Hardy look

BC Ferries, North America's largest ferry network, operates along the British Columbia Coast and to and from Vancouver Island. Two routes take overnight passengers in comfortable cabins for short getaways to some spectacular mountain and fjord scenery and to visit the Haida people on Queen Charlotte Island. Creative itineraries can be developed with the Alaska Marine Highway and with connecting BC Rail and Via Rail trains.

close to the ferry landing across the harbor, but a transfer is required.

In summer the *Queen of the North* leaves at 7:30 A.M. every other day for the 275-mile, fifteen-hour, nonstop passage. The first portion crosses a 50-mile stretch of open water called Queen Charlotte Sound, then enters Fitz-Hugh Sound to remain in protected waters for most of the balance of the day. The scenery is fjord land with mysterious arms that head inland, some traversed by a secondary BC Ferry service in summer. In the off-season the *Queen of the North* makes a few calls at towns without any road access, with **Bella Coola** being the exception. The coastal range will have snowcapped peaks during the early part of summer, and the deck temperatures may vary from being quite warm to chilly. En route you should see bald eagles, and you can expect to see some killer whales (orcas), porpoises, and seals. Many keen eyes will help you spot the wildlife.

Arrival at **Prince Rupert** is 10:30 P.M. for most summer sailings, and except late in the season, there should still be light in the sky. The landing is shared with the *Queen of Prince Rupert* and adjacent to the Alaska Marine Highway, but same-day connections are rare. Prince Rupert's motel district is about 1.5 miles away, and some motels overlook the harbor.

Sleep onboard if you are returning the next day to Port Hardy, or, as an alternative, take Via Rail's domeliner the *Skeena* to Prince George, spend the night, and connect to BC Rail over a spectacular route to North Vancouver. Or take the *Skeena* eastward to Jasper.

Prince Rupert and Skidegate to Queen Charlotte Islands: On this shorter route, sailings are usually during the day to the Queen Charlotte Islands, a six-and-a-half-hour run, with return to Prince Rupert overnight. Turnaround time is five and a half hours (Monday sailing from Prince Rupert is mostly overnight; Monday and Tuesday sailings from **Skidegate** are day.)

The mystical **Queen Charlotte Islands** are largely undeveloped, with wonderful misty forests, a rugged landscape, and the strong culture and artwork of the coastal Haida people. For more than a superficial visit, some sort of personal transportation is required, as there are no bus services.

BC Ferries' *Queen of the North* and *Queen of Prince Rupert*

Address/Phone: BC Ferries, 1112 Fort Street, Victoria, BC V8V 4V2; (250) 386–3431; fax: (250) 381–5452; www.bcferries.bc.ca or www.bcferries.com

The Ships: *Queen of the North*, built in 1969 as the *Stena Danica* and rebuilt for BC ferries in the 1980s, has a gross tonnage of 8,889 and a length of 410 feet. *Queen of Prince Rupert* was built in 1966 and has a gross tonnage of 5,864 and a length of 332 feet.

Passengers: Queen of the North 750 (210 berths); *Queen of Prince Rupert* 458 (90 berths); all ages and some non–North American passengers

Dress: Casual

Officers/Crew: Canadian

Cabins: Both ships have two- and four-berth outside and inside cabins with showers, and some are below vehicle deck with washbasin and toilet only

Fare: $

What's included: Cruise fare, port charges, and if booked, cabin and a meal plan (*Queen of the North* only)

What's not included: Transport to and from piers, drinks, meals not purchased in advance

Highlights: Some of the world's most beautiful scenery; lots of creative itineraries

Other itineraries: In addition to these two short getaways, which operate year-round with varying schedules, short ferry routes exist throughout coastal British Columbia, some incorporating through intercity buses between Vancouver-Victoria and Vancouver-Nanaimo.

AMERICAN CANADIAN CARIBBEAN LINE'S
GRANDE CARIBE
Erie Canal, St. Lawrence Seaway, and Saguenay River

The *Grande Caribe* is the creation of Luther Blount, a Yankee shipbuilder and shipowner who has been launching small cruise vessels since 1966, and at 185 feet it is ACCL's longest vessel ever. The one hundred passengers are mainly well-traveled American retirees ready to do without luxuries but not without camaraderie, which they share in rather tight quarters with a score of young American crew members.

The lounge, which also serves as theater and lecture hall, is forward on the upper of two accommodation decks. The dining room, one deck below, doubles as a card room and reading area. The American fare is fresh, well prepared, and served family style at one open sitting. Lunch is soup, salad, pasta, or sandwiches. Alcohol is not sold, but the ship has storage for passengers' own stock and provides setups gratis. The Sun Deck extends nearly the ship's full length and has a protected viewing area. The pilot house collapses approaching low bridges, and the patented bow ramp lowers for dry landings.

The fifty cabins—forty-one are outside with windows (some slide open) and portholes—have twin or double beds, and a few reduced-rate units have triple berths. Each cabin has air vents, limited hanging and shelf space, and minuscule bathrooms with hand-held showers. ACCL has a loyal clientele, thanks to the owner's innovative itineraries and moderate fares.

The Itinerary
The complete twelve-day Erie Canal to Saguenay cruise described here is altered in the fall to Erie Canal to Quebec City only (also twelve days), as sailing farther downriver is also north. Both fall foliage and the onset of snow come early to the lower St. Lawrence Valley.

No other cruise operated by the entrepreneurial firm of American Canadian Caribbean Line has proved to be so popular for so long, more than three decades. Embark in Rhode Island and twist and turn every which way via Long Island Sound, Hudson River, Erie Canal, St. Lawrence Seaway, and Saguenay fjord, ending beneath the Citadel at Quebec. The Grande Caribe is no luxury liner; instead, it's a spare vessel that carries a happy group of passengers who have little interest in the big ships and great enthusiasm for sharing America close up.

American Canadian Caribbean Line's *Grande Caribe*

Address/Phone: American Canadian Caribbean Line, P. O. Box 368 Warren, RI 02885; (401) 247–0955; fax: (401) 247–2350; www.accl-smallships.com

The Ship: *Grande Caribe* was built in the company's shipyard in 1997, has a tonnage of 99, a length of 183 feet, and a shallow draft of 6.5 feet.

Passengers: 100; age fifty-five and up and mostly Americans

Dress: Casual at all times

Officers/Crew: American

Cabins: 50 cabins, quite small; 9 inside; smoking on outside decks only

Fare: $$

What's included: Cruise and port charges, soft drinks, and setups for BYOB

What's not included: Airfare, shore excursions (very reasonably priced), tips

Highlights: The company's most popular route; social experience for passengers

Other itineraries: In addition to this twelve-day inland-waterways cruise, which operates June to October, ACCL offers many summer options in New England, eastern Canada, Great Lakes, Mid-America, Intracoastal Waterway, and winter cruises in Belize, Panama Canal, Caribbean, Orinoco River, and the Bahamas.

Embarking at **Warren,** Rhode Island, the *Grande Caribe* sails overnight, arriving in **New York** about dawn and passing down the East River within 2 blocks of my apartment; then, with a loop by the Statue of Liberty, it turns up the **Hudson River,** stopping at **West Point.** At **Troy** the pilot house is lowered for "low bridge on the Erie Canal." At **Waterford** the ship climbs 150 feet in a set of five locks to enter the canal proper, making stops and tying up at night, allowing the young American crew some freedom and passengers a chance to explore the delights of a small canal town. By breakfast the ship may already be underway, and from the open top deck, you can commune with the locals ashore, who are watching the unusual sight of a passenger vessel gliding by their front yards.

Turning into the **Oswego Canal,** the vast expanse of **Lake Ontario** is ahead, and soon one is threading among the beautiful **Thousand Islands.** Stops are **Clayton**'s Antique Boat Museum and splendid **Upper Canada Village,** with houses, churches, and public and farm buildings spanning one hundred years of Canadian architecture and small-town life. The tiny *Grande Caribe* shares the **St. Lawrence Seaway** with huge lake carriers and locks through to **Montreal** for a stop and a bow landing at Bay of Eternity in the dramatic **Saguenay Fjord.** From here the ship returns upriver to disembark at **Quebec City.** Passengers return to Rhode Island by bus in one day, and others come up to join the ship at Quebec.

MID-LAKES NAVIGATION'S *EMITA II*
Cruising the Canals of New York State

Mid-Lakes Navigation, run by five sons and one daughter of the company's founder, Peter Wiles Sr., has its home base in Skaneateles, New York. In three decades this small operation has brought due recognition to the state's treasured recreational waterways.

At first sight at the dock in Troy, just north of Albany, the 65-foot *Emita II*, a former Maine coastal passenger ferry, appears not much larger than a cruise-ship launch. The boat's top viewing deck, half protected by a new canopy, is attractively furnished with deck chairs and cushioned wooden benches. Mahogany trim accents the pilot house, and stairs lead down to the forward open deck and interior cabin. The dining room is aft, arranged with long, custom-built wooden tables, banquettes, and chairs. Oriental-patterned scatter rugs, a red deck, and orange life preservers in the overhead racks give the room and the forward library section both color and warmth.

All meals are taken aboard, and nights are spent ashore in nearby hotels and motels. Breakfast and lunch are buffet style, and dinner is served by waiters. One night features an outdoor summer supper, and entrees run to roast beef and Virginia baked ham; lunch is soup, salads, and sandwiches.

The Itineraries

While the Erie Canal from Albany (Troy) west to Syracuse and Buffalo is by far the best-known waterway, the company's forty-passenger packet boat, *Emita II*, also navigates the **Champlain Canal** from Albany (Troy) to Whitehall, from mid-June to mid-October. On the three-day Champlain Canal cruise, boarding begins in the morning at **Troy,** and Captain Dan Wiles sets the tone for the come-what-may trip with a short talk before departure.

Within minutes the boat comes to the first of a dozen locks that divide the Hudson River and the Champlain Canal into a series of controlled pools. The *Emita II* plows ahead at a leisurely pace of 8 miles per hour between wooded shores and rolling farmlands, where cows and children come down to the water's edge for a look. Powered yachts gather to share the transit through the toll-free locks. At Fort Edward the boat ties up for the night, and passengers spend two nights in **Glens Falls,** where the captain gives a slide-illustrated talk on canal history and current preservation efforts. On the second day the *Emita II* continues north along the pretty Champlain Canal to **Whitehall,** the turnaround point. The town's Skenesborough Museum recalls the city's past as the birthplace of the U.S.

Canal cruising, a popular way to go in Europe, is nearly unheard of in this country. One pioneering operator, Mid-Lakes Navigation Company, has offered two- and three-day trips along New York State's 527-mile canal system since 1968. The day is spent on the forty-passenger **Emita II** *and nights ashore in local accommodations.*

Navy and Marine Corps and as a once-important canal and rail center.

Besides the Champlain Canal trip, the *Emita II* makes three-day **Erie Canal** cruises from Albany to Syracuse along the Mohawk River. The highlights are the **Waterford Flight** of five locks, which lift the boat 150 feet, old factory towns such as **Amsterdam** and **Little Falls,** and the 22-mile Oneida Lake crossing. From **Syracuse** to **Buffalo** the *Emita II* passes through **Montezuma Wildlife Refuge** for possible sightings of bald eagles and Canada geese, restored canal towns such as **Fairport** and **Pittsford,** and the original canal's small locks and stone-arched aqueducts. These last structures were built by Frederick Law Olmsted of Central Park fame. In places the bridges are so low that the crew has to remove the boat's pilot house, and passengers have to crouch. On this stretch the boat docks at a canal park for the first night, and the hotel is just steps away. Both Erie Canal trips are one-way, with each night ashore in a different hotel and bus return to the port of embarkation.

Mid-Lakes Navigation's
Emita II

Address/Phone: Mid-Lakes Navigation Company, Box 61, 11 Jordan Street, Skaneateles, NY 13152; (315) 685–8500 or (800) 545–4318; fax: (315) 685–7566; www.mislakesnav.com

The Ship: *Emita II* was built in 1953 and then modified for day cruising. She has a gross tonnage of 65, a length of 65 feet, and a shallow draft.

Passengers: 40; mostly age fifty and up and many repeaters and whole-boat charters

Dress: Casual at all times

Officers/Crew: American

Cabins: Stay ashore in hotels/motels

Fare: $$

What's included: Cruise fare, port charges, all meals on boat, hotel stays, and transfers

What's not included: Drinks, tips

Highlights: Cruising historic canals while passing through rural and industrial landscapes

Other itineraries: In addition to the *Emita II*'s three above itineraries, operating between June and mid-October, the boat makes several Syracuse-Waterloo two-day cruises. The company also charters out Lockmaster English-style narrow boats for self-operated New York State canal cruising.

CLIPPER CRUISE LINE'S *NANTUCKET CLIPPER*

New England Islands to Chesapeake Bay

Clipper Cruise Line, based in St. Louis, got started in 1983, and its *Nantucket Clipper*, completed in 1984, is one of two similar shallow-draft cruisers. A young American crew gives friendly, professional service to mostly middle-age Americans from the West Coast and Sun Belt. In no time the ship takes on the atmosphere of an informal seagoing club.

The single lounge, decorated with bold colors and maple trim, faces forward with views ahead and to both sides. Ample seating makes this the social setting as well as the venue for local entertainers and enrichment programs about history and nature. The bar is to one side and the small library collection to the other. The dining room serves passengers and staff at one open sitting, with good table service and a few buffets. Chefs trained at the Culinary Institute of America use fresh ingredients to prepare an American menu that runs to excellent fish, grilled shrimp, veal, lots of different salads, and freshly baked desserts. The Clipper Chipper cookies are an afternoon staple. Hot and cold hors d' oeuvres are served before dinner in the lounge.

Cabins are all outside doubles with twin beds, radios, adequate stowage, and compact bathrooms with showers. Some passengers prefer a cabin that opens to a side deck, whereas others like the traditional door to a central corridor. A few lower-priced cabins have port-holes instead of windows, and noise from the engines is minimal, though noticeable, in the cabins located aft. Deck space includes a narrow wraparound promenade, a partly covered Sun Deck, and an observation deck at the bow. The ship has no swimming pool, fitness facilities, or casino. Instead, the *Nantucket Clipper* excels in providing an intimate, social, American-style vehicle to view coastal waters and islands.

The Itinerary

The *Nantucket Clipper* undertakes a variety of seven- to fourteen-day cruises along the Eastern Seaboard, and the ports will vary from cruise to cruise, so here are the highlights beginning in New England and sailing south. The ship's shallow draft permits close-in cruising, but during brief stretches in open seas, the unstabilized ship can roll.

The port of Quincy, just south of **Boston,** is used for embarkation and the base from which to visit Bean Town. Sailing into **Nantucket Harbor** re-creates the anticipated approach made by returning whaling ships, and with the *Nantucket Clipper* docked at its namesake town, it's but one block to one of the best preserved eighteenth- and early nineteenth-century seaports in America. Nearby **Martha's Vineyard** is larger and more varied in architecture, including Victorian gingerbread

Small-ship cruising takes you into ports not directly reached by the big ships, such as Nantucket and Martha's Vineyard islands, up the Hudson Valley, and south into the Chesapeake Bay; then add the splashy resort of Newport and cities like New York and Baltimore. The one-hundred-passenger Nantucket Clipper provides a convenient and comfortable way to see historic towns and scenic waterways from Massachusetts to Virginia.

Oak Bluffs. Newport, established as a showy summer resort, radiates wealth in the mansions along Bellevue Avenue, and several are open to the public.

Sailing into **New York** by the back door down the East River, the entire east side of Manhattan is revealed. Passing under the Brooklyn Bridge, the ship sails into the Upper Bay proudly dominated by Lady Liberty, and docks at the Chelsea Piers, a huge recreational sports complex. Sailing up the majestic **Hudson** between the Palisades and Highlands, a stop is made at **West Point** and perhaps **Kingston** for visits to a stately home with a view straight out of the Hudson River School of painting.

Cruises usually disembark and embark at New York (halfway point if making the fourteen-day cruise) for the voyage south along the New Jersey coast and through the **Chesapeake and Delaware Canal** for visits to **Baltimore Inner Harbor** and, at **Annapolis,** the U.S. Naval Academy and the oldest state capitol building. On the Chesapeake's Eastern Shore, **St. Michael's** has a wonderful maritime museum featuring the specialized craft that "fished" for blue crabs, steamer-type clams, and oysters and an example of a screw-pile (built on stilts) lighthouse on the grounds. Cruises usually end at **Old Town Alexandria,** Virginia, near Washington, and embark for ports into the South along the Intracoastal Waterway.

Clipper Cruise Line's
Nantucket Clipper

Address/Phone: Clipper Cruise Line, 7711 Bonhomme Avenue, St. Louis, MO 63105; (800) 325–0010 or (314) 727–2929; fax: (314) 727-6576; e-mail: SmallShip@aol.com; www.clippercruise.com

The Ship: *Nantucket Clipper*, built in 1984, has a tonnage of 95, a length of 207 feet, and a shallow draft.

Passengers: 100; mostly Americans fifty-five and up

Dress: Casual, with a jacket for the captain's reception

Officers/Crew: American

Cabins: 50 small doubles; all outside, most with windows, half opening onto a side deck

Fare: $$$

What's included: Cruise and port charges

What's not included: Airfare, shore excursions, drinks, tips

Highlights: Inshore, river, and island cruising, and an easy social life aboard

Other itineraries: In addition to these Eastern Seaboard cruises, which operate in the spring and fall, the *Nantucket Clipper* sails into the St. Lawrence River and the Great Lakes and along the Intracoastal Waterway to the Caribbean. The slightly larger *Yorktown Clipper* offers cruises between Panama, Baja California, the California Rivers, and the Inside Passage. The expedition-style *Clipper Adventurer* and *Clipper Odyssey* cover much of the world.

33

AMERICAN CANADIAN CARIBBEAN LINE'S
GRANDE MARINER
East Coast Inside Passage: New England to Florida

The *Grande Mariner* is the latest ship from Luther Blount's Rhode Island shipyard, and very similar to the earlier *Grande Caribe*. One hundred passengers, mainly well-traveled American retirees, are accommodated aboard, enjoying inland-waters cruising and one another's company rather than looking for the luxuries of a deep-sea cruise ship.

The lounge, located forward on the upper of two main accommodation decks, also serves as theater and lecture hall. One deck below, the dining room doubles as a card room and reading area after meals. The galley

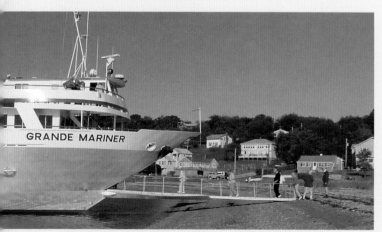

window opens into the dining room, where American fare is fresh, well prepared, and served family style at one open sitting. Lunch is usually soup, salad, pasta, or make-your-own sandwich.

No alcohol is sold, so passengers bring their own stock and the ship provides storage and setups gratis. The long Sun Deck has a protected viewing area, and the patented bow ramp lowers for dry beach landings.

The fifty cabins, of which forty-four are outside with windows (some slide open) and portholes, have twin or double beds. Several cabins aft on the Sun Deck open out onto the deck; otherwise they have access from a central corridor. Cabins have air-conditioning, limited stowage, and minuscule bathrooms with hand-held showers. As on all three ACCL vessels, there is a stair lift between decks, and smoking is permitted only on the open decks.

The Itinerary

Although this coastal cruise may begin in either Florida or **Rhode Island,** the narrative here will start in the Yankee North at the company headquarters and shipyard. Embarking the tiny ship, the course aims south into Long Island Sound, passing **New York**'s skyscrapers at

The Intracoastal Waterway stretches almost uninterrupted from Narrangansett Bay to south Florida, and a Gulf Coast section continues west to New Orleans and the Tex-Mex border. American Canadian Caribbean's Grande Mariner and fleetmates make the voyage every spring and fall, sailing past Manhattan's skyline, cruising the Chesapeake Bay and inside North Carolina's Outer Banks, and calling at historic ports from the antebellum South into the Sunshine State.

dawn, then out through the Narrows along the New Jersey coast for the only stretch of open ocean. Not far beyond Victorian Cape May, the *Grande Mariner* slices through the Delmarva Peninsula via the **Chesapeake and Delaware Canal** into the widening bay.

There are stops at **Baltimore Inner Harbor, Crisfield,** the capital for blue crabs, **Norfolk**'s busy waterfront, and the U.S. naval base at **Newport News.** The waterway opens wide through **Abermarle** and **Pamlico Sounds,** then narrows again south of Cape Hatteras, where happily the ship remains inside the breakers away from the graveyard of the Atlantic. When you stop at **Beaufort,** N.C., and **Beaufort,** S.C., you quickly learn, but may not remember, that they are pronounced quite differently (*bow-* and *bew*-fort, respectively). **Georgetown,** S.C., was once the largest port in the South, but today there's little sign of that, while **Charleston** and **Savannah** certainly impress as you approach and explore ashore.

The waterway is rural again in Georgia, with a stop at **St. Simon's Island;** then crossing into Florida, **St. Augustine** qualifies as America's oldest permanent European settlement. The ship is almost part of a convoy of yachts heading south for the winter, and there are many drawbridges that open for the waterborne traffic. The **Intracoastal Waterway** is especially busy along the Florida coast, with the cruise ending at **Palm Beach Gardens,** following two weeks of gradual climate change. Welcome to sunny Florida.

American Canadian Caribbean Line's
Grande Mariner

Address/Phone: American Canadian Caribbean Line, P.O. Box 368 Warren, RI 02885; (401) 247–0955; fax: (401) 247–2350; www.accl-smallships.com

The Ship: *Grande Mariner* was built in the company's shipyard in 1998, has a tonnage of 99, a length of 183 feet, and a shallow draft of just 6.5 feet.

Passengers: 100; age is fifty-five and up and mostly Americans

Dress: Casual at all times

Officers/Crew: American

Cabins: 50 cabins, all quite small with 6 inside

Fare: $$

What's included: Cruise and port charges, soft drinks, and setups for BYOB

What's not included: Airfare, shore excursions (very reasonably priced), tips

Highlights: An intracoastal route spanning the length of the East Coast offering a great variety of stops; a low-key social experience among like-minded passengers

Other itineraries: In addition to this fifteen-day inland waterways cruise, operating several times in spring and fall, ACCL offers summer options in New England, eastern Canada, Erie Canal, St. Lawrence Seaway, Great Lakes, and Mid-America, as well as winter cruises in Belize, Panama Canal, Caribbean, Orinoco River, and the Bahamas.

DELTA QUEEN STEAMBOAT'S *DELTA QUEEN*

Upper Mississippi River: St. Louis to St. Paul

Delta Queen Steamboat Company dates back more than one hundred years to the Greene Line of Steamers. The steamboat *Delta Queen,* first built in Scotland then completed in California in 1926, was first designed for overnight service between San Francisco and Sacramento, running opposite her mate, *Delta King,* now a hotel and restaurant on the Sacramento waterfront. She is a quintessential piece of Americana, evident the moment one treads her wooden decks and eyes the white-painted wood superstructure. The *DQ* may not be the opulent wedding cake like her big sister *American Queen,* but she is the real thing.

The lower of two forward lounges, graced with fluted columns and potted plants, is suitable for reading, playing cards, and having tea. The wooden grand staircase with shiny brass steps rises to the Victorian-style Texas Lounge with a bar, daytime games, a singer-pianist, and a popcorn machine. Dinner is served at two sittings. Service is casual and friendly and the food thoroughly American, featuring some Cajun-style soups and stuffed catfish among the usual meat, fish, and shellfish entrees. Portions are relatively small, yet sensible for diners who sample all five courses, and preparation ranges from good to excellent. The desserts, such as Mississippi Mud and pecan pie, are almost sinful.

Evening entertainment is popular, and following dinner, the lower-level dining room becomes a well-attended, old-fashioned music hall featuring ragtime, Dixieland, jazz, and blues. The engine room, where passengers are most welcome, is a spotless, eye-popping feast of brass fittings, multiple dials, and heaving machinery, and I love to go down to watch the slowly undulating Pitman arms turn the thrashing red wooden sternwheel.

Most of the eighty-seven staterooms are plain, with pipe racks for hanging clothes and functional baths. Most cabins open to covered or open decks with chairs on either side of the door. The better rooms feature stained-glass windows and open to the Betty Blake Lounge, a portrait and memorabilia gallery dotted with overstuffed chairs. The old-fashioned steam calliope over the bright red paddlewheel signals the steamboat's arrival at town landings, and the hearty toots to the shoreside warm even the most cynical hearts. People love to watch her pass, as she provides a glimpse of a bygone America. Some passengers are fiercely loyal to the *DQ* and would not consider sailing the other two "new boats."

The American steamboat triggers much the same emotional reactions as does the sight of a belching steam locomotive threading across the landscape or a hovering dirigible droning above a World Series game. Life on the Mississippi aboard the time-machine steamboat **Delta Queen,** *a National Historic Landmark, splashes along at the paddle-wheel pace of 6 to 8 miles per hour. You get a truly relaxing and thoroughly Middle American vacation celebrating big-band and Dixieland music, Southern and Cajun cooking, and the lore of the river, here along the scenic Upper Mississippi.*

The Itinerary

As the setting sun framed the **St. Louis** Gateway Arch one mid-August evening on my St. Paul–bound cruise, the *Delta Queen* eased away from the landing and headed upriver. In the week ahead we would sail 659 meandering miles and negotiate twenty-six locks en route to the headwaters of navigation. The average of 100 miles a day may take as many minutes in a car, but speed and distance become irrelevant after a full day on the river.

Most travelers quickly find a favorite spot on deck for taking in the slowly passing scenery. Forested banks, marshy coves, and high bluffs are the main characteristics of the **Upper Mississippi**. The approach to each town becomes a major event, and the *Delta Queen*'s throaty whistle and cheerful tunes from the century-old calliope announce the steamboat's arrival and draws people down to the river.

The Mississippi is a vibrant commercial waterway, and long strings of barges, pushed by towboats, move huge loads of grain, coal, scrap iron, and fuel. During locking operations people ashore share news, weather, and scenic highlights with passengers lining the rails. The passengers in turn answer questions about traveling aboard the *Delta Queen*. Daytime activities include kite flying and river lore and natural history talks at the bow and guided walks ashore. Stroll through Mark Twain's **Hannibal;** visit historic riverfront sites such as Villa Louis at **Prairie du Chien,** first established as a French fur-trading post; and walk into the red-brick Victorian lead-mining town of **Galena,** where U. S. Grant had a home that is open to visitors. The highlight at poky **Wabasha** is a visit to the Anderson House, where guests may rent a feline bedmate with their room. The *Delta Queen* ties up at **St. Paul** and many people choose to stay an extra night to visit the state capitol building, Fort Snelling, and railroad baron James J. Hill's house.

Delta Queen Steamboat's *Delta Queen*

Address/Phone: Delta Queen Steamboat Company, 5835 Blue Lagoon Drive, Miami, FL 33126; (800) 588–3609; fax: (504) 585-0690; www.deltaqueen.com

The Ship: *Delta Queen* was completed in 1926 for the Sacramento River trade and has been cruising the Midwestern rivers since 1948. The gross tonnage is 3,360, the length 285 feet, and the draft shallow.

Passengers: 174; age range fifty-five and up; mostly Americans

Dress: Jacket and tie optional for special evenings

Officers/Crew: American

Cabins: 87 cabins, all outside and most opening onto the open side deck; 19 have upper and lower berths, with the rest offering twin or queen-size beds

Fare: $$$

What's included: Cruise fare and port charges

What's not included: Airfare, shore excursions, drinks, tips

Highlights: Lazy river cruising aboard a floating National Historic Landmark

Other itineraries: In addition to this cruise aboard the *Delta Queen* which operates in the summer, the three steamboats together offer a huge range of itineraries on Midwest rivers, embarking in many different port cities and with cruises themed to big bands, great American performers, the Civil War, Kentucky Derby, fall foliage, and old-fashioned holidays, and many more. See *American Queen* and *Mississippi Queen*.

AMERICAN CANADIAN CARIBBEAN LINE'S
NIAGARA PRINCE
An Intricate Maze of Waterways: Chicago to New Orleans

American Canadian Caribbean Line, based on the Narragansett Bay at Warren, Rhode Island, is the creation of a Yankee entrepreneur named Luther Blount. In 1966 he initiated modern-day domestic coastal and inland cruises, and as the idea caught on, he designed purpose-built craft in his own shipyard.

The *Niagara Prince*, one of three nimble ships, can navigate the entire length of the Erie Canal, because it reduces its height off the water to just 16.5 feet by lowering the pilothouse, dismantling the funnel, and folding

the mast to slip under low, fixed bridges, built many years ago by the railroads in their efforts to kill off the competing barge canal business.

Unlike its running mates, the *Niagara Prince*'s dining room and lounge area ad-join each other rather than being located on separate decks. The dining tables and banquettes serve as additional lounge seating between meals for reading, cards, games, and puzzles. Video films and travel documentaries are shown at night on two screens. The roomy top deck has both covered and open portions. The food is good American cooking featuring excellent soups and salads, freshly baked breads and desserts, and entrees such as prime ribs, chicken stuffed with crabmeat, and yellowfin tuna. Lunch may be a build-your-own sandwich or salad and soup. For some diners the fixed-meal times of 8:00 A.M., noon, and 6:00 P.M. take getting used to. The ship is BYOB, and free setups and cold storage are provided.

All but two Main Deck cabins are outside, tiny doubles with two L-shaped lowers or upper and lower berths. The latter rooms may be used by single passengers. The higher grade Sun Deck cabins have sliding picture windows and twin or double beds, and six of the rooms open onto the narrow wraparound promenade. The curtained-off shower stall lies between the washbasin and toilet. Closet and drawer space are limited,

No North American itinerary includes more rivers and canals than American Canadian Caribbean's fifteen-day cruise, with a Civil War theme, between Chicago and New Orleans. The route follows a complex waterway system across the state of Illinois, then turns south into the Mississippi, up the Ohio and into the Cumberland, Tennessee, Tombigbee, and Mobile Rivers, finally joining the Intracoastal Waterway to New Orleans. The **Niagara Prince** *is a simple boat, not a luxury ship, and the passengers like it that way.*

but there is ample room beneath the bunks for storage, i.e., living out of a suitcase. Square footage is 72 to 96. First-timers will find no cabin keys, but soon they let the honor system prevail. Passengers are mostly well traveled, of retirement age, and looking for a social experience and new destinations. On my cruise out of Chicago, all but two passengers were ACCL repeaters. Normally, a 60 to 70 percent repeat level is not unusual.

The Itinerary

The *Niagara Prince* embarks at **Chicago's Navy Pier** and then crosses Illinois via the Calumet River, Calumet Sag Channel, Chicago Sanitary & Ship Canal, and the Des Plaines, Kankakee, and Illinois Rivers—interconnecting waterways used by rafts of barges transporting coal, scrap metal, salt, gravel, sand, and grain. On my cruise approaching the mighty Atchison, Topeka, & Santa Fe's Lemonte railroad bridge, the captain stood at the helm while his wife, the first mate, focused on the underside of the looming bridge and the eighty passengers lined the rails in hushed silence. Giving her husband the signal to proceed, the boat slid beneath with but a few inches to spare. Seconds later, a locomotive whistle blew, and Amtrak's crack *Southwest Chief* en route to Los Angeles thundered across.

Once beyond the metropolitan region, the settings change to state forests, wooded bluffs, and open farmland. The controlled waterway is interrupted with 600-foot-long locks that lower the ship from 2 feet to as much as 35 feet. Occasionally, one looks over levees to see cattle peacefully grazing on the fields below. An enjoyable bus trip includes the log village of **New Salem,** Illinois, where Abraham Lincoln had failed at running a business and then launched a rather more successful political career. Docked in the shadow of the Great Arch at **St. Louis,** and at the confluence of the Mississippi and Ohio Rivers near **Cairo,** pronounced "cayrow," one sees how different the river waters can look. A walking tour visits the historic river town of **Paducah,** Kentucky, and then in the Deep South, a call is made at **Waverly Plantation,** and two more calls offer Civil War buffs a look at the historic battle sites at **Demopolis** and **Shiloh.**

The *Niagara Prince* navigates the **Tennessee–Tombigbee Waterway,** which stirred up a lot of controversy as a pork barrel project when planned, then slips into **Mobile Bay** by the back door. The ship then turns west along the **Intracoastal Waterway** into **New Orleans.** When you look at a map, it is a wonder that any ship or boat could actually accomplish this circuitous route from Chicago to New Orleans.

American Canadian Caribbean Line's *Niagara Prince*

Address/Phone: American Canadian Caribbean Line, P.O. Box 368, Warren, RI 02885; (401) 247–0955; fax: (401) 247–2350; www.accl-smallships.com

The Ship: *Niagara Prince* was built in the company's shipyard in 1994 and has a length of 175 feet and a shallow draft of just over 6 feet.

Passengers: 84; age fifty-five and up, mostly Americans

Dress: Casual at all times

Officers/Crew: American

Cabins: 42 cabins, all quite small and just two insides

Fare: $$

What's included: Cruise and port charges, soft drinks, and setups for BYOB

What's not included: Airfare, shore excursions (very reasonably priced), tips

Highlights: An amazing route through Mid-America and the Deep South linking many waterways; a low-key social experience among like-minded passengers

Other itineraries: In addition to this fifteen-day inland waterways cruise, which operates several times a year, ACCL offers summer options in New England, eastern Canada, Erie Canal, the St. Lawrence Seaway, Great Lakes, Intracoastal Waterway, and winter cruises in Belize, Panama, Caribbean, Orinoco River, and the Bahamas.

DELTA QUEEN STEAMBOAT'S *AMERICAN QUEEN*

Cruising the Ohio River

Delta Queen Steamboat Company traces its origins back to 1890, the oldest U.S. flag cruise line, and today, with its fleet of three steamboats, the company celebrates Americana in music, food, small-town life, big cities, plantation homes, history, and steamboat lore.

I would take the *American Queen* anywhere as long as I could also enjoy the steamboat's remarkable ambience and interiors. Mounting the Grand Staircase for the first time and entering the Cabin Deck Lobby, I was dazzled by a stunning suite of rooms that could easily be the stately home of a nineteenth-century steel magnate or robber baron. Mahogany, silver, stained glass, etched glass, brass, marble, lace, leather, iron, plaster molding, tin ceilings, patterned wallpaper, thick carpets, oil paintings, chandeliers, stuffed animals, and a plethora of knickknacks outfit two Victorian parlors and a richly decorated club lounge.

The Grand Saloon aboard the *American Queen* turns an evening of entertainment into a major event for the staging of American musicals, jazz concerts, Dixieland, and big-band sounds. Designed after a small-town opera house, the theater has upholstered armchairs in curved theater boxes and deep cushioned lounge chairs on the lower level. Two massive globes ringed by gas-style lamps hang from a plaster ceiling of twinkling stars.

The J. M. White Dining Room recalls the main cabin lounge aboard the late nineteenth-century namesake steamboat with a pair of soaring two-deck-high sections

decorated with white filigree woodwork, colorful tapestries, and two huge, gilded antique mirrors. The food runs to American, Southern, and Cajun, with consistently satisfying prime ribs, roast duck, fried oysters, catfish stuffed with crab and wild rice, ravioli stuffed with shrimp, seafood gumbo, garlic and leek soup, Mississippi Mud Pie, and praline and pecan cheesecake.

On Cabin Deck above, the centrally positioned Mark Twain Gallery is a dark-paneled room that sparkles with display cases containing museum-quality collections of nineteenth-century maps, cameras, early radios, and showboat handbills and posters. River-related sheet music invites anyone to pluck the antique Steinway upright piano keys. In one corner a Victorian birdcage is home to a pair of chirpy tiger finches; and from an oversize armchair, there is a sneaky view down into the dining room.

To the right of the entrance foyer's Reed & Barton watercooler, the Gentlemen's Card Room welcomes both sexes to enjoy a game at cherry-wood tables encircled by a standing stuffed black bear, a working upright typewriter, a stereoscopic peep show, an iron fireplace, and Tiffany lamps ordered from an original nineteenth-century catalog. The Ladies' Parlor welcomes anyone to lounge on the swooning couch before a fireplace, its wooden mantle cluttered with black-and-white ancestral photographs and flanking vases. Floor lamps with linen shades, silver tea sets, a rosewood pump organ, and a floral wallpaper all add to the lovely room—a cozy

Delta Queen Steamboat Company spared no expense when they set out to build a spectacular floating Victorian wedding cake. The American Queen is as close as you will get to most people's idea of what an opulent, tall-stack steamboat should be, and an Ohio River cruise with lots of scenic variations is an appropriate itinerary to sample her.

spot for a read and for gazing out at the river through French doors or through a pretty curtained bay window.

The Front Porch of America, on Texas Deck, is aptly named for its sweeping views over the bow and furnishings of white wicker chairs and painted rockers. One deck above, the Chart Room is a hangout for the "riverlorian," who helps people get their bearings using flip charts and who spins tales every morning at eight.

Seven categories of cabins are beautifully decorated in elaborate Victorian style with patterned wallpaper and carpets, richly colored bedspreads, and wooden cabinets. Most cabins have cushioned wicker chairs and footstools and French doors that hook open to connect with the open deck. Twin beds are recessed into shallow arched niches, and bathrooms are tiled in black and white.

The *American Queen* is so much larger than her nineteenth-century predecessors that to slide under the numerous bridges on the Ohio and Upper Mississippi Rivers, the 109-foot-high twin feathered-topped stacks fold forward into cradles and the pilothouse cupola and rooster weather vane come off. Steam whistles are traditionally handed down from one boat to the next, and the *American Queen's* comes from the steamboat *Jason,* which accepted it from the *City of Memphis,* a boat that Mark Twain piloted.

The Itinerary

Pittsburgh, hemmed in by hills and sited where the confluence of the Allegheny and Monongahela Rivers form the Ohio, occupies the spot where steamboating originated in 1811. Embarkation takes place not far from the Golden Triangle, and once out of sight of the modern skyline, the Ohio becomes a feast of smokestack industry, towns that prospered because of the river location, soaring cliffs, and peaceful rural landscapes. The welcome mat is out at **Wellsburg,** West Virginia, a poky sort of place, whereas **Marietta,** Ohio, bustles by comparison along its tree-lined streets and at the Ohio River Museum's steamboat-era model and photo collection. The *W.P. Snyder, Jr.,* the last sternwheel steam-powered towboat, is open for a look into the crew's living quarters. At **Maysville,** on the Kentucky side, a coach tour visits three nearby covered bridges.

Cincinnati still exudes the importance of a river port as the skyline faces the mighty Ohio and waterfront parks link the landing with nearby Fountain Square. Tall Stacks, a huge civic celebration, draws thousands of spectators to see the gathering of steamboats every three years in October, the most recent one being in 1999.

Delta Queen Steamboat's
American Queen

Address/Phone: Delta Queen Steamboat Company, 5835 Blue Lagoon Drive, Miami, FL 33126; (800) 588–3609; fax: (504) 585–0690; www.deltaqueen.com

The Ship: *American Queen* was completed in 1995 and has a gross tonnage of 3,707, a length of 418 feet, and a shallow draft.

Passengers: 436; age fifty-five and up, mostly Americans

Dress: Jacket with tie optional at special dinners

Officers/Crew: American

Cabins: 222 cabins, 168 outside; some opening onto the side deck as well as an inside corridor; some with verandas and some with bay windows

Fare: $$$

What's included: Cruise fare and port charges

What's not included: Airfare, shore excursions, drinks, tips

Highlights: Outstanding recreation of floating American Victoriana, terrific music

Other itineraries: In addition to this cruise aboard the *American Queen,* which operates in the summer, the three steamboats together offer a wide range of itineraries on Midwestern rivers, embarking in many different port cities and with cruises themed to big bands, great American performers, the Civil War, fall foliage, and old-fashioned holidays, and many more. See the *Delta Queen* and *Mississippi Queen.*

DELTA QUEEN STEAMBOAT'S
MISSISSIPPI QUEEN
The Antebellum South

Delta Queen Steamboat Company is the largest operator of inland river cruises in North America, and its sternwheelers are American icons. The 414-passenger *Mississippi Queen*, built in 1976, is the second-largest stern-wheeler ever constructed after fleetmate *American Queen*. She seems more like a cruise ship than does the historic *Delta Queen*. This floating re-creation of nineteenth-century Americana has Victorian wall and fabric decor and furniture design alongside modern comfort and safety features.

The Paddlewheel Lounge rises two decks and overlooks the huge churning red wheel, and the Calliope Bar above also faces astern. The calliope is designed to impress the local town folks that a riverboat is coming, and the passengers take delight in feeling a tinge of importance at arriving in such a magnificent conveyance. The Grand Saloon, forward on the Observation Deck, serves well as the stylish brass-and-glass venue for a celebration of American music in the form of jazz groups, big bands, riverboat shows, Broadway revues, and cabarets. Port and starboard galleries house a card room-cum-lounge and a bar.

Dinner is at two sittings, and the best tables are by the large windows. The very good food is accented with regional flavors, particularly Cajun and Southern ones. Try the stuffed catfish, chilled blackened sirloin of beef, and crawfish en route for something different.

All 208 cabins have Victorian-style bedspreads and curtains, phones, two-channel radios, and thermostats. Half of the cabins have private verandas, and seventy-three are inside, with the lowest priced having upper and lower berths. Two of the largest face forward and flank the pilot house, and two more face aft over the wheel. Sixteen suites on Promenade Deck and two on Cabin Deck have sitting areas, twin or king beds, baths, and balconies.

The Itinerary

This **Lower Mississipp**i cruise has many variations in itinerary, but nearly all include the following calls once the steamboat gets beyond the industrial belt near **New Orleans.**

St. Francisville, built on high ground away from floods that destroyed the first settlement, may be seen on foot for its residential styles: antebellum, French colonial, Victorian, neoclassical, and dogtrot, a house divided by a breezeway. On upriver, **Natchez** has by far the largest collection of antebellum homes, numbering more than 200, and several house tours take in two or three of different styles. One, the largest octagonal

The Lower Mississippi from New Orleans north to Natchez and Vicksburg is the quintessential stretch of Old Man River, featuring what most travelers expect the South to represent, such as elegant plantation homes, Civil War battlefields, a dash of Cajun heritage, and steamboating. All three sternwheelers cruise here outside of the hot summer months, and for this antebellum itinerary, we'll have a look at the Mississippi Queen.

Delta Queen Steamboat's
Mississippi Queen

Address/Phone: Delta Queen Steamboat Company, 5835 Blue Lagoon Drive, Miami, FL 33126; (800) 588–3609; fax: (504) 585–0690; www.deltaqueen.com

The Ship: *Mississippi Queen* was completed in 1976 and has a gross tonnage of 3,360, a length of 382 feet, and a shallow draft.

Passengers: 414; age fifty-five and up; mostly Americans

Dress: Jacket and tie optional for special evenings

Officers/Crew: American

Cabins: 208 in a variety of configurations, including 104 with verandas

Fare: $$$

What's included: Cruise fare and port charges

What's not included: Airfare, shore excursions, drinks, tips

Highlights: Musical entertainment aboard and the antebellum South ashore

Other itineraries: In addition to this Lower Mississippi cruise varying between four and seven days, the three steamboats offer a variety of river itineraries and embarkation cities such as New Orleans, Memphis, St. Louis, Louisville, Cincinnati, Pittsburgh, and St. Paul. Theme cruises feature Dixieland music, the Old South, the annual "Great Steamboat Race," and a Kentucky Derby cruise, when she docks in Louisville. See the *American Queen* and the *Delta Queen.*

house in the United States, remains unfinished, but it comes with an amazing tale of a mother bringing up the children in the basement after her husband was killed in the Civil War. Then **Vicksburg,** the site of a great battle during the War Between the States, offers a military-park tour, the Gray and Blue Naval Museum, and a Civil War–era gunboat that was dredged up from the muddy Mississippi. The first Coca-Cola was bottled here to be sent out into the country.

If it's spring, river fog may rise in the early evening, and the steamboat will make for the nearest stout tree to tie up for the night until visibility improves. The *Mississippi Queen* conveniently makes levee landings, and, on the other side, there are classic antebellum homes to visit. **Houmas House** and **Oak Alley** both feature excellent costumed guides, good interior furnishings, and attractive gardens. They both provided settings for Bette Davis's horror film *Hush...Hush, Sweet Charlotte,* whereas Oak Alley also served Tom Cruise in *Conversations with a Vampire.* Following a visit to the latter, I walked along the levee and wandered back through tiny church communities set among cane fields.

Baton Rouge, the state capital, invariably leads the guides to reciting colorful accounts of Louisiana's Governor Huey P. Long, none requiring embellishing. The highlight here is Rural Life Museum, a collection of historic buildings that would have been out the back door of the plantation house, such as slave quarters, a barn, a small store, a one-room schoolhouse, an overseer's house, and a church. Another tour introduces Cajun music, language, customs, and food. The Lower Mississippi is not especially scenic, but this stretch provides an excellent glimpse into the antebellum and Civil War South.

RIVERBARGE EXCURSION LINES'
RIVER EXPLORER
Louisiana Bayou Cajun and Creole Cruising

RiverBarge Excursion Lines is the creation of Eddie Conrad, a New Orleans towboat and barge owner. Building on his commercial experience, he constructed two three-deck hotel barges—one *(DeSoto)* for the cabin accommodations and the other *(LaSalle)* housing the public spaces—lashed them together, and had them propelled by a towboat *(Miss Nari)*. The complete rig is a sight to behold, having a length of 730 feet and a width of 54 feet, fitting snugly into the locks of the Intracoastal Waterway.

The interior design is spacious, modern in decor, and features huge view windows. My favorite spot is the Guest Pilot House, an observation lounge facing forward, where there are lots of charts and maps to study and communications between river pilots to listen to. The *River Explorer*'s navigating pilot is one deck above, and he welcomes visitors when the barge is tied up.

The Lobby, aft of the Guest Pilot House, provides lounge and banquette seating, twenty-four-hour coffee, and a jumbo cookie jar. Pretty etched glass panels, which depict highway bridges crossing rivers, decorate the seat backs, and a giant steering wheel has been adapted as a centerpiece. The shop for regional and RiverBarge souvenirs is called the Louisiana Purchase, and the Governor Chavez is a midships lounge for borrowing books and videos and for playing board games and cards at three large octagonal tables. The Sprague,

a bi-level room with mezzanine, provides the setting for local musicians, storytelling, and bingo during the day and after dinner.

All meals, apart from outdoor barbecues, are served in The Galley, a huge, light-filled space on the lowest passenger deck. Breakfast is buffet, with a cook to prepare omelets. Lunch (called dinner here) is also a buffet, with hot and cold selections, occasionally geared to the region, such as catfish and shrimp dishes on the southern excursions. Dinner (called supper) is wait-served and features an appetizer, a soup, a salad, a choice of two entrees, and freshly baked cakes and pies for dessert. Preparation is good to excellent, and the food reflects what most American passengers like when eating out at a proper restaurant. The helpful and upbeat staff serves coffee, tea, drinks, and wine.

Cabins, named after states and arranged in order of their entry into the Union, are larger than average, all with the same layout; those on the higher of the two decks have narrow verandas. Beds are twins or queens with wooden headboards and good individual reading lights. Cabins have windows that slide open, TV/VCR, fridge, desk, two chairs, and decent hanging and drawer space for what is a very casual cruise. Bathrooms have full tubs and showers.

Outdoor space, both covered and open, stretches for 500 feet along nearly the complete length of the top

European barging vacations have grown in popularity over the last three decades, and the concept has finally made its way to the United States, albeit on a much grander and considerably less expensive scale. The 198-passenger **River Explorer** *navigates Mid-America's waterways from Cincinnati and Kansas City to the Mexican border, offering a great variety of year-round itineraries.*

deck, with bar service, hot and cold hors d'oeuvres before dinner, and a popcorn machine.

The Itinerary

Most cruises last between six and eight days and travel the Mississippi, Missouri, Ohio, Cumberland, and Tennessee Rivers and the Intracoastal Waterway, running parallel to the Gulf of Mexico. My eight-night cruise, themed to Cajuns and Creoles, embarked in **New Orleans** and explored remote bayou country and the lower regions of the mighty Mississippi.

The first night docked at New Orleans allowed an afternoon and evening in the French Quarter. Two hours after setting off down river, the barge passed through the Algiers Lock into the **Intracoastal Waterway** that runs west and southwest across Louisiana and Texas to the Mexican border. The shipping channel, slicing through swamps and marshlands, was completed in 1949.

Following an overnight anchorage well out of sight of human habitation, we transferred to small launches for an exploratory trip into a cypress swamp to spot alligators, nutrias (a kind of rodent), great blue herons, great white egrets, cormorants, and even water moccasins. Then after a night docked at **Morgan City,** a full-day excursion went deep into **Cajun country,** settled by French-speaking Acadians.

The visits included the Joseph Jefferson House, built in 1870; the state's oldest rice company; the historic village of **St. Martinville** of the poem "Evangeline" fame; and Vermilionville, a collection of original and reconstructed Acadian buildings that represent how the Cajuns lived, worked, worshiped, and played. A very good seafood dinner took place at a lively Cajun dance hall.

Cruising north parallel to the Atchafalya River, we enjoyed a barbecue lunch out on deck, which included Cajun spiced crayfish. By the afternoon of the fourth day, we left the bayous and entered the **Mississippi River** to tie up at **Baton Rouge,** the Louisiana state capital.

Most everything in Baton Rouge was within walking distance: the old state capitol building; the art deco capitol building; the USS *Kidd*, an authentically restored World War II destroyer; and two gambling boats. En route down the Mississippi, a final call at **Laura Plantation,** built in 1805, showed how a Creole family and their slaves lived.

Tying up at New Orleans in the afternoon of the final full day, we were allowed additional time to enjoy the city before disembarking the next morning.

RiverBarge Excursion Lines' *River Explorer*

Address/Phone: RiverBarge Excursion Lines, 201 Opelousas Avenue, New Orleans, LA 70114; (888) GO–BARGE; fax: (504) 365–0000; e-mail: rel@riverbarge.com; website: www.riverbarge.com

The Ship: *River Explorer* was built in 1998 and has a gross tonnage of 8,864, a length, including both barges, of 590 feet, plus a 140-foot towboat, and a shallow draft.

Passengers: 198; Americans, fifty-five and up

Dress: Casual at all times

Officers/Crew: American

Cabins: 99; all similar in size; one deck with verandas and one deck without

Fare: $$

What's included: Cruise, port charges, shore excursions, tips

What's not included: Airfare, drinks

Highlights: Seeing America close up from its waterways, aboard a roomy floating home

Other itineraries: In addition to this eight-day Cajuns and Creoles cruise, there are four- to ten-day cruises of the Mississippi, Missouri, Ohio, Cumberland, and Tennessee Rivers and the Intracoastal Waterway along the Gulf Coast to the Mexican border.

CLIPPER CRUISE LINE'S *YORKTOWN CLIPPER*
Exploring California by River

Clipper Cruise Line of St. Louis, in business since 1983, attracts a fairly homogeneous crowd of mostly well-traveled folks to its U.S. flag coastal ships *Nantucket Clipper* and *Yorktown Clipper* and its newly acquired expeditions ships *Clipper Adventurer* and *Clipper Odyssey,* carrying between 102 and 138 passengers.

Aboard the *Yorktown Clipper*, the wraparound forward observation lounge provides a cozy, clubby experience before meals and during informal talks. The big-windowed dining room operates with one open sitting at tables of four to eight. The chefs, trained at the Culinary Institute of America in Hyde Park, New York, prepare excellent domestic fare using high quality ingredients. There's an easy relationship between the passengers and the young American dining and cabin staff. Dinner's first course is served during cocktail hour, and the hot and cold appetizers include jumbo shrimp, steamed mussels, smoked salmon, and stuffed mushroom caps. In the restaurant the menu offers a soup, two kinds of salads, and a choice of four entrees, such as shrimp scampi, roast duckling, linguine with clam sauce, a pasta and a vegetable pie, ending with a freshly prepared dessert, cheesecake, or a variety of ice creams. Wines are moderately priced. As an alternative, the observation lounge serves a continental breakfast and a light soup, sandwich, and salad lunch. Entertainment may be a jazz group one evening, a film on another, and talks by the naturalist and chef, but aboard it's mostly socializing among like-minded passengers.

The sixty-nine compact cabins, all outside, typically have parallel twin beds (some L-shaped beds) set before two picture windows, and thirty-eight open onto the promenade for access to the passing scene. There's a desk-cum-vanity, a chair, a half dozen small drawers, two closets, and a tiny bathroom with shower. Outside, fourteen times around the teak promenade equals a mile, and the sun deck above is partly covered and has a bar, but no swimming pool or whirlpool.

The Itinerary

Departure is from **Redwood City,** located south of San Francisco. The *Yorktown Clipper* then cruises northward, passing "the city by the bay" and Alcatraz to anchor off **Sausalito** for the night. A half-day tour to the awe-inspiring **Muir Woods** provides a walk among the giant redwood trees, or you can go ashore independently to explore Sausalito's several miles of waterfront, intriguing houseboat communities, and the Army Corps of Engineers working research model of San Francisco Bay. By passing into the narrow Carquinez Strait and entering Suisin Bay, you can view six decades of U.S. shipping—World War II Victory Ships, twin-funneled troopships,

The inland waterways of Northern California provide convenient access to San Francisco, waterside Sausalito, Napa Valley wine country, Sacramento, with its beautiful capitol building and one of the country's finest railroad museums, and Yosemite National Park. The comfortable, American conveyance is Clipper's 138–passenger **Yorktown Clipper.**

Clipper Cruise Line's
Yorktown Clipper

Address/Phone: Clipper Cruise Line, 7711 Bonhomme Avenue, St. Louis, MO 63105; (314) 727–2929 or (800) 325–0010; fax: (314) 727–6576; e-mail: SmallShip@aol.com; www.clippercruise.com

The Ship: *Yorktown Clipper,* built in 1988, has a gross tonnage of 99 tons, a special U.S. coastal measurement, a length of 257 feet, and a draft of 8 feet.

Passengers: 138; age fifty-five and up, nearly all Americans

Dress: Casual at all times, perhaps a jacket at the captain's welcome party

Officers/Crew: American

Cabins: 69; all outside, most with picture windows, none with verandas but more than half with opening onto a side deck

Fare: $$$

What's included: Cruise only and port charges

What's not included: Airfare, shore excursions, tips, and drinks

Highlights: Destination-oriented itineraries; relaxed social atmosphere; great meals

Other itineraries: In addition to the above six-day California rivers cruise, offered in the fall, the *Yorktown Clipper* and *Nantucket Clipper,* between them, cruise to Alaska, British Columbia, Sea of Cortez (Mexico), Panama Canal, Caribbean, Orinoco River, East Coast via the Intracoastal Waterway, Chesapeake Bay, Hudson River, New England, Eastern Canada, and Great Lakes. Expedition ships *Clipper Adventurer* and *Clipper Odyssey* take in much of the world: Arctic, Antarctica, Amazon, northern Europe, the Mediterranean, the Far East, Southeast Asia, and Australasia.

handsome conventional freighters, steam tankers, and naval vessels.

Urban and suburban landscapes turn to flat farmlands protected by parallel levees forming the deepwater ship channel inland to the California state capital. Tying up at a wood-chip wharf just outside **Sacramento,** one group heads by road for an all-day tour to **Yosemite National Park** while another takes the free shuttle into **Old Sacramento,** a restored nineteenth-century riverfront commercial and tourist district. The main attraction is the California State Railroad Museum, where I love to walk through a gently rocking sleeping car, a traveling railway post office, and a 1938 Santa Fe Super Chief dining car set with two dozen examples of railroad china. Nearby, the seventy-year-old *Delta King,* the sternwheeler *Delta Queen*'s permanently tied-up sibling, serves as floating hotel, restaurant, and meeting facility. Within fifteen minutes' walk of Old Sacramento are a fine arts museum, a tour of the beautiful restored state capitol building, and a kind of archaeological dig of the soon-to-be restored Leland Stanford mansion.

A sail downriver to **Vallejo** connects to a mini-bus tour of several different **Napa Valley** wineries, including one using the champagne method. On the last full day, the *Yorktown Clipper* docks at Pier 35, **San Francisco**'s cruise terminal, for easy access to Fisherman's Wharf, Ghirardelli Square, Coit Tower, Alcatraz by boat, and city highlights by coach. After dinner the captain may take his ship under the Golden Gate Bridge, then back along the twinkling skyline, and finally beneath the Oakland-Bay Bridge to tie up at Redwood City.

LINDBLAD EXPEDITIONS' *SEA LION*
Columbia and Snake Rivers in the Wake of Lewis & Clark

Lindblad Expeditions, the brainchild of Sven Olaf Lindblad, whose father, Lars Eric, pioneered expedition-style cruising, offers some of the most creative itineraries afloat, employs wonderful naturalists and historians, and attracts well-heeled passengers keen on seeing the world and sharing the experiences.

The seventy-passenger *Sea Lion* and fleetmate *Sea Bird* are not very fancy, but then luxurious accommodations and lounging by the pool are not why most people book. The 152-foot-long ships, really boats, have just four decks, and apart from a half dozen lower-deck cabins with a tiny porthole high in the cabin, rooms are outside doubles with large windows, parallel or angled twins or queen-size beds. All have tiny private bathrooms. Bridge and Upper Deck rooms open onto a covered side promenade, and those on Main Deck open into a central corridor linking the forward observation lounge and bar to the dining saloon. In the spirit of honesty that prevails onboard, there are no cabin keys, and on my cruise no one seemed to worry. Open seating prevails at all meals, and dinner may offer grilled salmon and roast duckling. Breakfast features freshly baked muffins and croissants and special hot dishes, and lunch consists of very good soups and tasty, overstuffed sandwiches. Wines include reds and whites from vineyards overlooking the river.

The Itinerary
The inland water route passes between forested slopes, apple orchards, and vineyards, cuts through deep gorges and wildlife refuges, and negotiates eight commercial locks. The upriver expedition is no sedentary deck-chair cruise. Instead, the inflatable Zodiac rafts, with professional naturalists at the helm, take passengers ashore for visits to tiny riverside villages and salmon fish ladders, and on hikes and exploratory trips along small streams. The Pacific Northwest's **Columbia** and **Snake Rivers** are the country's second-largest system, after the Mississippi and Missouri, in terms of length and area drained. At the beginning of the nineteenth-century, Meriwether Lewis and William Clark descended the Columbia and Snake in canoes as part of their legendary Western expedition.

The *Sea Lion* embarks at **Portland,** Oregon, and the little ship eases away from its berth for an overnight sail downriver. At dawn in the half-light of a near full moon, I watched Pacific breakers pounding hard on the Columbia Bar, a sand spit that stretches partway across the river's misty mouth. Later the ship ties up at **Astoria**—a fur-trading post established by John Jacob Astor and now a lumber port dotted with Victorian houses—for visits to the Columbia River Maritime Museum and Fort Clatsop, the latter replicating the primitive conditions that Lewis and Clark faced during the very wet winter of 1805–1806.

The seventy-passenger **Sea Lion** *sails 450 miles upriver through a landscape that begins wet and well watered just in from the Pacific Ocean breakers and becomes drier, more rugged, and remote until the small ship can go no farther on the border between Washington and Idaho. An outstanding enrichment program aboard, during informal talks, in the Zodiac rafts and ashore on excursions add immeasurably to the river-voyage's enjoyment.*

During the night the *Sea Lion* sails upstream to the **Columbia Gorge,** narrows flanked by steep, forested cliffs, and then into a lock at the **Bonneville Dam,** a massive hydroelectric project completed during the Great Depression. A fish ladder allows the migrating steelhead trout and chinook, sockeye, and coho salmon to travel upriver to spawn and then die. While riding the **Mount Hood Railroad,** a 22-mile line winding into the mountains, 11,239-foot Mount Hood, Oregon's highest peak, rises to the south while Washington's 12,307-foot Mount Adams looms to the north.

Farther upstream, the Columbia River completely alters its character. The well-watered landscape gives way to semiarid steppes, gracefully tapered buttes, and diminishing signs of habitation. From Zodiac landing craft the expedition leader points out great blue herons bobbing on the water, marsh hawks in trees, three soaring bald eagles, a white pelican with a 9-foot wingspan, and several mule deer on the shore. Entering the **Snake River,** the *Sea Lion* passes between the banks formed by the largest basaltic lava flow in the world and anchors at the mouth of the **Palouse River.** The ship's crew prepares an outdoor barbecue of salmon and steaks around a bonfire.

One morning before sunrise, high-speed jetboats roar into Idaho's **Hells Canyon,** the deepest gorge in North America. The sluggish Snake River became increasingly turbulent on the way upstream, making it difficult to imagine the turn-of-the-century sternwheelers climbing through the white-water rapids, even with the aid of cables. The nimble jetboat noses up to 3,000-year-old Native American petroglyphs painted on the flat rocks, and we spot mountain bighorn sheep hundreds of feet up the cliff face. During the cruise downriver the ship may stop in midstream at an island set against a backdrop of orange and red rock cliffs. Underfoot, the ground cover exhibits the colors of yellow rabbit brush, pink and gray buckwheat, blue aster, and loose brown tumbleweed.

Lindblad Expeditions'
Sea Lion

Address/Phone: Lindblad Expeditions, 720 Fifth Avenue, New York, NY 10019; (212) 765–7740 or (800) 397–3348; fax: (212) 265–3370; email: explore@specialexpeditions.com; www.expeditions.com

The Ship: *Sea Lion* (and *Sea Bird*) were built in 1981 and have a gross tonnage of 99.7, a special U.S. Coast Guard measurement, a length of 152 feet, and a draft of 8 feet.

Passengers: 70; ages fifty and up, almost exclusively Americans

Dress: Casual at all times

Officers/Crew: American

Cabins: 37 outside tiny cabins, 26 opening onto the promenade and 5 on the lower deck with a portlight high in the room

Fare: $$$

What's included: All shore excursions, entrance fees, tips to guides ashore, port charges

What's not included: Airfares, alcoholic beverages, tips to crew

Other itineraries: In addition to the above seven-night Columbia and Snake itinerary, offered in May, September, and October, the *Sea Lion* and *Sea Bird* cruise up to Alaska and south to the Sea of Cortez and Baja California. The Polaris is based in the Galápagos Islands, and the deep-sea expedition ship *Endeavour,* the former *Caledonian Star,* sails to Antarctica, South America, and Europe.

DELTA QUEEN STEAMBOAT'S *COLUMBIA QUEEN*

Riverboat Cruise Deep into the Pacific Northwest

Delta Queen Steamboat Company began trading along the Columbia and Snake Rivers in April 2000, operating a small riverboat along trade routes that date back to the mid-nineteenth century. Although the *Columbia Queen* is considerably smaller than the Delta Queen Steamboat Company's three sternwheelers, the ambience and purpose are similar, a destination-oriented cruise with a strong onboard lecture and musical program, for mostly older Americans.

Externally, the 218-foot vessel bears little resemblance to the sibling Mississippi fleet, whereas the interiors echo a turn-of-the-century style using traditional and modern materials. My favorite place within was the Purser's Lobby, an oval, wood-paneled room with deep cushioned leather chairs and couch, ideal for browsing the surrounding shelves for books and references on the Columbia and Snake River region. Forward facing on the deck above, the Explorer Bar provides a setting for the historian's early morning talks about the epic journey Meriwether Lewis and William Clark made in 1805–06 en route from the East Coast to the Pacific Northwest, initial contacts with Native Americans, the first settlers and missionaries, removing hazards to river navigation, the coming of the railroads, and dam building. In the early evening, a pianist plays, and popcorn pops next to the sit-up bar, a Delta Queen tradition.

In keeping with the area's bounty, the ship's Victorian-style Astoria dining room serves both grilled and smoked Pacific salmon, lightly fried oysters, pies made from Washington apples, and chardonnays from both Oregon and Washington. The American-style cooking is every bit as good as aboard the Mississippi River steamboats, and the restaurant and bar service is both spirited and professional. Breakfast and lunch are open seatings, and dinner is served at reserved tables at 6:00 and 7:30 P.M. After dinner, the generously proportioned space becomes a showroom for an evening of purely American music, back-country cowboy humor, and performed tales of the Oregon Trail—all good fun.

A light breakfast is served on the Back Porch, furnished with rustic-style, white wicker chairs, a popular venue while churning up through the deeply forested Columbia River Gorge and rising in one of the eight locks, six of them individually higher than the 85-foot combined total of the Panama Canal's three Gatun Locks.

Eighty-one cabins are spread over three decks, and the outward facing ones open onto either the deck or a narrow covered side promenade, or they have tall windows that open inward like French doors. A typical AA category cabin, 37 in number, measures a roomy 165 square feet and has twin beds (convertible to king size) covered with Indian-style Pendleton blankets, oak

The 161-passenger **Columbia Queen** *plies the Columbia and Snake Rivers on seven-night voyages between the end of March and the end of November, offering one of the longest seasons of any operator. The riverboat's decor appropriately reflects the Indian and pioneering traditions of the Pacific Northwest.*

furniture, a desk, and a wardrobe. Big windows and a door to a semiprivate covered deck give quick access to the ever-changing scenery. All staterooms have satellite TV, VCRs with free use of videos, radios, hair dryers, irons, and ironing boards.

The Itinerary

The cruise tour begins with a night at the Embassy Suites' historic Multnomah Hotel in the center of **Portland,** a most attractive city to have a wander. Then on Saturday, the trip begins in earnest with a motor coach ride up snowcapped **Mount St**. **Helens** to see the devastation wrought by the 1980 eruption, followed by embarkation in the afternoon. Few passengers who come aboard the *Columbia Queen* have much inkling of just how dramatic a river journey can be.

At dawn on the first morning of the cruise, after an overnight passage from Portland, I awoke to the sight of Pacific breakers pounding the breakwater at the mouth of the **Columbia River.** The boat then turned inland to dock at **Astoria** for excursions to the ocean at **Cannon Beach,** Lewis and Clark's **Fort Clatsop,** and the Astoria Column with its sweeping mountain, sea, and river views. Traveling upriver through the **Columbia Gorge,** there's a stop at cliffside **Mary Hill Museum,** with its eclectic collection of Native American artifacts, Rodin sculpture, and Faberge eggs, and the salmon fish ladders and hydroelectric power stations at **The Dalles. Pendleton** offers a sample of its famous roundup, a tour down into the nineteenth-century Chinese ghetto built beneath the city streets, and the town's woolen mills. At the headwaters of navigation where Idaho, Oregon, and Washington borders meet, passengers switch to a jet boat for a ride up through **Hells Canyon** rapids on the **Snake River,** overlooked by herds of bighorn sheep. The National Park Service interprets the tragic story of the **Whitman Mission** massacre in 1847, and **Fort Walla Walla** exhibits village life in the 1800s. A drive up to the lower slopes of **Mount Hood** includes lunch and a tour of **Timberline Lodge,** a superb example of Depression-era architecture, arts, and crafts.

The *Columbia Queen* offers more comfortable cabins and elegant public rooms than Lindblad Expeditions' seasonal seventy-passenger *Sea Bird* and *Sea Lion,* though the latter's enrichment program is more extensive. Passengers drawn to the rivers are mostly fifty-five and up, seasoned travelers who enjoy each other's company and learning about the region's history, wildlife, ecology, and natural beauty.

Delta Queen Steamboat's
Columbia Queen

Address/Phone: Delta Queen Steamboat Company, 5835 Blue Lagoon Drive, Miami, FL 33126; (800) 588–3609; fax: (504) 585–0690; www.deltaqueen.com

The Ship: *Columbia Queen* was built in 2000, is 218 feet in length, and has a draft of 8 feet.

Passengers: 161; mostly Americans fifty-five and up

Dress: Casual, with a jacket on the captain's night

Officers/Crew: American

Cabins: 81; 58 are outside, and most of these open to a side deck or have French balconies

Fare: $$$

What's included: Cruise and shore excursions

What's not included: Airfare, port charges, drinks, and tips

Highlights: Varied landscapes and shore program; warm, friendly atmosphere aboard

Other itineraries: In addition to this eight-night cruise, Delta Queen operates three sternwheel steamboats on the Mississippi and tributaries and two brand-new coastal ships, *Cape May Light* and *Cape Cod Light*, along the U.S. and Canada's east coast, the St. Lawrence Valley, and the Great Lakes.

ST. LAWRENCE CRUISE LINES'
CANADIAN EMPRESS
Steamboating the St. Lawrence River

St. Lawrence Cruise Lines is a family operation based in Kingston, Ontario, that started in 1981 with the sixty-four-passenger *Canadian Empress.* Externally, the ship is odd-looking, whereas her interiors faithfully re-create the warm atmosphere of a turn-of-the-century Canadian steamboat. The Grand Saloon on Rideau Deck is a fine period combination dining room and lounge, from its pressed white tin ceiling to the red, orange, and yellow Axminster carpet.

Meals aboard may be one sitting or two, depending on the shore program. Main dishes at lunch and dinner include fresh fillet of perch, tender roast pork, and succulent roast beef. The soups are uniformly good, but the salads rather nondescript, and desserts are simple cakes, pastry, and puddings. The young waitresses, in keeping with the period decor, wear attractive long, formal, dark-blue skirts and white blouses at night and blue-and-white sailor suits during the day. Entertainment features a band for dancing and sing-along, followed by a shore-side campfire weenie roast.

The thirty-two cabins are priced in four different categories, but twenty-eight are virtually identical, differing in location. Most have parallel twin beds (four offer double beds) with the pillow-end set beneath the windows that open. The rooms are small, but during the day there is ample floor space, with one bed raised and the other becoming a sofa. Rosewood trim, red curtains and bedspreads, white walls, and white tin ceiling lend a pleasant air. All the cabins, apart from the four most expensive, have a pipe rack and hooks rather than a closet, and a curtain, rather than a separate stall, shields the shower from the toilet.

Observation decks placed fore and aft provide sheltered open-air viewing. The Sun Deck, running nearly the full length of the ship, offers yellow-and-white canvas directors chairs and yellow chaise lounges, a relaxing setting to watch a game on the giant checkerboard, the pieces maneuvered with the help of hooked poles.

The Itinerary

The *Canadian Empress* sails from **Quebec City,** with its ramparts, city walls, and Old World charm, for a rural stretch of the St. Lawrence punctuated with village churches. Montreal's Market Basin is conveniently situated for visiting **Old Montreal,** and soon after sailing,

Ever since the pioneering days of the sixteenth-century explorers, the mighty St. Lawrence River has formed the main entry route from the Atlantic to the Great Lakes. The scenic stretch between the former Canadian capital of Kingston and French-speaking Montreal and Quebec City includes the Thousand Islands, Upper Canada Village, and the locks of the St. Lawrence Seaway forming the principal route for the charming little Canadian Empress.

the ship enters the **St. Lawrence Seaway**'s first set of seven locks that create a series of controlled channels and pools. In minutes the *Empress* rises from the gloomy depths of a dank chamber on a flood of gravity-flow water to reveal the broad countryside beyond. Shortly after completing the transit through St. Catherine's Lock, the *Canadian Empress* ties up, still within sight of the city lights atop Mont Royal. Great Lakes iron ore and grain carriers slide silently by during the night, gently rocking the little ship.

Upper Canada Village, highlight of the trips ashore, is a composite of houses, public and farm buildings, and churches spanning more than a hundred years of Canadian architecture. This working community came about in 1961, to save something important from each of the eight towns that would soon be submerged by St. Lawrence Seaway construction. In the circa-1800 Ross-Baffin House, women explain how to make colorful quilts for the village beds and how to hook rugs for the floors. The Greek Revival Chrysler Hall offers a beautiful slide presentation showing Upper Canada Village at work and at play in all four seasons. Next door the bakery ovens produce fresh loaves of bread that will soon appear on *Canadian Empress* tables at lunchtime.

Fort Wellington served as a British garrison during the War of 1812 and later as a Royal Canadian Rifle Regiment to protect shipping. On the U.S. side the Frederic Remington Art Museum displays the master of Western American Art's paintings, watercolors and bronzes depicting heroic and savage scenes of cowboys, soldiers, and Indians. The Antique Boat Museum houses the largest collection of inland water recreational boats in the world.

On the final day the *Canadian Empress* cruises among the fairyland of the rocky and wooded **Thousand Islands,** on which stand an enormous variety of simple and elaborate, shingled, clapboard, and stone summer houses. The American Narrows once attracted Helena Rubenstein, Mary Pickford, Irving Berlin, and John Jacob Astor. The granddaddy of all, **Boldt Castle**—a huge eclectic, medieval-style fortress—was never finished, and a trip ashore explores 120 rooms, formal gardens and outbuildings. The cruise ends approaching **Kingston,** its well-proportioned skyline punctuated by the attractive limestone buildings of the Royal Military College, Old Port Henry, and City Hall.

St. Lawrence Cruise Lines' *Canadian Empress*

Address/Phone: St. Lawrence Cruise Lines, 253 Ontario Street, Kingston, Ontario, Canada K7L 2Z4; (613) 549–8091 or (800) 267–7868; fax: (613) 549–8410; www.StLawrenceCruiseLines.com

The Ship: *Canadian Empress,* built in 1981, has a displacement tonnage of 321, a length of 108 feet, and a shallow draft of 4.9 feet.

Passengers: 66; age fifty-five and up, divided between Americans and Canadians

Dress: Casual; jacket and maybe a tie one night

Officers/Crew: Canadian

Cabins: 32; tiny but all outside with windows, a few forward with portholes

Fares: $$

What's included: Cruise, shore excursions

What's not included: Airfare and, if required, rail fare to embarkation port, drinks, tips

Highlights: Varied scenery, the Seaway, Upper Canada Village, friendly ambience on ship

Other itineraries: In addition to this six-night cruise from Quebec to Kingston, the ship also offers five-night cruises between Kingston and Ottawa. The season runs from early May to the end of October.

ONTARIO WATERWAY CRUISES'
KAWARTHA VOYAGEUR
Exploring the Trent-Severn Waterway

In 1982 a farming family named Ackert went into the cruising business by offering overnight trips here and along the 125-mile Rideau Canal, the latter connecting Kingston and Ottawa, Canada's former and present capital. Between mid-May and mid-October, the forty-five-passenger *Kawartha Voyageur* offers three different five- and six-night itineraries.

At first sight docked at a downtown Peterborough marina, the trim blue-and-white vessel resembles an overgrown houseboat. Stepping aboard, the main deck corridor leads to twenty-three outside cabins, minute by deep-sea cruise ship standards. Twenty-one doubles are fitted with twin beds, open shelves, pipe racks for hanging clothes, a curtained-off sink and toilet, and a large screened window that opens. Commodious showers with dressing rooms are located at the end of the passageway. Two additional cabins cater to the handicapped and single traveler. On the deck above a cheerful observation lounge occupies the forward end with a one-sitting dining room amidships and a tiny library alcove off to the side. Aft is the galley and crew quarters for the captain, first mate, and an all-female

crew. An open deck above runs the full length, and additional covered decks are located fore and aft on the main deck.

The dinner meats come from the family butcher, such as baked ham with candied yams, chicken breasts in melted Swiss cheese with brown and wild rice, and farm sausages with sauerkraut. The bran muffins, banana bread, lemon meringue pie, and English trifle are all baked onboard. Though there is no choice of menu, most passengers eat this kind of food at home, so the only "no thank you" would be for seconds. On average the mostly retired passengers are equally divided between Canadians and Americans who come to enjoy a slow-paced, scenic cruise with other genial folks. Many return to complete all three itineraries—Peterborough–Big Chute, Peterborough-Kingston, and Kingston-Ottawa.

The Itinerary
Embarking at **Peterborough,** Ontario, then not an hour into the cruise, the *Kawartha Voyageur* encounters a massive concrete structure and slides into an open chamber, and as the gates close behind, several

A glance at the map of Ontario Province shows the land lying between the Great Lakes Huron and Ontario laced with watery patches and meandering streams. To encourage the region's commerce and tourism, nineteenth-century Canadian visionaries joined the two lakes by digging a series of short canals and constructing forty-three locks that became the continuously navigable, 240-mile Trent-Severn Waterway. The tiny Canadian-flag Kawartha Voyageur follows this route, which includes narrow channels slicing through the center of town, fast flowing rivers, sizable lakes, and the engineering marvel of a pair of hydraulic–lift locks.

small boats settle into a second parallel tub 65 feet above. Without getting too complicated, an extra foot of water in the upper chamber causes it to descend while raising its opposite, and soon passengers standing at the stern are peering over a precipice to the channel far below.

Captain Marc Ackert, along with his brother John, constitute the second generation to own and operate the boat, while their wives, Heather and Joy, do the supplying and run the home office in **Orillia,** the largest town we visited. When the boat is tied up at a marina, they would often show up, with one or more children in tow, to bring needed stores and to socialize. During the day intrepid Captain Marc Ackert takes us ashore to the nineteenth-century home of Stephen Leacock, Canada's Mark Twain, warns us to sit down when we are about to pass under a low bridge, points out an osprey nest, offers freshly baked cookies to lock masters to speed our way through twenty-two locks, and entertains us at the keyboard one night after dinner. He lets us loose on small canal towns to shop or search for historical curiosities and tells us when we might go for a walk between closely spaced locks. We tie up at night, usually adjacent to a quiet park, and get underway after breakfast, threading along wooded waterways dotted with summer camps and through areas devoid of human habitation. Then without warning, the boat comes to a vast expanse of water, makes the crossing, and enters yet another twisting channel.

On the final morning we dock adjacent to the **Big Chute Marine Railway,** an ingenious mechanism for lifting boats around a Severn River waterfall. Boats slide into a submerged transfer platform, and once tied down, the structure rises on rails out of the water, crosses a highway protected by gates and flashing lights, and then descends to settle back into the river below. What takes five days to cover by water is but two and a half hours by bus, returning passengers to their cars or to connecting transportation.

Ontario Waterway Cruises'
Kawartha Voyageur

Address/Phone: Ontario Waterway Cruises, Box 6, Orillia, Ontario, Canada L3V 6H9; reservations (800) 561–5767 and inquiries: (705) 327–5767; e-mail: info@ontariowaterwaycruises.com; www.ontariowaterwaycruises.com

The Ship: *Kawartha Voyageur* was built in 1983, enlarged in 1995, and has a length of 108 feet and a shallow draft.

Passengers: 45; mostly fifty-five and up, split between Americans and Canadians

Dress: Casual at all times

Officers/Crew: Canadian

Cabins: 23; 21 tiny twins, 1 handicapped-equipped, and 1 single

Fare: $$

What's included: Cruise, port charges, excursions and bus back to the starting point

What's not included: Airfare, drinks, tips

Highlights: Scenic waterway cruising

Other itineraries: Besides this five-night cruise between Peterborough and Big Chute, operating between mid-May and mid-October in both directions, the *Kawartha Voyageur* makes five-night cruises between Kingston and Ottawa and Kingston and Peterborough.

ATLANTIC OCEAN

CELEBRITY CRUISES' *ZENITH*
Bermuda Cruising

Celebrity Cruises began as an upscale offshoot by the Greek Chandris family, and now the company is part of, but separate from, Royal Caribbean Cruises, Ltd. The *Zenith*'s understated elegance comes through in the beautifully appointed, tastefully decorated, and immaculately maintained public spaces and cabins. Service is polished but not pretentious.

Celebrity ships all have a common layout that is apparent throughout the fleet, whether it is on the 47,000-ton *Zenith* or the larger 73,000-ton *Galaxy* and *Mercury* described in the Caribbean sections. Aboard the *Zenith*, Deck 12, atop the ship, offers sports facilities with a jogging track and very recently expanded Health Club facilities that look out over the ocean. Deck 11 has the pool amidships and a lido dining area aft, including an outdoor grill and twenty-four-hour pizza service with cabin delivery in a cardboard box. The Fleet Bar, located above the bridge, offers a magnificent 180-degree view, a quiet spot during the daytime and for dancing in the evenings. The room pays homage to older Chandris ships.

The two-tiered show lounge occupies the forward space on Decks 7 and 8 and has excellent sight lines no matter where you choose to sit. Amidships on Deck 8

is Harry's Tavern, a wonderful European-style piano bar. Michael's Club is Celebrity's answer to the old-fashioned smoking room, beautifully appointed with overstuffed chairs and a steward present who will hand roll cigars. Outside the dining room the Rendez-Vous Lounge and Tastings, a champagne and caviar bar, are gathering places for a drink before dinner.

Food on Celebrity ships rates among the best available at this moderate price level. The ingredients are fresh, and the presentation is terrific and sometimes fanciful. Delectable soups and wonderful seafood and beef entrees are overseen by Michel Roux, who has been Celebrity's head of catering since 1990 and runs his own three-star (Michelin) restaurants.

If you want nonstop excitement and constant action, do not pay for passage on a Celebrity vessel, where daytime activities tend to be subdued, and evening entertainment in the show lounge is limited by the Bermudian government's restriction against use of professional entertainers while the ship is in port. Instead a variety of musical events to listen or dance to takes place in each lounge every evening.

Most cabins on the *Zenith* are identical, with the exception of the two Royal Suites and twenty Deluxe

A cruise to Bermuda is different from most one-week itineraries because there's only one destination and the ship stays in port, at Hamilton and St. George's, for the better part of four days, allowing lots of time to come and go while the ship acts as the hotel. Two nights and a day are spent at sea each way to and from New York, so the ship experience and Bermuda make a fine balance. Celebrity Cruises has the best food, service, and ambience, making the **Zenith** *a great choice.*

Suites, and none have balconies. The cabins measure 172 square feet, and regardless of whether you select an inside or outside stateroom, they are tastefully decorated with color-coordinated bedspreads, curtains, and upholstery and have two lower twin-size beds, which can be pushed together into one large bed or arranged in an L configuration for more floor space. A dressing table with drawers doubles as a desk, and there's a television, telephone, radio, safe, minibar, and glass-top sitting table with two chairs. Bathrooms are larger than average, and hair dryers are provided.

The Itinerary

Cruises begin with a grand departure from **New York** and offer two nights and a day at sea to settle into the ship's routine before docking in **Hamilton** at Front Street. From this convenient location it's easy to explore **Bermuda** on a tour, by taxi, moped, scooter, bicycle, or by a well-organized bus and ferry network. Rental cars are not available in Bermuda. Duty-free shopping in Hamilton is good, with high quality clothing, perfumes, bone china, and Irish linens available for sale in attractive settings.

The pastel-colored residences make a pretty picture on foot and when seen from afar by ferry to the **Royal Naval Dockyard,** which houses the maritime museum and is a center for crafts, shops, and nightclubs. Nearby **Somerset** has lots of restaurants and more shops.

Understandably, the pink coral beaches are a major draw, as is the snorkeling amid well-developed, beautiful reefs that offer a great variety of sea life and fascinating shipwrecks, some at snorkeling depths. Windsurfing, fishing, golf, tennis, and horseback riding may all be arranged by calling around. You can also hike the **Bermuda Railway Trail** from just outside Hamilton in the direction of St. George's, another port of call, and Somerset.

Celebrity Cruises' *Zenith*

Address/Phone: Celebrity Cruises, 1050 Caribbean Way, Miami, FL 33132; (305) 539–6000 or (800) 437–3111; www.celebritycruises.com

The Ship: *Zenith* was built in 1992, has a gross tonnage of 47,255, a length of 681 feet, and a draft of 24 feet.

Passengers: 1,374; mostly American couples in their late thirties to sixties; some families, too

Dress: Suits or tuxes for formal nights; jackets for informal night; slacks and collared shirts for casual nights

Officers/Crew: Greek officers; international crew

Cabins: 687, of which 541 are outside; none have verandas

Fare: $$

What's included: Cruise fare only

What's not included: Airfare, port charges, tips, drinks, shore excursions

Highlights: Stylish ship and great menus; Bermuda as a destination

Other itineraries: In addition to these seven-night Bermuda cruises, operating between April and October, the fleet also cruises the Caribbean, South America, Alaska, and Europe.

PRINCESS CRUISES' *PACIFIC PRINCESS*
Three Bermuda Ports Aboard the Love Boat

The 20,636-ton *Pacific Princess*, purpose-built in 1971 as the *Sea Venture* for Bermuda service, is distinctly smaller and less glamorous than the new Princess megaships. She will be withdrawn from service at the end of the 2002 season and replaced with another ship, but until then she remains a favorite choice for veteran cruisers and should delight first timers. At first sight, she appears dowdy by today's decorative standards, but her layout is cozy and charming, and she has an especially friendly crew. British-registered, she carries 640 passengers, a British captain, and an international crew of 350.

The forward Starlight Lounge on Sun Deck is the favorite viewing spot, and the Terrace Room one deck below and aft is a quiet retreat for reading and watching the ship's wake. Small-scale after-dinner shows take place in the Carousel Lounge, the Princess Theater shows films, and the captain officiates here at an interdenominational Sunday worship service, a long tradition on British ships. The Pacific Lounge opens onto the aft pool, and a second pool is located beneath a retractable glass roof, protection during inclement Atlantic Ocean weather. The poolside buffet prepares omelets to order at breakfast and provides an excellent salad bar at lunch. The Coral Dining Room, with an Italian chef in charge, offers a good continental menu and a very English afternoon tea. Other attractions are a comfy library with a view out to the promenade deck, a casino, shops, a gym, a sauna, and massage treatments. The cabins are a good average size, with 250 of the 320 outside, some with baths but none with verandas. Sofa beds are the norm, and all rooms come with TVs and bathrobes.

The Itinerary

No other ship has ever called at three Bermuda ports, and as this is really a destination cruise, access to all the island's attractions is particularly convenient. Late on a Sunday afternoon, the *Pacific Princess* sets sail from **Manhattan**, sailing down the Hudson River past the skyline, Ellis Island, and the Statue of Liberty to the open sea. Two nights and a day are spent cruising the Atlantic and settling into the shipboard routine before

Bermuda beckons visitors to its pink-sand beaches, pastel-colored towns, lots of sporting activities, and after dark entertainment. The Pacific Princess, the original TV "Love Boat," sails from New York between early May and late October to call at no less than three Bermuda ports—St. George's, Hamilton, and the Royal Naval Dockyard.

Princess Cruises' *Pacific Princess*

Address/Phone: Princess Cruises, 24305 Town Center Drive, Santa Clarita, CA 91355; (661) 753–0000 or (800) 774–6237; fax: (661) 259–3108; www.princesscruises.com

The Ship: *Pacific Princess* was built in 1971 as the *Sea Venture;* it has a gross tonnage of 20,636, a length of 554 feet, and a draft of 25 feet. She will be withdrawn from service at the end of the 2002 season.

Passengers: 640 passengers; mostly Americans age forty and up and not many children

Dress: Formal, informal, and casual for the three nights in ports

Officers/Crew: British captain; international crew

Cabins: 350 cabins; 250 outside and none with verandas

Fare: $$

What's included: Cruise only

What's not included: airfare, port charges, tips, drinks, and shore excursions

Highlights: A traditional small to midsize ship; three different ports on one island

Other itineraries: Besides these seven-day sailings to Bermuda between early May and late October, at other times of the year the *Pacific Princess* sails transatlantic to and from the Mediterranean, cruises in the Indian Ocean, and circumnavigates Africa. Other Princess ships are found in Alaska, the Caribbean, the Mediterranean, and indeed throughout most of the world.

the ship docks at **St. George's,** the island's original capital and the second oldest English New World town after Jamestown, Virginia. The first ship to arrive here in 1609 was the British sailing vessel *Sea Venture,* which ran on a reef, and involuntarily deposited the island's first settlers. *Sea Venture* also happens to be the original name for the *Pacific Princess,* which lands its passengers at a pier.

Early on Wednesday morning, the *Pacific Princess* casts off and makes for Front Street, **Hamilton,** docking by 9:00 A.M. Everything is within walking distance—the upscale shops featuring English woolens, linen, porcelain, and crystal; pubs; the Bermuda Cathedral; Parliament Building; Fort Hamilton for its panoramic views; and, for hikers, the 21-mile Bermuda Railway Trail.

Then at noon on Thursday, the *PP* sails across Grassy Bay to the **Royal Naval Dockyard,** a former British military base and now home to the Bermuda Maritime Museum, an arts center, a crafts market, a nightclub, and several restaurants. For those who prefer organized activities, there are guided walking tours, snorkeling trips, beach packages, glass-bottom boat rides, and a choice of golf courses.

The return sailing leaves Bermuda at noon on Friday, spends a day at sea, and arrives back in **New York** early on Sunday morning.

CUNARD LINE'S *QUEEN ELIZABETH 2*
The Ultimate Crossing: New York to England

Cunard Line is virtually synonymous with transatlantic travel, having plied the Great Circle route between England and America since 1840. Over the years, some of the most famous passenger ships ever built have sailed under the Cunard banner, including the *Lusitania,* the *Aquitania,* the *Queen Mary,* and the *Queen Elizabeth.* Today, even though owned by Carnival Corporation, the company steeps itself in its history and British formality, keeping the transatlantic era very much alive. In late 2003, a new Cunard liner, the *Queen Mary 2,* will debut, ensuring an almost uninterrupted seventy-year continuum of North Atlantic queens.

With her strong hull, variety of public spaces, and teak promenade decks, the *QE2* is truly a liner well suited for the Atlantic run. The ship is more formal on a crossing, with four straight nights when tuxedos are in the majority. The focus is never the next day's port, but rather the New or Old World at either end, blissfully several days away.

As a holdover from the former class system, your cabin grade determines your restaurant. While the menus are basically the same throughout, there is a noticeable difference in quality, service, and ambience. The Mauretania restaurant is the largest and offers two traditional seatings. One category above is the single-sitting Caronia, resplendent in mahogany wood trim after a December 1999 makeover. The ship's smallest

restaurants, the Britannia and Princess Grill, both seat just over one hundred people, and ordering off the menu is an added feature. At the very top is the Queens Grill, complete with its own private lounge. The three grills provide an unmistakable feeling of exclusivity, and each is reached by a private entrance. The Lido Restaurant provides three casual meals a day.

Over the years, the *QE2* has undergone many renovations and refits, transforming a product of the late 1960s into a celebration of the mid-1930s. The ship has never looked better. Of particular note is the Chart Room, a wonderful transatlantic setting adorned with the *Queen Mary*'s original piano.

There is an amazing variety of spaces onboard, from elegant, large rooms to cozy corners in bars. The Queens Room, the ship's ballroom, boasts the biggest dance floor at sea and is a cherished venue for a formal afternoon tea. An elaborate library and bookshop are supervised by the only seagoing professional librarians. The remodeled spa and gymnasium are deep down in the ship, offering a saltwater indoor pool and thalossotherapy (a fresh heated seawater treatment). The 550-seat, two-story theater screens films and hosts lectures by well-known experts on topics ranging from maritime history to America's influence on Russian culture. The two-story Grand Lounge is used for cabaret and play productions, the Yacht Club caters to

For some, the ultimate voyage is a transatlantic crossing onboard **Queen Elizabeth 2.** *Reveling in tradition and history, contented passengers enjoy five full days at sea, which soon melt indistinguishably one into another. This ship was built for Atlantic crossings, and repeat passengers swear that the sense of travel with a purpose makes this experience much more than just a cruise.*

the late-night crowd, and the Golden Lion pub supplies beer aficionados contentment well into the night.

Outside shuffleboard, a driving range, deck tennis, and basketball keep the active happy, while a Nursery and Teens Club provides reassurance for harried parents. Since the *QE2* is used as relocation transportation, the ship offers a garage and pet kennels.

Cabins come in all shapes and sizes, and with the coupling of the restaurant to your cabin grade, this is a most important choice. The minimum-grade cabins, inside with upper and lower berths, are small and not what one expects on a luxury ship, but they allow the less well-heeled to travel. Cabins increase in size from there, and most have personality with odd shapes and quirky designs. Grill category cabins will have wood paneling, and the original One Deck suites are just gorgeous, complete with walk-in closets, satin-lined walls, and oval-shaped windows.

The *QE2* has developed one of the most loyal followings afloat, and past passengers return time and time again. For anyone wishing to experience a trip into the grand style of the past, a crossing on the most famous ship in the world is absolutely not to be missed.

The Itinerary

The *QE2* sails regularly between Southampton and New York from April to October, and some years into December. Passengers spend five full days at sea. The appeal and romance of being on the immense North Atlantic is unmistakable, and the *QE2* steaming at 26 knots exudes a sense of power and strength.

Leaving **Southampton,** the ship sails down the **Solent,** passing the **Isle of Wight.** During the ensuing days, the weather turns colder and then warmer again as the ship arcs north along the Great Circle route. When the weather is fine and sunny, the open decks are full of passengers promenading, while others rest contentedly to read or snooze in wooden deck chairs, warmly wrapped in steamer rugs. On choppier days, the ship rises and falls on the sea swells and creaks within to remind you that you are aboard a ship that knows these waters well.

On the morning of the sixth day, most passengers are up early as the *QE2* arrives in **New York City.** A quick passage up the harbor brings you to the **Statue of Liberty,** the **Battery,** and the **World Trade Center,** docking just west of Midtown. As passengers disperse, the *QE2* remains in port for only eight hours, before again setting off across the Atlantic, conveying a whole new group of excited passengers.

Cunard Line's
Queen Elizabeth 2

Address/Phone: Cunard Line, 6100 Blue Lagoon Drive, Suite 400, Miami, FL 33126; (305) 463–3000 or (800) 7–CUNARD; fax: (305) 463–3010; www.cunardline.com

The Ship: *Queen Elizabeth 2* was built in 1969. It has a gross tonnage of 70, 327, a length of 963 feet, and a deep draft of 32 feet.

Passengers: 1,740; Americans, British, and Europeans of all ages, especially during the summer vacation months

Dress: Formal on the middle four nights, with almost all passengers in the grills wearing tuxedos; informal the first and last night

Officers/Crew: British officers; international crew

Cabins: 925, in a wide variety of shapes and sizes, 150 singles, 30 with verandas. Cabin category determines your restaurant.

Fare: $$$ to $$$$$

What's included: Cruise fare, transfers, and return airfare

What's not included: Port charges, drinks, tips

Highlights: A true Atlantic crossing; social life and a wide variety of activities onboard

Other itineraries: In addition to the frequent Atlantic crossings offered between April and October and December 2002, the *QE2* sails occasionally from New York or Southampton to cruise the Caribbean, Mediterranean, Canary Islands, or Europe. Recently, the ship began offering line voyages between Southampton and Cape Town. January to April, the ship undertakes her annual world cruise. The *Caronia* also makes more leisurely Atlantic crossings and cruises in Northern Europe, the Mediterranean, and South America.

CUNARD LINE'S *CARONIA*
Florida to England via the Southern Route

The name may be different and the flag now British but Cunard's *Caronia* remains the same classic liner in the European tradition that draws legions of loyal passengers back year after year. First built in northeast England as the 24,292-ton *Vistafjord* in 1973, she was the final ship delivered to Norwegian America Line. She immediately went into full-time worldwide cruising for between 550 and 620 one-class passengers. In 1980 she was sold to K/S Norwegian America Cruises A/S, and in 1983 the Cunard Line bought the ship and the Sagafjord, now Saga Rose.

The *Caronia* remains the choice for world travelers who like European-style service, low-key stage entertainment, ballroom dancing, classic concerts, and proper afternoon tea. For me, the real beauty of the transatlantic crossing is almost no interruption of life aboard.

Walking aboard, one enters a European-style boutique hotel, with large floral arrangements set against handsome wood paneling.

The most attractive space is the semicircular Garden Lounge, where the windows arc 180 degrees and the dominant colors are soft muted grays and blue greens. The room sweeps upward toward the bow, and the perimeter seating is higher than the circular center section, occupied by comfortable seating, a dance floor, and a bandstand. In the afternoon, one of the best formal teas at sea takes place. Stewards wheel carts laden with crustless sandwiches, pastries, and creamy scones, while a pianist plays in the back-

ground. After dinner, the formally dressed gather for an after-dinner drink and classical concert. An informal buffet-style tea takes place in the Ballroom, and both events are extremely well attended.

The high-ceilinged Ballroom is a throwback to the days when the main evening entertainment was dancing to a good band. Gentlemen hosts are on hand before and after dinner. The room also hosts vocalists, instrumentalists, and local groups who come aboard in port. A traditional cinema hosts special-interest lectures and screens first-run films, and not far away is a small casino. The library, while offering a very good hardcover and reference collection, is tiny, with just a couple of chairs and a sofa, so most people read elsewhere.

The Piccadilly Club serves several functions. It's a quiet lounge, a place for bridge instruction, and a late-night club, while the upper level is the Tivoli Restaurant. Every evening, dinner served to just thirty-five diners by reservation.

The Franconia Restaurant is designed to take the full complement of passengers and top officers at one sitting. There are many tables for two, including next to the windows, and when the ship is not full, tables for four seat two.

Because most of the passengers are American, British, and German, the menu caters to these nationalities with lots of fish, roast sirloin of beef, lamb, pheasant, venison, and very good pasta dishes. The menus do

*The 679-passenger **Caronia**, with the classic lines and ambience of a North Atlantic liner, is the next best ship to the **Queen Elizabeth 2** to undertake an ocean crossing. In fact, some will prefer her for the smaller size and less sense of importance. Hers is a more leisurely southern route.*

not repeat, even on long cruises. The staff is predominently European and well trained to serve passengers for whom dining is one of the major reasons to cruise.

The Lido buffet faces onto the afterdeck. The selections at breakfast and lunch vary daily, and locally purchased fresh fish or shellfish might appear at lunch. Seating is limited.

Since the *Caronia* is a classic older ship, the cabins vary greatly, even within the same category. Among the best features are the seventy-three single cabins, small yes, but designed for the person traveling alone. Most of the largest cabins and suites are high up on the Promenade, Sun, and Bridge Decks. Some have verandas, some face down onto the side promenade, and my favorite faces forward over the bow.

The wraparound promenade deck has shady recesses for reading and dozing, but the small after-facing tiered decks are the most sought after locations for a read or conversation while gazing down on the swimmers in the outdoor pool and over the stern to the ship's wake.

As the *Caronia* was built to cruise in cool waters, the ship has one of the few indoor pools and saunas, two decks below the lowest passenger cabin level. The spa is small and constricted by the limited space, but the number of treatments available is quite generous.

The Itinerary

The *Caronia* often takes the southern route to Europe for the late spring, summer, and fall season in Northern Europe and/or the Mediterranean. In March 2002, the ship will sail from Fort Lauderdale on a thirteen-day crossing with just two ports of call.

The first break in the rhythm is a two-day call at **Bermuda,** with lots of time to explore the island's coral sand beaches, upscale resorts, golf courses, the maritime museum at the **Royal Naval Dockyard,** the **Railway Trail,** and the shops along Front Street. Because it is still early in the season, the *Caronia* will be the only ship in port.

Several days later the ship calls at **Ponta Delgada,** the main city in the Portuguese **Azores.** Make up a foursome and hire a car and driver for the day to make a counterclockwise circuit, passing through beautiful countryside, following twisting lanes that parallel cliffs overlooking the sea, and visiting towns where the church dominates the main square.

The weather cools as the *Caronia* aims northeast to enter the **Bay of Biscay,** the **English Channel,** and the **Solent** to arrive in Britain at the very beginning of spring, finally docking in **Southampton.**

Cunard Line's *Caronia*

Address/Phone: Cunard Line, 6100 Blue Lagoon Drive, Suite 400, Miami, FL 33126; (800) 7–CUNARD; fax: (305) 463–3010; www.cunardline.com

The Ship: *Caronia* was built as the *Vistafjord* in 1973. It has a gross tonnage of 24,492, a length of 627 feet, and a draft of 27 feet.

Passengers: 679; Americans, British, and Germans age fifty and up

Dress: Formal evening, informal jacket and tie nights, and casual in port

Officers/Crew: British captain; European officers; European and international crew

Cabins: 376; 324 outside, 25 with verandas, and 73 singles (54 outside, 19 inside)

Fare: $$$

What's included: Cruise fare and port charges

What's not included: Airfare, tips, drinks, and shore excursions

Highlights: A classic ocean liner experience, European formality

Other itineraries: Besides this thirteen-day Atlantic crossing, which operates in March, the *Caronia* will return to South America in November. It cruises there through the winter, then spends the northern spring, summer, and early fall mostly in the Mediterranean.

STAR CLIPPERS' *ROYAL CLIPPER*
Mediterranean to the Caribbean under Sail

Approaching by tender, five tall bare poles rise above everything else in the harbor, then the full length of a shapely steel hull appears, stretching from a rounded overhang at the stern forward to the angular raked bow. A thick black stripe runs the full length, and black gun-port squares below give the ship an extra sense of importance. If one did not have a passenger ticket in hand, this ship might pass for a man-of-war, or at least a commercial cargo carrier.

The 228-passenger *Royal Clipper*'s purposeful appearance contrasts sharply with its 168-passenger running mates, *Star Flyer* and *Star Clipper,* both resembling large, white-hull racing yachts. The *Royal Clipper* is a full-rigged ship, with square sails on all five masts, while the earlier four-masters are barkentine rigged. At 439 feet, the *Royal Clipper* is 79 feet longer and qualifies as the longest and largest sailing vessel ever built, besting the Russian training ship *Sedov* in length and the German Flying P Line *Preussen* (1902–10) in overall size at 5,000 gross tons. She carries 56,000 square feet of Dacron sail, compared to 36,000 for the *Star Clipper* and *Star Flyer.* The twenty-member deck crew uses electric winches to angle the twenty-six square sails, and electric motors to furl and unfurl the square

sails stored in the yardarms and the eleven staysails, four jibs, and one gaff-rigged spanker.

On the Main Deck, an upward sloping observation lounge has a view of the forward deck and sees use for meetings, informal talks, and Internet connections. The main lounge, located amidships, is as comfortable as they come, with banquette, soft couch, and chair seating, a sit-up bar and a central well that looks down into the dining room two decks below. Through the aft doors, the covered Tropical Bar recalls the earlier pair, as does the paneled Edwardian library with its electric fireplace, though on a much larger scale.

The handsome paneled dining room with brass wall lamps, reached via a freestanding staircase from the lounge, has a large upper level surrounding a central well with some tables and the buffet. Tables are rectangular, round, and banquette style. An omelet chef cooks to order at breakfast and a carvery features roast beef, ham, and pork at lunch. Seating is open for all meals, and the lunch buffets are the biggest hit. The menu for the first day at sea includes jumbo shrimp, foie gras, artichoke hearts, herring, potato salad, lots of salad fixings, hot and cold salmon, meatballs, and sliced roast beef. The dining room is set low enough so

The most dramatic way to cross the Atlantic has to be aboard the square-rigged **Royal Clipper,** *a brand-new five-master that in mid-2000 became the third ship in the Star Clippers fleet. Twice a year, in the spring and again in the fall, the world's largest sailing ship ever built repositions between the Caribbean and the Mediterranean.*

that in any kind of sea, the water splashes washing machine–style over the portholes. For an actual underwater view, Captain Nemos, the gym, spa, tiled Turkish bath, and beauty salon, has lounge seating to the side where one can look for the creatures of the sea.

The deluxe suites are reached by walking along a central mahogany-paneled companionway, with a thick sloping mast penetrating the corridor at the forward end. The luxurious cabins, mahogany-paneled with rosewood framing and molding, contrast with an off-white ceiling and the upper portion of two walls. Pale gold-framed mirrors enlarge the space, and brass-framed windows bring in light to bathe the far corner sitting alcove. Brass wall lamps and sailing ship prints give the feel of a ship's cabin, upward sloping at that, not a hotel-style room on a hull.

A heavy wooden door leads to a private furnished teak veranda with shrouds passing upward from the ship's side. The huge marble bathroom comes with a Jacuzzi bath, which, like the TV and minibar, happily hidden from view, nods to an upscale cruise ship. There are fourteen of these 255-square-foot deluxe one-room suites, plus two even larger 320-square-foot owner's suites located at the stern and two 175-square-foot deluxe cabins that open onto the afterdeck. The most numerous standard cabins (eighty-eight) in categories 2 to 5 are 148 square feet and vary mostly by location. They have marble bathrooms with showers, TVs, satellite telephones, radio channels, private safes, and hair dryers. Six inside cabins round out the accommodations.

The real show is up on the Sun Deck. The full length of the Burma teak deck is cluttered with electric winches, halyards, belaying pins, lines, shackles, ventilators, lifeboats, and deck chairs arranged around three swimming pools. The center pool, 24 feet in length, has a glass bottom that drops into the piano lounge and serves as a skylight to the dining room three decks below.

A hydraulic platform stages the water sport activities, and the ship offers banana boats, water-skiing, diving, snorkeling, and swimming from the 16-foot inflatable raft. An interior stairway gives access to the marina. Two sixty-passenger tenders, resembling military landing craft, take passengers for beach landings. Two 150-passenger fiberglass tenders ferry passengers between the anchored ship and pier.

The Itinerary

On the westbound ocean crossing, the *Royal Clipper* embarks in **Cannes** and makes calls in Spain, such as the island of **Majorca** and **Malaga, Granada,** then **Casablanca** in Morocco and **Las Palmas** in the Canaries.

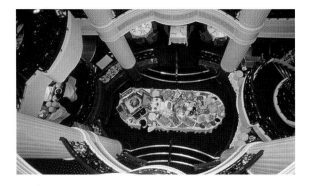

The last landfall signals the start of why people really come, the eleven unbroken days at sea, under sail.

In optimum wind conditions, the ship can attain 20 knots, but the schedule calls for half that. When there is no wind, the twin Caterpillar, 2,500-horsepower diesel engines can propel the ship at up to 14 knots. The exhaust leaves from the very top of the hollow mizzen and spanker masts, the highest being 197 feet above the waterline. However, the captains, being sailing ship enthusiasts, use the engines sparingly.

While passengers do not handle the sails as on the windjammers, they enjoy being part of the navigation by collecting on a raised platform with the helmsmen and one of the duty officers above the bridge and chart room. A lot of conversations ensue, and relationships develop over the periods of many days at sea. Crew members give lessons in sailing and rope tying. Passengers, wearing safety belts, may climb the steel masts to a crow's nest 60 feet above the deck, and they may also crawl out on the netting that cascades from the bow sprit. Suspended over the sea, they can watch the bow wave below and the masts swaying against the clouds and sky.

Every day at 10:00 A.M., the captain conducts story time, relating tales of the sea, defining nautical terms, and announcing special events. When the conditions are right, passengers can embark in one of the tenders to watch from a distance the ship proceeding under full sail. From a small boat at water level, the view of the *Royal Clipper* bearing down on you, fully dressed with all forty-two sails catching the wind and sun, is beyond words.

For those who have not crossed the Atlantic by sea, there is variation on the crossing-the-line ceremony, in which passengers and crew are initiated by King Neptune, his mermaid queen, and the ship's doctor. One day I intend to make that ultimate ocean voyage under sail.

Star Clippers' *Royal Clipper*

Address/Phone: Star Clippers, 4101 Salzebo Street, Coral Gables, FL 33146; (305) 442–0550; (800) 442–0551; brochures: (800) 442–0556; fax: (305) 442–1611; www.starclippers.com

The Ship: *Royal Clipper* was built in 2000. It has a gross tonnage of 5,000, a length of 439 feet, and a draft of 18.5 feet.

Passengers: 228, all ages, Americans and European; English is the lingua franca

Dress: Casual at all times

Officers/Crew: German captain; European officers; international crew

Cabins: 114; all but 6 outside, 14 with verandas

Fare: $$

What's included: Cruise only

What's not included: airfare, port charges, tips, drinks

Highlights: The ultimate in a sailing ship experience; social bonding aboard

Other itineraries: Besides these two annual transatlantic crossings, which take place in the spring and fall, Star Clippers offers sailing ship cruises aboard the *Royal Clipper* and *Star Clipper* in the Caribbean, with all three ships in the Eastern or Western Mediterranean. In the fall, the *Star Flyer* sails through Suez to cruise Malaysia and Thailand, returning via the Indian Ocean in April.

THE BAHAMAS
AND CARIBBEAN ISLANDS

DISNEY CRUISE LINE'S *DISNEY WONDER*
Bahamas Cruising for All Ages

Disney debuted its eagerly anticipated *Disney Magic* in 1998, promising creative innovations to family cruising. After some initial teething problems (including few activities for adults and poor food), the *Disney Magic* and *Disney Wonder* have settled down quite comfortably into a routine that pleases families, honeymooners, and Disney fans of all ages. While Disney's insistence on the ships being "just so" caused them to be delayed and over budget, the company also ended up with lavishly decorated ships with real pizzazz and style.

Inspired by classic ocean liner design, the 1999-built *Disney Wonder* looks very smart with her black hull, long bow, and twin funnels proudly adorned with Mickey's ears. Exploring further, you will find fanciful Disney touches everywhere, including an elaborate scrollwork of Steamboat Mickey on the bow, a larger-than-life Donald Duck hanging over the stern, painting the hull, and a bronze statue of Ariel from *The Little Mermaid* gracing the three-story atrium. However, these flourishes are fun and whimsical and do not overwhelm those with only a passing interest in cartoons.

In fact, much of the art nouveau decor is so stylish that it is hard to remember you are on a family-oriented cruise ship. Staircase railings are festooned with elaborate scrollwork and the Promenade Lounge, with its wood veneer paneling, soothing dark colors, and chic furniture is a delightful, elegant retreat from either the Caribbean sun or overactive kids.

In order to attract both families and those without kids, the ship has an "Adults Only" section with three types of entertainment. The Cadillac Lounge, a burgundy-colored piano bar with the fins of a 1958 DeVille on either end of the bar, is an atmospheric spot for predinner cocktails, while Wavebands, a large nightclub decorated with vintage radios and records, becomes popular late at night. Barrel of Laughs is a popular dueling pianos club you won't find on any other cruise line.

Of the three pools onboard, the most attractive one, nestled between the forward funnel and the mast, is off limits to kids. A modern health club and the ESPN skybox (cleverly located inside the forward funnel) keep most adults happy. As part of Disney's fanaticism for family entertainment, there is no casino onboard. Surprisingly, the segregation of kids and adults works well and is rigidly enforced.

Of course, kids have plenty of room to frolic, with activities broken into six age groups including a dedicated nursery. A large computer and science lab entertains the eight- to twelve-year-olds, while a mock pirate ship is the scene for games of make-believe with the

When Disney jumped into cruising, they brought with them their distinctive squeaky-clean fun and several new ideas. As expected, they have been a hit with families, who often combine the three- and four-night cruises with a package in Orlando. The biggest surprise, however, is how much fun these classically inspired ships can be for adults and non-Disney fanatics.

younger set. Teens find a hip coffeehouse all to themselves, filled with foosball tables, a big-screen TV, and large chairs for hanging out. With more than fifty youth counselors on some sailings, activities can be really creative, including kids-only shore excursions, animation classes, ship-wide treasure hunts, late-night supervised games on deck, and making commercials onboard. Two pools are also open to families, including one with Mickey's gloved hand supporting a slide. A movie theater shows Disney films throughout the day, while the Walt Disney Theatre performs well-received Broadway-style Disney favorites after dinner.

Cabins are large and designed for families, with some even accommodating five people. A unique feature is the one and a half bathrooms in every cabin (except categories 11 and 12).

Another Disney innovation is rotation dining, whereby you, your tablemates, and your waiters rotate each night through three dining rooms. One night you are in elegant Triton's, the next night you are transported to a tropical jungle in Parrot's Cay. Younger kids will probably like Animator's Palette the best (the walls, ceiling, and even the waiters' uniforms start off in only black and white but gradually change color through the meal). Food is standard cruise ship fare throughout, although the adults-only alternative restaurant, Palo's, is well worth the $5.00 charge for both its stunning Italian design and far superior food.

The Itinerary

Most passengers take the cruise as part of a combined Disney resort package, and Disney has made the transition between ship and shore as seamless as possible. Not only does a fleet of custom Disney buses transport you from your hotel to the spectacular art deco cruise terminal in **Port Canaveral,** but the same key you used for your hotel will work in your cabin on board as well.

After a late afternoon sailing, you arrive the next morning in **Nassau** for shopping at the **Straw Market,** gambling, or a visit to the Atlantis resort. The ship stays until 1:30 A.M., and in the evening there is a party on deck that culminates with streamers and confetti.

At **Castaway Cay,** Disney's private island, the ship actually docks. This is the only cruise line private island where anchoring offshore is not necessary. Certain areas of the island are sectioned off for kids or adults only. After a beach barbecue and last dip in the protected lagoon, it is time to head back to the ship and set sail for Port Canaveral.

Disney Cruise Line's
Disney Wonder

Address/Phone: Disney Cruise Line, P.O. Box 10210, Lake Buena Vista, FL 32830; (407) 566–7000 or (888) 325–2500; www.disneycruise.com

The Ship: *Disney Wonder* was built in 1999 and has a gross tonnage of 83,000, a length of 964 feet, and a draft of 25 feet.

Passengers: 1,750; many more if all third, fourth, and fifth berths are occupied; mostly American families with kids and couples in their thirties to fifties who love the Disney concept

Dress: Jackets for men are expected in Triton's and Palo's; collared shirts are fine in other restaurants. No shorts, jeans, or T-shirts in any restaurants.

Officers/Crew: International

Cabins: 875; 720 outside, 388 with verandas. Most cabins have one and a half bathrooms and a sitting area with a convertible couch to sleep three, four, or even five.

Fare: $$$

What's included: Cruise fare, port charges

What's not included: Airfare, tips, drinks, and shore excursions; water sports, bicycles, and strollers on Castaway Cay

Highlights: Fantastic children's facilities and an attractive, creative, and fun ship for families; superb private island

Other itineraries: *Disney Wonder* does both a three- and four-night itinerary, with alternate four-night voyages substituting a day at sea with a port call in Freeport. The *Disney Magic* does a seven-night itinerary calling at St. Thomas, St. Maarten, and Castaway Cay, with alternate trips to the Western Caribbean ports of Key West, Grand Cayman, Cozumel, and Castaway Cay.

PRINCESS CRUISES' *GRAND PRINCESS*

Eastern Caribbean Megaship Cruising

Princess Cruises, owned by the giant P&O Steam Navigation Company of London, is one of the largest and most innovative lines in the cruise business. For the first eighteen months of its life, the 109,000-ton *Grand Princess* was the world's biggest and most expensive ($450 million) cruise ship. With eighteen towering decks the ship is taller than the Statue of Liberty (from pedestal to torch) and too wide to fit through the Panama Canal.

The public areas range from the clubby, dimly lit Wheelhouse Bar, a repository of historic P&O paintings and maritime memorabilia, to Skywalkers, a spectacular observation lounge and nightclub suspended in a cylindrical pod 150 feet above the ocean at the rear of the ship. Entertainment venues include a two-story show lounge for big-cast Broadway-style musicals, a smaller lounge to present hypnotists and singers, and a third for dancing to a live band. The dazzling Atlantis Casino is one of the largest at sea, and Snookers is a woody sports bar. Connecting the principal public areas is an elegant three-story atrium, where a resident string quartet entertains passersby with classical music, recalling a grander era of sea travel. The ship carries two full-time florists to create and care for impressive flower arrangements and a large variety of live plants.

The *Grand Princess* has lots of dining options, and overall the food is good—not great—but the variety is laudable. The casual Horizon Terrace feels much smaller than it actually is, and clusters of buffet stations feature stir-fry, a carvery for sides of beef, turkey, and pork, salads fixings galore, heaps of fruit, and cheeses from around the world. Buffet-style breakfast, lunch, and dinner, as well as between-meal specialties, make this a twenty-four hour-a-day eatery. The three restaurants are named for Italian artists Leonardo da Vinci, Botticelli, and Michelangelo, and the decor reflects their artworks. Choices run to five entrees including prime rib, king crab legs, halibut in a citrus-caper butter sauce, rack of lamb with Dijon sauce, and pan-roasted rabbit with rosemary and sage, plus vegetarian choices. Reservations are taken for the Southwestern and Italian specialty restaurants. For noshing during the day, there's always pizza and grill food on the main pool deck, and Häagen-Dazs by the scoop or in a sundae for a charge.

The *Grand Princess* has no fewer than 710 cabins with verandas, but as they are tiered, passengers above look down on those below. All have refrigerators, TVs that broadcast CNN and ESPN, and terry-cloth robes. The twenty-eight wheelchair-accessible cabins make for a wider choice than that offered by any other ship.

The shipboard activities more than fill the three sea days, and the list is a long one. For a start you can play a nine-hole miniature golf course, a golf simulator, basketball, volleyball, and paddle tennis, or disappear

*The **Grand Princess**'s space-age profile is like nothing else at sea. Intimidating from afar, yet, in reality, the ship's well-laid-out interior is easy to navigate, and, even with a capacity load, this ship never feels crowded. The GP is truly a destination itself, and St. Thomas, St. Maarten, and Princess Cays take a backseat to life aboard.*

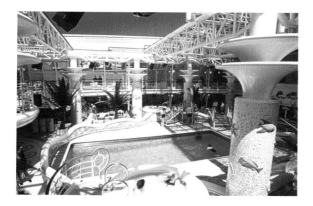

into a gigantic virtual-reality game room, where you can climb aboard for hang gliding, downhill skiing, fly-fishing, or motorcycle riding. Punctuated around the 1.7 acres of open deck space, there are four great pools, nine hot tubs, and oodles of space for sunbathing. The Plantation Spa offers massages and has saunas, steam rooms, aerobics classes, and an ocean-view gym and beauty parlor. Indoor activities include art auctions, bingo, cards, trivia games, port talks, beauty and spa demonstrations, and first-run movies.

Kids enjoy a two-story, indoor-outdoor Fun Zone, with toys, tricycles, games, splash pool, hot tub, computers, and a ball bin. Teens who like privacy have a disco and their own patch of deck space with chaise lounges. The captain performs legal marriages in an attractive wedding chapel on every cruise.

The Itinerary

Embarkation is at **Fort Lauderdale.** After a sea day to settle in, the first call is **St. Thomas,** a busy shopping mecca with pockets of nineteenth-century houses. Sailing leisurely overnight, the ship arrives off Dutch **St. Maarten.** The French side has charming residential sections and good beaches. The pace again slows with two nights and a day at sea and a final call at **Princess Cays.** This palm-fringed private island is set up for a barbecue, lying in a hammock, beach walking, swimming, and water sports such as snorkeling, jet skiing, and banana-boat rides for an extra charge. The last afternoon and night is at sea, with an early morning arrival back at **Fort Lauderdale.** An alternative weekly itinerary makes a western Caribbean loop, calling at Cozumel, Grand Cayman, Princess Cays, and the newly developed port of Costa Maya for less frequented Mayan ruins and good sand beaches.

Princess Cruises'
Grand Princess

Address/Phone: Princess Cruises, 24305 Town Center Drive, Santa Clarita, CA 91355 (661) 753–0000 or (800) 774–6237; fax: (661) 259–3108; www.princesscruises.com

The Ship: *Grand Princess* was built in 1998 and has a gross tonnage of 109,000, a length of 951 feet, and a draft of 26 feet.

Passengers: 2,600; mostly Americans in their thirties to seventies

Dress: Suits or tuxedos for formal nights, jackets for semiformal nights, and slacks and collared shirts for casual nights

Officers/Crew: British and Italian officers; international crew

Cabins: 1,300; 938 outside and 712 with private verandas

Fare: $$

What's included: Cruise fare and port charges

What's not included: Airfare, shore excursions, drinks, tips, lots of onboard extras

Highlights: Miniature golf course, golf simulator, virtual-reality game room, restaurants

Other itineraries: In addition to this seven-day Eastern Caribbean cruise, and on the alternative Western Caribbean cruise, the new *Golden Princess,* a sister-ship, makes twelve-night Mediterranean cruises between Barcelona and Istanbul from June through September.

CARNIVAL CRUISE LINES' *CARNIVAL VICTORY*
Eastern and Western Caribbean Megaship Cruising

Carnival Cruise Lines took a giant step in size with the building of the highly popular Carnival Destiny-class, and the third ship in this series, the *Carnival Victory,* boasts more than 500 veranda cabins and is extraordinarily popular. When the upper berths are filled, this ship's capacity climbs to 3,400, and when you add 1,000 crew members, you have 4,400 souls living on something less than 1,000 feet long. But they occupy a dozen passenger decks, more for the crew, and the ship is wide, in fact, too beamy to pass through the Panama Canal.

Four glass elevators soar through the ship's nine-deck atrium, which is more tasteful and less glitzy than the one aboard her predecessors. The three-deck Caribbean lounge can seat 1,500 for extravagant Las Vegas–style shows performed on a revolving stage and backed by an orchestra that rises out of the pit on a hydraulic lift. One club has a two-tiered dance floor surrounded by walls of video monitors, and the sports bar brings in the games on huge TV screens. The casino counts two dozen gaming tables and more than 300 slot machines, and for an intimate retreat, slip into the revolving piano bar.

The two bi-level dining rooms, the first for Carnival, have trios serenading during dinner, but the rooms are crowded, and the waiters work hard to keep up with the demand. The Mediterranean Buffet, designed as an international food court on two levels, seats more than 1,250 and serves everything the heart desires, including wok-prepared Chinese food, cooked-to-order pasta, and grilled hot dogs and hamburgers, and has a twenty-four-hour pizzeria.

Four outdoor pools, including one exclusively for children, a three-deck 214-foot spiral water slide, and seven whirlpools draw hundreds to the open decks which can get crowded on the days at sea. The Lido Deck pool has the protection of a retractable dome and the novelty of a swim-up bar. The huge Nautica Spa features two more whirlpools, a large gym, aerobics, and massage, loofah, sauna, and steam rooms. Children are well looked after at Camp Carnival, a two-deck suite of play areas and activities.

The 1,379 cabins are the most spacious and sophisticated in the Carnival fleet, with TVs that call up a selection of films for a charge, coffee tables, good closet space, hair dryers, and big showers. The ship has family cabins that sleep five and lots more that are interconnecting; more than half the outside cabins have balconies. No ship in the fleet is more popular than the *Carnival Victory*.

The largest cruise ships qualify as major destinations in their own right, and the 102,000-ton **Carnival Victory** *aptly fits this description. It's a twelve-deck city at sea overflowing with things to do during a week in the Caribbean or shorter cruises from New York to eastern Canada. First timers, families, and anyone looking for nonstop fun will enjoy this one.*

The Itinerary

Two alternating itineraries operate year-round and include three full days at sea. The ship's eastern Caribbean swing leaves **Miami,** spends a day at sea, and calls at **San Juan** for a flamenco-rumba show or city-sights tour, but you can easily do **Old San Juan** on your own, as it begins at the end of the pier. Sailing the short distance to **St. Croix,** there are more than a dozen choices including a beach party, a 12-mile guided bike tour, botanical garden visit, and catamaran sail. **St. Thomas,** next door, offers a party raft cruise with underwater viewing, snorkeling, and swimming, a trip up to Paradise Point for an island view, and shopping on a tour or on your own. The last two days are at sea, cruising slowly back to Miami.

On the ship's western Caribbean circuit, a full day is spent at sea before docking at **Cozumel,** where a ferry link to **Playa del Carmen** provides access to snorkeling, scuba diving, horseback riding around a ranch, and a trip down the coast to the walled Mayan city of **Tulum.** A second sea day is spent sailing eastward for a day onto **Grand Cayman.** The shore program includes several tours to Stingray City, to which are added an island tour, a catamaran cruise, and scuba diving. It's an overnight sail to Jamaica, where the most popular tours in **Ocho Rios** are to Dunn's River Falls to scurry 600 feet up the slippery rocks, in the shape of a giant staircase; a peaceful, 3-mile river-tubing ride; and horseback riding along the beach and into the shallow waters. Then enjoy the ship for two final nights and a full day at sea.

Carnival Cruise Lines' *Carnival Victory*

Address/Phone: Carnival Cruise Lines, 3655 NW 87th Avenue, Miami, FL 33178; (305) 599–2600 or (800) 327–9501; fax: (305) 406–4740; www.carnival.com

The Ship: *Carnival Victory* was built in 2000 and has a gross tonnage of 102,000, a length of 893 feet, and a draft of 27 feet.

Passengers: 2,758; mostly Americans in their twenties to sixties

Dress: Suits or tuxes for two formal nights; slacks and collared shirts for casual nights

Officers/Crew: Italian officers; international crew

Cabins: 1,379; 853 outside and 508 with private verandas

Fare: $$

What's included: Cruise and port charges

What's not included: Airfare, shore excursions and water sports, drinks, tips

Highlights: Nonstop activities, entertainment, pool slide

Other itineraries: In addition to the *Carnival Victory*'s seven-day Caribbean cruises, Carnival has many other itineraries in the Caribbean, Bahamas, Mexican coast, and Alaska.

CARNIVAL CRUISE LINES' *PARADISE*
Smoke-Free Caribbean Cruising

Carnival Cruise Lines stays on top of industry trends—balconies, pizza, patisseries—and creates some new ones of its own, in this case a completely smoke-free ship. There is no lighting up anywhere for passengers or crew, not even on the open decks. The penalty for those who do is a $250 fine, disembarkation at the next port of call, forfeiture of the cruise fare, and a return home at one's own expense. Nonsmokers love the idea, and those who don't have more than a dozen other Carnival ships from which to choose. The result is a more mellow atmosphere, because the bars and discos on the *Paradise* are noticeably less bustling and wind down earlier in the evening. Still, the *Paradise* is full of fun and displays that fantasyland collage of color, texture, and flashing lights for which Carnival is so famous, if slightly more subtle.

Some of the public rooms are downright elegant and use quality materials—leathers and suede, marble, tile, and stained glass. The Normandie show lounge, for instance, has an attractive art deco motif with copper friezes and wall accents, cherry and rosewood details on seating and wall designs, and a massive chandelier, a feast for the eyes before the curtain is ever raised on the elaborate Vegas-style musicals. The ship's Blue Riband library is a graceful tribute to the great ocean liners of the past, featuring a full-size replica of the Blue Riband trophy (awarded to the fastest Atlantic liner), displays of ship memorabilia, and a ceiling mural of the great Atlantic shipping lanes. The Rex disco is cute, with faux animal-skin upholstery and carpeting, and the piano bar has an American flag and funnel motif. Like all eight Fantasy-class ships, the *Paradise* has a six-story atrium flanked by glass-sided elevators, but this one features a bar and live music trio on the ground floor.

In addition to two formal, well-planned dining rooms, there's a huge buffet-style lido restaurant serving breakfast, lunch, and dinner to casual diners who would rather skip the formality of the main restaurant. Here, yummy pizzas, Caesar salads, and garlic bread are served twenty-four-hours a day, and self-serve frozen yogurt and soft-ice-cream machines are open most of the day. For passengers with an exotic palate, there's a bona fide, complimentary homemade sushi bar. Carnival's cuisine has really improved and is easily on par with the rest of the mainstream pack. Expect all-American favorites like surf-and-turf, prime rib and rib-eye steaks, as well as lots of pastas, grilled salmon, broiled halibut, Thai pork, and lamb dishes. There are also healthier "Nautica Spa" and vegetarian options on each menu.

Nobody throws a better party than Carnival, and in the case of the **Paradise***, it's entirely smoke-free. This extraordinarily successful company has the concept of fun, flashy, action-packed cruises in theme-park-like settings down to a science. The last of the Fantasy-class ships, the new* **Paradise** *boasts a décor vaguely reminiscent of the great Atlantic ocean liners, albeit more focused on the predictable neon and wild color combinations.*

Some passengers seem bent on dressing as casually as possible, even wearing jeans and T-shirts to dinner or rushing back to their cabins after the meal to change into tank tops and sandals. Some things the line does are tacky, too, such as using white plastic wine and ice buckets, plastic cups for beer on deck, and prepackaged creamers and butter pats.

The 12,000-square-foot Nautica Spa has everything—mirrored aerobics room, large windowed gym, men's and women's locker rooms, sauna and steam rooms, and whirlpools. There are three swimming pools and a water slide, and the Sun Deck offers jogging track covered with a rubberized surface.

Standard cabins are a good size at 190 square feet, and all cabins, even the least expensive inside ones, have good storage, a safe, TV, desk and stool, chair, and reading lights for each bed, plus bathrooms with roomy showers and mirrored cabinets for toiletries.

The Itinerary

Aboard a Carnival cruise, the destination is more the ship itself, with ports of call playing a decidedly secondary role for many passengers. Alternating eastern and western Caribbean itineraries, sailing year-round from Miami, are well-worn and similar to those of many other ships.

The eastern cruise spends three days at sea between port calls, and first pauses for a morning in Nassau, then after a day at sea, another full day at San Juan for El Yunque rain forest, the Bacardi Rum tour, and an early dinner out on your own in **Old San Juan** or a flamenco show. For the combined visit it's a short sail to **St. Thomas,** which offers shopping, a neighborhood stroll, snorkeling, and the Atlantis Submarine dive to 150 feet. Or take a ferry to St. John for Virgin Islands National Park and the great beach at Trunk Bay. Then what many people love most is three nights and two full sea days en route to Miami.

On the western loop with three sea days, **Playa del Carmen** and **Cozumel** are ports for the beach, snorkeling, diving, and the swimming lagoon at **Xel-Ha** and Mayan ruins at shorefront **Tulum.** A sea day sailing eastward brings you to **Grand Cayman** for upscale shopping for black coral jewelry, perfumes, and accessories and for snorkeling, stingray feeding, and a day on gorgeous Seven Mile Beach. After an overnight cruise to **Ocho Rios** on Jamaica, take a plantation tour or a 75-foot yacht cruise ending at Dunn's River Falls for a wet climb up rocks, shaped like a giant staircase, or bike down 1,500-foot Murphy Hill past eight river springs that give Ocho Rios its name. Unwind at sea en route to Miami.

Carnival Cruise Lines'
Paradise

Address/Phone: Carnival Cruise Lines, 3655 NW 87th Avenue, Miami, FL 33178; (305) 599–2600 or (800) 327–9501; fax (305) 406–4740; www.carnival.com

The Ship: *Paradise* was built in 1998 and has a gross tonnage of 70,367, a length of 855 feet, and a draft of 26 feet.

Passengers: 2,040; mostly Americans in their twenties to sixties

Dress: Suits or tuxes for two formal nights; slacks and collared shirts for the five casual nights

Officers/Crew: Italian officers; international crew

Cabins: 1,020; 618 outside and 26 with private veranda

Fare: $$

What's included: Cruise and port charges

What's not included: Airfare, shore excursions and water sports, drinks, tips

Highlights: Nonsmoking cruise, entertainment, sushi bar, pool slide

Other itineraries: In addition to these seven-day *Paradise* cruises, Carnival has many other itineraries in the Caribbean, Bahamas, Mexican coast, and Alaska.

CELEBRITY CRUISES' *GALAXY* AND *MERCURY*
Stylish and Affordable Caribbean Cruising

Celebrity Cruises began as an upscale brand for Chandris Lines, and soon the lower level Fantasy Cruises was phased out. In 1997 Royal Caribbean International bought Celebrity Cruises, but thus far the line is being operated as a separate brand.

The *Galaxy* and *Mercury* are spacious and comfortable and exhibit a kind of glamorous, vaguely art deco style associated with classic ocean liners. The decor casts a chic and sophisticated mood, with lots of warm wood tones as well as rich, tactile textures and fabrics in deep primaries, from faux zebra-skin to soft leathers. The ships attract a wide range of ages and backgrounds.

Celebrity might be best known for its cuisine, which is indeed better than average. Dinners are served in high style in the ships' gorgeous two-deck main dining rooms, with a wall of glass facing astern to the ships' wakes and, if you're lucky, a moonlit night. The menu is likely to feature something along the lines of pan-fried salmon with parsleyed potatoes, Pad Thai (noodles and veggies in a peanut sauce), tournedos Rossini with foie gras and Madeira sauce, or prime rib with horseradish and baked potato.

Breakfast, lunch, and dinner (by reservation only) are served in the buffet-style Lido restaurants. For snacking there's also ice cream, high tea, and pizza

available, and pizza can be delivered in a cardboard box to your cabin. In place of traditional midnight buffets, the ships offer "Gourmet Bites," hors d'oeuvres served by waiters in the public lounges between midnight and 1:00 A.M. Waiters are poised and professional, and sommeliers circulate in the dining room and in the Lido restaurants.

Activities during days at sea may include enrichment lectures on topics like personal investing, body language, or handwriting analysis; wine tastings; bingo; art auctions; arts and crafts; spa and salon demonstrations; and dancing lessons. If you prefer solitude, some semblance of peace and quiet can be had on the far corners of the Sky Deck and on the aft Penthouse Deck. Inside there are many hideaways, including Michael's Club, the card room or the edges of Rendez-Vous Square.

Each ship has a well-stocked playroom, called the Fun Factory, and an attached outside deck area with wading pool. During summer and holidays supervised activities are offered all day long for four age groups between three and seventeen. The AquaSpas are among the best facilities at sea. The focal point is a 115,000-gallon thalassotherapy pool, huge hot tubs with warm jets of water. Although managed by Steiner, as on most other ships, there are more exotic treatments offered on these ships such as mud packs, herbal

The 1,870-passenger sistership **Galaxy** *and* **Mercury** *are two of the most elegant big ships at sea, offering appealing and rare combinations of fun and refinement, two of the best spas, and gorgeous public rooms. The* **Mercury** *does the more typical seven-night western Caribbean route out of Fort Lauderdale, while the* **Galaxy** *spends a week in the southern Caribbean embarking in San Juan.*

steam baths, and water-based treatments. In the good-sized, windowed gyms, landscapes unfold on the color monitors of the ships' high-tech, virtual-reality stationary bikes. There are also aerobic classes in a separate room, an outdoor jogging track, a golf simulator, and a sports deck with basketball, paddle-tennis, and volleyball courts. There are three swimming pools; one is covered by an all-weather retractable roof.

In addition to the Broadway-style musicals performed on two stages there are live dance bands and pianists performing in other lounges, as well as innovative entertainment like a strolling a cappella group and a strolling magician, who perform in various lounges and public areas.

With its crushed-velvet couches and leather wing-back chairs, Michael's Club is a quiet, sophisticated spot for cigars, cordials, and conversation. The disco within the top-deck observation lounge is open until about 3:00 A.M. The cozy, dimly lit nightclub is the spot for cabaret, dancing, and karaoke. First-run movies are screened in the theater, and both ships have spacious, sultry casinos.

Pleasing cabin decor is based on monochromatic themes of muted bluish-purple, green, or red and light-colored furniture. Although inside cabins are about par for the industry standard, outside cabins are larger than usual, and four categories of suites are particularly spacious. Suite passengers are privy to a tuxedo-clad personal butler who serves afternoon tea and complimentary hors d'oeuvres from 6:00 to 8:00 P.M., handles laundry and shoe shining, and will serve you a full five-course dinner in your cabin. Cabin TVs are wired with an interactive system, from which you can order room service from on-screen menus, select the evening's wine, play casino-style games, or browse in "virtual" shops.

The Two Itineraries

The *Mercury*'s seven-night cruise sails from **Fort Lauderdale** on a Sunday and calls at **Key West, Calica, Cozumel,** and **Grand Cayman** and includes two full sea days. Beginning in late 2002, the itinerary changes and the ship sails from **Miami** to Grand Cayman, Cozumel, **Progreso,** and Key West.

The *Galaxy*'s seven-night cruise departs **San Juan** and calls at **St. Croix, St. Lucia, Barbados, Antigua,** and **St. Thomas.** From November through February, the ports of call are St. Thomas, **St. Kitts,** Barbados, and **Aruba.**

Celebrity Cruises' *Galaxy* and *Mercury*

Address/Phone: Celebrity Cruises, 1050 Caribbean Way, Miami, FL 33132: (305) 539–6000 or (800) 437–3111; www.celebritycruises.com

The Ships: *Galaxy* was built in 1996 and *Mercury* in 1997, and they have a gross tonnage of 77,713, a length of 866 feet, and a draft of 25 feet.

Passengers: 1,870; mostly American couples in their late thirties to sixties, some honeymooners and families, too

Dress: Suits or tuxes for the formal nights, jackets for semiformal nights, and slacks and collared shirts for casual nights; no shorts, jeans, or T-shirts in the restaurants

Officers/Crew: Greek officers; international crew

Cabins: 948; 639 outside and 220 with verandas

Fare: $$

What's included: Cruise fare only

What's not included: Airfare, port charges, excursions, water sports, drinks, tips

Highlights: AquaSpas are some of best at sea. Modern art collection is one of most interesting and provocative in the industry.

Other itineraries: In addition to these two Caribbean itineraries, which operate between late November and March, both ships spend the summer in Alaska, doing cruises in the Inside Passage and across the Gulf. The *Zenith* cruises to Bermuda.

ROYAL CARIBBEAN'S *VOYAGER OF THE SEAS*

The Western Caribbean's Largest Cruise Ship

Royal Caribbean clearly won the "Who can build the biggest and best" competition with its new 137,000-ton *Voyager of the Seas,* a full 25 percent larger than the competing *Grand Princess* and *Carnival Destiny.* More importantly, however, the company started with a blank slate and came up with a ship that is more than just an oversized sistership—rather, she is a true trendsetter that leaves most passengers dazzled. Like her smaller fleet mate *Sovereign of the Seas,* the *Voyager* may well be remembered as a daring new ship that set a precedent for all ships to follow.

Unlike other megaships, which often try to hide their size through smaller public rooms, the *Voyager* makes no pretensions about being large—she is huge and she wants everyone to know it. From the Royal Promenade to the three-story dining room to the expansive upper deck space, the ship is full of grand sweeping vistas and cavernous spaces, constant reminders of how big she is. Of course, size does have its downsides as well, including less personal service and occasional waits for elevators or disembarkation.

The first thing that passengers notice upon boarding is the fascinating Royal Promenade, a 500-foot, four-story walkway running down the middle of the ship. Cafes and shops line the path, while three decks of "Promenade View" cabins look down onto the scene through large bay windows. The space is constantly brimming with passengers strolling by, stopping to listen to the piano player in the bar, or simply striking up a conversation at a sidewalk cafe. The space works well, and like any town center it takes on different moods throughout the day and into the evening, especially when street performers and buskers are about.

Just aft of the Royal Promenade is the ship's three-story dining room, easily one of the most spectacular rooms to put to sea within the last twenty years. Crowned by a striking chandelier and flanked by window walls on either side, the three levels are linked by a dramatic grand staircase. Unfortunately, despite attempts to improve the quality, the food does not live up to the decor in the main dining room, and it is hard to get a reservation for a better menu in the smaller alternative Portofino restaurant.

Much attention has been given to the ship's ice-skating rink, which is used for both shows and free skating for passengers. There is also a rock-climbing wall 200 feet above the keel on the after end of the funnel, and it is equally fun just to watch the passengers doing the actual climbing. For the active set, there is also a full-size basketball court, a miniature golf course, an in-line skating track, and a large spa. From the elaborate children's facilities to the wedding chapel to the Johnny Rocket's 1950s-style diner, there really is something for everyone.

Do you believe bigger is better? If so, then your ship has come in with the **Voyager of the Seas,** *one of the world's two largest cruise ships. More than just impossibly huge, this ship is innovative and full of energy, with enough activities to please all ages during a cruise in the Western Caribbean. From rock-climbing walls and miniature golf to ice-skating rinks, there is always something to do.*

Traditionalists will delight in the ship's open deck space, including a wraparound promenade deck that actually cantilevers over the side, giving a unique perspective on the steel hull crashing through the seas. Even the bow is open to passengers, and it is fantastic to go all the way forward at night and gaze back at the darkened superstructure and spinning radar antennae.

Cabins are of good size and generally well laid out, and many have balconies with steel partitions on one side offering true privacy from at least one of your neighbors. In addition to the standard inside and outside cabins, there are many "Promenade View" cabins (which are slightly more expensive than standard inside cabins) that offer bay windows looking down onto the Royal Promenade. For those who can't get enough of city life, these cabins are perfect—although other passengers can see in just as easily as you can see out unless the curtains are drawn.

Listing the additional spaces on board will not do justice to the ship. This ship is visually fascinating, and the extensive use of glass permits some interesting people-watching vistas looking either within or out from the ship. This is not your standard cookie-cutter cruise ship, and the creativity shows.

The Itinerary

The *Voyager of the Seas* sails Sundays year-round from **Miami,** and hits the larger Western Caribbean ports and includes two sea days.

The first day is spent at sea, allowing passengers time to get acclimated and to find their way around. On Tuesday, the ship anchors off **Labadee,** which is Royal Caribbean's private "island," although it's actually a private, secluded stretch of the Haitian coastline. Passengers can enjoy the day sunning on the beach or renting a small sailboat. The next day is spent in **Ocho Rios,** Jamaica, where passengers can climb the famous Dunns River Falls or enjoy a guided bamboo raft journey down a tropical river.

Popular **Grand Cayman** offers some upscale shopping in **Georgetown** in addition to **Stingray City,** where tame stingrays surround swimmers offering them food. **Seven Mile Beach** and renowned diving on "The Wall" will satisfy those who yearn to spend all their time in the water or on the beach.

The last port is the resort island of **Cozumel,** Mexico. For those who are not into the excellent snorkeling and diving opportunities here, there are the Mayan coastal ruins at **Tulum** or a day trip to resorty **Cancun.** With a last day at sea, here's another chance to rediscover the ship all over again.

Royal Caribbean's
Voyager of the Seas

Address/Phone: Royal Caribbean International, 1050 Caribbean Way, Miami Fl 33132; (305) 539–6000 or (800) 327–6700 for brochures; fax: (305) 374–7354; www.royalcaribbean.com

The Ship: *Voyager of the Seas* was built in 1999. It has a gross tonnage of 137,000, a length of 1,020 feet, and a draft of 29 feet.

Passengers: 3,114 double occupancy; mostly Americans of all ages. As many as 3,608 passengers have been onboard at once, a peacetime record for any ship.

Dress: Suits or jacket and tie for the formal night and jackets for informal nights

Officers/Crew: International

Cabins: 1,557; 939 outside, 757 with balconies, and 138 "Promenade View" cabins looking into the Royal Promenade

Fare: $$

What's included: Cruise fare only

What's not included: Airfare, port charges, tips, drinks, shore excursions

Highlights: An exciting, innovative ship with enough options to please everyone.

Other itineraries: In addition to this year-round seven-day cruise, the equally huge *Explorer of the Seas* sails year-round on an Eastern Caribbean itinerary. Royal Caribbean cruises the Mexican Riviera, Alaska, and Europe. The Royal Journeys program sends the *Legend of the Seas* around the world, including Australia.

SEA CLOUD CRUISES' *SEA CLOUD*
Eastern Caribbean Island Hopping under Sail

After taking delivery of the new yacht in 1931, E. F. Hutton and his wife, Marjorie Post, spent most of the next four years aboard sailing the world, including to the Galápagos Islands, where they acquired a tortoise named Jumbo, who became a permanent resident of the ship. Several years later, following the couple's divorce, Mrs. Hutton rechristened the ship *Sea Cloud,* and leased it to the U.S. government for $1.00 a year during World War II. After having several private owners, the *Sea Cloud* was abandoned in Panama by the late 1960s, then purchased in 1978 by some German businessmen who brought her back to the Kiel shipyard and had cabins added for cruise service to take up to sixty-nine paying passengers.

Cabins number 1 to number 8 are original, looking more like suites at the Ritz Carlton or Waldorf Astoria than any found aboard even the most luxurious cruise ship. Marjorie's Suite (cabin number 1) displays an opulence reminiscent of Versailles: a blue-canopied bed in antique white with gold-leaf ornamentation, Louis Philippe chairs, a finely etched floor-to-ceiling dressing mirror, a marble fireplace with an elaborate mantel, chandeliers, plaster ceilings with intricate moldings, and a grand Carrara marble bathroom. Port-side, cabin number 2's dark paneling with deep-red furnishings, a large mahogany secretary, and high-backed chairs leaves no doubt that this was E. F. Hutton's domain. Distinctive furnishings help differentiate each original portholed cabin, all having a fireplace, a writing desk, a sitting area, and a marble bathroom.

Although the name *Sea Cloud* elicits images of grand living, most passengers occupy one of the twenty-six new cabins, added in 1979 and refitted in 1993. Nautically styled and roomy, they have wood paneling, brass fittings, fabrics in pastel colors, large windows, and marble bathrooms with shower.

One wouldn't normally think of an "open house" as a popular onboard cruise activity, but, to most passengers aboard the *Sea Cloud*, it is the week's highlight sailing the Caribbean. On the penultimate evening, champagne and canapés are served on Main Deck, and the passengers dress for the occasion and tour the cabins. Whether one occupies the original or the added, it seems to have no impact on social life aboard.

Buffet breakfasts and formal dinners are served at open-seating tables for six to eight in the original dining room and saloon. Dark paneling, oil paintings, and fireplaces create an atmosphere of dining in a large private

When the tall ship **Sea Cloud** *was completed in a Kiel, Germany, shipyard in 1931 as* **Hussar (V)**, *it qualified as the world's largest private yacht. Then to ensure it was also the most impressive, Mrs. Marjorie Merriweather Post, the ship's original owner and heiress to the Post Cereal fortune, had a fourth mast added. Now cruise passengers can experience something of the time when the super rich had the resources and time to create and enjoy something truly beautiful, and money was no object.*

home. For dinner formal table settings of navy blue, gold, and white china embossed with the ship's logo, silver napkin rings, candlelight, and fresh flowers add to the elegant scene. Local specialties, such as fresh Antigua spiny lobster, complement the delectable nouvelle cuisine fixed menu. Luncheon buffets are beautifully presented outside on the Promenade Deck, and helpful crew members carry the laden trays above to the Lido Lounge, protected from the midday sun under a blue awning. Entertainment before and after dinner is presented here by a popular piano player, and one evening crew members sing salty sea chanties.

The Itinerary

Embarking in **Antigua,** the *Sea Cloud* motors out of the harbor, and then the call, "All hands on deck!" brings passengers above to watch the deck crew climb the masts to unfurl the sails. One by one, thirty billowing sails fill with wind, and the ship is underway. The time at sea is passed hanging about the wheelhouse, lying on cushioned benches either side of the bridge eyeing the progress, or sitting with a book in a shady spot. The Promenade Deck fantail is fitted with huge royal-blue cushions, comfy for sunbathing and lying on one's back to gaze up at the brilliant stars at night.

The usual pattern sees passengers ashore most mornings, onboard for lunch, and under sail for the afternoon. The port of calls are usually Bequia, Grenada, Carriacou, Soufriere on St. Lucia, and Terre d'en Haut on Iles des Saintes. At **Bequia** you can visit the giant sea turtles in their natural, and protected, habitat or spend a day snorkeling and swimming on uncrowded beaches. St. George, on **Grenada,** is a pretty harbor town with a busy market square, and **Carriacou** offers a scenic mountain and garden drive. Soufriere, on beautiful **St. Lucia,** leads to a botanical garden, a waterfall, a volcano, and sulfur springs. A short, steep hike from **Terre d'en Haut,** on Ile des Saintes, brings you up to historic Fort Napoleon, for a spectacular view of the yachting harbor with the *Sea Cloud* as the centerpiece. The ports are fun, but life aboard the largest former private yacht is the real draw.

Sea Cloud Cruises' *Sea Cloud*

Address/Phone: Sea Cloud Cruises, 32–40 North Dean Street, Englewood, NJ 07631; (201) 227–9404 or (888) 732–2568; fax: (201) 227–9424; e-mail: seacloud@att.net; www.seacloud.com. Agents are Abercrombie & Kent International, (800) 757–5884 for brochures or (800) 323–7308; and Elegant Cruises & Tours, Inc. (800) 683–6767.

The Ship: *Sea Cloud,* originally built as the *Hussar* in 1931, was rebuilt into a cruise ship in 1979. She has a gross tonnage of 2,532, a length of 360 feet, and a draft of 17 feet.

Passengers: 69 well-heeled Americans, often part of a group

Dress: Passengers smarten up for dinner and dress semiformally for the penultimate evening.

Officers/Crew: American or European captain; international crew

Cabins: 34; a wide range of choice, all outside with windows or portholes

Fare: $$$$

What's included: Unless part of a group, cruise only, some sightseeing, soft drinks, plus wines at lunch and dinner

What's not included: Airfare, port charges, shore excursions, drinks, tips

Highlights: Experiencing the opulence of a former private yacht under sail and the company of like-minded passengers

Other itineraries: In addition to this seven-night cruise in the Caribbean, operating during the winter months, there is a second Caribbean loop, as well as one transatlantic voyage from the Mediterranean to the Caribbean in November. In 2001 the newly built *Sea Cloud II,* taking ninety-six passengers in more uniform accommodations, began Caribbean and Mediterranean cruising.

WINDSTAR CRUISES' *WIND SPIRIT*
Motorsailing the Eastern Caribbean

Windstar Cruises, founded in 1986, operates four high-tech motor sail ships, the sails being a highly decorative feature that unfurl with the push of a button on the bridge and give an extra couple of knots when the winds are favorable.

With the distinctive profile of a large yacht and a maritime atmosphere within, the *Wind Spirit* immediately pleases the eye when boarding. The main lounge, located aft, has a sailing ship–style skylight over the dance floor that rises into an attractive centerpiece for the open deck above. It becomes the social venue before and after meals with light entertainment after dinner. An adjacent room offers a two-table casino and slot machines, but this is not a late-night ship. Many passengers enjoy selecting from several hundred videos or CDs and squirreling away in their cabins.

The wood-paneled dining room offers open-seating flexibility, and dress is always casual, with jackets and ties seen only at the captain's table. Entrees may feature linguine with frutti di mare, crisp duck breast, and grilled filet mignon. In good weather only dinner is served here, while the Veranda provides glassed-enclosed protection for breakfast and lunch with sheltered tables out on deck and under parasols. Food is available from a menu or the buffet; at breakfast, a chef prepares omelets and pancakes and, at lunch, a pasta or a superb bouillabaisse. Bread pudding is a daily lunchtime staple.

Dinner takes place under the stars one evening, a romantic outdoor setting with tables arranged around the pool and with dancing on deck between courses. The spread includes jumbo shrimp, mussels, crab, lots of salad fixings, and freshly grilled tuna, lobster tails, steak, lamb chops, and chicken breasts.

The daytime gathering spot is the lido, partly a covered lounge with sit-up bar, and partly an open area with a small pool for dipping, a whirlpool, deck chairs, and cushioned mats. The water-sports program is a big draw and includes diving instruction and snorkeling in several ports and complimentary use of sailboats, sailboards, banana boats, and kayaks that are launched from the marina deck. Gym equipment includes aerobic trainers, two treadmills, two bicycles, a rowing machine, weights, and a sauna.

A Windstar cruise rates high as a casual, upscale, social experience with lots to do in the water and on excursions ashore. Time aboard is pleasantly unstructured, and the majority of passengers are active couples in their forties to sixties, including many repeaters.

The ship's seventy-four roomy outside cabins on two decks are similar, with beds, either twins or queen-size, set beneath twin portholes. Amenities include TVs—with news, features, and three movie channels—and a built-in combination of a CD player, VCR, minibar, and refrigerator. A dining table folds out for in-cabin dining from a full menu at mealtimes. The bathrooms have teakwood floors and circular, steel-gray shower and toilet stalls.

The Itinerary

The week's itinerary is planned around water sports, beach outings, and slow-paced sightseeing, a terrific combination for a week of unwinding.

At **St. Thomas,** the embarkation port, the harbor may be crowded with huge cruise liners, but once the *Wind Spirit* slips out of the harbor, another world is ahead. **St. John,** also in the U.S. Virgin Islands, is an overnight call where the ship gently swings at anchor. Spend the morning on a scenic island drive to the Virgin Islands National Park and the afternoon at the beach, one of the Caribbean's finest. Anchoring off **Marigot,** St. Martin, on the French/Dutch island's less commercial side, the most popular activity features a spirited sailing race aboard an America's Cup 12-meter boat with you acting as crew.

On nearby and upscale **St. Barts,** there's a chance to go horseback riding and snorkeling, and, for a change of venue, check out Gustavia's restaurants lining the small harbor. They all have menus out front, and once you have made a choice, go inside to make a reservation for dinner, as the ship does not sail until 11:00 P.M. Tortola and Jost Van Dyke, both in the British Virgin Islands, are serenely peaceful places. Cruising to **Tortola,** take a taxi to Mount Sage National Park for a hike along the Rain Forest Trail or the Mahogany Forest Trail. **Jost Van Dyke** is an ideal destination for a morning on the beach. The ship anchors overnight at **Virgin Gorda,** and from the stern marina, you can go for a sail or take out a kayak. The most popular excursion is to the Baths, an area of massive boulders by the sea, where there are narrow rock cuts and caves to explore.

Windstar Cruises' *Wind Spirit*

Address/Phone: Windstar Cruises, 300 Elliott Avenue West, Seattle, WA 98119; (206) 281–3535 or (800) 258–7245; brochures: (800) 626–9900; fax: (206) 286–3229; www.windstarcruises.com

The Ship: *Wind Spirit* was built in 1988 and has a gross tonnage of 5,350, a length of 440 feet, and a draft of 13 feet.

Passengers: 148; mostly American, forty and up

Dress: Casual

Officers/Crew: British officers; Filipino and Indonesian crew

Cabins: 74; all similar, roomy outside with portholes, apart from one owner's suite

Fare: $$$

What's included: Cruise fare and port charges, basic tips

What's not included: Airfare, drinks, shore excursions, extra tips

Highlights: A carefree and casual lifestyle in small Caribbean ports

Other itineraries: In addition to this seven-day Caribbean cruise aboard the *Wind Spirit,* which operates between December and April, the fleet includes two sisterships, the *Wind Song* and *Wind Star* and the 14,745-ton, 312-passenger Wind Surf (formerly *Club Med I*). Itineraries, mostly seven days, are offered in the Mediterranean, Caribbean, and Costa Rica, plus longer Signature Voyages, transatlantic crossings, and a new program in New Zealand.

STAR CLIPPERS' *STAR CLIPPER*
Caribbean Cruising under Sail

The *Star Clipper* and sistership *Star Flyer* were conceived by Swedish yachting enthusiast Mikael Krafft as near replicas of mid-nineteenth-century fast clipper ships. Built in Ghent, Belgium, in the early 1990s, the pair qualify as two of the largest and tallest sailing ships ever built, and in summer 2000 were joined by the brand-new, five-masted *Royal Clipper.*

In price and accommodations the *Star Clipper* falls between the simpler Windjammer Barefoot fleet and the upscale four Windstar Cruise vessels. At sea the ship is generally under sail from late evening to early or mid-morning the next day. Passengers may help with the lines, but there is no pressure to do so. When the wind dies, the 1,370-horsepower Caterpillar diesel engine kicks in.

The Tropical Bar provides the *Star Clipper's* social center, located amidships on a sheltered deck under a protective canvas awning. One of the two public rooms is an Edwardian-style library, with a wall of mahogany-fronted bookcases flanking a fireplace and comfy seating for reading and cards on a rainy day. The other, with light wood-paneled walls and recessed seating, serves as a piano lounge, with a pianist seated beneath circular skylights cut into the bottom of the suspended swimming pool.

In good weather the lounge and library see little use during the day, and most passengers gather around the wheelhouse and the two sun-deck swimming pools or at the midships bar. In the morning the captain holds forth at story time, when he recites sailing-ship traditions and rules of navigation and discusses the day's program.

Meals are served to both officers and passengers at one open sitting in a wood- and brass-accented dining room. Breakfast and lunch are buffet style, with a good choice of hot and cold items, while dinner is served by a waiter with the menu offering a fish, meat, and vegetarian entree. The food is of good quality and well prepared but by no means gourmet. Dress is casual but never ragged.

Cabins, nearly all outside and some shaped by the ship's hull, are of moderate size and have a sailing-ship feel, using wood trim, electric lamps mounted in gimbals, and decorative brass counter railings. Amenities include phones and televisions and tiny bathrooms with water-saving push-button showers.

The Itinerary

The Treasure Islands week embarks and disembarks at **St. Maarten,** the Dutch and shopping half of the island shared with St. Martin, the more peaceful French

The barkentine-rigged Star Clipper offers a close equivalent to a true sailing experience, yet done in comfort and at affordable rates. From November through April the four-mast tall ship, taking 170 passengers, cruises a string of eastern Caribbean islands on alternating one-week itineraries, embarking at St. Maarten.

Star Clippers' *Star Clipper*

Address/Phone: Star Clippers, 4101 Salzebo Street, Coral Gables, FL 33146; (305) 442–0550 or reservations: (800) 442–0551; brochures: (800) 442–0556; fax: (305) 442–1611; www.starclippers.com

The Ship: *Star Clipper* was built in 1992 and has a gross tonnage of 2,298, a length of 360 feet, and a draft of 18.5 feet.

Passengers: 168; all ages; some Europeans, but English is the lingua franca

Dress: Casual at all times

Officers/Crew: European officers; international crew

Cabins: 84; 78 outside, most relatively compact; no verandas

Fare: $$

What's included: Usually cruise only, although cruise tour rates will include air, hotels, some meals, some sightseeing, and transfers

What's not included: For cruise only, airfare, port charges, tips, drinks

Highlights: A terrific outdoor sailing experience; small yachting ports; thoroughly relaxed, social atmosphere

Other itineraries: Besides this and an alternative seven-night Caribbean cruise, which operates between November and April, the *Star Clipper* offers two Western Mediterranean itineraries and spring and fall transatlantic positioning voyages. The sistership *Star Flyer* operates in the Greek islands and along the Turkish coast from May to October, then travels via the Suez Canal to cruise the coasts of Malaysia and Thailand, returning through the Indian Ocean in April. The five-masted *Royal Clipper*, completed in 2000 and the largest sailing vessel ever built, also cruises the Caribbean, Mediterranean, and Atlantic.

side. The first call is at the upscale resort island of **Anguilla,** then the beaches at **Sandy Cay** and **Soper's Hole** provide opportunities for swimming, snorkeling, and windsurfing. Norman Island is where Robert Louis Stevenson wrote *Treasure Island,* and **Virgin Gorda,** an overnight stay, is noted for its **Baths,** an area of massive boulders by the sea, with narrow rock cuts and caves to explore.

At **St. Kitts** there is an island tour to old plantation sites, great views from Brimstone Hill, golfing, and a chance to shop at **Basseterre.** Off **St. Barts,** always a favorite stop, the little harbor island at **Gustavia** provides an appropriate setting for the *Star Clipper.* It being the biggest sailing ship to call, you can expect a lot of curious onlookers. There are moderately priced and expensive restaurants within walking distance of the landing, and the shopping here is good and less frenetic than on **St. Maarten** where the cruise ends.

When the weather permits, a very special treat is offered, a Zodiac ride to observe just how splendid the *Star Clipper* looks slicing majestically through the water, with all sixteen sails catching the wind. From a water-level position ahead of the bow, passengers watch the ship bear down on them; and viewed from the stern, the ship appears to be leaving you behind. The *Star Clipper* is a democratic experience—it's not easy to tell the difference between passengers with money and those who have saved up for this easygoing cruise with visits to small ports.

WINDJAMMER BAREFOOT CRUISES' *LEGACY*
Eastern Caribbean Sailing Fancy-Free

The famous Captain Mike Burke, now retired, founded the company in 1947. He purchased a slew of ships with interesting histories, transformed them into one-of-a-kind sailing vessels, and for years hosted party cruises popular with singles. Burke's children run the company now and, over the past few years, have been making a conscious effort to shake off the vestiges of the old self and create a more mainstream experience. Windjammer has recently hired its first hotel manager to improve the overall quality of the dining and cabin service, has added a kids' program (arts and crafts, snorkeling trips) on the Legacy during the summer months, and has plans to build additional new sailing ships.

Launched in 1997, the *Legacy* is the line's newest acquisition, its biggest and most modern. Built in France in 1959 as a research vessel called the *France II*, the ship was acquired by Windjammer in 1989 and converted into a traditional tall ship. The brightest and most spacious in the fleet, the *Legacy* is a departure from Windjammer's fleet of old-timers. It has comfortable cabins with bunk-style beds and good-sized private bathrooms, a cheerful dining saloon with large, round booths, and a roomy expanse of outdoor deck space. There's space to move around and then some.

Dining is informal family-style and ranges from unmemorable to really tasty. All breads and pastries are homemade, and at dinner, after soup and salad are served, passengers can choose from two main entrees, such as curried shrimp and roast pork with garlic sauce. Unlimited carafes of red and white wine are complimentary. Tasty breakfast, like Eggs Benedict as well as the normal fare, and lunch, such as lobster pizza and apple salad, are served buffet style. At Jost Van Dyke the crew lugs ashore a picnic lunch for an afternoon beach party.

The Itinerary

The *Legacy* makes its way to off-the-beaten-track Caribbean ports of call like **Virgin Gorda**, **Jost Van Dyke**, **Culebra**, and **St. John** (as well touristy ones like **St. Thomas** and **St. Croix**), anchoring offshore a mile or two and shuttling passengers back and forth by tender. Landings may require wading through knee-deep water to get ashore. Several excursions, like island tours and snorkeling, are offered in each port. The ship is usually the biggest vessel in port, and you'll feel like a quiet visitor, not an interloper.

With a palpable pirate-ship feel, the four-masted barquentine (powered by both sails and engines) and

A Windjammer cruise aboard the 122-passenger **Legacy** *is a let-your-hair-down adventure on a beautiful, four-masted barquentine sailing seven-night Caribbean cruises round-trip from Fajardo, Puerto Rico, to off-the-beaten-track ports in the British, U.S., and the Spanish Virgin Islands.*

its yards of sails, chunky portholes, and generous use of wood lures passengers into a fantasy world of fairytale adventure. Guests are invited to help pull in the sails, crawl into the bow net, which juts out over the water, and sleep out on deck whenever they please (mats are provided). There are few rules and lots of freedom. The *Legacy* delivers an ultrainformal seafaring adventure rich in eccentricities. For example, there are no keys for the cabins (you can only lock cabins from the inside), rum punch is served in paper cups, daily announcements are written in magic marker on a bulletin board, and the purser doubles as the nurse and gift-shop manager.

Corny yet cute rituals make the trip feel like summer camp for adults: for instance, the doubloon system at the bar (a debit card of sorts that is punched with holes each time you buy a drink), the hymn "Amazing Grace" loudly broadcast over the PA system each time the ship's sails are hoisted, and morning "story time," when the captain regales guests with the day's schedule and some funny tall tale he's concocted on the fly.

Besides this morning dose of down-home entertainment, you're on your own until happy hour. Just about every day is spent in port somewhere, and the occasional day at sea might feature a knot-tying demonstration and a bridge tour. The entertainment is the ship itself and the camaraderie among passengers. At 5:00 P.M. every day gallons of complimentary rum swizzles are generously offered with hors d'oeuvres like spicy meatballs, chicken fingers, and cheese and crackers. Guests gather on deck, often still in their sarongs and shorts, mingling in the fresh sea air, with taped music playing in the background. Sometimes an impromptu song or skit takes shape from a couple of fun-loving, down-to-earth guests. After dinner head up to the bar for drinks—you won't spend more than $3.00 a pop—or grab a chaise lounge or mat and hit the deck. One or two nights a week a local pop band is brought on board for a few hours of dancing, and there's a weekly barbecue buffet dinner, and a costume party. Generally the ship stays late in one or two ports so that passengers can head ashore to one of the island watering holes. From honeymooning couples in their twenties to grandparents in their seventies, Windjammer attracts a broad range of adventurers, who return again and again.

Windjammer Barefoot Cruises' *Legacy*

Address/Phone: Windjammer Barefoot Cruises, 1759 Bay Road, Miami Beach, FL 33119; (305) 672–6453 or (800) 327–2601; fax: (305) 674–1219; www.windjammer.com

The Ship: *Legacy* was built in 1959 as the research vessel *France II* and was converted in 1997 to a windjammer. It has a gross tonnage of 1,165, a length of 294 feet, and a draft of 23 feet.

Passengers: 122; all ages and mostly Americans

Dress: Casual at all times

Officers/Crew: American and British officers; West Indian crew

Cabins: 62 cabins, outside with either a window or porthole and relatively compact

Fare: $$

What's included: Cruise only, rum punch at happy hour, and wine at dinner

What's not included: Airfare, port charges, shore excursions, tips, bar drinks

Highlights: Carefree, very casual onboard atmosphere; unstructured; few rules

Other itineraries: In addition to the Legacy's seven-night Caribbean cruises, round-trip from Fajardo, Puerto Rico, visiting the British, U.S., and the Spanish Virgin Islands, the fleet includes four other windjammers (*Flying Cloud, Mandalay, Polynesia,* and *Yankee Clipper*) plus the passenger supply vessel *Amazing Grace,* which sails year-round in the Bahamas and Caribbean.

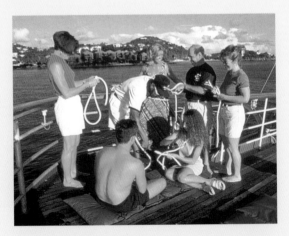

VALTUR TOURISM'S *VALTUR PRIMA*
Cruise to Cuba and the Western Caribbean

The *Valtur Prima,* virtually unknown in North America, gets high marks from several recent travelers for providing a comfortable, enjoyable European-style cruise. The ship takes only 540 passengers and caters to mostly German-, Italian-, and Spanish-speaking passengers in their thirties to sixties. They board in Havana, while Americans and some Canadians board at Montego Bay, Jamaica, on a Friday.

Built as the *Stockholm* in 1948 for the Swedish American Line, the ship passed through several owners before being completely rebuilt from the hull up in 1994. The profile is a combination of a classic, riveted ocean liner hull, with a somewhat ungainly, contemporary superstructure atop and sponsons (stability extensions to the hull) attached to the stern. While the ship is very stable, you can expect some engine noise, akin to a hum. Also expect European smoking habits, except in the nonsmoking dining room.

Public rooms exhibit a contemporary Italian style with bold colors, such as rose, pink, and blue, simple fabric patterns, and extensive use of marble surfaces on the floors and stairwells. Most spaces are on Capri Deck and include Le Maschere Lounge, the venue for entertainment, geared to multinational passengers and done mostly in mime with eight dancers acting out skits. Most attractive is the Duetto Lounge & Bar, located on the upper level of the arced stairway, where a duo performs, on the keyboard and in song, before and after dinner. The Admiral's Club is the cigar lounge; and a handsome card room and library—but with a poor selection of books—offers comfy overstuffed furniture. The modest casino has blackjack and roulette tables and slots, and two shops sell very high quality designer clothing and Italian jewelry.

Dining is at one sitting, with dinner generally served between 7:30 and 8:30 P.M., and Americans sit together at tables for two to eight. The atmosphere is cheerful, and the service is by Cubans, who make up the entire hotel staff. The menu is very good continental fare, and a special pasta of the day is prepared in the dining room. Il Giardino Café, done in green and white, is the casual restaurant, with a station preparing omelets at breakfast and fresh pasta at lunch. Other features are Italian cold cuts, good seafood, shrimp, lobster, and sardine salads, and hamburgers. Complimentary beer, Italian red and white wine, and soft drinks are served at both lunch and dinner.

Aft on Capri Deck is a small swimming pool, and musicians play here at an open covered deck at various hours. While the wraparound promenade deck is wonderfully sheered fore and aft, deck space, especially aft, is limited. The top deck houses a small spa and gym, and pool games keep people happy during the time at sea.

The cabins, on average, are larger than those found on most middle-market ships, and the amenities include twin and queen-size beds, bathtubs, bidets, TV with European programs, fridges (stocked and with a

*If you ever thought about visiting Cuba, but thought you were not permitted to do so, think again. The **Valtur Prima,** a smallish Italian-owned ship, sails from Montego Bay every week and spends a day and a half in Havana during the course of a week's cruise. The shore excursion is hosted, so that takes care of having to spend money ashore, which is illegal for most U.S. citizens.*

charge for use), minibars, decent closet space, hair dryers, and robes. The two-room suites with balconies are wonderful and come with Jacuzzi tubs, which the junior suites also share. There is a $2.50 charge for room service, and the ship operates using U.S. dollars.

The Itinerary

The week's cruise offers a great balance between port and sea time. U.S. passengers board at **Montego Bay,** Jamaica, sailing at 7:00 P.M. on a Friday. The call at **Grand Cayman** lasts from 7:00 A.M. to 1:00 P.M., with ample time for snorkeling and scuba diving, a walk to a beach, and some good shopping.

The ship arrives at **Havana** at 3:00 P.M. on a Sunday with thirty-three hours docked in **Old Havana** within walking distance of the central district. The hosted shore excursion by air-conditioned bus visits the former capitol building, **El Morro** (Castle), modeled after the U.S Capitol, and Old Havana and includes shopping stops, but most U. S. citizens are not permitted to spend money while in Cuba. However, certain groups, such as teachers and journalists may spend limited amounts.

On the second full day, there is additional time to explore on your own by foot to see the decayed magnificence of the historic city center and walk the **Prado** and **Malecon,** the latter road paralleling the sea, with waves crashing against the breakwater. The streets are lively and the people exceptionally warm, friendly, and inquisitive, and you will relish in seeing the number of pre-1960 heavy American cars, Soviet-style models from the 1960s, 1970s, and 1980s, and contemporary European cars, many used by private taxi drivers.

Upon sailing about midnight on Monday, there is nearly a full sea day to **Calica,** a port on the **Yucatan Peninsula,** with time in the evening for a nightclub tour to **Playa del Carmen** or **Cancun.** On Wednesday there is a choice of excursions by bus to **Chichen Itza** (three hours each way, $95), including admission charge to the Mayan site and a good buffet lunch. A shorter forty-five-minute drive goes to **Tulum,** a coastal Mayan site ($85), and the tour includes lunch and a beach stop. The independent minded can also rent a jeep.

Sailing at 6:00 P.M. from Calica, the ship next calls from 8:00 A.M. to 2:00 P.M. at the Cuban **Isle of Youth,** a private beach stop for swimming, topless sunbathing, water sports such as kayaking, and an optional lobster lunch for $20. Then it's an overnight return to **Montego Bay,** arriving at noon with the convenient option to stay on the ship until flight check-in time.

Valtur Tourism's
Valtur Prima

Address/Phone: West Indies Cruises Ltd., 5560 Explorer Drive, Mississauga, Ont L4W 5M3 (877) 818–CUBA (2822); fax: (905) 238–6177; www.westindiescruises.com

The Ship: *Valtur Prima* was originally completed as the *Stockholm* for Swedish American Line in 1948. It was then sold to East German owners and completely rebuilt in 1994 to become the *Italia Prima* and now its present name for the Valtur Tourism charter.

Passengers: 541, mostly Germans, Italians, and Latin Americans, with small numbers of British, Americans, and Canadians; age thirty to sixty

Dress: One jacket and tie night, rest casual

Officers/Crew: Italian officers; Filipino deckhands; Cuban hotel staff

Cabins: 260, with 221 outside and 8 with verandas

Fare: $$

What's included: cruise only; free visa issued on a separate paper upon arrival in Havana

What's not included: port charges, shore excursions, $7.00 a day suggested tips, bar drinks

Highlights: Visiting Havana; an onboard European atmosphere

Other itineraries: None; however, another Cuban port may be added to the itinerary.

LATIN AMERICA

VOYAGER CRUISE LINE'S
WILDERNESS ADVENTURER
Small-Ship Adventure Cruising on the Sea of Cortez

Voyager Cruise Line is a relatively new sister company to Alaska's Glacier Bay Tours and Cruises, a small-ship line owned by an Alaska Native corporation based in Juneau.

A small, boxy, utilitarian ship, the *Wilderness Adventurer* sailed as American Canadian Caribbean Line's *Caribbean Prince* before transferring to the current owners in 1996. Like other ships built by ACCL founder Luther Blount, it was constructed more as a vehicle than as a destination in itself. Cabins are as plain as you'll find on any ship, with simple platform beds and head-style bathrooms (sink, toilet, and shower all in one small curtained space). A dining room and connected bow-end lounge/bar are the only public rooms.

Rather than decor or amenities, though, it's the ship's outdoors-oriented features that draw passengers. Like all Blount-designed vessels, the *Wilderness Adventurer* has an extremely shallow draft, which, coupled with a ramp that folds from its bow, allows the captain to nose right up to dockless islands and beaches to disembark passengers. The ship also carries a fleet of stable, professional, two-person sea kayaks, and its stern is fitted with a dry-launch platform that allows passengers to begin their kayak excursion right from the ship.

Meals are served in open seatings, with a set menu at breakfast and lunch and two entree options at dinner (passengers are asked to decide on their selection the night before). While not gourmet, the cuisine is generally delicious and plentiful, with Mexican dishes scattered through the week. In the evenings passengers tend to gather on the shaded top deck for drinks and snacks. Unlike those aboard most ships, relations between passengers and crew are extremely informal, and within days the groups become so friendly that only the crew's uniforms and undertone of professional responsibility distinguish them. You'll find off-duty deck hands and passengers watching nature videos together in the lounge and naturalists gathering with guests to watch the starlit night sky or marvel when, as happened during cocktail hour one evening on my sailing, a whale leaps from the water right off the ship's starboard side, reflections of the setting sun scattering off its back.

Carrying only seventy-two passengers and with an onboard atmosphere as relaxed and casual as an Alaska B&B, the **Wilderness Adventurer** *sails a seven-day itinerary in Baja California's Sea of Cortez that's all about the outdoors. Passengers choose from daily kayaking, hiking, snorkeling, and whale-watching excursions on Baja's coast and coastal islands, and accredited naturalists accompany to provide commentary.*

The Itinerary

The *Wilderness Adventure* sticks mainly to uninhabited or sparsely inhabited islands in the **Sea of Cortez,** anchoring each morning and allowing passengers a full day of hiking, kayaking, and snorkeling. Excursions are freely structured, with passengers setting the pace and sometimes the route, and naturalists offering commentary and only occasionally warning guests away from dangerous areas.

The ship departs from bustling **La Paz,** capital of southern Baja, and sails north, making for **Isla San Jose** and **Isla San Francisco,** pristine volcanic islands where the only signs of humans are footprints and a few salinas, shallow salt pits dug by visiting fishermen to preserve their catch. A small group hikes up the highest peak in the surrounding hills and then watches the

kayakers pass by hundreds of feet below.

In its weeklong itineraries, the ship visits only one real port, quiet **Puerto Escondido,** from which passengers make two excursions on consecutive days: to the 300-year-old mission town of **Loreto** and two hours overland to **Magdalena Bay** on the Pacific coast. There, passengers board tiny, eight-person fishing boats and head out into the bay for a few hours of up-close whale watching. The gray whales who come here with their newborn calves are so friendly that they'll often swim right up to the boats and allow themselves to be patted. Those on my trip were more reticent, but several, including two calves, did swim to within a few feet, at one point diving just below our keel, all 40-plus feet of mother whale gliding below, perfectly in view.

The remaining days of the cruise are spent back out among the islands, which offer passengers stunning contrasts. In one day at **Los Islotes** and **Isla Espiritu Santo,** one could hike in the morning up a steep canyon among cacti and scuttling desert lizards and then kayak in the afternoon to within 100 yards of a colony of sea lions, while pelicans fly overhead. A Mexican beer at sunset tops off the lovely day. Consider adding a five-day Copper Canyon rail extension aboard the South Orient Express during the day and at remote hotels at night.

Voyager Cruise Line's
Wilderness Adventurer

Address/Phone: Voyager Cruise Line (aka Alaska's Glacier Bay Tours & Cruises), 226 Second Avenue West, Seattle, WA 98119; (206) 623–2417 or (800) 451–5952; fax: (206) 623–7809; www.voyagercruiseline.com

The Ship: *Wilderness Adventurer* was built in 1984 as the *Caribbean Prince,* and has a gross tonnage of 89, a length of 157 feet, and a draft of 6.5 feet.

Passengers: 68; mostly American, all ages, interested in the outdoors, and active

Dress: Casual at all times

Officers/Crew: American

Cabins: 30 of 35 cabins are outside, and all are small and Spartan; no verandas

Fare: $$

What's included: Cruise, port charges, all excursions, transfers, and use of kayaks and snorkeling equipment

What's not included: Airfare, tips, drinks

Highlights: A fantastic opportunity to get close to nature while also having the comfort of a warm, casual ship to come back to at the end of the day

Other itineraries: In addition to this seven-day Sea of Cortez cruise, operating between January and March 2001, the *Wilderness Adventurer* makes one-week cruises in Alaska's Inside passage, round-trip from Juneau, under the Glacier Bay Tours & Cruises banner. Three additional small ships offer different Alaskan itineraries, land tours, and positioning trips south to Seattle.

ROYAL CARIBBEAN'S *VISION OF THE SEAS*
Megaship Mexican Riviera

Counting the world's biggest cruise ships, the 137,000-ton, 3,100-passenger *Voyager of the Seas* and *Endeavor of the Seas,* Royal Caribbean has fourteen ships in its mostly-mega fleet, and another four are in the works. The 78,491-ton, 2,000-passenger *Vision of the Seas* is the newest and last member of the line's Vision Class, all built between 1995 and 1998.

The *Vision of the Seas*, like its sisters, is bathed in glass (especially good in Alaska), with glass canopies and windbreaks, skylights, and floor-to-ceiling windows with sweeping views. The focal point is a soaring, seven-story atrium with a huge, dramatic sculpture within and lots of shops around it. Overall, the ship is designed with warm woods and brass, fountains and foliage, crystal, soft leathers, and eye-catching artwork. The *Vision* is easy to navigate, despite its size. Glass elevators take passengers up through the Centrum atrium into the stunning Viking Crown Lounge, the line's signature, glass-sheathed observation-lounge-cum-disco, perched high above the rest of the ship. The Schooner Bar is a casual piano bar with lots of wood and rope, befitting its nautical name, and ditto the Champagne Bar, at the foot of the atrium, where you can listen and dance to a trio while sipping wine or a glass of bubbly. Full musical revues are staged in the two-story show lounge, which has an orchestra pit that can be hydraulically raised and lowered. Likewise, the sprawling

casino is dressed in Vegas-style flash and splash and assures gambling folk of an atmosphere conducive to at least having fun trying to beat the odds.

The ship's vast open areas include the Sun Deck's two swimming pools (one covered by a retractable glass roof), six whirlpools, and the Windjammer buffet-style restaurant. Poolside, you'll find loud, live music serenading the party along with silly contests that most passengers seem to just love. The soothing ShipShape spa is truly one of the most attractive around, and adjacent is a spacious solarium with a pool, chaise longues, floor-to-ceiling windows, and a retractable glass ceiling. Surprisingly, the gym is small for the ship's size. Families will like the extensive, supervised kids' activities for four age groups, including a children's playroom, a teen center and disco, and a video arcade.

The large dining room spans two decks that are interconnected with a very grand staircase and flanked with walls of glass nearly 20 feet high. Each has contemporary and tasteful decor, replete with stainless steel, mirrors, dramatic chandeliers, and a massive grand piano for dinnertime serenading. The food is generally tasty enough for a ship of this size, featuring choices like oven-roasted crispy duck served with rhubarb sauce or grilled pork tenderloin on a bed of stewed tomatoes and eggplant. A light and healthy vegetarian dish and pasta are offered at each meal.

The name aptly describes this ship. Royal Caribbean's **Vision of the Seas** *is an attractive ship through and through. It's a class act in the megaworld, not overboard in the neon-and-glitz department, but lots of fun and high energy, making this ship an exciting place to cruise the Mexican Riviera, its resort and fishing ports, coastal scenery and beaches, and inland villages and mountains.*

Standard cabins are compact, although larger than the cramped cubicles featured aboard the company's older ships. Nearly one fourth of the cabins have private verandas, and all have TVs (offering some twenty channels of video, four music channels, three for movies, and three with satellite programming), preprogrammed radios, and safes. Bathrooms are small.

The Itinerary

Exploring the **Mexican Riviera** on this floating resort couldn't be more enjoyable. Sailing seven-night cruises round-trip from **San Diego,** you can savor the spice of Mexico's culture, its dramatic rocky shoreline, and great beaches at a string of Pacific coast ports.

Cruising south, two nights and a day at sea bring the ship within sight of the dramatic rock formations of **Cabo San Lucas** peninsula. During the port call snorkel, take a seat in a glass-bottom boat or semisubmersible to view the reefs and sea life and spend the day at a beach resort for sunbathing and swimming. While waiting for the tender back to the ship, browse the open-air craft market. Sailing overnight to **Mazatlan,** a city that's worth exploring on foot or a tour for its main square, historic district, huge produce market, and lots of handicrafts and practical clothing for these hot climes for sale. Take a drive inland to picturesque colonial villages and mission churches set among the **Sierre Madre Mountains,** go deep-sea fishing for marlin and sailfish, and take in a folkloric show.

Just down the coast beautiful **Puerto Vallarta** is often the favorite call for its setting, winding cobblestone streets, tropical gardens, and now-distant connections to Elizabeth Taylor and Richard Burton and *Night of the Iguana.* Enjoy two full sea days back north to San Diego.

Royal Caribbean's
Vision of the Seas

Address/Phone: Royal Caribbean International, 1050 Caribbean Way, Miami, FL 33132; (305) 539–6000 or (800) 327–6700 for brochures; fax: (305) 374–7354; www.royalcaribbean.com

The Ship: *Vision of the Seas* was built in 1998, has a gross tonnage of 78,491, a length of 915 feet, and a draft of 25 feet.

Passengers: 2,000; mostly American, all ages, especially during school holidays

Dress: Suits or tuxes for the formal nights; jackets for informal nights, and slacks and collared shirts for casual nights

Officers/Crew: International

Cabins: 1000 average size, 593 outside, 25 per cent with verandas

Fare: $$

What's included: Cruise and port charges

What's not included: Airfare, shore excursions, drinks, tips

Highlights: Spa and solarium, overall design, lots of outdoor activities aboard and ashore

Other itineraries: In addition to these seven-night *Vision of the Seas* Mexican Riviera cruises, operating from late October 2001 to April 2002, the ship cruises Alaska in summer and occasionally the Panama Canal. Other Royal Caribbean ships cruise the Caribbean, New England/Canada, Europe, and Asia.

CRUISE WEST'S
TEMPTRESS EXPLORER
Costa Rica's Pacific Coast

Cruise West's *Temptress Explorer* focuses on protecting the natural environment while enabling tourists to visit unusual sites in Costa Rica, Belize, Guatemala, and Panama.

Originally built as a U.S. supply ship, the *Temptress Explorer* was converted into a passenger ship in 1995 and sails exclusively along Costa Rica's Pacific coast. The ship takes up to ninety-nine passengers in a friendly atmosphere on an all-inclusive program of shore excursions. The passengers are likely to include families, couples of all ages, and singles.

The forward observation lounge has comfortable chairs and couches for quiet reading, watching the sights, or browsing the corner library's local reference books and donated paperbacks. Socializing takes place at the Tortuga Bar on Upper Deck, where drinks are complimentary. Entertainment may be local musicians or dancing under the stars.

Open-sitting meals are served in a pleasant dining room at tables and at banquettes next to large panoramic windows. Continental breakfast is available on deck, but most passengers choose the dining-room buffet for fresh fruit, croissants, pastries, cold cereals, and hot dishes to order such as huevos rancheros or French toast. Lunch is served buffet style on the Upper Deck or on the beach at tables with red-checkered tablecloths. The choices may be cold cuts and salads and entrees such as sea bass, roast turkey, chicken, and pizza. For dinner passengers sign up for one of three flavorful entrees such as tenderloin steak with mushroom sauce, mahimahi with tartar sauce, and fettuccine with tomato sauce.

The attractive cabins are simply furnished with either twin or queen beds, matching night tables, a double closet and storage drawers below, a five-shelved unit, and a demilune table beneath a mirror. Rich Costa Rican woods are used in the furniture highlighted by the maroon red, dark green and navy blue–striped bedspreads. Cabin windows open to bring in the sounds of the birds and the sea. The bathroom is functional and has a shower. At day's end a briefing session, held in the Toucan Lounge, lays out the upcoming shore activities, which invariably means an early wake-up knock.

The Itinerary

Experienced and highly competent local naturalists lead groups of fourteen to sixteen on hikes rated as easy, medium, and difficult, depending on length and

*Few roads reach the remote coastline and pristine national parks of Costa Rica's Pacific rim, where a diversity of wildlife abounds. The **Temptress Explorer** literally deposits you into a world of nature where you can experience the pleasures of being able to kayak, snorkel, and go scuba diving or deep-sea fishing. During the week passengers visit a wide variety of ecosystems full of exotic plants, native birds, four species of monkeys, and tree sloths.*

terrain. Shore excursions begin at the swim platform, the launching spot for the Zodiacs and for taking a kayak or banana boat or water-skiing.

The *Temptress Explorer* sails from **Los Seuños,** Herradura Bay, to the Nicoya Peninsula and the privately owned **Curu Wildlife Refuge.** The dry, tropical-forest vegetation allows relatively easy spotting of howler monkeys and native birds such as trogons, blue-tailed manakins, and motmots. On **Isla Tortuga** passengers swim or snorkel from the white sandy beach, or they can try the Canopy Ride, where people "fall" from a platform in the treetops with the aid of a harness attached to a cable-and-pulley system.

In the evening the ship sails south overnight to **Corcovado National Park,** one of the most remote parks in Costa Rica. Located 75 miles north of the Panamanian border, it covers 108,000 acres and is one of the richest, most diverse tropical regions in the world. Although biologists have identified 285 species of birds, 500 species of trees, 139 species of mammals, and 116 of amphibians and reptiles, we were content with spotting howler monkeys, scarlet macaws, morpho butterflies, and pizotes (raccoonlike animals).

An early morning hike from **San Pedrillo Ranger Station** to a waterfall took us through a forest of buttressed root trees, strangler vines, guava and cashew trees, and *Brosium utile,* or milk tree, so named because of the edible white latex that runs through its trunk. A short walk brought us to Rio Claro and a swimming hole on the beach. Slightly upriver, hanging vines provided a perfect spot for Tarzan-style dives into the crystal water. At Caletas in **Corcovado Conservation Area,** there was horseback riding along trails and the beach. Offshore, **Isla Cano,** an ancient burial site, is excellent for snorkeling. Deep-sea-fishing and scuba diving enthusiasts spent the morning on a chartered boat.

Midweek we anchored in **Golfo Dulce** off **Golfito,** once an important port for the United Fruit Company. We visited two privately owned preserves, the lush rain forests and beautiful gardens at **Cana Blanca,** a peaceful, family-owned resort complete with its own resident scarlet macaw; and **Casa Orquideas,** a landscaped botanical garden.

On the last day we visited **Manuel Antonio National Park** to finally spot the elusive two-toed sloth high on the branches of a ceiba tree, iguanas, white-faced or capuchin monkeys, and agoutis (native rodents). During a final afternoon swim and snorkel beneath Cathedral Point came the sound of howler monkeys in the distance.

Cruise West's
Temptress Explorer

Address/Phone: Cruise West, 2401 4th Avenue, Suite 700, Seattle, WA 98121; (800) 426–7702; fax: (206) 441–4757; e-mail: info@cruisewest.com; www.cruisewest.com

The Ship: *Temptress Explorer* was first built in 1970 and completely rebuilt in 1995 and has a length of 185 feet and a draft of 12.5 feet.

Passengers: 99; average age fifty; families welcome; 95 percent American

Dress: Very casual

Officers/Crew: Costa Rican

Cabins: 46 double cabins and 4 suites; all with large picture windows

Fare: $$$

What's included: Cruise, port charges, drinks, excursions, water sports, laundry service

What's not included: Airfare, tips

Highlights: Exploring remote areas of Costa Rica's Pacific coast; seeing lots of wildlife

Other itineraries: In addition to this seven-day cruise, three- and four-day options are available aboard the *Temptress Explorer,* which operates from December to August, and there are other Central American itineraries. Cruise West also opperates cruises from Baja California north to Alaska and around the Pacific Rim.

CRYSTAL CRUISES' *CRYSTAL HARMONY*
The Panama Canal and Caribbean

Established in 1990, Crystal Cruises' ships are among the largest in the luxury sector, and the sisters provide a refined cruise for passengers who appreciate superb service and top-notch cuisine. Overall, the decor is breezy, light, and cheerful, with lots of white and beige as well as dabs of pinks, mints, and blues.

Crystal is owned by Nippon Yusen Kaisa (NYK), Japan's largest container-shipping enterprise, and yet most passengers will not be aware of this fact. More than anything, Crystal is international, with a strong emphasis on European service. The Japanese flavor comes through subtly in the excellent Asian alternative restaurant, in the theme buffets, and the handful of Japanese passengers.

The *Crystal Harmony* is a social, active ship with four restaurants, a half dozen bars and entertainment lounges, a sizable gym and spa, two pools (one covered by a retractable glass roof), an uninterrupted jogging circuit, a paddle-tennis court, Ping-Pong, shuffleboard, golf driving nets, and a putting green.

The *Harmony*'s two reservations-only alternative restaurants— Kyoto, a Japanese restaurant, and Prego, an Italian one—are two of the best at sea. Kyoto, completely authentic, offers miso soup, beef teriyaki, and pork dishes, served with chopsticks and little rests; sake, in tiny sake cups; and sushi, presented on thick, blocky glass platters.

The main dining room, with its stylish, white Doric columns and roomy table arrangements, serves dinner in two seatings, whereas breakfast and lunch are one. Dishes may be a roasted duck with apricot-sage stuffing, served with a Grand Marnier orange sauce, or broiled Black Angus sirloin steak or seared sea scallops and jumbo shrimp served with a light lobster beurre blanc over a bed of pumpkin risotto. A low-fat selection is broiled fillet of Chilean Sea Bass served with steamed vegetables. Crystal inventories one of the most sophisticated selections of fairly priced California wines on the high seas. Service by the team of ultraprofessional, gracious European male waiters is excellent.

Themed luncheon buffets—Asian, Mediterranean, or a western barbecue—are excellent and generously spread out by the pool. For a casual lunch you can order beef, chicken, and salmon burgers, pizza, tuna melts, chicken wraps, Caesar salad, and fruit from the pool-side Trident Grill. For afternoon tea the revenue is the ultrachic Palm Court, a sprawling space on a high deck bathed in floor-to-ceiling windows and with

*Crystal Cruises operates the two of the largest upscale ships in the industry. Carrying 960 passengers each, the **Crystal Harmony** and **Crystal Symphony** aren't huge or hulking, but they do offer many more facilities for entertainment, socializing, dining, and fitness than their smaller high-end peers. Both food and service are on par, and Crystal's Asian food is tops. With these ships life aboard is as important as the destination, so a Panama Canal cruise with many days at sea is an ideal choice.*

pale-blue and white furniture in leather and rattan as well as a harpist in residence.

Count on several enrichment lectures such as those given by a Panama Canal historian, a movie critic, or a celebrity guest speaker. Learn to swing or do the rumba and merengue, play bridge and trivia games, partake of arts-and-crafts sessions like glass etching, or take golf lessons. The computer lab has twenty work stations, and classes are offered on basic introduction, understanding the Internet, how to buy a computer, and using e-mail, with access readily available.

Shows encompass classical concertos, comedy acts, dancers, and lead singers performing Cole Porter or Rodgers and Hammerstein. Other venues host ballroom dancing, a pianist in the paneled and very romantic Avenue Saloon, and first-run movies.

Despite their high price tag, the large majority of Crystal's cabins are smaller than these aboard the small luxury competitors. About half the accommodations have small verandas, measuring about 6 by 8 feet. Drawer space is adequate, hanging closets are tight, bathrooms compact, and soundproofing is fair. All cabins have a sitting area, a bathtub (a compact one on the lower category cabins) and shower, TVs broadcasting CNN, ESPN, and other channels, a VCR, a minibar, a hair dryer, and a safe.

The Itinerary

The *Crystal Harmony* is a fine, roomy, well-laid-out ship to take you through the Canal and to spend five or six days at sea. Recline on your private balcony, head to one of the quiet, concave slices of the aft tiered decks, or get cozy in one of the ocean-facing banquettes in the Palm Court/Vista Lounge observation lounge.

Sailings of mostly eleven and twelve nights between **New Orleans** or **Fort Lauderdale** and **Acapulco** call variously at **Playa del Carmen/ Cozumel,** for the Mayan ruins at **Tulum;** or **Chichen Itza** and **Grand Cayman,** for shopping and the beach; and **Puerto Caldera,** Costa Rica, for a rain-forest tour. The highlight, of course, is the daylong **Panama Canal** transit with three sets of one, -two and three-chamber locks, the peace and serenity of the Gatun Lake, and the narrow passage through the Gaillard Cut in the Continental Divide. A Panama Canal company narrator will provide lots of interesting material during the passage between the seas. Then, in the **Pacific,** the successive, rhythmic days at sea show how Crystal shines.

Crystal Cruises' *Crystal Harmony*

Address/Phone: Crystal Cruises, 2049 Century Park East, Suite 1400, Los Angeles, CA 90067; (310) 785–9300 or (800) 820–6663 for brochures; fax: (310) 785–3891; www.crystalcruises.com

The Ship: *Crystal Harmony* was built in 1990, has a gross tonnage of 49,400, a length of 790 feet, and a draft of 25 feet.

Passengers: 960; mostly North Americans, age fifty-five plus

Dress: Fit to kill; formal nights, jackets and ties on informal nights

Officers/Crew: Norwegian and Japanese officers; European and Filipino crew

Cabins: 480; 461 outside, 260 with private verandas.

Fare: $$$$

What's included: Cruise fare only

What's not included: Airfare, port charges, drinks, shore excursions, tips

Highlights: Japanese and Italian restaurants, waiter/bar service, lots of onboard amenities

Other itineraries: In addition to these eleven- to thirteen-day Panama Canal cruises, which operate in January and October–November, the *Crystal Symphony* also undertakes Panama Canal trips; between the two ships, the pair cruises most of the world, including northern Europe.

HOLLAND AMERICA LINE'S *VEENDAM*
The Panama Canal and More

Holland America Line, one of the world's oldest shipping companies, has long had a solid reputation of friendly service and well-run ships. The 55,451-ton *Veendam,* built in 1996, is the fourth ship in the *Statendam* series.

Two levels of public rooms, punctuated by a glass sculpture rising dramatically through the three-deck atrium, run the length of the ship along Promenade and Upper Promenade decks, creating a rhythmic flow as passengers seek out their favorite spots and pass to and from the two-story dining room. An impressive double staircase links the two, and a Filipino orchestra serenades diners from an upper-level platform, with the sound quality well distributed. Holland America perpetuates its tradition of good, uncomplicated food, and service by the Filipino and Indonesian staff is attentive. For informal dining the spacious lido restaurant has picture windows and seating under cover near the pool.

The bi-level show lounge, well designed with good views (except from the rear balcony), presents elaborate Broadway-style entertainment. A band plays for listening and dancing in the attractive Ocean Bar, the ship's social center. The Crow's Nest provides the indoor perch for the canal transit, and it doubles as a daytime lounge for tea and as a nighttime disco. The piano bar is a cozy hideaway, whereas the Explorer's Lounge is open to passersby.

The roof of the central pool retracts in good weather, and sandwiches and satay are served informally at lunch. A gym, massage and steam rooms, saunas, and a juice bar look over the stubby bow. A jogging track encircles the mezzanine above the lido, and a much longer walk can be made on the Lower Promenade Deck.

Cabins are arranged over five decks, and those on the topmost two have verandas. To provide as many outside cabins as possible, the result is a long, narrow room with small sitting areas, TVs, VCRs, and minibars.

The Itinerary

Most passengers booking the canal cruise for the first time focus on that one day, but every line brackets the experience with Caribbean and Pacific coast of Central American ports. In the *Veendam*'s case the ship sails from **Fort Lauderdale** and first calls (last call in the reverse direction) at Holland America's private Bahamian island, **Half Moon Cay,** for a barbecue, snorkeling, swimming, hiking nature trails, or relaxing on the beach.

The all-day transit of the Panama Canal qualifies as one experience not to be missed. In a series of three sets of locks, the ship is lifted up over the continent's spine and then lowered to sea level; in between there are incredible engineering triumphs to see as well as lush tropical vegetation when sailing through the Gatun Lake and Gaillard Cut. While the **Veendam** *makes some of the transits, there are a half dozen other Holland America ships making twice-a-year positioning voyages between the Caribbean and Alaska.*

St. Thomas, in the U.S. Virgin Islands, is well set up for the tourist shopper, but you can also take a boat over to nearby **St. John** for the beautiful beaches at Trunk Bay or Hawksnest Bay. Sailing due south to **Oranjestad,** the island of Aruba provides another outdoor day at a hotel beach or at the shopping plaza next to the ship, but all this is a prelude to the big event—the **Panama Canal** transit.

Two pilots from the canal company come aboard early in the morning to guide the ship into the first set of three Gatun Locks, with electric engines called mules taking the lines to ease the ship forward. The side-by-side chambers provide a two-way transit whereby your ship is raised 85 feet while another, heading to the Caribbean, is lowered. Once clear of the third lock, the ship proceeds through Gatun Lake, a giant reservoir for the gravity-flow system. The channel narrows at Gamboa, the canal headquarters, to slice through the Continental Divide; then the ship enters the single Pedro Miguel and finally the double Miraflores Locks. About eight to ten hours after leaving the Caribbean, the pilots disembark off Balboa, and the ship sails freely into the broad Pacific, turning north along the Central American coast.

San Juan del Sur, Nicaragua, a new port of call, leads to Masaya National Park for a visit to the rim of the Santiago Crater, the colonial city of Granada on the shore of Lago de Nicaragua, and an island cruise on this huge freshwater lake. Disembarkation is at **Puerto Caldera,** a tiny, deep-water port in Costa Rica, for transfer up to San Jose. If you prefer, you can linger in this natural paradise on a post-cruise package.

Holland America Line's
Veendam

Address/Phone: Holland America Line, 300 Elliott Avenue West, Seattle, WA 98119; (800) 426–0327; fax: (206) 281–7110; www.hollandamerica.com

The Ship: Veendam was built in 1996 and has a gross tonnage of 55,451, a length of 719 feet, and a draft of 25 feet.

Passengers: 1,266; mostly Americans, age fifty-five and up

Dress: Formal, informal, and casual nights

Officers/Crew: Dutch officers; Indonesian and Filipino crew

Cabins: 633; 502 outside and 150 with verandas

Fare: $$$

What's included: Cruise only, unless a fly-cruise package is purchased, basic tips

What's not included: Airfare, port charges, shore excursions, drinks, extra tips

Highlights: The Panama Canal transit on a most attractive ship with lots to do

Other itineraries: In addition these nine-day Panama Canal cruises, which operate January to March, the *Veendam* cruises to Europe. Holland America's large fleet covers the globe: Alaska, Hawaii, around the world.

ABERCROMBIE & KENT'S *EXPLORER*
Exploring the Upper and Lower Amazon

Abercrombie & Kent began as an East African safari company and entered the cruise business by chartering riverboats, barges, and small cruise ships and now operates the *Explorer* year-round, the first purpose-built expedition ship when she entered service in 1969. Newer expedition vessels are larger, more spacious, and have additional sophisticated amenities, but this little vessel is just fine for a calm-water Amazon itinerary.

The main observation lounge can seat all passengers at one time for the naturalists' recaps and announcements for the day ahead; bar service is offered on the starboard side, and a good reference library exists to port. A lecture hall, aft on the deck above, screens documentaries and slide-illustrated lectures that form an integral part of the voyage. The experienced staff include botanists, hydrologists, zoologists, anthropologists, and historians, and their names and biographies often appear in the main brochure. Aft on this deck is a small pool, and outdoor space is adequate for a port-intensive cruise. Passengers have access to the bridge for navigational information and chats with the officers.

The dining room seats passengers at one sitting, where they mix with the naturalist staff. The food is European and American, well prepared but not gourmet, and from a more limited menu than those found on larger ships. Breakfast and lunch provide buffets, and coffee and tea are available all day. Cabins are small outsides with twin beds, a desk-cum-vanity and stool between, limited storage space, and small bathrooms with showers.

The Itineraries

The big ships ply the Amazon's 1,000-mile lower reaches between Manaus and its mouth at Belem, while more nimble expedition vessels churn an additional 1,200 miles upriver to **Iquitos,** a sprawling port city located deep in the Peruvian rain forest. Iquitos, a rather tatty place, enjoyed a brief burst of prosperity during a turn-of-the-century rubber boom.

Iquitos to Manaus: Cruise ships bound downstream to ports in Colombia and Brazil dock at a floating pontoon, securely tied against a powerful current. The core of the more adventurous small-ship cruises are Zodiac excursions, most scheduled for early in the day. At

Amazonia contains one third of the world's rain forest, and although the Nile is slightly longer, the Amazon discharges sixty times more freshwater, fully one third of the world's supply. The river, above the Brazilian port of Manaus, is a wide, wondrous stream surging through an unbroken tropical setting inhabited by elegant, large-billed toucans, playful river dolphins, and isolated Bora and Tikuna Indians. Abercrombie & Kent's expedition ship, the one-hundred passenger Explorer, is an ideal, small, fully-equipped ship sailing with a topflight naturalist staff.

the town of **Pevas,** you visit an artist's house that commands the Amazon-jungle equivalent of a Hudson River view. The owner's landscape paintings draw on the colors of the bromeliads in the forest and the light of the puffy cumulus clouds and darker vertical thunderheads.

During the day of cruising, with no channel markers of any kind, Peruvian pilots navigate the ever-changing river using charts covered with penciled notations and a very good memory, much as Mark Twain did on the Mississippi in the nineteenth-century steamboat days. The elevation drops only 180 feet over the 1,262 miles from Iquitos down to Manaus.

Calling at a **Bora Indian Village,** the guides lead you ashore to wander through a compound of wooden houses built on stilts to allow the air to circulate beneath the floors and to keep them dry during the rainy season. Some of the villagers simply watch in silence from an open window or repose in a hammock strung across the veranda, while others come closer to barter their face masks, patterned baskets, and bark paintings for articles of our clothing, flight bags, and knick-knacks.

At the tri-country junction of Peru and Brazil, there's a landing in the third country of Colombia at **Leticia,** where a thriving market exists for the local residents as well as tourists. Then calls at the **Tikuna Villages** reveal children proudly holding pet spider monkeys, baby sloths, and small lizards, happily posing for pictures without asking anything in return. These villages are largely self-sufficient, and around the perimeter are

healthy-looking Brazil nut and banana trees, garden plots of corn, manioc, and yams, and pigs snorting around in the dirt. On walks into the rain forest, the guide may cut open a termite nest in search of the elusive queen. In a clearing some tourists find hardy vines to swing from while yodeling Johnny Weissmuller style. High up in the trees where most action in the forest takes place, you may see howler monkeys.

Darkness falls rapidly in the tropics, and once the powerful searchlight from the bridge is turned on, the bright beam becomes a tube filled with flying insects and darting birds, and it spotlights floating vegetation and hardwood logs. The riverbanks become a solid black wall, interrupted by an occasional lantern or cooking fire.

Following nine nights on the Upper Amazon, the *Explorer* ties up alongside the pontoon landing at **Manaus,** a ramshackle city of more than one million inhabitants and best known for its opulent, neoclassical opera house and wrought-iron, Eiffel-designed market pavilion, relics of the rubber boom long since passed.

Manaus to Belem: Below Manaus the **Rio Negro,** a large tributary whose high content of tannic acid gives the waters an usually dark tint, mixes with the lighter silt of the Amazon. The Amazon broadens out into a wide highway, the main transportation artery through Amazonia, where the traffic consists of colorful, two-deck wooden boats carrying produce to market and passengers between hundreds of ports on more than 50,000 miles of navigable rivers.

Boca da Valeria, a small village of only seventy-five inhabitants, welcomes callers to inspect their riverside lifestyle, and the town of **Parintins** is known for its folkloric events that include a samba performance recalling the traditions of Carnival in Rio. The blue waters of Rio Tapajos join the Amazon at a little place called **Alter do Chao,** where, believe it or not, passengers may swim from a sandy beach without fear of piranha attacks.

The mouths of the Amazon are a confusing complex of navigable waterways that lead to the Atlantic. Ships en route to Belem turn into the narrow, looping **Breves Canal,** a natural waterway that the rain forest often appears to close off. But it's just another bend in the channel, and the way is clear though the overhanging tree branches that just beg to be pulled. The Amazon cruise ends at **Belem,** a city of one million inhabitants and a crossroads of river, coastal, and ocean-going trade. The sprawling market displays scores of edible species of fish, fruits, and vegetables, plus folk-medicine remedies and handicrafts such as baskets, pottery, and clothes.

Abercrombie & Kent's
Explorer

Address/Phone: Abercrombie & Kent International, 1520 Kensington Road, Oak Brook, IL 60523; (630) 954–2944 or (800) 323–7308, brochures only: (800) 757–5884; fax: (630)-954–3324; e-mail: info@abercrombiekent.com; www.explorership.com or www.abercrombiekent.com

The Ship: *Explorer,* built in 1969 as the *Lindblad Explorer,* later became the *Society Explorer.* The ship has a gross tonnage of 2,398, a length of 238 feet, and draft of 14 feet.

Passengers: 100; Americans, some British; age fifty and up

Dress: Casual

Officers/Crew: European officers; Filipino crew

Cabins: 50; small, with twin beds, all outside

Fare: $$$

What's included: Cruise, port charges, transfers, shore excursions, tips

What's not included: Airfare add-ons available, drinks

Highlights: Highly professional staff, remote Upper Amazon itineraries

Other itineraries: In addition to these Amazon cruises, which operate from late March to early May, the *Explorer* spends the winter cruising in Antarctica, the summer in northern Europe, and undertakes a one-of-a-kind, annual, thirty-five-day North-South mid-ocean Lost Islands of the Atlantic voyage. A&K also offers cruises and tours all over the world.

AMAZON TOURS & CRUISES'
ARCA AND *RIO AMAZONAS*
Upper Amazon Expedition-Style Cruising

Amazon Tours & Cruises, in business for more than a quarter century, is run by an American living in Iquitos, Peru. Although the firm's riverboat fleet numbers a half dozen, only the two largest, making the full six-night cruises to and from Iquitos, Peru, are described here.

The twenty-nine-passenger *Arca*, the smaller of the two, is a three-deck riverboat that was most recently upgraded in 1995. Public areas include non-air-conditioned covered and uncovered lounges, a bar, and a partly covered top deck. The dining room is air-conditioned, as are the sixteen cedar- and mahogany-paneled cabins, ten with upper and lower berths, and three triples with lower berths; all cabins have private showers.

The *Rio Amazonas*, the largest in the fleet, is a true veteran of the Amazon with a battered white steel hull to prove it. First built in 1896 as a passenger-cargo boat, then rebuilt into a river cruise vessel in 1981, it was last refitted in 1994. The public spaces include an air-conditioned dining room and a small library, a lounge and bar and a Sun Deck with open and covered seating, hammocks, and a hot tub. The air-conditioned cabins, all outside with showers and baths, have two lower beds; three are triples.

Both vessels have buffet-style dining. The food includes fresh fish, vegetables, and fruit, but some food is preserved to avoid spoilage in this tropical climate.

The Itineraries

Cruises operate downstream and upstream, with some different landings for each three-night segment between Iquitos and the small Peruvian port of Santa Rosa opposite Leticia (Colombia) and Tabatinga (Brazil). Either or both riverboats may be used. The days are always warm, with rain likely once a day from December through March. Jungle walks are invariably hot and sticky, but when cruising and at night, the temperatures are surprisingly moderate. Air-conditioning during meals and while asleep provides additional relief.

Downstream: Iquitos, located east of the Andes, may qualify as the world's largest city with no road access to the outside world. Navigable rivers provide local transportation. This sprawling city experienced a very brief rubber boom, and there is some evidence of past wealth but not much, so it is a relief to begin the downriver cruise. There are no channel markers, so the pilots simply memorize the river. The water level can

River cruising on the Peruvian Upper Amazon aboard a small expedition vessel provides a completely different experience from traveling the Brazilian Amazon below Manaus aboard a large cruise liner. On the remote upper stretches, people come from all over the world to enjoy rain-forest walks, visits to Indian villages, bird-watching, piranha fishing, and views of this amazing riverine wilderness.

change 30 to 40 feet between the dry and rainy seasons, and any buoys would simply be carried away by the high and fast-flowing waters.

The first full day is spent visiting **Indian villages,** isolated communities that depend on the river for transportation, water, and fishing. There is a a tour of the stilted compounds and blowgun demonstration. At the larger town of **Pevas,** built mostly on high ground, there is a chance to visit an artist's house. The landscape paintings draw on the colors of the bromeliads in the forest.

The second full day begins with a rain-forest walk to see the giant water lilies and perhaps howler monkeys. While they are easily heard, without a good guide or binoculars they are often hard to spot. Piranha fishing is not as frightening as it may sound, but the setting, a dark backwater pond beneath a thick canopy of tree branches, can be an eerie experience. If the catch, including catfish, is large enough, the cook onboard will prepare it for dinner. The afternoon is spent visiting a missionary village, and, after sunset, small boats take passengers into a reedy swamp for Amazon caiman spotting, using flashlights to set the eyes aglow.

Passengers on the three-night cruise transfer across the Amazon to **Leticia,** Colombia, for onward flights; a new group boards here, joining those making the round-trip voyage.

Upstream: The boundaries of Brazil, Colombia, and Peru come together at the turnaround location, and the river traffic is busy. The first afternoon may include a rain-forest walk or a river tributary exploration.

The first full day provides a fishing trip, using hand lines, deep into the forest canopy for catfish or piranha. In the afternoon there is a visit to a leper colony at **San Pablo** and time to buy wood carvings, dolls, and artwork. After dark the launches follow a tributary, and there will be red-eyed caiman to spot with the aid of flashlights.

The second day revisits **Pevas** and a last chance to trade items for local handicrafts of handmade masks and bark paintings. As the current can be strong, the upriver cruise provides less time ashore.

If you are taking only one segment, it is highly recommended to add a stay at one of the lodges or campsites. Whatever stretch is chosen, the line is a highly experienced Amazonian operator, and its river vessels offer comfortable accommodations and a very good value.

Amazon Tours & Cruises' *Arca* and *Rio Amazonas*

Address/Phone: Amazon Tours & Cruises, 275 Fontainebleau Boulevard, Suite 173, Miami, FL 33172; (305) 227–2266 or (800) 423–2791; fax: (305) 227–1880; e-mail: info@amazontours.net; www.amazontours.net

The Ships: *Arca* was built in 1980, has a gross tonnage of 95, a length of 99 feet, and a shallow draft. *Rio Amazonas* was first built in 1896, then rebuilt in 1981, and has a gross tonnage of 350, a length of 146 feet, and a shallow draft.

Passengers: *Arca,* 29; *Rio Amazonas,* 44 (maximum capacity); age thirty and up, Americans and Europeans

Dress: Casual

Officers/Crew: Peruvian

Cabins: Arca, 13; Rio Amazonas, 21; twin beds, upper/lower berths, some with a third upper berth; all air-conditioned, outside, and with shower and toilet

Fare: $$

What's included: Cruise fare, port charges, excursions

What's not included: Airfare, drinks, tips

Highlights: Remote and roadless Upper Amazon; exotic bird life, Indian villages

Other itineraries: In addition to these year-round three- and six-night cruises, the company runs four smaller vessels and one new larger one, some for charter, on other parts of the Upper Amazon, its tributaries, and the Rio Negro. Lodge and jungle camp stays can be added.

ROYAL OLYMPIA'S *OLYMPIA VOYAGER*
Cruising the Lower Amazon and Caribbean

The *Olympia Voyager* is a true thoroughbred and is a completely new start for Royal Olympia, along with the 2001-built sistership *Olympia Explorer*. Staffed with mostly Greek crew, this is one of the few ships that retains a national identity.

While most choose the cruise for the unique itinerary, in this case the Lower Amazon and Caribbean, the ship itself is also appealing. The *Olympia Voyager* successfully blends modern technology with fresh but classically influenced interiors, and her relatively small size appeals to those who do not want a floating resort at sea.

Executed by the same designers that do Celebrity's ships, the upscale interiors use cherry wood paneling and illuminated glass. Starting at the top, the Anemnos Disco doubles as an observation lounge offering 270-degree views and afternoon tea. It's a fine perch while cruising in tropical waters.

The ship's social hub is the Piano Bar, with a walkway running through the middle of the room, allowing people to look in and naturally congregate. The Alexander the Great Lounge, a simple one-story showroom, sees use for lectures and evening entertainment. There

is also a plush smoking room with large, soft couches and a small casino, library, and spa and gym area. The ship's only real drawback is a lack of good deck space, including virtually nonexistent promenade space.

The Dining Room, serving good to average food, is situated aft and cleverly divided into three areas, allowing an intimate feeling no matter where you are seated. With blue and rust chairs set against a rich blue carpet, this is a very inviting room. The buffet, one deck above, is one of the more attractive lido areas afloat and serves a good selection for breakfast and lunch, including some excellent Greek specialties. A pizza parlor adjacent to the swimming pool offers excellent varieties from early afternoon to well into the evening hours.

Standard cabins are only 140 square feet, slightly smaller than those found on many megaships, but well laid out with TVs, safes, and minibars. There are only twelve veranda cabins on board, although the balconies are unusually deep and can easily accommodate a cocktail party. Of particular note, however, are the ship's sixteen bay window suites, which have floor-to-

Visions of the Amazon jungle bring forth images of anacondas slithering through a green hell, saw-toothed piranhas attacking cattle as they drink from the river, and developers slashing and burning the virgin South American rain forest. Reality is something quite different, and the dangers that lurk in one's mind are largely hidden in the forest or safely beneath the muddy waters. A Lower Amazon cruise on a midsize liner may give you the appetite for something more exotic upstream. This Royal Olympia cruise operates to and from Fort Lauderdale, taking only seventeen days.

ceiling windowed alcoves projecting out from the hull of the ship. Twelve of these have been replaced by veranda cabins on the newer *Olympia Explorer.* Cabins all the way aft on Decks 2 and 3 can experience some vibration and noise at top speed.

While you shouldn't expect a luxury service, it is usually cheerful and efficient, with many of the crew having served proudly with the company for many years. Zipping through the Caribbean and up the broad Amazon is exciting, and watching the ship's powerful, fuming wake chasing astern is also exhilarating. Passengers who come for a port intensive cruise and who want some insight into the area they are traveling will be very satisfied with this new ship.

The Itinerary

The *Olympia Voyager* is a 28-knot, high-speed ship, and this seventeen-day itinerary from and returning to **Fort Lauderdale** for many years used to take twenty-eight days aboard *Stella Solaris.*

After sailing from South Florida, there is a day and a half at sea to become acquainted with the ship and take in some of the enrichment program outlining what lies ahead. Then, for the next three days, there are calls at **San Juan,** for an excursion to **El Yunque** rain forest, to **El Morro,** the fortress guarding the harbor, and on foot to **Old San Juan** with dinner on the town; a more relaxing day on **Tortola,** British Virgin Islands and on **Barbados,** with the sharp contrast between the pounding Atlantic breakers on the western shore and the calm waters and sandy beaches on the eastern side.

The mouths of the **Amazon** are a confusing complex of navigable waterways that lead in from the Atlantic. The river is a wide highway, literally the main transportation artery through Amazonia, where colorful two-deck wooden boats carry produce to market and passengers between hundreds of ports on more than 50,000 miles of navigable rivers.

During this first day on the river, lectures may include discovering the official source of the Amazon high in the Peruvian Andes and the threats facing the animals, birds, and Indians of Amazonia. Indians are in great danger because of neglect, politics, and invasion by outsiders in search of land, timber, and gold. One of the largest groups, the Tikuna of the Upper Amazon, had its first European contact in 1532 and today numbers 23,000; another group, the Assurini, whose first contact was in 1972, numbers only fifty-seven. At Boca de Valeria, passengers can visit a Caboclo village, a typical example of native culture.

Upstream, the Lower Amazon cruise ends at **Manaus,** a ramshackle city of more than one million inhabitants and best known for its opulent neoclassical opera house and wrought-iron Eiffel-designed market pavilion, relics of the early twentieth-century rubber boom. Tied up to the city's pontoon, the *Olympia Voyager* looms over the dozens of arriving and departing wooden riverboats. Manaus has no road access to the rest of Brazil for most of the year due to rained-out roads, and for many the rivers become the highways. The **Rio Negro,** darkly tinted with steep vegetation,

meets but does not immediately mix with the lighter, silty Amazon a few miles below the city, creating a distinct line that trails across the surface for several miles.

Returning downstream, the next call is at **Santarem,** the largest city between Manaus and Belem. There, you may spot gray and pink river dolphins, kingfishers, and colorful parrots. Most of the wildlife, however, is elusive and when seen is likely to be a pet boa constrictor, sloth, alligator, or spider monkey in the arms of a child. Exiting the Amazon, ships en route to Devil's Island and the Southern Caribbean take the more northerly route, crossing the equator at **Macapa** then out to open waters.

Out in the Atlantic, **Devil's Island** is much more beautiful and interesting than one would imagine, with its pounding surf, tropical forests, and unsettling prison ruins, the structures once serving as a notorious French penal colony made famous in *Papillon*.

Twenty-four hours later, **Trinidad,** a crossroads of shipping, has a varied population makeup, including a substantial number of Indians from the Asian subcontinent, many of whom have been here for generations. Visit the **Asa Wright Nature Center** and the **Caroni Bird Sanctuary,** two conservation centers and homes for many colorful tropical birds. **Martinique** is France with a black face in the Caribbean, and **St. Thomas** provides a final call and an easy reentry into the United States.

Royal Olympia's
Olympia Voyager

Address/Phone: Royal Olympia Cruises, 805 Third Avenue, New York, NY 10022; (212) 688–7555 or (800) 872–6400; fax: (888) 662–6237; www.royalolympiacruises.com

The Ship: *Olympia Voyager* was completed in 2000. It has a gross tonnage of 25,000, is 590 feet in length, and has draft of 24 feet.

Passengers: 836; mostly Americans, age fifty-five and up

Dress: More formal than in the Mediterranean, also with informal and casual nights

Officers/Crew: Greek officers; international (but predominantly Greek) crew

Cabins: 418, of which 12 have balconies and 16 are bay window suites; 12 of these are balcony cabins on the *Olympia Explorer*

Fare: $$$

What's included: Cruise fare, port charges

What's not included: Airfare, tips, drinks, shore excursions

Highlights: A packed Amazon and Caribbean itinerary on a sleek new ship with good cultural emphasis on the destinations

Other itineraries: In addition to these seventeen-day Amazon and Caribbean itineraries, which operate between December and March, the *Olympia Voyager* and the *Olympia Explorer* cruise the Orinoco, South America, the Panama Canal, and the Atlantic on crossing to and from the Mediterranean. In the spring, summer, and early fall, both ships and the rest of the fleet cruise the Eastern Mediterranean from Venice and Piraeus.

CANODROS' *GALAPAGOS EXPLORER II*
The Galápagos Archipelago

Canodros, S.A. bought the *Renaissance III* in 1997 and renamed her *Galapagos Explorer II* to replace an older ship of the same name for three-, four-, and seven-night itineraries.

The Main Lounge on Deck 3 serves as the lecture hall for briefings before shore excursions and for dancing to local bands or one made up from the crew. The piano bar aft on Deck 4 is popular, as all drinks are complimentary, except wines and champagne.

The attractive dining room on Deck 2 is partitioned into three distinct areas, with tables set for two, four, and six or eight. Open seating is the rule at breakfast and lunch, but passengers are asked to sit at the same table for dinner. Breakfast is buffet, catering to American and European tastes, plus South American delicacies such as fried plantains with cheese. At dinnertime the fixed menu might include melon and prosciutto, soup, salad, entrees such as Galápagos lobster with curry sauce, filet mignon with mushroom sauce, or fresh local fish and a dessert. Food is tasty but not gourmet; the staff is friendly and willing, but the standard of English is minimal. Lunch is usually served on Deck 5 with buffet, bar, and tables around the pool. Selections include salads, soup, a local Ecuadorian dish, and spaghetti or sweet and sour pork. Next to the pool the Jacuzzi is popular after shore expeditions.

The fifty cabins are spacious suites lined with dark paneling and decorated in pastels. Three picture windows provide ample daylight, and a sitting area, with a sofa, chair, and small glass-topped table, encourages passengers to read and relax. Additional amenities include two drawers that lock, two full-length closets, a hair dryer, a telephone, a minibar and a TV/VCR.

The Itinerary
On a typical seven-day cruise, you visit ten of the thirteen islands in the archipelago, and you will see species uniquely adapted to these islands as described by Charles Darwin in *The Origin of Species* (1859).

A few hours after landing on the tiny airstrip at **San Cristobal,** you may be crouching on a dark sand beach staring eye to eye at sea lions while, above, brown pelicans swoop down to the clear blue water looking for their evening meal. Blue-footed boobies perch on nearby cliffs, and frigate birds soar above the pangas (dinghies) as the sun sets between the twin peaks of Kicker Rock. Wildlife seems completely oblivious to human visitors, a surprise and perhaps the highlight of a Galápagos trip.

The rhythm of life onboard begins with an early morning wake-up call and buffet breakfast. Then it's all aboard the pangas by 8:00 A.M., dressed accordingly for dry or wet landings. During briefings by the Ecuadorian expedition leader, you get an idea of what wildlife is likely to be seen, while the environments vary from

About 65,000 tourists come annually to observe a remarkable collection of animals and the adaptations to their individual environments. Marine iguanas, sea lions, Sally Lightfoot crabs, blue-footed boobies, masked boobies, Galápagos penguins, sea turtles, tortoises, flamingos, and thirteen finch species all can be found living in this protected environment. The Galapagos Explorer II is the most luxurious of the Galápagos fleet.

beaches of different colors—red, olive green, white—to flat lava rocks, steep cliffs, and rocky coastlines.

Wooden stairs lead to superb views on **Bartolomé** out to surrounding islands and the many lava spatter cones, remnants of volcanic activity. Down on the beach you have a chance to slip into the water to enjoy swimming among sea lions and watching a variety of brightly colored fish darting in and out of the rocks, with curious Galápagos penguins rushing by at speeds up to 40 miles per hour.

The beautiful white-sand beach at Gardner Bay on the island of **Española** proves to be a challenging wet landing. The reward is a pristine setting shared with sea lions, endemic scavenger hawks, oystercatchers, and finches. At Devil's Crown, off **Floreana,** some of the party on my trip were lucky to spot a white shark.

At **Point Espinoza** on the northern end of **Fernandina,** the terrain is dominated by scaly marine iguanas, a twentieth-century miniature version of the ancient dinosaur and the world's only true marine lizard. These creatures, which look prehistoric, huddle in groups and move slowly in and out of the shallow water, spitting saltwater to aid the digestion of seaweed. The spiny ridges down their backs determine the sex, with males having higher and more predominant features, and their bodies blend so well with the land that it is difficult to avoid stepping on them. A strong stench is present, due to the many iguana carcasses. The scene includes flightless cormorants perched on algae-covered rocks and sea lions and Sally Lightfoot crabs moving about rock pools and on the beach.

Civilization appears when landing at **Puerto Ayora,** the main town on **Santa Cruz Island.** At the Charles Darwin Research Station, you get the chance to observe tortoises (the Spanish word is *galápagos*) from different islands, separated into environments that replicate their natural ones. They are now studied and bred in captivity, where once they almost become extinct by sailors using them for fresh meat during long Pacific Ocean voyages. When the offspring are strong enough, they are returned to their natural habitats; as a result, their numbers are increasing significantly.

On a trip into the highlands, the sights are banana and papaya plantations, cattle and horse farms, and scalesia trees covered in Spanish moss, a habitat far removed from the sea. A visit to Steve's Farm gives the opportunity to observe giant tortoises in their natural environment, where they come to drink from the water holes as they have done for hundreds of years.

Canodros's
Galapagos Explorer II

Address/Phone: Galapagos Inc., 7800 Red Road, Suite 112, South Miami, FL 33142; (305) 665–0841 or (800) 327–9854; www.canodros.com. Elegant Cruise & Tours: (800) 683–6767

The Ship: *Galapagos Explorer II,* built in 1990 as the *Renaissance III,* came under new ownership in 1997. Gross tonnage is 4,077, length 290 feet, and draft 12 feet.

Passengers: 100; all ages; mostly Americans and some Europeans and South Americans

Dress: Casual at all times

Officers/Crew: Ecuadorian

Cabins: 50 luxury outside suites with sitting areas

Fare: $$$

What's included: Cruise fare, port charges, flights between Ecuador mainland and the Galápagos, shore excursions, drinks (except wines)

What's not included: Airfare to Ecuador, overnight accommodations between flights, wines, tips to guides and ship's staff

Highlights: Seeing unique wildlife species in native habitats, most without fear of humans

Other itineraries: In addition to year-round cruises, Canodros, S.A. operates Kapawi, an ecological reserve in the Amazon Basin of southeastern Ecuador. Tours of three or seven nights can be arranged in conjunction with itineraries of the *Galapagos Explorer II.*

LINDBLAD EXPEDITIONS' *POLARIS*
The Galápagos Islands

Lindblad Expeditions was founded by Sven-Olaf Lindblad, the son of Lars Eric Lindblad, the pioneer of expedition-style cruising. The eighty-passenger *Polaris* has cruised worldwide and now spends most of the year in the Galápagos.

The Vega Lounge and well-stocked bar can seat all passengers at once for lectures and briefings, the latter taking place before dinner, when cocktails and hot hors d'oeuvres are served. Several TVs positioned around the room show videos after dinner. Adjacent, the Polaris Room is the ship's reference and reading library, with a good selection of books and games. The partially covered aft deck has old-fashioned, heavy wooden deck furniture. Above the Sky Deck is an open space over the bridge with wood benches and deck chairs. On a clear night the expedition leader will point out the stars and constellations.

The dining room is a delight, located forward with large wraparound windows with a captain's table for ten to twelve persons and others for two to seven. Meals, served at one open seating, are buffet style at breakfast and lunch and from a menu at dinner. Food is good but not necessarily memorable. The shop carries clothing and souvenirs related to the destination, and there is a sauna with separate times for men and women, as well as unisex hours.

Passengers go ashore in pangas, with a naturalist for every twelve passengers. The expedition leader and naturalists travel with the ship and mingle onboard and at meals.

The Itinerary
The itinerary for this chapter is shared with the *Galapagos Explorer II*.

The Galápagos Islands, located well out into the Pacific Ocean off the coast of Ecuador, are noted for wildlife that is found nowhere else in the world and that is oblivious to human intrusion. You can walk among masked boobies and prehistoric marine iguana and swim with playful sea lions and darting Galápagos penguins. A cruise of several days to one week is the only convenient way to visit several islands, and the **Polaris** *provides a most professional conveyance.*

Lindblad Expeditions' *Polaris*

Address/Phone: Lindblad Expeditions, 720 Fifth Avenue, New York, NY 10019; (212) 765–7740 or (800) 397–3348 or (800) GALAPAGOS; fax: (212) 265–3370; e-mail: travel@expeditions.com; www.expeditions.com

The Ship: *Polaris*, originally built in 1960 as the day ferry *Öresund*, was rebuilt into the cruise ship *Lindblad Polaris* in 1982, then simply *Polaris* after 1986. The ship has a gross tonnage of 2,138, a length of 238 feet, and a draft of 14 feet.

Passengers: 80; age fifty and up, mostly Americans

Dress: Casual at all times

Officers/Crew: Ecuadorian

Cabins: 41; mostly small, all outside with windows, portholes on A Deck

Fare: $$$$

What's included: Cruise fare and port charges; airfare between Miami and Guayaquil and between Guayaquil and Baltra, two hotel nights at Guayaquil, all shore excursions, entrance fees

What's not included: Drinks, tips to crew and guides, pooled at the end of the trip

Highlights: One of the finest natural history cruises; species unique to the Galápagos

Other itineraries: In addition to the above seven-night cruise aboard the *Polaris*, which is offered weekly except some dates in April, May, and September, the *Sea Lion* and *Sea Bird* cruise the Columbia and Snake Rivers, the British Columbia coast up to Alaska and in the Sea of Cortez and Baja California, Mexico. The deep-sea expedition ship *Endeavour,* the former *Caledonian Star,* sails in Antarctica, South America, and Europe, and the *Hapi I* cruises the Nile.

SEABOURN CRUISE LINE'S *SEABOURN PRIDE*

Down South America Way

Seabourn Cruise Line, now part of Cunard Line and both owned by the Carnival Corporation, operate a similar trio of all-suite ships, the *Seabourn Pride, Seabourn Legend,* and Seabourn *Spirit*. Although a Seabourn cruise is about as sophisticated an experience as one will find at sea, the atmosphere is less stuffy and more friendly and relaxed than in the past.

The principal public spaces revolve around The Club, a trio of glass-partitioned rooms, offering an intimate lounge setting, a cozy bar, and a small casino for blackjack, poker, and roulette. The location is popular before dinner, with hot hors d'oeuvres served and live music; after dinner a small group performs cabaret acts, and a band plays for dancing. The tiered main lounge is used for the captain's parties, films, special-interest lectures, and piano concerts. A quiet spot is the observation lounge for an unimpeded view forward and for checking the ship's position. A tiny library stocks books and videos to take out.

Outside, the attractive lido deck has sun-protected areas for chairs, two heated whirlpools, and a little-used swimming pool awkwardly sited in a shadowy pit. Constitutional walks and jogging take place on the circular deck above.

Dining aboard a Seabourn ship may be as private or as social as one would like, an option that extends to all times of the day. On two formal nights a week,

the top officers host tables, and, on informal evenings, there may be invitations from the cruise staff or the enrichment lecturers. The main restaurant meals are uniformly excellent, with memorable dishes being the fresh fish, veal dishes, and beef tenderloin. For an Italian dinner, with reservations required, the Veranda Café has a set menu that might include antipasto, minestrone, linguine al Don Alfredo, tender osso buco, and tiramisù. Complimentary wines are served at lunch and dinner. The indoor-outdoor Veranda Café never repeats its lunch menu and is equally a lovely spot for breakfast, especially at a table under the awning-covered after-deck poised over the stern. Once during the cruise, an outdoor barbecue will feature a cold buffet of jumbo shrimp, smoked mussels, smoked salmon, oysters, caviar and salad fixings galore, while the hot carvery will offer sliced roast beef, duck, and ham.

The Seabourn suites are most inviting, with blond wood grain outlining the furnishings and cabinetry and natural light pouring through the 5-foot-wide picture window. Thirty-six suites now have French balconies in place of the window. The refrigerator is stocked and replenished daily with sodas, beer, and, as ordered prior to the cruise, one complimentary bottle of red and white wine or spirits. The walk-in closet has ample hanging space and a safe, but drawer space is limited and shallow. The bed is queen-size (or two twin-size)

South America is a most difficult place for wide-ranging independent travel, and a cruise aboard the 204-passenger **Seabourn Pride** *will take you in supreme comfort to mostly Brazilian ports that would be hard to reach any other way. You have the choice of cruising northbound or southbound along the East Coast between the Caribbean and Rio de Janeiro.*

with good, focused reading lights, and the lounge has a sofa, two chairs, two stools, and a coffee table that could be raised for in-suite entertaining and dining.

The Itinerary

The ports are a mix of the usual and exotic and will vary from year to year; on the southbound cruise, some passengers will embark in **Fort Lauderdale** to call at five Caribbean ports en route to **Barbados,** where the South American portion then begins in earnest. Two days at sea precede the call at **Devil's Island,** a much more beautiful and interesting place than one might imagine, with pounding surf, tropical forests, and unsettling prison ruins—the buildings once a notorious French penal colony made famous in the book *Papillon.*

Although the Nile is slightly longer, the **Amazon** discharges sixty times more freshwater, fully one third of the world's supply. The muddy delta pushes hundreds of miles into the open ocean, and when sailing south, the ship will eventually cross that line. The mouths of the Amazon are a confusing complex of navigable waterways that lead into the Atlantic. The ship turns into the narrow, looping **Breves Canal,** a natural waterway through the rain forest that often appears likely to come to an impasse, but it's just another bend in the channel, and the way is clear.

The city of **Belem** boasts one million inhabitants and a history dating back more than 300 years, and its port is a crossroads of river, coastal, and oceangoing trade. The sprawling market displays scores of edible species of fish, fruits, and vegetables, as well as folk-medicine remedies and handicrafts such as baskets, pottery, and clothes. In a more organized setting, a botanical garden helps explain some of the plants seen along the river, and a zoo harbors the elusive animals hidden from view in the jungle.

Sailing south you come to Brazil's most easterly city, **Recife,** a sprawling city built over three islands, which is best noted for its collection of seventeenth-century churches displaying fine wooden sculpture, elaborate high altars, splendid *trompe l'oeil* ceilings, primitive-style murals, and beautiful Portuguese tiles. On down the coast **Salvador de Bahia** is the most beautiful port, which you can visit on a walking tour. The architecture of this 400-year-old colonial upper city reflects the former Portuguese capital's opulence. Two more days of cruising brings the ship into **Rio de Janeiro,** dramatically sailing past Sugar Loaf into Guanabara Bay. Be sure to linger a couple of days to stroll the broad beaches of Ipanema and Copacabana and to view the city from Corcavado.

Seabourn Cruise Line's
Seabourn Pride

Address/Phone: Seabourn Cruise Line, 610 Blue Lagoon Drive, Suite 400, Miami, FL 33126; (305) 463–3000 or (800) 929–9391; fax: (305) 463–3010; www.seabourn.com

The Ship: *Seabourn Pride* was built in 1988 and has a gross tonnage of 9,975, a length of 440 feet, and a draft of 17 feet.

Passengers: 204; mostly Americans in their fifties, some Europeans and South Americans in the mix

Dress: Formal, informal, and casual nights

Officers/Crew: Norwegian officers; mostly European crew, plus some Filipinos

Cabins: 102; all outside suites, the majority identical except for location. Thirty-six French balconies (window-type double doors set before a railing) have been added to some suites in place of sealed windows.

Fare: $$$$$

What's included: Cruise fare, port charges, wine and drinks, gratuities

What's not included: Airfare, transfers, shore excursions

Highlights: Exotic ports and a most luxurious ship to come home to at day's end

Other itineraries: In addition to this fifteen-day cruise from Barbados to Rio and a fourteen-day northbound equivalent, which operate in February and March, the Seabourn trio offers itineraries that cover the globe, including Vietnam.

ORIENT LINES' *MARCO POLO*
Passages from the East to West Coast of South America

Orient Lines, originally a British-owned company, is now a separate brand for Star Cruises, also owners of Norwegian Cruise Line. The 840-passenger *Marco Polo* was designed for worldwide cruising. First built in 1965 for the Soviet Black Sea Shipping Company as a rugged ice-strengthened transatlantic liner, the ship was completely rebuilt in 1993 as the *Marco Polo,* happily retaining her handsome ocean liner profile.

Public rooms, with an understated decor, and the outdoor swimming pool and lido bar occupy one deck and include the forward Ambassador Lounge, the venue for enrichment lectures on such topics as Indian and European influences and South American politics, plus entertainment. Further aft is the Polo Lounge, a piano bar; the Palm Court, furnished with cane chairs for afternoon tea; Le Bar, a cozy watering hole; a card room; a well-stocked library; and a small casino.

Raffles offers varied high-quality buffet selections for breakfast and lunch and gets magically transformed at night for an Oriental dinner (extra charge for tip and wine). The outdoor grill prepares steaks, sausages, and hamburgers by the pool. On the decks above are the Charleston Club's dance band and disco and the well-equipped Health Club and Beauty Center. The Sky Deck Jacuzzis, overlooking the stern, become a popular gathering spot when the ship is leaving port. Deck space is attractively tiered, and wooden steamer chairs line the wide teak Promenade Deck. The circular Boat Deck above, while narrow, is for serious walkers.

The Seven Seas Restaurant provides two sittings at dinner and a tasty selection of salads and soups such as curried pumpkin and lentil. Entrees include grilled sea shrimp, Alaska salmon with almonds and ginger crust, and seared prime beef with tempura vegetables.

The 425 cabins have mostly twin beds, some convertible to queen-size, with light-wood trim, TVs with VCRs, three-channel radios, phones, good storage, and hair dryers. Large staterooms and suites have tub baths.

The Itinerary

Argentina to Chile: Happily, there are still frontiers that offer travelers an unusual and uncrowded cruising experience, and Argentina's **Patagonia** and the **Chilean fjords** are just such places. Together they possess great scenic beauty, unusual wildlife, a thinly scattered population, and limited access.

The cruise tour begins with two full days in the stylish European city of **Buenos Aires.** Argentina's capital is a feast of flamboyant Victorian and beaux arts build-

South America is an ideal cruising region that lets you bypass the hassles of international land and air travel. This itinerary may be taken as a whole or in one of its two parts, Buenos Aires–Valparaiso and Valparaiso–Panama Canal–Caribbean–Barbados. The cruises are bracketed by land packages that add depth to the travel experience. Marco Polo is a great value. The midsize liner attracts an English-speaking union of Americans, British, and Australians who come for the creative itineraries and easy social ambience.

ings. The outdoor cafes and restaurants, handsome limestone apartment buildings, and smart shopping arcades seem even more French than those in Paris. The rich hire dog walkers; smartly dressed ladies lunch with friends; schoolboys wear blue blazers, ties, and white shirts; and no one likes to eat before ten o'clock. In Recoleta, a smart residential neighborhood, Eva Peron is buried in a cemetery of elaborate mausoleums.

The cruise begins in earnest by sailing across the muddy Rio de la Plata to **Montevideo,** Uruguay's capital. The nearby resort of **Punta del Este** attracts jet-setting South Americans.

Sailing into the South Atlantic, the *Marco Polo* calls at **Port Stanley** and **West Point** in the **Falkland Islands,** a British colony with the look of a northern Scottish isle. Sheep raising and fishing are the main occupations, and the islands are home to cute rockhopper penguins and southern elephant seals.

Sailing westward around **Cape Horn,** the land to starboard is **Tierra del Fuego,** shared by Argentina and Chile. At **Ushuaia,** a catamaran cruise into the Beagle Channel visits an island covered with seals. The next call, **Punta Arenas,** is Chile's southernmost city, the center for the sheep farming industry and gateway to **Patagonia.** Climb La Cruz Hill for great views of the surrounding forests, lakes, sand cliffs, **Strait of Magellan,** and **Tierra del Fuego.**

Glaciers come down to calve into the sea, and when the channel widens the *Marco Polo* leaves the sheltered waters and aims westward and northward to the Pacific and the Chilean fjords. There are more than 5,000 islands in the Chilean archipelago, and most channels have had no soundings. Navigation is made even trickier by unexpected mountain downdrafts that strike ships broadside. A call is made at the fishing village **Puerto Chacabuco,** set along a coast of soaring fjords and Andean peaks, then you'll sail north to **Puerto Montt,** located at the northern end of the Chilean fjords in the lake district. **Lake Llanquihue,** the country's largest lake, is overlooked by the conical 8,000-foot **Osorno** volcano, one of more than two thousand in Chile alone.

Cruising back into the Pacific, this leg of the cruise ends at **Valparaiso,** Chile's main port and now the location for the country's parliament. The lower and upper sections of Valparaiso are connected by more than one dozen hundred-year-old elevators or funicular railways, a diversion for those so inclined. Five miles distant is **Vina del Mar,** one of the continent's foremost resorts with an elegant seafront, a presidential summer palace, and a

splendid casino, maintaining a strict dress code, set among formal gardens.

Santiago, the capital, is 75 miles inland, a modern city at the foot of the snowcapped **Andes,** with enough attractions to warrant the additional nights tacked onto the cruise. You can travel by a good subway system to visit the cultural center housed in a now-disused railway station, arcaded Plaza de Armas, the 1805 Palacio de la Moneda, now a museum for paintings and sculpture. In the evening the arty Bellavista District is the place for street life, shops selling lapis lazuli, art galleries, theaters, cafes, and restaurants.

Chile via Panama to Barbados: Santiago, Chile's sprawling capital, is nestled in the Andes Mountains east of the main seaport of **Valparaiso,** where the *Marco Polo* is waiting to sail. This northbound itinerary is nicely spaced, with a day at sea between most ports. At Coquimbo, Gustav Eiffel (of Eiffel Tower fame) built one of the churches, while nearby **La Serena** is a beach resort with no less than twenty-six churches.

The coastline changes dramatically as the ship reaches **Arica,** Chile's northernmost city, rising among the foothills of the Andes. To the east the **Atacama Desert** qualifies as the driest place on earth, while beyond are the **High Andes.** The archaeological museum displays mummies that are reputed to be older than those in Egypt, and the desert hills have pre-Columbian petroglyphs. There's a terrific city and sea view from the Morro, a fort, and in Arica be sure to visit iron San Marcos Cathedral and the equally splendid custom house.

After cruising up the coast to **Callao,** the commercial port for **Lima,** it's a short drive to Peru's colonial capital quarter. Lima now counts roughly seven million inhabitants, and tours are highly recommended here and at all the ports along the coast. In Lima, the cathedral on the Plaza de Armas has a splendid interior with finely carved seventeenth-century stalls, silver-covered altars, and beautiful wall mosaics. **Miraflores,** a trendy, expensive suburb and Lima's social center, is worth a visit for beaches and the upscale shops built around a handsome park.

Salinas is a popular Ecuadorian beach resort, and to the north are **Machalilla National Park,** a dry tropical forest, and **Isla de la Plata,** home to a colony of blue-footed boobies. There is also a flying excursion inland to Quito, the capital.

Before sailing though the Panama Canal, the ship docks in **Balboa,** the port for **Panama City.** Its San Felipe district is a United Nation's World Heritage Site featuring a mixture of Spanish, French, and early American architecture. A tour visited a village on stilts in the rainforest.

Taking on the pilots early the next morning, the ship begins the **Panama Canal** transit with the 85-foot climb through the two Miraflores Locks and a half hour later moves into the single Pedro Miguel Lock. The ship then begins a peaceful sail amid lovely tropical surroundings to the Gaillard Cut through the Continental Divide and past the canal headquarters at Gamboa and into **Gatun Lake.** At the eastward end, the three-step, 85-foot drop through the Gatun Locks lowers the ship to sea level again. By mid-afternoon the pilots disembark at **Cristobal-Colon** and the ship sails into the Caribbean.

After an overnight sail, **Puerto Limon,** Costa Rica's Caribbean port, is the gateway to the inland cloud forests, home to over 800 species of birds including the flamboyant quetzal. Two nights and a day at sea bring the ship to the north coast of South America and Colombia's main port of **Cartagena.** The city's 1533-built San Felipe Fortress and twisting streets were designed to foil the pirates who came to steal the gold bound for the Spanish crown. There's one last call at **Oranjestad** on the island of **Aruba,** whose attractions range from beaches and desert plants species to Dutch-style architecture and a last chance for some shopping before the ship sails east to **Barbados,** the cruise disembarkation port.

Orient Lines' *Marco Polo*

Address/Phone: Orient Lines, 1510 S.E. 17th Street, Suite 400, Fort Lauderdale, FL 33316; (954) 727–6660 or (800) 333–7300; fax: (954) 527–6657; e-mail: info@orientlines.com; www.orientlines.com

The Ship: *Marco Polo* was originally built in 1965 as the Soviet-flag *Alexandr Pushkin,* then completely rebuilt from the hull up in 1993. She has a gross tonnage of 22,080, a length of 578 feet, and a deep draft of 27 feet.

Passengers: 840 double occupancy; age range is fifty and up, mostly English speaking

Dress: Some formal nights, otherwise jacket and tie, with casual nights in port

Officers/Crew: Scandinavian captain; mostly European officers and Filipino crew

Cabins: 425, most average size; 294 are outsides, none with verandas

Fare: $$$

What's included: Cruise, hotel nights, sightseeing, transfers

What's not included: Low airfare add-ons from U.S. gateways, port charges, shore excursions, tips, drinks

Highlights: Exotic itinerary to some remote coastal locations at an affordable package price. Great ambience on board.

Other itineraries: In addition to the twenty-day cruise tour from Buenos Aires to Santiago and the twenty-one-day cruise tour from Santiago to Barbados, combinable into one thirty-four day trip, which operate from February into April, the *Marco Polo* spends the summer in Northern Europe and the Mediterranean and winter in Antarctica. Running mate *Crown Odyssey* cruises in the Mediterranean and east of Suez to India and onto Southeast Asia, Australia, and New Zealand.

SILVERSEA CRUISES' *SILVER WIND*
Around the Bottom of South America

The newest line in the ultraluxury cruise market, Silversea Cruises made a splash in 1994 when it introduced the brand-new, 296-passenger *Silver Cloud* and *Silver Wind* followed by the 388-passenger *Silver Shadow* and *Silver Whisper.* The ships combine the spaciousness and entertainment options of a larger ship with the best of intimate, yacht-like cruising.

Public areas, inside and out, are stylish and open. Dusty blues, teal greens, and deep burgundies and violet are blended with lots of Italian marble and the odd tile mosaic tabletop. Entertainment is low-key, but there are decent options, considering the small size of the ship. Afternoon tea is served in the windowed Panorama Lounge and evenings a pianist plays there. Broadway-style production numbers with a four-dancer cast are performed in the two-story Venetian show lounge, and most nights a dance band plays oldies or a DJ spins rock and roll in the intimate, softly lit Bar. Organized activities include trivia contests, port talks, movies, and wine tasting. Mostly people socialize, read, play on the computer in the library, or roam around the roomy decks.

The outdoor deck space is sweeping, and there's never overcrowding in and around the pool, two hot tubs, and ocean-view gym. The oddly placed observation lounge, sequestered on the top deck, is a quiet place to read or play a round of cards. On cooler itineraries, like this one, it becomes ideal for watching the scenery slide by.

The formal, open-seating dining venue is delicately decorated in pale pink and gold, and elegant candlelit tables are set with heavy crystal glasses, chunky Christofle silverware, and doily-covered silver show plates. Rivaling the best restaurants in New York City or Paris, delectable dishes like grilled tournedos of beef with foie gras and truffles and marinated crab with leek salad and star anise are prepared in conjunction with Le Cordon Bleu Culinary School. Several nights a week, the Terrace Café, where buffet-style breakfast and lunch are served, is transformed into a cozy, reservations-only alternative-dining venue, featuring mostly regional Italian cuisine. Here the ambience is darker and more intimate, and there are a good number of tables for two.

All 148 suites have sitting areas, roomy walk-in closets, bathtubs, vanities, TVs and VCRs, and stocked minibars. Natural light pours in through the glass veranda doors, casting a warm glow on the creamy-beige fabrics and the abundant golden-brown-colored wood. Swirled peachy-gray marble covers the bathroom from head to toe.

Few cruises offer such spectacular scenery in such remote settings as the **Silver Wind's** *Southern Hemisphere cruises between Chile and Argentina, sailing down the Pacific side through the Chilean fjords, then up through the Atlantic along the Patagonian coast. At the bottom of the continent, the ship cruises Cape Horn and the Strait of Magellan and visits the wonders of Torres del Paine National Park.*

The Itinerary

Embarking in **Valparaiso,** 75 miles from Chile's capital at Santiago, the *Silver Wind* sets sail for **Puerto Montt,** located in the lake district at the northern end of the Chilean fjords. Just to the east, **Lake Llanquihue,** the country's largest lake, is overlooked by the conical, 8,000-foot Osorno volcano.

Sailing south in protected waters, the ship comes to the weathered **Chiloe Island** town of Castro where unpainted wooden houses perch on stilts. Leaving the *Silver Wind* in the ship's launches, a complimentary excursion enters **Laguna San Rafael,** a saltwater lake connected to the sea by a narrow tidal channel. Cruising amid broken ice, the launch eases toward 25-mile-long San Valentine glacier. The pack ice reveals a wonderful kaleidoscope of colors and shapes.

Two more days are spent cruising the fjords and the **Beagle Channel,** often within site of glacial remnants of the Ice Age, to **Ushuaia,** Argentina, on Tierra del Fuego, where a catamaran heads out to island rookeries for a close-up view of lounging, smelly sea lions and the protected nests of black-and-white cormorants. After a cruise past **Cape Horn,** the ship returns to protected waters and calls at **Punta Arenas,** Chile, for a two-day stay.

The excursion to **Torres del Paine National Park** is an absolute must, where you will encounter herds of guanaco (an American relative of the camel that resembles the llama), Darwin's flightless rhea, Chilean flamingos, black-necked swans, buff-necked ibis, and the soaring Andean condor, with a 10-foot wingspan. Gauchos with their horses sit by the roadside brewing tea. A footpath leads to a rolling, tufted green-and-yellow alpine meadow that recedes toward a deep chasm, behind which rise jagged granite peaks, each topped with a layer of brown lava. The higher, snow-covered mountains are draped with hanging glaciers.

From Punta Arenas the ship sails along the **Strait of Magellan** and out into the Atlantic Ocean to **Puerto Madryn,** a town settled by Welsh in the mid-nineteenth century. To the south **Punta Tombo** is a refuge for up to one million Magellanic penguins, who swim ashore to lay their eggs in dusty, shallow burrows. The last day is spent negotiating the muddy River Plate while en route to the European-style city of **Buenos Aires,** a civilized and sophisticated cap to the sixteen-day cruise. Plan to stay on to take in this most European of cities.

Silversea Cruises' *Silver Wind*

Address/Phone: Silversea Cruises, 110 East Broward Boulevard, Fort Lauderdale, FL 33301; (954) 522–4477 or (800) 774–9996; fax: (954) 522–4499; www.silversea.com

The Ship: The *Silver Wind* was built in 1995 and has a gross tonnage of 16,800, a length of 514 feet, and a draft of 17 feet.

Passengers: 296; mostly North American couples in their late fifties to seventies

Dress: Formal nights; informal jacket evenings; jackets and slacks for casual nights

Officers/Crew: Italian officers; European and Filipino crew

Cabins: 148; all outside and all but 38 with verandas

Fare: $$$$$

What's included: Cruise fare, port charges, one shore excursion, unlimited wines and liquors, tips, and sometimes airfare

What's not included: Most excursions and airfare when not part of a package

Highlights: The outstanding beauty of Chile and Argentina; veranda suites, cuisine, service, ship's interiors

Other itineraries: In addition to this sixteen-day *Silver Wind* itinerary between Valparaiso and Buenos Aires, which operates in both directions between December and March, there are South American cruises on other stretches of both coasts. With two new larger ships now in service, Silversea truly covers the world in great style, including East and South Africa and Australia/New Zealand.

CRUCEROS AUSTRALIS' *TERRA AUSTRALIS*
Cruising the Chilean Fjords

Terra Australis (from Latin, meaning southern lands) was built in 1984 as the *Savannah* for cruising American coastal waters and now operates for Cruceros Australis in southern Chile. Although the *Terra Australis,* a small coastal ship, does not have stabilizers and is not designed for ocean cruising, and the Strait of Magellan can experience rough seas, the ship normally operates in sheltered, calm waters.

The large observation lounge, furnished with well-padded sofas and chairs, is a passenger favorite because of its picture windows and the Magellan Bar. The navigation bridge is open most of the time, and the officers welcome a chat. Located just above the diesel engines, the dining room can be noisy when the ship is underway, but the high standard of food and service overcome the rumble just below. Tables are set with white tablecloths and a vast array of china, silver, and glassware, and the waiters are smartly dressed in black pants, white jackets, and black bow ties. Seating is open. Memorable entrees are the seafood salads at lunch and fresh fish at dinner, accompanied by Chilean wines.

Evening entertainment includes bingo, parties, and slide lectures illustrating the history and ecology of southern Chile and Argentina and what places the passengers will be visiting. The staterooms' large picture windows open, and the all-outside accommodations are surprisingly spacious for such a small ship.

The Itinerary

Flying south from the United States to **Santiago,** Chile, may be tiring but there is minimal jet lag with little time change. Plan to spend a few days here before joining the *Terra Australis* at **Punta Arenas.** Sailing on a Saturday evening into the **Strait of Magellan,** by the following morning the ship has reached the narrow Agostini Fjord, surrounded by the snowcapped Andes mountains. An interesting excursion via Zodiac motors you to Videla Glacier, where vintage Scotch whisky is served, chilled with ice from the 20,000-year-old Millenarian Glacier.

In the **Beagle Channel** the ship cruises rather close to six glaciers—Espana, Francia, and Romanche, plus Alemania, Holanda, and Italia—lined up in a row along the mountainous north coast. The weather over these ice fields can change without warning from reasonably warm and sunny to hurricane-force downdrafts and blizzard conditions that have sent many ships onto the rocks. The call at **Puerto Williams,** a small Chilean naval base and the "Southernmost City in the World," is to visit a small museum and to hike some good trails. The yacht club, housed in a retired cargo ship, hosts rugged, deep-sea sailing vessels, some having made the journey across the stormy Drake Passage from Antarctica.

At daybreak on Tuesday the *Terra Australis* arrives at **Ushuaia,** Argentina, a location also billing itself as

The extreme southern regions of Chile and Argentina rank among the world's most beautiful and isolated places, with breathtaking vistas, deep fjords, huge glaciers breaking off into the sea, and bird life and wildlife. A week's cruise on 102-passenger **Terra Australis** *provides an unusual opportunity to visit an area where tourists seldom venture.*

the "Southernmost City in the World." It's an emerging frontier town with an interesting historical museum, and there are some optional tours to a nearby national park for a barbecue and by catamaran out to small, rocky islands covered with slumbering sea lions. Later, the ship continues to **Tierra del Fuego,** landing at Harberton, a sheep farm established in 1886, for an Argentinean-style barbecue.

Wednesday marks *Terra Australis'* farthest point of the cruise, and, weather permitting, you will land by Zodiac at **Puerto Toro,** a small village on the eastern coast of Navarino Island. From there the ship heads westward through the Beagle Channel for the spectacular **Garibaldi Fjord,** overlooked by the peaks of the Cordillera de Darwin, a glacier of the same name, and several waterfalls. The adventuresome and sure-footed passengers can go ashore to climb Pirincho Island.

On Friday the final visit is to the penguin colony and lighthouse on **Magdalena Island,** just in from the Atlantic Ocean. Magdalena is home to 85,000 Magellanic penguins, whose little heads pop out of their holes as visitors stroll by. Every now and then a gang of several dozen storms across the landscape to go for a swim and get a bite to eat.

Disembarkation takes place at **Punta Arenas** on Saturday morning, and some passengers opt for a worthwhile tour to **Torres del Paine National Park.** This park is justifiably famous for its soaring granite towers, ice fields, plunging waterfalls, tranquil lakes, and quiet green valleys where herds of guanacos graze and an occasional condor soars overhead.

Cruceros Australis's
Terra Australis

Address/Phone: Cruceros Australis, Avenida El Bosque Norte 0440, Piso 11, Oficina 1103, Las Condes, Santiago, Chile; 56 2 4423110; fax: 56 2 2035173; e-mail: terra@australis.com; www.australis.com

The Ship: *Terra Australis* was built in 1984 as the U.S.-flag *Savannah* and has a gross tonnage of 1,899, a length of 220 feet, and a shallow draft.

Passengers: 114; North and South Americans and Europeans, age forty and up

Dress: Casual

Officers/Crew: Chilean, with a good standard of English

Cabins: 55; all outside, with large windows that open

Fare: $$

What's included: Cruise fare and port charges, some excursions, wine with meals; complete packages with air, land available

What's not included: Airfare, optional excursions, drinks, tips

Highlights: Spectacular scenery, remote destination, including glaciers, icebergs, mountains, sea life, few tourists

Other itineraries: The above one-week cruise, which operates between September and April, may be taken as a three- or four-day segment and combined with a most worthwhile tour to Torres del Paine National Park. For other Chilean fjord trips see www.chileancruises.com.

PACIFIC OCEAN

ROYAL CARIBBEAN'S *LEGEND OF THE SEAS*
Sailing to Down Under

With a gross tonnage of 70,000, the 1,800-passenger, sixteen-deck *Legend of the Seas* qualifies as a megaship, but she still offers plenty of peaceful nooks and crannies, removed from the bustle of the large public rooms.

A favorite indoor spot is a deep leather library chair where one can read, snooze, and watch the gentle surf pile up along the Great Barrier Reef. Around the central atrium, several small and cozy areas invite you to sit and pass the time at sea. My choice was the Card Room, decorated with sculptures and paintings of court jesters, while the library, port-side on same deck, was a close second. The Crown and Anchor Study houses sixteen computers, cleverly clustered in groups of four per table and separated by smoked glass partitions. As evening approached, we adjourned to the "highest bar afloat," the Viking Crown Lounge, to watch the sunset and try naming the passing islands in Whitsunday Passage.

Later at night, flashing lights and souped-up music transformed the serene daytime Viking Crown Lounge into a disco under the stars. We also enjoyed the piano player in the Schooner Bar and listened to dance music by a trio in the Anchors Aweigh Lounge. Audiences in the That's Entertainment Theater enthusiastically welcomed a troop of Australian entertainers, the first time RCI has included local artists. Other attractions included ballroom dancing, karaoke hour, and a popular

Call My Bluff team that had passengers guessing who was for real.

The huge window views throughout the vessel include the double-decked Romeo and Juliet dining room, where the waves are a backdrop to the theme nights dictating the menus. On American night, prime rib is an excellent choice with strawberry shortcake for dessert, and for the French celebration featured items are escargots, coq au vin and lobster tail. Local specialties include John Dory fish.

One evening, after a long day ashore, we decided to eat in the Windjammer Café, located all the way forward above the bridge on Deck 9. The evening buffet selection always includes a roasted meat and such dishes as veal medallions, baked grouper, a vegetable paella, and pasta of the day, complemented by a large selection of salads. A pizza, hotdog, and hamburger bar overlooking the Solarium pool serves from 10:00 A.M. to 7:00 P.M.

With summer weather in the Southern Hemisphere, the good-sized outdoor decks and attractive pool and whirlpools are popular venues. In addition, the Solarium, air-conditioned and covered with a retractable glass dome, provides an alternative to the heat and humidity of the Tropics. Games and activities focused around the pool proved popular, and aft on the top deck, an eighteen-hole miniature golf course

Megaships can considerably bring down the price of a cruise, especially far from North American shores, as most faraway cruises are costly. Royal Caribbean's **Legend of the Seas** *undertakes a program called Royal Journeys that spans the world, and this one embarks in Singapore for the Australian coast and Sydney.*

was a great novelty. Each hole is named after a well-known course, and a humorous explanation as to its notoriety provides entertainment for those waiting to tee off. Inside, daytime activities include the Academy at Sea's photography, theater production, and hospitality training courses. An up-to-the-minute gym and aerobics room, together with extensive spa and massage facilities, adds to the long list of amenities.

Typical of the accommodations was our roomy midships Deck 8 cabin—twin beds with pastel blue and rose coverings, a cozy seating area with a sofa and two armchairs opening onto a spacious balcony, ample closet space, a minibar, a TV, and a tub bath.

The Itinerary

This eighteen-night itinerary of the *Legend of the Seas* from Singapore to Sydney, with calls at Bali, Darwin, Cairns, and Brisbane, beckons you to settle into the comfortable deck chairs or onto your private balcony and watch the world pass by.

Singapore is a most civilized Asian city in which to unwind from the long flight and slip easily into an alien culture, with well-run hotels, lots of good eateries, and Orchard Street for shopping. For something different, take the zoo's night safari, when the nocturnal animals come out to feed and explore their rain forest environment.

Threading through the Indonesian archipelago, the *Legend of the Seas* calls at **Bali** for an excursion that leads inland to **Ubud**, where the Hindu culture produces all manner of art and crafts and even the most mundane domestic items are creatively decorated. The terraced rice paddies have a timeless air and represent a well-organized society.

Darwin, the first Australian port of call, is the country's northernmost city and the center for Aboriginal culture and art, most evident at the Museum and Art Gallery of the Northern Territory. The town center reveals many historic buildings, some reconstructed after a 1974 Christmas Day cyclone virtually flattened the place. At nearby **Kakadu National Park**, a 9,000-square-mile World Heritage Site, sacred aboriginal rock paintings in earthy reds, oranges, and black show scenes of huntsmen and animals.

Sailing south inside the **Great Barrier Reef** and parallel to the **Cape York Peninsula**, the *Legend of the Seas* next docks adjacent to the center of **Cairns**, a city of 127,000, where tropical blossoms in vibrant reds and yellows line the broad streets. During the overnight stay, one can choose from a snorkeling trip out to the **Barrier Reef**, a scenic train ride up the

spectacular Barron River Gorge, or browsing for souvenirs such as stuffed kangaroos, wide-brimmed digger hats, and boomerangs.

One of the more adventurous trips is a daylong four-wheel-drive safari to **Daintree** and **Cape Tribulation National Park**, reached by driving north along the spectacular coastline with glimpses of the Great Barrier Reef peaking above the pale green waves. On a Daintree River trip, you see crocodiles basking on the roots of the mangrove trees, while yellow orioles and egrets observe from their perches. Later, after walking through the rain forest and carefully avoiding stinging vines, you'll enjoy a delicious barbecue lunch of grilled perch, juicy steaks, and salads served amid stag horns and thousands of wild orchids.

At **Tjapukai Aboriginal Cultural Park**, men painted in ceremonial body markings perform a *corrooboree*, the traditional ancient dance. In the tribal village, the art of throwing a returning boomerang may be elusive, while the aboriginal instructors make it look so simple! They also demonstrate the use of the didgeridoo, a long cylindrical musical instrument that emits a haunting sound.

Two days later, before dawn, the passengers line the decks as the ship passes the Alexandra Headlands and enters the mouth of **Brisbane River**. Situated just 500 miles south of the Tropic of Capricorn, **Brisbane** has a subtropical climate that encourages an easygoing outdoor lifestyle. With help from the Tourist Information booth in Queen Street Mall, it's easy to plan a self-guided walking tour that includes the magnificent Victorian-style Central Railway Station and City Hall, the latter topped by a clock tower that gives the time for those in King George Square. On the way to the Botanic Gardens, one passes the colonial-style Queensland Club facing the Parliament House, a colonnaded French Renaissance–style building with an imposing mansard roof. Then to rest weary feet, board a Brisbane River ferry to glide by private homes known as Queenslanders, characterized by wide sprawling verandas and built up on stilts to catch the slightest breeze during the long, hot, and humid summers.

In a leafy suburb of Brisbane, the **Australian Woolshed** gives a glimpse into the outback experience. You can watch sheepdogs deftly rounding up their flock to have them shorn of their thick wool coats. In a wide-open field, you'll mingle with kangaroos, some with joeys in their pouches, and peer at the long-legged emus and cuddly koala bears hidden among the leaves of eucalyptus tree branches. The visit includes a "cuppa" tea served from a billy (tin can) heated over the coals and a bite of damper, or bushman's bread.

On the last morning before dawn, the *Legend* sails between the Heads, the dramatic entrance to **Sydney Harbor,** which 200 years ago Captain Arthur Phillip called the finest harbor in the world. Today it's the spectacular Opera House, designed to mirror the sails of a ship, that greets passengers. The ship slides under the Sydney Harbor Bridge to dock in Darling Harbor, and a brass band and chorus welcomed us with *Waltzing Matilda,* Australia's unofficial national anthem.

Most passengers stay on for a few days to explore sights of Sydney. From the Rocks, site of the first settlement in 1788, you can walk across the **Sydney Harbor Bridge** or even climb to the top for a breathtaking view. Sydney harbor ferries depart Circular Quay for **Taronga Park Zoo** and **Manly Beach,** and it's a quick train or bus ride to Bondi Beach, famous the world over for its spectacular surfing and the tanned surfing set. There are visits to the Opera House and a walk through the harborside Royal Botanic Gardens and inland to Hyde Park and the **Art Gallery of New South Wales** for Australian and Aboriginal art. A short monorail ride transports you from the city center to **Darling Harbor** for a day at **Sydney Aquarium** to check out the crocodiles, sharks, stingrays, and seals, then next door to the **National Maritime Museum** and the hands-on exhibits of applied arts and science in **Powerhouse Museum.**

Departing Sydney, the *Legend of the Seas* calls at **Melbourne** and **Hobart,** Tasmania, before crossing the **Tasman Sea** to circumnavigate New Zealand's **North and South Islands.** Royal Caribbean's now annual cruising program gives compelling reasons to experience the lands Down Under by sea.

Royal Caribbean's
Legend of the Seas

Address/Phone: Royal Caribbean International, 1050 Caribbean Way, Miami, FL 33132; (305) 539–6000 or (800) 327–6700; fax: (800) 722–5329; www.royalcaribbean.com

The Ship: *Legend of the Seas* was built in 1995. It has a gross tonnage of 69,130, a length of 867 feet, and a draft of 25 feet.

Passengers: 1,800, age fifty and up; many Americans but also Europeans, British, and Australians

Dress: Formal, informal with jackets, and casual

Officers/Crew: Norwegian officers; international crew

Cabins: 900 good-size cabins, with 575 outside and 231 with verandas

Fare: $$

What's included: Cruise fare

What's not included: Airfare, port charges, tip, drinks, shore excursions

Highlights: Moderately priced big-ship cruising in exotic locales

Other itineraries: Besides this sixteen-day cruise from Singapore to Sydney, which operates in both directions in December, January, and February, the *Legend of the Seas* makes cruises around New Zealand, the Indian Ocean, the Mediterranean, and Northern Europe. Royal Caribbean also cruises in the Caribbean, in the Mexican Riviera, trans–Panama Canal, and to Alaska.

CAPTAIN COOK CRUISES' *REEF ENDEAVOUR*
Australia's Great Barrier Reef

Captain Cook Cruises operates small cruise ships in several Australian locations and in the Fiji Islands. The closest North American equivalent in size and layout would be the *Nantucket Clipper* or the *Yorktown Clipper,* but the passenger list is an international one of all ages from North America, Europe, Australia, and New Zealand.

Public rooms include a forward-facing observation lounge, and, high up on the Sun Deck, a second, smaller observation lounge; aft are two spa pools, a sauna, a gym, and an outdoor bar. The main lounge, furnished with cane seating, has a bar and a grand piano; mouth-watering hors d'oeuvres are served here before dinner, and the room opens back onto the outdoor pool and lido area. In addition, there's a small library, a gift shop, and a self-service laundry.

The amidships dining room on D Deck runs the width of the ship, with buffet-style, open-seating breakfasts and lunches and with waiter-served, one-seating dinners. During my barrier-reef cruise, I enjoyed a seafood terrine, grilled barramundi (a local fish), and roast beef with Yorkshire pudding, accompanied by good Australian wines. Breakfast offers honey-dew, rock melon, passion fruit, kiwi, mango, pawpaw (papaya), papino (pear and melon), juices, cereals, eggs to order, American and English styles of bacon, as well as sausage, toast, danish, and freshly baked croissants. One hot-and-cold lunch buffet displayed more seafood than I have ever encountered—cold whole salmon, smoked salmon, red emperor, prawns, raw oysters, curried mussels, scallops, whitebait fritters, mud crabs with huge claws, and Moreton Bay bugs (a saltwater crayfish). It would be sinful not to overeat. An outdoor deck barbecue featured steak, sausage, spareribs, chicken, and prawns.

The seventy-five similar outside cabins, arranged on four decks, fall into three categories, varying more in location than size. Most have a door opening onto the side promenade. The D-Deck cabins have portholes and open onto an inside passageway. Wooden furniture consists of a desk, a low table, a chair, two night-tables, a good-size closet, and limited drawer space. All bathrooms have showers.

Stretching across the sea for more than 1,250 miles, Australia's Great Barrier Reef easily qualifies as the world's largest marine park. The best way to see its many facets—undersea life, the colorful coral, sand cays, and inhabited and uninhabited islands—is on a cruise that lasts several days. The 150-passenger **Reef Endeavour** *is the largest and most elaborate vessel in these waters, with good programs ashore and a lively, casual social life aboard.*

The Itinerary

The *Reef Endeavour* leaves from **Cairns,** northern Queensland, twice a week on three- and four-day cruises that can be combined into a full week. The reef, located at an average distance of 40 miles from the coast, is not one continuous coral wall, but comprises 1,500 major and 1,000 minor separate living reefs ranging in age from two to twenty million years old and is home for more than 1,500 species of fish.

On the four-day cruise the *Reef Endeavour* sails south to **Fitzroy Island** for a rain-forest walk, followed by a full day anchored off **Hedley Reef** for scuba diving, snorkeling with gear provided by the ship, and viewing the undersea world from a glass-bottom boat. With the ribbon reef protection from the pounding Pacific Ocean, I saw fish as colorful as their names—clownfish, yellowtail fusilier, blue angelfish, moorish idol, surgeonfish, butterfly fish, sergeant major, sweet lip, fox-faced rabbit fish, plus feather starfish, blue starfish, sea cucumber, and giant clams with openings 2 or 3 feet across—in a setting of blue-tip and golden staghorn, and brain, honeycomb, boulder, and lettuce-leaf coral.

As the ship enters the beautiful **Hinchinbrook Channel,** flanked by an island and the very mountainous Queensland coast, the marine biologist talks about the nearby saltwater mangrove swamp that provides home for mud crabs, saltwater crocodiles, hammerhead and whale sharks, dugongs (similar to a manatee or sea cow), box jellyfish, and lots of fishes. In the skies above are ibis, reef herons, shags, and spoonbills. Later in the day, anchored off **Dunk Island,** a national park, a rain-forest walk might reveal bush turkeys and birdwing, tiger, and Ulysses butterflies, and a rewarding climb affords a sweeping panorama of islands, forested coastline, and seascape stretching to the far horizon.

The three-day cruise heads north to **Cooktown,** a former gold-rush site with a colorful history and architectural relics, then out to **Two Isles,** an uninhabited, except for bird life, coral cay. **Lizard Island,** location for the poshest resort on the Barrier Reef, offers a morning hike to the highest hill and a day of snorkeling and, diving, and as a finale, the best variety of sea creatures inhabit **Ribbon Reef No. 5,** at the edge of the continental shelf.

Captain Cook Cruises' *Reef Endeavour*

Address/Phone: Captain Cook Cruises, No. 6 Jetty, Circular Quay, Sydney NSW 2000 Australia; (011) 61–2–92–06–1122; or (888) 292–2775 for information and brochures only; fax: (011) 61 2 92 51 4725; e-mail: captcookcrus@captcookcrus.com.au; www.captcookcrus.com.au

The Ship: *Reef Endeavour* was built in 1995, has a gross tonnage of 3,125, a length of 243 feet, and a shallow draft.

Passengers: 150; all ages; Australian, European, and American, with English the lingua franca

Dress: Casual at all times

Officers/Crew: Australian

Cabins: 75; all outside, most with windows and doors that open onto a promenade

Fare: $$

What's included: Cruise fare, port charges, most excursions

What's not included: Airfare, drinks, optional shore excursions such as diving

Highlights: Spending time along the Great Barrier Reef, one of the world's natural wonders; Australian hospitality

Other itineraries: The above cruise may be segmented into three or four days. Captain Cook Cruises operates other small ships from Sydney, along the Murray River in South Australia, and in the Fiji Islands (both cruise ship and sail cruise).

KANGAROO EXPLORER CRUISES'
KANGAROO EXPLORER
Catamaran Coastal Cruising in Far North Queensland

The *Kangaroo Explorer*, family-owned by Kangaroo Explorer Cruises, is a former research vessel built in 1990 and converted to a thirty-five passenger catamaran with compact but comfortable accommodations. Because the boat is small, less than 83 feet, it can buck and roll in the strong prevailing winds and heavy seas.

The Main Deck lounge doubles as the restaurant and bar, where fresh family-style meals run to rack of lamb and reef fish at dinner and salads, sandwiches, and quiche for lunch. The simply furnished cabins on three of the four decks have double beds, twins, some upper berths, windows or portholes, and private shower and toilet. The top deck has a glass-enclosed observation lounge and a partly covered afterdeck. That's about it.

The Itinerary

The *Kangaroo Explorer* makes seven-night, one-way northbound and southbound cruises running parallel to the coast between **Cairns** and the northern tip of Queensland's **Cape York Peninsula.** The rugged shoreline looms forbiddingly, as it did for English explorer Captain James Cook when his ship careened on Endeavour Reef more than 200 years ago.

The first stops are still within civilization (just barely) at historic **Cooktown,** with its century-old buildings, attractive tropical gardens, and museum dedicated to Cook. A stop is made at **Cod Hole** to swim and snorkel with the giant potato cod and moray eels and to explore the vertical coral outcroppings at Pixie Pinnacle. Then beyond **Lizard Island,** known for its upscale resort, few encounters are likely except fishing boats and a few yachts.

The *Kangaroo Explorer* uses its *Joey Explorer* to visit remote sand cays, populated by nesting sooty terns and common noddies, for swimming and a barbecue featuring prawns, steak, sausages, and reef fish. A remote stop leads to a hill hike for views of the coastline, reef, and far out into the Pacific. The Great Barrier Reef is well away from the coast, and anchoring on the protected side away from the Pacific breakers, you can fish

Here's a Great Barrier Reef cruise that goes truly off the beaten track to the remote Cape York Peninsula in Far North Queensland. Passengers are few in number aboard this tiny catamaran, but the attractions of the Barrier Reef, small islands, and sand cays for fishing, snorkeling, swimming, and birding are many.

from the boat's bow and stern. Using octopus as bait, cast for red and spangled emperor and spotted cod. Whatever is a keeper gets cleaned and boned for dinner.

On the last day the *Kangaroo Explorer* rounds the tip of Cape York Peninsula and enters the **Torres Strait,** a treacherous channel dotted with a thousand islands that divide Australia from New Guinea. Before World War II the area was a treasure-trove for Japanese pearl divers, but today's catch is crayfish. At **Thursday Island,** at one time an important military base and now inhabited by Torres Strait islanders, passengers disembark and either fly directly back to Cairns or join a week's overland camping expedition by four-wheel-drive vehicle south through remote Cape York Peninsula. Look into this possibility for a most unusual second week.

Kangaroo Explorer Cruises' *Kangaroo Explorer*

Address/phone: Kangaroo Explorer Cruises, P.O. Box 7110, Cairns, Queensland 4870 Australia; (011) 61 7 40 32 4000; fax: (011) 61 7 40 32 4050; e-mail: kevin@kangaroocruises.com.au; www.kangaroocruises.com

The Ship: *Kangaroo Explorer*, a catamaran, first built in 1990 and then converted to a passenger vessel, measures 83 feet in length and has a very shallow draft.

Passengers: 35; all ages, mostly from Australia and New Zealand

Dress: Casual at all times

Officers/Crew: Australian

Cabins: 16; all outside, with private shower and toilet

Fare: $$

What's included: All excursions, wine at meals; one-way flight Cairns/Thursday Island

What's not included: Individual drinks, modest government reef tax

Highlights: Exploring a remote part of Queensland and the Great Barrier Reef

Other itineraries: In addition to the above seven-night, year-round cruise between Cairns and Thursday Island, the cruise may be shortened to four days by joining the boat at Lizard Island, and a camping safari and lodge stays may be added.

SILVERSEA CRUISES' *SILVER CLOUD*
Australia and New Zealand

Silversea Cruises began in 1994, when the *Silver Cloud* and *Silver Wind* entered service about a year apart, and verandas in the majority of cabins were a great new feature. Now the company has introduced the larger *Silver Shadow* (2000) and *Silver Whisper* (2001), taking up to 388 passengers. The tiered Venetian Show Lounge on the *Silver Cloud* is an outstandingly beautiful room. Fanciful artistic lighting contrasts nicely with the rich blue-and-red upholstery on the banquettes and chairs. The entertainment may include a male and female vocalist, a pianist, or a comedian, but Las Vegas flesh-and-feathers-style shows are not a part of this scene. The company has also teamed up with *National Geographic* magazine to present a first-rate lecture program.

The social center is unquestionably the spacious main bar, spanning the full width of the ship with a central sit-up bar and a corner dance floor and bandstand. Other public spaces include a small casino, a shop, a combined card and conference room; open-shelf library for books and videos; a suite of rooms offering a fitness center, massage, a sauna, and a beauty salon; and a greenhouse-style forward observation lounge. Amidships on Deck 8, deck chairs surround a largish outdoor pool and two whirlpools with a sit-up

bar at the forward end. Above, a wraparound mezzanine provides additional sunning space and a jogging track.

Dining aboard the *Silver Cloud* offers variety in menu and location. The simplest offering is early morning coffee and pastries in the Deck 8 Panorama Lounge, located aft, as are all the public rooms. The lounge, which offers sweeping views in three directions, is a refined venue for afternoon tea, predinner cocktails, and a quiet place to read. The Terrace Café's breakfast and lunchtime buffets can be enjoyed inside in a semiformal setting or at four large round tables outside under a canvas awning, my favorite spot. Some evenings feature, by reservation only, a splendid Italian dinner, with additional theme evenings depending on the cruising region. The open-seating main restaurant on Deck 4 is another public room with a strong Italian flavor. Murano-glass capitals decorate the columns, convex illuminated ceiling panels offer soft lighting, and a raised, concave central dome is flanked by metal filigree. The continental and Italian menu caters well to the passenger list, which is mostly American, with some Europeans and Aussies.

The 295-square foot veranda suites number 102 of the 148 cabins. Upon entering, one is struck by the

The all-suite concept on the high seas took on considerably larger dimensions when the 296-passenger **Silver Cloud** *and sistership* **Silver Wind** *appeared, yet they have more than managed to maintain the same high standards and the all-inclusive price. This stylish pair reflects an Italian ancestry—the owners and the shipyard— and they present two of the finest cruise experiences on the high seas, so it's down under to Australia and New Zealand.*

plush decor, light woods trimming the furniture and walls, and the private veranda with its teak deck, two cushioned chairs, and a table. Only the 38 lowest-priced Vista Suites lack verandas. The bedroom is divided from the sitting area by an archway with a drop curtain, and the marble bathroom combines a tub and shower. The lounge has a desk, a minibar, a well-stocked refrigerator, a TV/VCR, a three-seat sofa, two armchairs, and a small coffee table that can be enlarged for in-cabin meals.

The Itinerary

The *Silver Cloud* or a running mate schedules a number of Southern Hemisphere summer cruises, including Australia and/or New Zealand. Sailing out past the **Sydney** Opera House and between the North and South Heads is simply breathtaking, and after a day at sea the ship puts into **Melbourne,** a city with an older, softer feel than fast-paced Sydney. Buy a day pass and ride the famous green-and-yellow trams that glide along Collins Street, the principal center-city shopping precinct, with routes fanning out to the botanical gardens, smart suburbs, and seaside **St. Kilda's.** Across the **Bass Strait** on the island of **Tasmania,** the countryside is England with a soft rural landscape, rough stone houses and churches; and near **Hobart,** you'll see **Port Arthur,** which at one time had the reputation of being Australia's toughest penal colony.

During the three days crossing the **Tasman Sea to New Zealand** social life aboard takes hold; then a completely new world opens up when the ship slides into **Doubtful, Dusky, and Milford Sounds,** gorgeous deep fjords that are part of a vast South Island national park. Sailing around to **Dunedin,** a city settled by Scottish Presbyterians, visit Larnach Castle, a Scottish-style hilltop home, and take a nature cruise below the coastal cliffs to view seals, seabirds, and a royal albatross nesting ground. Up the east coast to **Lyttleton** and nearby **Christchurch,** an English-style garden city laid out by Anglican immigrants, offers punting on the River Avon, art and natural history museums, and on weekends, a bustling arts and crafts show, ethnic-food stalls, a flea market, and buskers (street entertainers).

At the end of the cruise, the *Silver Cloud* sails on to **Auckland,** New Zealand's largest city, where most of the sights—Mount Eden, the Auckland Museum (with a terrific Maori collection including war canoes), and lively inner-city neighborhoods—lie a short distance from the ship.

Silversea Cruises' *Silver Cloud*

Address/Phone: Silversea Cruises, 110 East Broward Boulevard, Fort Lauderdale, FL 33301; (954) 522–4477 or (800) 774–9996; fax: (954) 522–4499; www.silversea.com

The Ship: *Silver Cloud,* completed in 1994, has a gross tonnage of 16,800, a length of 514 feet, and a draft of 17 feet.

Passengers: 296; mostly Americans age forty-five and up, but also some Europeans, others

Dress: Formal, informal, and casual nights

Officers/Crew: Italian officers; mostly European crew

Cabins: 148 outside suites, all but 38 with verandas

Fares: $$$$$

What's included: Air-sea program, port charges, hotel stay, transfers, all drinks and wines at lunch and dinner, gratuities, usually a special excursion

What's not included: Excursions

Highlights: Stylish atmosphere, top-of-the-line food and services; a varied itinerary

Other itineraries: In addition to this fourteen-day cruise, operating January through March, to which land packages may be added, Silverseas cruises to Europe, East and South Africa, Asia, and North and South America, New England, and Canada.

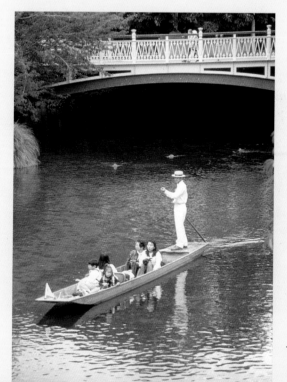

ORIENT LINES' *CROWN ODYSSEY*
Circumnavigating New Zealand's North and South Islands

Orient Lines developed a fiercely loyal following with its first ship, the *Marco Polo,* for its unusual itineraries, good food and service, and comfortable ambience at a reasonable price. Their success led to the addition of the *Crown Odyssey,* originally built in 1988 as Royal Cruise Line's globetrotting flagship. The 34,250-ton ship is ideally suited for longer sea voyages, with large cabins (many with tub baths), broad deck space, and classical touches. Passengers who sail with Orient Lines appreciate the included pre- and post-cruise hotel packages, giving them an opportunity to spend more time at their destination than on the average cruise.

Throughout the ship, there is a tremendous feeling of spaciousness and inherent, relaxed comfort. Poised high is the fabulous Top of the Crown Lounge, a 360-degree observation room with floor-to-ceiling windows. It is an uplifting experience to enter when the ship is at sea, with the sunlight filling the room and passengers enjoying the view.

Most public rooms are concentrated on one deck, starting with the forward Stardust Lounge. The entertainment is average but the enrichment program offers good speakers on a wide range of topics dealing with New Zealand and its relation to the rest of Asia and the world. Further aft is the ship's true social center, the Monte Carlo Piano Bar, adjacent to the noisy casino.

At the after end is the Yacht Club, the newly remodeled lido offering three casual meals a day. The after end is sectioned off on certain nights to become the ship's alternative restaurant, featuring popular Oriental-themed dinners. The room looks out through a wall of glass onto the stern and pool area, and the sheltered sitting section is a perfect place to start the day.

One deck above, a small bar looks through a glass wall to a protected terrace. The little nook on the port side is the Palm Court, furnished with cane furniture and lush, green plants. A very comfortable library, stocked with books and both British and American papers, shares the starboard side with a small Internet cafe. A proper 210-seat movie theater rounds out the public spaces.

The ship provides huge areas of open deck space, including a wide, wraparound promenade deck that is well used by exercising passengers. The beautifully tiered after section of decks sees use for a variety of activities, from quiet reading to shuffleboard to intense games of checkers. Finally, the ship offers a rarity these

Most of what travelers want to see in New Zealand—great alpine scenery, majestic fjords, variety of bird life, Maori culture, and charming cities with English and Scottish origins—can be conveniently included in a North and South Island cruise and a short land tour. The Crown Odyssey, a midsize, moderately priced liner, draws Americans, British, and Australians for the creative itineraries, good food, and relaxed onboard ambience.

days—an attractive indoor pool flanked by two whirlpools and coupled with the gym and spa.

Cabins are all the same standard size, except for the suites, and the price differentials only get you a larger window or a bathtub. Again, because the ship was built for long-distance cruising, the standard cabins are both spacious and cheerful. A variety of bay window suites are also very attractive, with a nice enclosed sitting area framed by a wall of glass. There are also sixteen suites with exceptionally roomy balconies.

The ship's main dining room has two wings extending forward, making a very large room seem smaller than it really is. Extensive use of mirrors and hard surfaces creates far more noise than one would like, especially in the sunken center section of the room. Nonetheless, food is generally good to very good and is served by efficient and friendly Filipino waiters. Throughout the ship, there is a cheerful spirit onboard, and the head waiter often strolls through the room playing his guitar. Every night, the Yacht Club is also open for casual dining, and on some nights an additional, more informal Italian dinner is served on the open deck.

Because of the small size of the ship and a complement of like-minded passengers who are genuinely interested in where they are going, a real camaraderie develops among the international but almost always English-speaking clientele. There are few nicer, more comfortable ways to travel the world, and the *Crown Odyssey* begins to feel more like your home after a few days.

The Itinerary

Some around New Zealand itineraries are as described below, and others may re-order port calls and cross the Tasman Sea to include Melbourne and Sydney. **Auckland** is the country's largest city and principal overseas arrivals terminal. The mainly low-rise city, made up of distinctive neighborhoods, sprawls about several extinct volcanoes, forming parks through which to climb for the views. One, the Domain, is the location for the Auckland Museum, a repository of Maori artifacts, which include a meetinghouse and war canoes. From the handsome downtown Ferry Building (1912), boats fan out across the harbor for hikes into **Rangitoto Island**'s volcanic park, to historic **Devonport,** and to **Waiheke Island** for its vineyards, beaches, and a drive through hilly sheep-farm country.

This cruise embarks in **Christchurch** (from the Port of Lyttleton), an English-style garden city laid out in the mid-nineteenth-century by middle-class Anglican immigrants. The **River Avon,** bordered by a tree-lined linear park, meanders through the city and its botanical gardens, providing a pretty setting as well as opportunities for boating and punting. A useful tourist tram loops past the cathedral, art and natural history museums, antique center, and leafy neighborhoods. On weekends the former university complex is a bustling site for an arts and crafts show, ethnic-food stalls, a flea market, and buskers (street entertainers).

Down the east coast **Dunedin,** a solid, architecturally distinctive university city settled by Scottish

Presbyterians, has a thriving commercial center, historic homes, the well-executed Settlers Museum, and Larnach Castle, a nineteenth-century Scottish-style, private hilltop home. A nature cruise passes beneath the coastal cliffs to view seals, seabirds, and a royal albatross nesting ground. Sailing around the bottom of the South Island, **Dusky, Doubtful,** and **Milford Sounds** are deep fjords carved out by glaciers, and their sheer cliffs are drenched in waterfalls. During a cruise into these sheltered waters, I have seen dolphins, seals, and penguins.

The *Crown Odyssey* sails north along the coast, paralleling the spine of the New Zealand Alps, and rounds the top of the South Island to enter Cook Strait, docking at **Picton.** The port, which provides the ferry link to Wellington, is the gateway for a drive out to **Marlborough,** New Zealand's most important wine region. **Wellington**'s harbor, across the strait, provides a grand entrance, and the capital city, rimming the basin, is set against a backdrop of wooded hills. The botanical garden, with access by tramway, and attractive nineteenth-century neighborhoods are within easy walking distance of the center. Fronting directly on the harbor, **Te Papa,** the new national museum, has put Wellington on the must-see list for its creative interpretation of European, Maori, and Chinese history and culture.

Up the North Island's east coast, **Napier,** a city largely rebuilt after a 1931 earthquake, presents one of the world's finest examples of urban art deco architecture. After an overnight sail to **Tauranga,** it's an hour to **Rotorua,** a turn-of-the-century spa with boiling hot springs, sheep demonstrations at the Agrodome, a rain-forest habitat for the kea and the flightless kiwi, and the center for **Maori** art, crafts, architecture, dance, and music.

In a serenely beautiful setting north of Auckland, the **Bay of Islands** holds the world's records for kingfish, marlin, shark, and tuna and is one of the few places to find the great Kauri trees used by the Maoris to build their long war canoes. On the last morning the *Crown Odyssey* sails into **Auckland**'s fine harbor to dock adjacent to the city center and next door to the fine Ferry Building.

Orient Lines' *Crown Odyssey*

Address/Phone: 1510 S.E. 17th Street, Suite 400, Fort Lauderdale, FL 33316; (954) 527–6660 or (800) 333–7300; fax: (954) 527–6657; e-mail: info@orientlines.com; www.orientlines.com

The Ship: *Crown Odyssey* was built in 1988 for Royal Cruise Line. It has a gross tonnage of 34,250, a length of 614 feet, and a draft of 24 feet.

Passengers: 1,052, with up to half of the passengers from abroad, although almost all will be English-speaking

Dress: On this longer itinerary, the ship is decidedly more formal than in the Mediterranean.

Officers/Crew: International officers; Filipino crew

Cabins: 526, of which 412 are outside and 16 have verandas

Fare: $$$

What's included: Airfare, pre- and post-cruise hotel package with tours, transfers

What's not included: Port charges, drinks, tips, shore excursions

Highlights: New Zealand's beauty at an affordable package price; very happy ship with similarly interested passengers

Other itineraries: In addition to this fourteen-day New Zealand cruise tour that operates in March, the *Crown Odyssey* also sails in the Indian Ocean, Southeast Asia and Australia, and the Mediterranean in summer.

AMERICAN HAWAII CRUISES'
SS *INDEPENDENCE*
Classic U.S. Flag Cruising in Hawaii

American Hawaii Cruises is part of American Classic Voyages, which also operates the Delta Queen Steamboat Company. The 30,090-ton SS *Independence* is one of the very few twin-funneled vessels still in service. Her sister, the *Constitution,* featured in the movie *An Affair to Remember* and Grace Kelly's ship when traveling to Monaco to marry Prince Rainier, sank under tow to the scrap yard in late 1997.

A Hawaiian theme permeates the ship's decor, from the collection of framed pictures (portraits, birds, flowers, and landscapes) lining the corridor walls to the fine artifacts in the Kama'aina Lounge. These include musical instruments, tiki sculptures, an outrigger canoe, story murals, and cane furnishings. My favorite spot is a seat along one of the two glass-enclosed promenades, or lanais, which, furnished with cushioned bentwood easy chairs set in front of the French doors and under slow-moving ceiling fans, is pure W. Somerset Maugham.

Five-tiered decks step down to the stern, providing vast open spaces for relaxing, strolling, and taking in the ship's considerable maritime character. Cabins come in every imaginable configuration, so different from the modular design found on newer ships. The former tourist-class space on what was once a three-class ship offers economical upper and lower berths (tight quarters at 95 square feet), while the ship's original solarium on the Bridge Deck has been converted into six big-window suites with skylights. Single travelers have the choice of twenty-five inside and outside cabins bearing no single supplement.

On one cruise, my B-grade stateroom featured a lounge area with three portholes, settee, cane chair, three-drawer dresser, and two single beds, separated by a night table, nestled snugly in an alcove. The small, white-tiled bathroom had a circular shower, and in spite of the cabin's well-aft position, the steam turbines operated as smoothly as the day they were built.

Based in Maui, American Hawaii's SS **Independence** *makes year-round weekly circuits of the Hawaiian Islands. Completed in 1951 at the peak of U.S. ship design, she's the only deep-sea U.S.-built, U.S.-flag passenger ship still operating, a must for anyone interested in sailing a classic liner. While a bit of a dowager, she does offer one of the best shore-excursion programs afloat. United States Lines'* **Patriot** *joined the Hawaiian cruise trade in late 2000, and takes over the* **Independence's** *weekly Saturday departures from Honolulu.*

Two dining rooms provide two seatings at tables for two to eight people. Best entree courses were Hawaiian seared sea scallops with a gingered black bean sauce, mahi mahi with fresh mango salsa, and oven-baked albacore tuna with macadamia-nut butter sauce. For dessert try the coconut milk custard, white chocolate mousse cake, and blueberry cheesecake with raspberry puree. Service from the all-American crew is generally friendly and professional. As an alternative to the dining rooms, the buffet offers pancakes and waffles with coconut syrup and omelets and eggs to order at breakfast, hamburgers and hot dogs at lunch, and abundant fresh pineapple, papaya, mango, cantaloupe, and honeydew melon. Operating in domestic service, the wine and drinks, while not duty-free, are reasonably priced, and state rules prohibit a casino.

Entertainment reflects Hawaiian music and dance, with local troupes made up of small children, teenagers, and adults coming aboard in ports accompanied by a ukulele and slack-key guitar. A popular soloist sings Broadway show tunes, and a resident

group offers typical cruise ship–style singing and dancing. The *kumu*, a traditional Hawaiian storyteller and teacher, lectures about Hawaiian culture and history in the Kama'aina Lounge, furnished in Hawaiian plantation-house style. A packed Sunday worship service interweaves American and Hawaiian traditions and language in prayers and hymns, including a rousing bilingual rendition of "Amazing Grace."

The Itinerary

The ship embarks on a Saturday at the port of **Kahalui** on **Maui,** and at the gangway passengers are welcomed with a traditional floral lei. During its weeklong inter-island circuit, the *Independence,* depending on the season, will spend most of Sunday at sea en route to the Big Island or depart in the late afternoon, allowing you time to drive the coastal Hana Highway or climb to the 10,000-foot rim of **Haleakala.**

On **Hawaii** a trip from **Hilo** up to the thin-air level on **Mauna Kea** includes a visit to one of the astronomical observatories and a chance to take a short but always bracing walk to a sacred Hawaiian site perched at the 13,796-foot summit. During the coastal run to **Kona,** the island's resort side**,** the ship passes close to a fiery tongue of lava that lights up the night as it flows toward the sea. Anchoring off the Kona coast, there's a choice of three different snorkeling trips, scuba diving, deep-sea fishing, parasailing, or lolling on the beach. For something completely different, the Kona Coffee tour starts with a visit to a traditional coffee and macadamia nut farm led by two Japanese immigrants who lived and worked here and finishes up with a tour of a small-scale coffee-bean roasting plant.

The *Independence* docks for two days at **Honolulu**'s Aloha Tower Pier, where colorful murals recall Boat Days, when the big white Matson liners arrived and sailed on four-day voyages to and from California and across the wide Pacific to New Zealand and Australia. From the tower's observation platform, the entire harbor opens up and with a wide-angle lens, there's a super photo opportunity to capture the *Independence.* Within walking distance, the maritime museum recalls the islands' Polynesian discovery and sea heritage and the **Iolani Palace** give tours of the final home to the Hawaiian royal family. Take a tourist trolley, local bus, or taxi into **Waikiki**'s shopping and hotel strip or out to **Pearl Harbor** to see the **USS *Arizona* Memorial** and the place of Japanese surrender on the deck of the battleship *Missouri.*

The captain earns his keep bringing the *Independence* into the narrow twisting channel and tight turn-

American Hawaii Cruises' SS *Independence*

Address/Phone: American Hawaii Cruises, 5835 Blue Lagoon Drive, Miami, FL; (800) 588–3609; fax: (504) 585–0690; www.cruisehawaii.com

The Ship: *Independence,* completed in 1951, has a gross tonnage of 30,090, a length of 682 feet, and a draft of 26.5 feet.

Passengers: 867; ages range from couples in their twenties to the retired, skewed to the higher end; lots of children during school holidays; on average, 65 percent of the passengers are making their first visit to Hawaii.

Dress: Jacket with tie optional one night, otherwise casual

Officers/Crew: American

Cabins: 414 in many configurations, half outside, no verandas; 25 are single cabins

Fare: $$$

What's included: Cruise only, including port charges

What's not included: Airfare, Hawaii state tax, tips, drinks, and shore excursions

Highlights: The shore excursion program; sailing a classic American liner

Other itineraries: In addition to the above year-round seven-night cruises, three- and four-night segments are also available, and the line can arrange pre- and postcruise hotel stays. A second U.S. flagship, the *Patriot* of the United States Lines, in December 2000 began sailing weekly from Honolulu.

ing basin at **Nawiliwili,** the main port for **Kauai.** A good free beach is a ten-minute walk. Organized tours by bus and four-wheel-drive vehicle visit the rainbow gorge of **Waimea Canyon,** and helicopter flights skim the dramatic **Na Pali** coastal cliffs. By renting a car, easily arranged on board, it's just over an hour's drive to **Kea Beach** and the start of the coastal footpath, a most satisfying cliff hike of moderate difficulty that can be as short as an hour or take up the entire day. Between late December and April, humpback whales can be seen cavorting near the breakers or spouting further out at sea. After a last night at sea, the ship returns to **Maui.**

Half-day tours start at about $30, and full-day tours begin at $75, with the most expensive being helicopter flights and the Cessna transfer to **Molokai** for a guided tour to **Kalaupapa Settlement** by one of the patients of the leper colony. For independent touring, several merchants provide free shuttles to shopping centers, and car rental agency vans serve the piers. Swimming is free, and with so much to do and eighty tours from which to choose, one could easily come back in a year or two and enjoy a completely different set of outings.

HOLLAND AMERICA LINE'S *STATENDAM*
Southern California to Hawaii

Holland America Line dates back to 1873, operating transatlantic passenger service for the first one hundred years, and now has one of the largest and most attractive fleets in the industry. Purchased by Carnival Corporation in 1988, an infusion of money resulted in a spate of new ship orders, the first being the 55,451-ton *Statendam* in 1992.

This ten-deck ship accommodates 1,266 passengers, and the public rooms are located on Sports, Lido, Upper Promenade, and Promenade decks. These include the Crows Nest forward on the Sports Deck, a delightful observation lounge during the day and an intimate nightclub in the evening. The Lido Deck offers health and fitness facilities, a large pool area (covered during cool weather by a retractable roof) amidships, and the spacious Lido Restaurant aft. Upper Promenade is anchored forward by the Van Gogh show lounge's balcony seating and the *Rotterdam* dining room's upper level aft. In between are shops, the Casino, the Ocean Bar for a drink and dancing, a card room, a library, and the Explorer's Lounge, also with a dance floor. On the Promenade Deck the orchestra level of the show room and the dining room's main level bracket the front desk, Java Café, and the Wajang Theater, which serves freshly popped popcorn at show time.

Carnival's influence is most apparent in the high quality of the shows performed nightly while at sea. These "Las Vegas-style" productions are full of energy, bright lights, and good staging. The show room is also the venue for popular local Hawaiian entertainment that boards in at least two ports. In the two-level dining room, the traditions of Holland America shine. The dignified Indonesian waiter service is the perfect complement to the culinary delights presented at each meal, and a Filipino band serenades at dinner.

The 633 cabins and suites, spread along five decks, range from 187-square-foot inside cabins to four-room penthouse suites measuring 1,126 square feet. Most cabins are outside, and two decks feature private verandas. Avoid cabins located above the theater if you retire early.

The Itinerary

By law only U.S.-registered ships may carry passengers between Hawaiian ports; hence, the Dutch-registered *Statendam* embarks at **San Diego** for the four-day ocean voyage to then call at five Hawaiian ports before sailing back to San Diego, a nifty combination cruise and double crossing. The days at sea are filled with traditional shipboard activities and by Holland America's lecture series, which includes such topics as finance, world

Circle Hawaii visiting five different ports, sailing onboard the **Statendam** *round-trip from San Diego, California, a fifteen-day cruise with four full days at sea each way. This high seas and island cruise recalls the halcyon days of Matson Line's traditional Pacific voyages in the 1930s and 1950s.*

politics, self-improvement, Polynesian life, Hawaiian royalty, and Hawaiian culture. One elegant evening hosts the superbly orchestrated "Black and White Ball," when all the ship's officers appear in formal white waistcoats. The crossing is a prelude to the beauty and spectacular experience of Hawaii, where, at each port, there is a wide range of shore excursions, some including lunch and a luau with traditional Hawaiian dancing.

From **Hilo** on the "Big Island" of **Hawaii,** take in the Queen Lili'uokalani Gardens or drive through the tropical forest to gaze into the Kilauea crater from Volcano House, perched right on the rim of the world's largest volcano. For a nonorganized tour rent a car or take one of the free shuttle buses to a shopping mall and the beach. Especially dramatic is the after-dark view, from the deck, of hot lava flowing down the slopes into the sea.

Sailing past Diamond Head to dock at the Aloha Tower in **Honolulu,** tour Iolani Palace, the only royal palace in the United States; drive out to Diamond Head, and shop on Kalakaua Avenue. At Pearl Harbor see the film that recalls the Japanese attack on December 7, 1941, then board a boat out to the USS *Arizona* Memorial and visit the recently opened USS *Missouri*, the battleship on which the Japanese surrendered.

At **Nawiliwili** on the garden island of **Kaui**, take a jeep safari to the rim of Waimea Canyon, the Grand Canyon of the Pacific, and a helicopter flight over the breathtaking Na Pali Coast; then enjoy a water-level view as the *Statendam* sails past. On **Maui** in April there is a good chance to see humpback whales up close, or ascend nearly 10,000 feet to visit Haleakala, Maui's largest volcano. At **Kona** on the far side of the "Big Island" of **Hawaii**, visit the 250,000-acre Parker Ranch, the largest single-owner cattle ranch in the United States; see Kealakekua Bay—even snorkel here—where Captain James Cook lost his life in 1779; and explore Pu'uhonua o Honaunau, a sacred Hawaiian "City of Refuge," with its sanctuary for defeated warriors, wooden carvings and ancient temples. Following the intensive sightseeing, relax and enjoy the ship's social life on the way back to the mainland.

Holland America Line's
Statendam

Address/Phone: Holland America Line, 300 Elliott Avenue West, Seattle, WA 98119; (800) 426–0327; fax: (800) 628–4855; www.hollandamerica.com

The Ship: *Statendam* was built in 1992, has a gross tonnage of 55,451, a length of 719 feet, and a draft of 25 feet.

Passengers: 1,266; mostly Americans, fifty-five and up

Dress: Formal, informal, and casual nights

Officers/Crew: Dutch officers; Indonesian and Filipino crew

Cabins: 633; 502 outside and 150 with verandas.

Fare: $$$

What's included: Cruise only

What's not included: Airfare, port charges, shore excursions, drinks, tips

Highlights: Attractive ship on which to spend many sea days; lots to do ashore in Hawaii

Other itineraries: In addition to these fifteen-day Hawaii cruises from San Diego, which operate January to April and October to December, the *Statendam* cruises to Alaska. Other Holland American ships cruise the Caribbean, the Panama Canal, and South America, and the *Amsterdam* and *Rotterdam* cruises around the world. Holland America's large fleet covers the globe.

RENAISSANCE CRUISES' *R3* AND *R4*

Linger Longer in French Polynesia

Renaissance Cruises has taken delivery of eight identical ships carrying up to 684 passengers. *R1* entered service in mid-1998, *R2* joined later in the year, *R4* joined in 1999, and *R8* joined in 2001. The sophisticated English hotel-style atmosphere may seem a bit odd in the South Pacific. The lounges and bars are wood-paneled with oriental-style carpets, and marble mantel fireplaces. The lovely library has a greenhouse-like atmosphere, with a painted dome ceiling of birds in flight. The observation lounge-cum-sports bar provides an air-conditioned setting to absorb the stupendous scenery after a hot day ashore.

Four restaurants offer open seating at dinner and the food is excellent, especially for the moderate price. Although the atmosphere is formal, the dress code in the 348-seat Club Restaurant is casual. Or choose from selections at the wood-paneled Grill, the Italian restaurant, or the Panorama Buffet, designed for a quick dinner.

Cabin categories A through D, nearly 70 percent of the accommodations, have private verandas; categories E, F, and G have ocean views; and just 25 cabins in category H are inside without windows or portholes. The bathrooms with showers are small.

The Itinerary

For the cruise highlights refer to the week aboard the *Paul Gauguin* (next section), but add more time in some ports and **Huahine,** the former island home of Polynesian royalty in a setting of steep mountain peaks and deep blue lagoons.

In the second half of 1999, Renaissance Cruises placed its R3 and R4 in gorgeous French Polynesia, offering year-round, moderately priced, seven- and ten-day destination-oriented itineraries from Tahiti to Moorea, Huahine, Raiatea, and Bora Bora. On ten-day cruises approximately two days are spent at anchor in each port.

Renaissance Cruises' *R3* and *R4*

Address/Phone: Renaissance Cruises, 1800 Eller Drive, Suite 300, Fort Lauderdale, FL 33335; (954) 463–0982 or (800) 525–5350; fax: (954) 463–0985; www.renaissancecruises.com

The Ship: *R3* was completed in 1999, has a gross tonnage of 30,200, a length of 593 feet, and a draft of 19.5 feet.

Passengers: 684; mostly Americans, age fifty and up

Dress: Casual

Officers/Crew: European officers; European and international crew

Cabins: 342; mostly outside, 232 with private verandas

Fare: $$

What's included: Cruise, airfare from Los Angeles, and transfers

What's not included: Port charges, shore excursions, drinks, tips

Other itineraries: In addition to the above seven- and ten-day *R3* and *R4* cruise, which is offered year-round, the R Class cruises between Lisbon and Barcelona, and operates in the Eastern Mediterranean between Athens and Istanbul. Additional R Class ships operate in Northern Europe, Asia, and South America.

RADISSON SEVEN SEAS CRUISES'
PAUL GAUGUIN
Cruising in Paradise

The 320-passenger *Paul Gauguin* flies the French flag and is sold through Radisson Seven Seas Cruises. Overall, the ship is more French modern than South Pacific in decor, but the corridors are a gallery of intriguing photographs of turn-of-the-century Tahiti, and a small Fare Tahiti museum displays a few Paul Gauguin drawings and carved ceremonial canoe paddles, wooden flyswatters and a trio of ironwood shark hooks. The pool is a generous size for a small ship, and deck chairs abound, but with little protection from the intense sun. For the active types the ship's marina opens up for water-skiing, windsurfing, kayaking, scuba diving, and snorkeling, but the latter two sports must be done away from the ship.

Most public rooms, including the two restaurants, are stacked aft and have wraparound windows. On the two highest decks, two pretty observation lounges offer venues for a quiet read during the day, a formal afternoon tea with piano music, drinks before meals, private parties, a cabaret, and a late-night disco.

L' Étoile, the principal restaurant, has a high ceiling and spacious open seating for the continental dinner menu. Above, the cheery 130-seat La Veranda offers a menu and a buffet for breakfast and lunch, while dinner, by reservation, alternates between two French menus. On one night the cold starter was a dollop of Sevruga caviar set atop a charlotte of potatoes, followed by lobster ravioli in dim sum, grilled sea bass and grilled tenderloin of beef, with crème brûlée and a Tahitian vanilla sauce for dessert. Complimentary wine accompanies both lunch and dinner. Le Grill, located outside and under cover near the midships pool, serves all three meals.

The tiered show lounge offers a wonderfully inventive multi-instrumental singing Filipino quintet and three great shows of dancing and singing islanders, from a two-year-old making her debut to teenagers and grandmothers.

Every cabin is outside, with generous-size bathrooms and tubs, and 50 percent have private verandas for enjoying breakfast and the cool early-evening breezes before dinner.

The TV comes with a VCR, and the minibar is stocked with beer, soda, tonic, and water (except for the beer, these are replenished daily without charge), as well as complimentary bottles of gin, vodka and scotch.

Post-Impressionist French artist Eugène-Henri-Paul Gauguin should have been so lucky to have sailed in the ship named after him when making the long voyage between Metropolitan France and French Polynesia. This ship takes you in style from one beautiful anchorage to another during a week's cruise from Tahiti.

The Itinerary

For ten months of the year, the 513-foot ship sails Saturdays from **Papeete,** Tahiti, on a seven-day sub-equatorial loop that takes in the four **Society Islands** of Raiatea, Taha'a, Bora Bora, and Moorea, with much of the week spent lazily at anchor in one gorgeous aqua-blue-water bay after another and just two nights underway. Most passengers, completely seduced by the islands' incredible beauty, seem to like it that way, and while riding at anchor, the ship gently swings about 120 degrees, revealing continually changing views of jagged mountain peaks, palm-fringed reefs, and the pounding surf just beyond.

The shore program offers a lot of variety, and because French Polynesia is an expensive region, the organized excursions are on the pricey side. At **Raiatea** a motorized outrigger canoe speeds along the coast to the Society Island chain's only river, from where it is said that the Polynesians set out to populate Hawaii, Easter Island and New Zealand. Nearby, the seventeenth-century temple **Marae Taputapuatea** served as the center of religion and sacrifice until the Christian missionaries arrived and largely destroyed it. The ruins are being gradually pieced back to better demonstrate the island's heritage.

The adjacent island of **Taha'a** offers a jeep safari deep into the hills over a rutted road fringed by pink and red ginger, white gardenia, red hibiscus, and tiare, the fragrant flower the Polynesians wear over their ear. There's a stop to watch coconuts sliced open for sampling the sweet water, milk, dried coconut, and the mushy young meat. Another taste, a bit bland, is breadfruit, the crop that Captain Bligh and the *Bounty* had come to collect for replanting as a food crop for the West Indian slaves. Taha'a, a typical volcanic island,

Radisson Seven Seas Cruises' *Paul Gauguin*

Address/Phone: Radisson Seven Seas Cruises, 600 Corporate Drive, Suite 410, Fort Lauderdale, FL 33334; (954) 776–6123 or (800) 333–3333; fax: (954) 722–6763; www.rssc.com

The Ship: *Paul Gauguin* was completed in late 1997, has a gross tonnage of 18,800, a length of 513 feet, and a draft of 17 feet.

Passengers: 320; age forty and up, mostly Americans

Dress: Casual at all times

Officers/Crew: French officers; European and Filipino crew

Cabins: 160; all outside, 80 with verandas

Fare: $$$

What's included: Cruise, wine at meals, stocked minibar, tips

What's not included: Airfare, port charges, shore excursions, drinks at the bars

Highlights: Cruising among some of the most beautiful islands in the world; sophisticated yet relaxed on-board ambience

Other itineraries: In addition to the above seven-night cruise aboard the *Paul Gauguin,* which operates ten months of the year, the ship makes an occasional fourteen-night cruise to the Marquesas Islands in December. Radisson Seven Sea's 180-passenger *Song of Flower* cruises in Asia and Europe and the 350-passenger catamaran *Radisson Diamond* cruises in Europe. The line also markets the 184-passenger *Hanseatic,* the new 490-passenger *Seven Seas Navigator,* and the 720-passenger *Seven Seas Mariner.*

is surrounded by a protective reef, and palm-bedecked sandy islands called *motus* offer swimming, snorkeling, and a barbecue lunch ashore.

Anchoring off **Bora Bora,** with its fantastic pointy mountain spires, outrigger canoes head out to the fringing reef, where the guides feed the black-tipped reef sharks and stingrays ranging close by (in shallow waters stingrays, if fed, do not mind being stroked). A jeep ride leads to terrific island views and locations where World War II American cannon point to sea. Author James Michener was stationed here in 1942, and his *Tales of the South Pacific* refer to Bora Bora as "the most beautiful island in the world."

Moorea may be the favorite island of most visitors, but it's a close call. Snorkeling brings the sight of picasso triggerfish and butterfly, angel, surgeon, and parrot fish. On land, plantation agriculture shows fields of pineapples, mangos, papaya, guava, bananas, taro, vanilla, melons, and avocados. Days can be hot and humid, but the water is always nearby, and on clear nights the sky reveals the Southern Cross, False Cross, Orion's Belt, and Castor and Pollux.

At the end of the cruise, visit Tahiti's fine museum, with its displays of sailing craft, tiki sculpture, and maps of Polynesian immigration and European exploration. Another museum is dedicated to Paul Gauguin's life rather than his artistic works. Even after a short visit, it is easy to see how one might be taken over by the islands' incredible lure and the genuine friendliness of the local Polynesians.

EUROPE

CRYSTAL CRUISES' *CRYSTAL SYMPHONY*
Northern European Capital Cities

Crystal Cruises, owned by Japan's NYK Line, offers European service to a largely American clientele. The newer *Crystal Symphony,* built in Finland rather than Japan as with the *Harmony,* is designed for worldwide cruising and spending delightful days at sea.

The primarily European hotel and restaurant staff provides impeccable service throughout the ship in the restaurants, lounges, and on deck. The most popular lounge is the Palm Court, on this ship, one large wrap-around room that serves as the venue for sightseeing in cool northern climes, reading, enjoying formal afternoon tea, and drinks before and after dinner during the long summer evenings. On this same Lido Deck, there's an outdoor lap pool, a second indoor-outdoor pool and adjoining Jacuzzis, lots of deck chairs in a wide variety of groupings, a snack and ice-cream bar, and an indoor-outdoor buffet. The deck above has one of the largest ocean-view spas at sea, with an elaborate fitness center, saunas, steam rooms, aerobics, and body treatments, plus a paddle-tennis court, a golf driving range, and a putting green. The jogging/walking deck at the promenade level runs the full length of the superstructure.

Dining is a delight, and the two special dinner options by reservation are Prego, a smartly decorated Italian restaurant, and the Jade Garden, Chinese on this ship rather than Japanese as aboard the *Harmony.* The main dining room has two seatings, unusual for a ship of this caliber, but the food is excellent, and the wine list, emphasizing California, is fairly priced.

All cabins are outside, and well over half have private verandas. Amenities include a sitting area, queen or twin beds, a desk, a TV and VCR, a refrigerator, a safe, and bathrooms with stall showers and tubs. Room service from an extensive menu is available twenty-four hours.

The Itinerary

In summer the *Crystal Symphony*'s Baltic Sea cruises call at Scandinavian capitals and St. Petersburg, embarking at Dover, England, and Stockholm, Sweden.

Departing **Stockholm,** one of Europe's best preserved low-rise capitals, the ship gingerly threads through a vast wooded archipelago into the Baltic with a sea day en route to **St. Petersburg** for a two-day stay. Highlights are the artworks in the Hermitage Mu-

Upscale, classy, and much larger than all other high-end cruise ships, the **Crystal Symphony** *and sister* **Crystal Harmony** *provide lots of space, amenities, and activities for any itinerary. During a relatively short summer season, the* **Crystal Symphony** *visits Scandinavian capitals and Baltic Sea ports, featuring a two-day stay at St. Petersburg.*

seum, the Winter Palace, St. Isaac's Cathedral, Peter and Paul Fortress, and an evening at the ballet.

Docking next to the center of **Helsinki,** you can visit the Finnish capital on foot, beginning with the Kauppatoru (Market Square) for its fruits, vegetables, flowers, and handicrafts; and just around the harbor, the old market hall sells meat and fish. One of Finland's great architects, Eliel Saarinen, built the massive stone railway terminal, adorned with great red-granite figures, where trains depart for the lake district, Moscow, and St. Petersburg.

Sailing west through the Baltic, Warnemunde is the port for the long day trip to Europe's largest construction site, **Berlin,** the new German capital. Walk the Unter den Linden, the city's grand boulevard, to the Brandenburg Gate, where, just beyond, the Reichstag, after a long hiatus, is once again the seat of government. Several of the world's most powerful corporations have taken over Potsdamer Platz, reviving one of the city's great crossroads.

Good walkers can enjoy the promenade from **Copenhagen**'s cruise terminal into the city center for the classy Stroget (pedestrian streets), Amalienborg Palace, the royal residence for 200 years, the tightly packed line of outdoor cafes and restaurants along the Nyhavn, and Tivoli, the 150-year-old amusement park, restaurant, and entertainment center in a garden setting that inspired Walt Disney to create his stateside equivalents.

About two hours after leaving Copenhagen, sail past Hamlet's Castle at **Helsingor.** Then you continue overnight and a 60-mile cruise up the Oslofjord to **Oslo,** Norway's capital, where again you dock conveniently within walking distance of the center. Take the ferry for an outing among Norway's maritime heritage centers to see the expedition raft *Kon Tiki*, the polar exploration ship *Fram*, traditional viking ships, and cruise-liner models. Following a leisurely two-night sail, the cruise ends at **Dover,** nestled beneath the famous white cliffs, just ninety minutes from London.

Crystal Cruises' *Crystal Symphony*

Address/Phone: Crystal Cruises, 2049 Century Park East, Suite 1400, Los Angeles, CA 90067; (310) 785–9300 or (800) 820–6663 for brochures; fax: (310) 785–3891; www.crystalcruises.com

The Ship: *Crystal Symphony* was built in 1995, has a gross tonnage of 51,044, a length of 781 feet, and a draft of 25 feet.

Passengers: 940; mostly North Americans age fifty-five plus

Dress: Fit to kill; formal nights, jackets and ties on informal nights

Officers/Crew: Norwegian and Japanese officers; European and Filipino crew

Cabins: 470; all outside and more than half with private verandas

Fare: $$$$

What's included: Cruise fare only

What's not included: Airfare, port charges, drinks, shore excursions, tips

Highlights: Alternative Chinese and Italian restaurants, excellent waiter/bar service, lots of onboard amenities

Other itineraries: In addition to these twelve- and thirteen-day Scandinavian/ Baltic cruises, which operate in June and July, the *Crystal Symphony* and *Crystal Harmony* undertake Panama Canal trips, and between them they cruise most of the world.

HEBRIDEAN ISLAND CRUISES'
HEBRIDEAN PRINCESS
Scotland's Western Isles

Hebridean Island Cruises, a well-kept secret in North America, got its start in 1989, when a 600-passenger Scottish ferry was transformed into a posh, floating country house for a maximum of fifty mostly British guests. She came under new ownership in 1997, and the public rooms have been completely redecorated, making her even more attractive.

The cozy public rooms evoke the feel of an old-fashioned country inn, nowhere more so than in the forward observation lounge, with its comfy upholstered armchairs and settees and rustic brick-and-timber fireplace. A small bar is off to one side. The library has leather and tartan-upholstered seating. Two other lounges feature afternoon tea and cigar smoking amid wicker furniture. Some evenings are formal, and, in warm weather, passengers gather aft on deck for champagne receptions with hot hors d'oeuvres. Top-deck spaces also include comfy, wind-protected chairs for reading.

The restaurant operates like a hotel dining room. Passengers sit with friends or at tables for two, but singles are seated with fellow singles and usually an officer. Presentation and service are top-notch. The menu is typically British, featuring a Sunday roast with Yorkshire pudding at lunch, sliced duckling at dinner, black pudding and kippers at breakfast, and fresh strawber-

ries on meringue for dessert. Other dinner choices include Scottish highland game and mushroom pie, sautéed and smoked salmon, and raw oysters. Unfamiliar Scottish delicacies that may startle the palate are haggis, a mixture of calf or lamb hearts, lungs, and liver with onion, suet, and seasonings, and kedgeree, a rice and smoked-fish combination.

The twenty-nine individually designed and furnished cabins, carrying the names of Scottish isles, lochs, sounds, and castles, vary widely, but all show fabric frills above headboards and around windows that open. TVs, refrigerated bars, coffee and tea makers, irons and ironing boards, trouser presses, hair dryers, dressing tables, and ample stowage are standard throughout. Two cabins on the lowest deck share baths, and there are eleven dedicated inside and outside singles. The ship is not air-conditioned, but this is seldom a problem in these northerly waters. Although the fares are as high as they get, the *Hebridean Princess* is a one-of-a-kind treasure appealing to the well-heeled, many of whom come back year after year.

The Itinerary
A guide accompanies all cruises, and excursions include visits to stately homes, country gardens, fishing villages, and remote, rugged islands. Passengers

There is nothing on the high seas quite like the **Hebridean Princess,** *a genteel country-house hotel for just fifty passengers that combines a sophisticated social life aboard with daily visits to the islands off northwest Scotland. As this ship could not be more British, Anglophilia is essential.*

should come prepared for Scottish mists and uncertain weather, and the ship anchors or ties up at night except on an occasional overnight sail to the outer islands and across the North Sea to Norway's fjords. The *Hebridean Princess* most often boards in **Oban,** a popular Scottish seaside resort about two hours by train northwest of Glasgow. Port descriptions here are meant to be typical examples, as itineraries vary from cruise to cruise.

A two-hour sail takes you to **Tobermory Bay** on the **Isle of Mull** for a guided tour of the neat, white-washed town, founded by the British Fisheries Society. Underway, the ship cruises into **Loch Stuart,** over-looked by the rugged and scenic beauty of **Ardna-murchan Peninsula,** where its point is the most westerly mainland in the British Isles, beating out much-better-known Land's End by 20 miles.

The **Sound of Sleat,** separating the mainland from the **Isle of Skye,** leads to the pastel-fronted island capital of **Portree** for a bit of a wander. In **Upper Loch Torridin** the surrounding peaks create a dramatic setting for an overnight anchorage. The village of **Plonkton** offers the unusual sight, in these northerly parts, of an arc of palm trees, and later in the day from the dock at the **Kyle of Lochalsh,** a drive explores **Cuillin Hills** across the sea on Skye.

Cruising past Rhum and Eigg, the ship anchors off **Muck** for a beach landing and a walk across the island to have a proper afternoon tea with local residents. A cruise up **Loch Linnhe** may offer a glimpse of Scotland's highest peak, **Ben Nevis,** snowcapped for much of the year. Northwest Scotland's remarkable climate has encouraged the creation of some beautiful gardens, including those at **Torosay Castle,** which exhibit, depending on the time of one's visit, glorious spring flowers or colorful autumnal leaves. The *Hebridean Princess* spends one more night at anchor, then slips into Oban in the morning.

Hebridean Island Cruises' *Hebridean Princess*

Address/Phone: Hebridean Island Cruises, Griffin House, Broughton Hall, Skipton, North Yorkshire, BD23 3AN England; 011 44 1756 704704 or (800) 659–2648 (9:00 A.M.–5:15 P.M. U.K. time); fax: (011) 44 1756 701455; e-mail: reservations@hebridean. co.uk; www.hebridean.co.uk

The Ship: *Hebridean Princess* was rebuilt in 1989 from the Scottish ferry *Columba* and has a gross tonnage of 2,115, a length of 235 feet and a shallow draft of 10 feet.

Passengers: 50; age fifty and up, largely British with perhaps a handful of Americans

Dress: Formal some nights, jacket and tie on others

Officers/Crew: British

Cabins: 29; wide range of shapes and sizes but all prettily furnished

Fare: $$$$$

What's included: Cruise and port charges, excursions, tips, drinks on special nights

What's not included: Airfare, drinks

Highlights: Sailing aboard a most genteel, floating, country-house hotel to a beautiful part of the world, weather cooperating

Other itineraries: In addition to the one-week cruise among the Inner Hebrides, the *Hebridean Princess* offers many different six- to nine-night Scottish itineraries, plus trips to Norway, Northern Ireland, and the Isle of Man from March through November. The seventy-eight passenger, 4,200-ton *Hebridean Spirit* joined the fleet in mid-2001, offering wider-ranging cruises to Norway, the Baltic, the Mediterranean, and through Suez into the Red Sea and Indian Ocean.

P&O SCOTTISH FERRIES' *ST. SUNNIVA*

To the Isles North of Scotland

For more than a century, a fleet of "North Boats," now owned by the venerable P&O Steam Navigation of London, has linked Scotland's Orkney and Shetland Islands with the mainland. The ships are designed to sail in some of the world's roughest seas, but when the weather cooperates, the island scenery is absolutely gorgeous.

Once a week in the summer, the blue-and-white, 4,200-ton *St. Sunniva* boards ferry and cruise passengers, pets, vehicles, freight, and the mail from a pier near the center of Aberdeen, a handsome, gray stone Scottish city located at the edge of the North Sea.

The public rooms include a seventy-seat restaurant, a bar/lounge with afternoon and evening entertainment, a room for reading and cards, and a self-service restaurant. A shop carries souvenirs and necessities, and there is sheltered seating aft and a boat deck for strolling.

All meals are semi-self-service, and an orderly number system prevents queuing after the initial sitting is full. Dinner might offer a choice of grilled rainbow trout, double lamb chops, or braised steak, accompanied by steamed fruit and a spice pudding and, for dessert, freshly baked cakes and pies. Waiters serve the appetizers, coffee, and fairly priced wines, including some fruity Scottish reds and whites. Service is efficient, and the food well-prepared, with no pretensions.

Passenger cabins on the *St. Sunniva* are plainly furnished and have compact facilities, with showers. My cabin had two berths and a settee under a large window looking forward over the bow, but the majority face to the side or are windowless.

The Itinerary

The harbor at **Aberdeen**, packed with oil-rig-supply vessels and numerous fishing boats, is a tight squeeze for the *St. Sunniva* on its way out to the North Sea. The ship turns north along the coast, passing the headland at **John O'Groats** during the afternoon. Late in the evening the *St. Sunniva* docks at **Stromness** on Orkney, the island's second city, allowing time for an evening walk along the rabbit warren of quiet lanes.

In the morning a coach excursion visits the Italian chapel, crafted from scrap metal by Italian prisoners of World War II; the weathered, red sandstone Norman cathedral of St. Magnus; and **Maes Howe,** a neolithic burial chamber built before 2700 B.C. Most of the island is gently rolling farmland and grazing fields for cattle and sheep, but the shoreline has sharp edges.

The Orkney and Shetland Islands form two remote archipelagos best known for their steep cliffs, nesting grounds for seabirds, clusters of mysterious standing stones, ancient fortifications, and sheep crofting. In the summer months the St. Sunniva makes a moderately priced, three-day minicruise to both island chains, and passengers with extra time can disembark at Lerwick, the second port, and return on a later sailing. NorthLink Orkney and Shetland Ferries, Ltd., will take over these sailings in late 2002.

Upon sailing at midday the ship passes close to Europe's highest vertical cliffs, featuring a 1,565-foot pinnacle of rock known as the **Old Man of Hoy** that serves as nesting grounds for thousands of noisy gannets, kittiwakes, puffins, razorbills, and oystercatchers. Near sunset the vessel cuts close to Sumburgh Head, the most southerly point of the Shetland Islands, and exchanges salutes with the P&O ferry *St. Clair,* bound overnight to Aberdeen.

After dinner the ship docks at **Lerwick,** the principal town of the one-hundred-island chain. The Shetlands are much wilder, with crofting (small farm holdings) and fishing its main industries. At anchor are scores of Russian and Polish fish-factory ships, known locally as klondykers, that arrive every summer to buy and process herring and mackerel.

In the morning a headland walk leads to the ruins of **Clickimin Broch,** a first-century, fortified stone tower built in a shallow loch by the Picts. In the afternoon a local coach heads into the countryside, dotted with stacks of freshly cut peat and ruins of old stone crofts. There are sweeping views to both sides out to the North Sea and to the Atlantic. A stop is made at **Jarlshoff,** Sir Walter Scott's early nineteenth-century name for an ancient site that had seen 3,000 years of habitation from the stone age to the seventeenth century.

On the last leg the *St. Sunniva* sails in the evening, passing **Mousa Broch,** the largest of some 500 ancient fortifications found in these islands, and **Fair Isle,** known for its bird sanctuary rising dramatically from the sea and for its patterned wool sweaters. By 8:00 A.M. the next morning, the ship has tied up at Aberdeen.

P&O Scottish Ferries'
St. Sunniva

Address/Phone: P&O Scottish Ferries, P.O. Box 5, Jamieson's Quay, Aberdeen AB11 5NP, Scotland; (011) 44 1224 589111; fax: (011) 44 1224 574411

The Ship: *St. Sunniva,* built in 1972 as the Danish ferry *Djursland,* was converted for night sailings by P&O and has a gross tonnage of 4,211, a length of 342 feet, and a draft of 14.5 feet.

Passengers: 409 total occupancy. The majority of passengers are British, and the minicruise passengers often come in groups.

Dress: Casual at all times

Officers/Crew: British

Cabins: 248 berths in small outside and inside cabins with private facilities

Fare: $

What's included: Minicruise includes port charges, meals

What's not included: Shore excursions, drinks, tips

Highlights: Inexpensive way to see spectacular scenery, remote islands, and lots of birds

Other itineraries: Besides this three-day minicruise aboard the *St. Sunniva,* operating between June and August, this ship and the *St. Clair* sail regularly to and from the same ports, making it relatively easy to arrange stopovers.

NORWEGIAN COASTAL VOYAGE'S *NORDKAPP*
Norwegian Coastal Voyage

The locals refer to their domestic passenger and cargo service as the *Hurtigruten*—fast route. For more than one hundred years, a fleet of ships owned by several different companies has operated a water highway linking three dozen towns along the rugged Norwegian coast between Bergen in the south and the North Cape and beyond. Norwegian Coastal Voyage markets them all in North America. The ships' role as the primary means of access has diminished, and while many Norwegians still travel this way and expedite their cargo, the *Hurtigruten's* future lies with local and overseas tourism.

The eleven ships are quite different. Three distinct ship types include two traditional passenger-cargo ships from the 1950s and 1960s, six new, much larger cruise-style vessels completed between 1993 and 1997, and a 1980s-built, then enlarged, trio whose amenities reflect the newest fleet mates.

At 11,300 tons, the 1996-built *Nordkapp* can take up to 490 cabin passengers. Most cabins are of a uniform design, with large windows, two lower beds, a vanity, decent storage space, and private facilities. The *Nordkapp* is beautifully decorated in attractive bold colors and with distinctive Norwegian paintings of landscapes, seascapes, and historic steamers, plus lots of glass and mirrors, creating a most cheerful atmosphere. The large, 110-seat panorama lounge, done in

blues and greens, has sweeping views in three directions, and aft a spacious lounge/bar looks out to port and starboard. A second deck of public rooms includes a lounge with musical entertainment offered during the high season, conference rooms, a quiet reading room, a twenty-four-hour cafeteria, a souvenir shop, a children's playroom, and a long gallery lounge leading aft to a big, windowed dining room that seats 240.

The size of the ship and the presence of tour groups often make meeting other passengers more difficult than on the more intimate ships. There is limited outdoor seating on three afterdecks and a wraparound deck for walking. Cargo is wheeled through doors in the ship's side, and watching the handling is less a pastime than on the older crane-loading ships.

The food is Norwegian, which means, besides standard continental-breakfast items, eggs and bacon (on some mornings), cold meats, cheeses, and a variety of herring. Lunch, also a buffet, is the most elaborate meal, with a choice of several hot and cold entrees such as salmon, halibut, lamb chops and veal, as well as soup, salads, cheeses, and desserts. Dinner is a set three-course menu, but a certain sameness sets in after a week aboard. Alcohol is heavily taxed. A bottle of beer costs about $6.00 and wine starts at $25.00 per bottle. If you like a drink before dinner, bring your own.

The Norwegian Coastal Voyage offers a comfortable, moderately priced way to visit an expensive country and to get to know Norway, its people, towns, and wonderful mountain and island scenery. These are working ships, without the entertainment or gambling found on big cruise liners.

The Itinerary

Tourists are attracted to Norway's scenery, which does not disappoint in good weather. The route is a coastal one, and the ships do not penetrate the deepest fjords, except for summertime visits to the Geiranger Fjord, but there are some quite spectacular narrow passages that the big cruise ships cannot negotiate.

The thirty-five ports, called at different hours northbound and southbound, range from small villages and good-size fishing ports to major market centers, most rebuilt after World War II. Time in port ranges from fifteen minutes to several hours but a quick walk is nearly always possible.

The cities vary considerably in their offerings. **Aalesund,** destroyed by fire in 1904, was rebuilt into a handsome Norwegian-style of art nouveau. **Trondheim** has a much older center, a magnificent eleventh-century medieval cathedral, and a wooden waterfront. An excursion is offered both northbound and southbound, including the Museum of Music History on the latter.

Crossing the **Arctic Circle** is marked with a globe set on an island, and the ship celebrates the event with proclamations and an ice-water "ceremony."

The **Lofoten Islands,** a popular subject for maritime artists, rise dramatically out of the sea as the coastal express approaches from **Bodo.** Depending on the weather the ship is likely to sail into the narrow **Troll Fjord** and turn 180 degrees in a very tight basin surrounded by steep cliffs oozing water that become cascading waterfalls in the wetter seasons.

One of my favorite excursions leaves the southbound ship at **Harstad,** stops at a thirteenth-century stone church, continues into interior farming regions, crosses a fjord by ferry, and rejoins the ship at **Sortland. Tromso** is a delightful university city. The Arctic Cathedral, built in a layered A-frame style, possesses Europe's largest glass mosaic.

The landscape becomes more rugged and less populated, and, at **Honnigsvåg,** if snow isn't blocking the road (normally open by mid-May), there is an excursion to the **North Cape** that passes reindeer and an encampment of the indigenous Sami people and then culminates in a glorious view northward over the sea.

Rounding the top of Norway, the ship skirts some of Europe's highest sea cliffs, populated with nesting gannets. Again the coastal steamer is exposed to the open sea, so be prepared for hours of pitching before reaching **Kirkenes.** This is where most one-way passengers leave to fly south or come north to join the trip. Round-trippers will stop at the same ports but at different times of the day, so those missed at night come during the day.

Norwegian Coastal Voyage's *Nordkapp*

Address/Phone: Norwegian Coastal Voyage, Inc., 405 Park Avenue, New York, NY 10022; (800) 323–7436 or (212) 319–1300; brochures: (800) 666–2374; fax: (212) 319–1390; www.coastalvoyage.com

The Ship: *Nordkapp* was built in 1996 and has a gross tonnage of 11,200 and a length of 414 feet.

Passengers: 490; all ages; mostly forty and up, traveling as individuals or groups (aboard the newer ships); largely Norwegian, German, and British, with some Americans and other Europeans

Dress: Casual

Officers/Crew: Norwegian

Cabins: 217, all outside, plain but decent size

Fare: $$

What's included: Varies, from cruise only, including port charges, to a complete package, airfare, hotel, transfers, and a prepaid shore-excursions package

What's not included: Tips, drinks, and airfares when not part of a package

Highlights: Norway's spectacular coast; cargo handling, especially aboard the older ships; maritime atmosphere aboard the old ships; Norwegian art aboard the newer ships

Other itineraries: The coastal voyage may be taken as an eleven-day round-trip, calling at thirty-five ports each way, leaving Bergen almost every night at 10:30 P.M. throughout the year. One-way five- and six-day sea-air trips are available between Bergen and Kirkenes and can be combined with hotel stays and the highly recommended Bergen-Oslo train ride. The northbound itinerary has better port timings for Aalesund, Trondhiem, Tromso, and the North Cape. The midnight sun is visible in clear weather above the Arctic Circle between mid-May and late July, whereas the Northern Lights are most often seen in winter. The summer months see many deck passengers, but by early September they are mostly gone.

DFDS SEAWAYS' *CROWN OF SCANDINAVIA*
Ferry Cruising between Copenhagen and Oslo

DFDS (Det Forende Dampskibs Selskab—The United Steamship Company), Denmark's largest and oldest passenger shipowner, began sailing the Capital Cities Route in 1866. The company now operates a fleet of seven overnight cruise ferries on routes between Denmark, England, Sweden, Norway, Germany, and Holland. Advertising proudly proclaims DFDS as "Masters of the Northern Seas," and there is no disagreement here.

In recent years this route annually carried about 750,000 passengers, of which Norwegians and Danes accounted for about 75 percent. Many British and American passengers also use this service, and language presents no problems, as English is generally spoken throughout Scandinavia. Sailings are geared to the business traveler and tourist, with daily departures at 5:00 P.M. from terminals close to both city centers and arrivals at 9:00 A.M. next day.

Crown of Scandinavia is the largest and newest passenger ferry in the fleet, the last in a series of four ships built at Split in Croatia for various Scandinavian owners. Delivered in July 1994, she runs alongside the slightly smaller *Pearl of Scandinavia,* dating from 1981. Boarding by car or on foot, the passenger arrives at the spacious reception area to be directed to the cabin. *Crown of Scandinavia*'s 662 cabins include, unusual for

a ferry, twenty-two with verandas, and a further forty-six larger cabins feature extra facilities and limited room service, designated as Commodore Class. Every cabin has a shower and a toilet.

Dining options cater to all price ranges. The most popular is the Seven Seas restaurant, with its panoramic forward view, serving buffet dinners and traditional Scandinavian smorgasbord. Dinner with wine costs about $65 for two. The window seats at breakfast are quickly taken during the transit up the Oslofjord. My preferred dining option is the elegant, Chinese-style setting of Sailors Corner, with its dark cherry furniture and paneling. Grilled meats, fish, and shellfish are specialties here, and a drink, wine, and coffee are included in the three-course price ($105 for two). Always book a table in either restaurant on embarkation. As an alternative, the Scandia Café provides light meals and snacks.

The well-patronized Admiral Pub, adjacent to the Sailors Corner, is modeled on a dark wood–furnished English bar, a style featured on a number of Scandinavian ferries. The main lounge is the Columbus Club, with three bars, a dance floor, and a nearby casino. Entertainment includes a singing group, bingo, and shipboard horse racing. In the afternoon this lounge provides a good position to view the passing scenery,

Overnight ferry cruises abound throughout Northern Europe, making attractive spontaneous getaways for a couple of nights. The 272 nautical-mile voyage from Copenhagen to Oslo aboard DFDS Seaways' Crown of Scandinavia *combines good scenery, fine food and service, and elegant surroundings. At the other end spend the day or linger longer, and return by a later sailing.*

and outside the extensive sundecks provide more viewing platforms. Other facilities aboard include cinemas, a disco, a Jacuzzi, a sauna, an indoor pool, a children's playroom, and teen activities.

The Itinerary

The pier in Copenhagen is conveniently sited close to the city center and within walking distance of several attractive hotels. Before boarding have a look at the ship-model collection in the main lobby of the adjacent company headquarters.

As the ship sails from **Copenhagen,** the royal palace, the *Little Mermaid,* and the cruise-ship quay can be seen on the port side and the mooring for the Danish Royal Yacht to starboard. Shortly after entering the **Öresund,** Middleground Fort is rounded and a course set for **Helsingborg** in Sweden, where the ship arrives at about 6:45 P.M., this is a brief call to pick up passengers and vehicles for Oslo. Helsingborg is a busy ferry port annually handling more than thirteen million passengers, most traveling to **Helsingor** in Denmark.

Ten minutes after sailing from Helsingborg, the *Crown of Scandinavia* passes to port **Kronborg Castle** at Helsingor, famous as the setting for *Hamlet.* Soon the ship enters the **Kattegat,** following the Swedish coastline northward for about another hour. During the night the **Skaggerak** is crossed, and arrival at the mouth of **Oslofjord** is at about 5:00 A.M.

The 60-mile passage to **Oslo** takes about four hours, and at 7:30 the ship enters the narrowest part after passing **Oscarsborg Fortress.** At 9:00 A.M. the *Crown of Scandinavia* docks adjacent to the thirteenth century **Akershus Castle,** a short walk from the city center. On arrival all passengers (including the roundtrippers) must disembark, but returning passengers can leave luggage aboard. The nightly departures permit flexible planning.

DFDS Seaways' *Crown of Scandinavia*

Address/Phone: DFDS Seaways, 6555 N.W. 9th Avenue, Suite 207, Fort Lauderdale, FL 33309; (954) 491–7909 or (800) 533–3755; fax: (954) 491–7958; e-mail: resinfo@dfds.com; www.seaeurope.com

The Ship: *Crown of Scandinavia* was built in 1994 and has a gross tonnage of 35,498 and a length of 559 feet.

Passengers: 2,400 full capacity; mostly Danish and Norwegian, but English spoken

Dress: Casual

Officers/Crew: Mostly Danish, some Filipinos

Cabins: 662, inside and out, with a total of 2,126 beds

Fare: $

What's included: Cruise only; Commodore class includes breakfast

What's not included: Meals, drinks, tips

Highlights: Lots to do and eat aboard; scenic approaches to and from both capitals

Other itineraries: In addition to this overnight ferry cruise between Copenhagen and Oslo, which operates every day of the year except Christmas Eve and Christmas Day, DFDS operates popular overnight sailings between Denmark, Germany, the Netherlands, and England with coordinated train connections at both sea terminals.

SILJA LINE'S *SILJA SERENADE* AND *SILJA SYMPHONY*

Cruise Ferries in the Baltic

The Silja Line, headquartered in Helsinki, has been trading in ships for larger new ones as often as Americans trade in their cars. Presently the world's largest cruise ferry, the *Silja Europa* has a gross tonnage of 59,914 and passenger capacity of 3,013; sisters *Silja Symphony* and *Silja Serenade* are slightly smaller at 58,400 tons and take up to 2,852.

On the *Serenade* and *Symphony*, Decks 2 to 12 are fitted with cabins, restaurants, cafes, bars, nightclubs, a cinema, lots of shopping, a casino, a children's playroom, a video arcade, saunas, small pools, whirlpools, and several levels for vehicles of all shapes and sizes.

Dining options include no less than three à la carte restaurants: Maxim à la Carte, with a large menu; Casa Bonita for steaks; and Happy Lobster, a fish and seafood eatery. The latter features smoked, slightly salted, grilled, and poached fish, mustard herring, Baltic herring, fish roe and shrimp, and if desired, Finlandia vodka. Buffet Serenade and Buffet Symphony (smorgasbord) have an incredible range of food for one set price, with reserved timed entry to avoid queues. Snack bars and cafes for light meals and hot hors d'oeuvres are scattered about the ship.

Most spectacular is the Promenade, a shopping and restaurant arcade running fore and aft for 475 feet, five decks and 60 feet high, decorated with mobiles and topped with skylights. Glass-enclosed bridges run across the horizontal atrium.

Entertainment and drinking venues are Atlantis Palace, a tiered cocktail lounge and nightclub with dance music; a casino for roulette, blackjack, and slots; Stardust, for karaoke and disco, located under the funnel; a British-style pub; and a panorama bar and pastry café overlooking the stern. High up, the Sunflower Oasis is the spa with small pools and whirlpools, and low down is a bank of saunas. Siljaland is a play area for children, and the electric bazaar features the latest video games. Seminars and corporate meetings are big business, and the Conference Center can be adapted to large or small gatherings.

Nine hundred eighty-five cabins with 2,980 berths fall into eight categories, the top being Commodore class, set high up and forward; others include standard outsides with windows, insides, promenade-view cabins, and budget accommodations below vehicle decks. Deck 12 is open for viewing in all directions, and the

The word ferry does not normally conjure up the thought of a cruise, but once aboard one of the giant Scandinavian Silja Line ships, all that will change. Sailing nightly between Sweden and Finland, these ships offer more dining options than many cruise liners and most of their amenities, plus wonderful archipelago scenery along the way. Incorporating these short cruises into your travel plans is simple, whether driving or using a rail pass.

enclosed central portion looks down into the Promenade Arcade. Deck 7 permits a walk under lifeboats completely around the ship.

The onboard atmosphere is that of an urban entertainment center, with everything geared to encouraging passengers to spend money and have a good time doing it. It's one late-night party, but with cabins located on separate decks, passengers wishing to sleep can do so.

The Itinerary

The Silja Line and its arch competitor, the Viking Line (sporting bright-red hulls), offer daily year-round overnight service between Stockholm and Helsinki, and both overnight and daylight sailings between Stockholm and Turku, some departures calling at the scenic **Åland Islands.** The most popular trip leaves Stockholm at 5:00 P.M., sails overnight to Helsinki, arriving at 9:30 A.M. for a day in the Finnish capital, and then overnight back to Stockholm.

Departing **Stockholm,** the ship threads for three hours through an amazing wooded archipelago—some islands residences for daily commuters into the city, others summer and weekend camps, and many uninhabited. The outdoor experience is best enjoyed in the late spring and summer, when the lingering daylight stretches almost to midnight. The approach to **Helsinki**'s inner harbor the next morning is among rocky islands.

If making the return sailing, you keep your cabin and spend the day ashore sightseeing the Finnish capital, its waterfront markets, neighborhoods, and individual styles of architecture. If staying longer, consider the daylight, all-island route from **Turku,** Finland's second port, 125 miles and two hours by train from Helsinki. The sophistication and size of these cruise ferries exist nowhere else in the world.

Silja Line's *Silja Serenade* and *Silja Symphony*

Address/Phone: Norwegian Coastal Voyage, Inc., 405 Park Avenue, New York, NY 10022; (212) 319–1300 or (800) 323–7436; fax: (212) 319–1390; www.coastalvoyage.com

The Ships: Sisters *Silja Serenade* and *Silja Symphony,* built in 1990 and 1991, have a gross tonnage of 58,400, a length of 656 feet, and a draft of 23 feet.

Passengers: 2,852 maximum capacity; all ages, mostly Swedes and Finns but also Germans, other Europeans, and some Americans (language not a problem)

Dress: Casual

Officers/Crew: Finnish officers; Scandinavian crew

Cabins: 985; modern and simply furnished, outsides and insides

Fare: $

What's included: Cruise fare only

What's not included: Everything is extra unless part of a package.

Highlights: A floating restaurant, cafe and nightlife center; island scenery in summer

Other itineraries: Besides the above overnight cruise, Norwegian Coastal Voyage, Inc. represents other ferry operators with Scandinavian and North Sea routes.

SWAN HELLENIC'S *MINERVA*

Iberian Cultural Cruise: British Style

Swan Hellenic, a long-established British firm based in London, has traditionally drawn its clientele from the upper end of the British market, plus a modest percentage of North Americans to its cultural-enrichment cruises in Europe, the Nile Valley, and Asia.

The 12,500-ton *Minerva* was built from the hull and engines of an unfinished former Soviet-block listening—read *spy*—ship. Owned by a group of investors based in Monaco, she is chartered by the Peninsular and Oriental Steam Navigation Company of London, engaged in shipping since 1836, and parent firm for P&O Cruises, Princess Cruises, and Swan Hellenic.

The company asked the fiercely loyal past passengers and Swan staff to help custom-design the new ship, which made its debut in 1996. The *Minerva*'s posh surroundings are meant to woo both a younger clientele (age forty and up) and more Americans. Cruising with Swan Hellenic does not come cheaply, and discounting is not a feature of the line.

It's Britain afloat from stem to stern aboard the *Minerva*. Original paintings, prints, antique maps, and passenger-donated photographs line the public room and corridor walls.

The well-stocked, wood-paneled library (only the *QE2* carries more books) offers travel guides, references, and novels for all destinations and lots of comfy easy chairs. Leather chairs give the smoking room a clubby feel, and the card room's suede-covered walls provide a hushed setting for serious bridge players. The main lounge, with conversational seating, draws an evening crowd for after-dinner coffee and for dancing to a four-piece band; rearranged, it becomes the venue for the daytime lecture program at sea.

The formal Wheeler Bar, employing a resident pianist, twins appropriately with the sophisticated oak-paneled dining room, while on the deck above, the Orpheus Room's airy blue-green colors and potted plants pairs well with the cheerful, informal Bridge Cafe.

At the one-sitting dining the barrier between the reserved British and more open Americans quickly disappears. The Bridge Café, an alternative to more formal jacket-and-tie dining, provides buffet dinners indoors and outside around the pool. With a new chef, the menus have greatly improved. The Promenade Deck has an extrawide wraparound promenade for walking, but there is limited shade from the sun.

Cabins, with twin beds that push together to form a queen, have a small desk, chair, TV, telephone, adequate closet and drawer space, bathrooms with showers, and, in the highest categories, tubs. Thirty-four of the 170 are inside without windows.

*A Swan Hellenic cruise is the most culturally rich experience on the high seas, and the 344-passenger **Minerva** makes two voyages a year between Northern Europe, the Iberian Peninsula, and the Western Mediterranean. It pays to be an Anglophile because most of the passenger list will be British, many of whom are fiercely loyal to the Swan experience.*

The Itinerary

Swan Hellenic cruises offer onboard seminars. Names and short biographies of the historians, archaeologists, anthropologists, geologists, and clergy appear in the brochure. Most hail from British universities. For this Iberian cruise, topics range from historic connections between Britain and Iberia to the wine trade. The program forms an integral part of the cruise experience, and lecturers join passengers at meals and accompany them ashore. The ports of call vary every year, but include calls in France and Iberian ports on the Atlantic and Mediterranean coasts. All cruises start or end in England, paired with a one-way charter flight between the ship and London.

Sailing up the **Loire,** the ship stops at **Nantes,** which has a fine cathedral, a good museum housed in a medieval castle, and beautifully maintained botanical gardens; an excursion is offered out to the Muscadet vineyards. Docking adjacent to the handsome city of **Bordeaux** allows for walking tours to see the neoclassical architecture, wide boulevards, and narrow streets of Old Town. During the transit along the **Gironde,** the wine expert points out the south bank's Médoc vineyards.

Sailing westward through the Bay of Biscay to **Vigo,** northwest Spain, you make the historic pilgrimage to **Santiago de Compostela,** where, at the magnificent Roman Catholic cathedral, Swan arranges for the giant incense burner, requiring eight men on the ropes, to perform its dramatic swings over head, soaring to the rafters.

The Douro River city of **Oporto** is famous for its port-wine production, narrow, cobbled streets, and outstanding Baroque architecture. The old-fashioned capital city of **Lisbon** spreads over hills above the **Tagus River.** The residential neighborhoods are best enjoyed with a bus-and-tram day pass. Great museums and waterfront monuments demonstrate Portugal's pioneering maritime feats of exploration.

The attractive port of **Cadiz** leads inland to **Seville** for its great Gothic cathedral, Moorish Alcazar Palace, and quiet residential squares. From coastal **Malaga** the excursion visits **Granada**'s Alhambra Palace and magnificent Arab-style formal gardens. Disembarking at **Barcelona,** you'll have time to enjoy cafes and restaurants lining the medieval streets, a Gothic district, and the Picasso Museum.

Swan Hellenic's *Minerva*

Address/Phone: Swan Hellenic Cruises, Kartagener Associates Inc., 631 Commack Road, Suite 1A, Commack, NY 11725; (877) 219–4239; fax: (631) 858–1279; www.swanhellenic.com

The Ship: *Minerva* was built in 1996 from an unfinished Ukrainian hull and has a gross tonnage of 12,500, a length of 436 feet, and a draft of 19.6 feet.

Passengers: 344, double occupancy; age forty and up, largely British.

Dress: Jacket and tie expected on evenings at sea in the main restaurant

Officers/Crew: British captain and European officers; mostly Filipino and Ukrainian crew

Cabins: 170; mostly average size and 12 with verandas

Fare: $$$$

What's included: Cruise and port charges; program of shore excursions for every port, all tips aboard and to guides ashore, charter flight between London and the ship

What's not included: Airfare between the United States and London, optional shore excursions, drinks

Highlights: Excellent enrichment program; terrific organization aboard and ashore

Other itineraries: In addition to the above cruise between England and the Iberian Peninsula, which is offered in late spring and late summer, the *Minerva* makes year-round nonrepeating eight-to-twenty-five-day cruises in the Mediterranean, around Britain, to Norway and the Baltic, and late fall voyages via Suez and the Red Sea to a winter season in South and Southeast Asia.

RADISSON SEVEN SEAS CRUISES'
RADISSON DIAMOND
Port Hopping across Europe

Radisson Seven Seas Cruises owns the *Radisson Diamond* and *Song of Flower* (180 passengers) and markets the *Paul Gauguin* (320 passengers), *Seven Seas Navigator* (490 passengers), *Seven Seas Mariner* (720 passengers), and *Hanseatic* (184 passengers), a fleet of top cruisers that cover the globe.

Upon boarding the *Radisson Diamond*, one enters the foyer and atrium of a sophisticated European hotel furnished with demilune tables set with large floral bouquets against mirrored walls. Two glass-enclosed elevators rise five decks next to an arcing staircase.

The public rooms are an odd lot and they see less use than on most ships. The tri-level observation lounge looks forward through two decks of glass; however, sight lines are poor for the entertainment, which consists of a small band for dancing, a singing duo, a pianist, and perhaps a comedian. Just aft, a central corridor divides the casino's fifty slot machines from the blackjack and stud-poker tables. On the deck above, the Club piano bar, although stylishly furnished, suffers from no windows and is lightly patronized. The big-windowed fitness room looks over the stern, and outdoor deck space is terrific, with a variety of open, covered, sheltered, and divided deck-chair seating areas shared with a whirlpool, a splash pool, and a sit-up bar.

The two-deck-high aft dining room is one of the most attractive afloat, with 270-degree large window views and a center portion fringed with colorful mythological friezes on three sides. The room seats 330 at an open sitting, and I never failed to get a well-placed table for two. The menu includes appetizers such as escargots, jumbo shrimp, and seafood pancakes, a different salad every night, and entrees that included beef tenderloin in a creamy peppercorn sauce, grilled lobster tails, and pork chops in a wonderful sage sauce. Memorable desserts included a warm cheese strudel, strawberry cream cake, and the parfaits. Poured wines are complimentary. The grill's alternate buffet at breakfast and lunch rates high in terms of quality and variety. Lunch features a daily theme—Chinese, Japanese sushi, Indonesian sate, Mexican—plus freshly grilled swordfish, tuna, steaks, and sausages. At night the grill section becomes a reservations-only Italian bistro with a set menu and singing waiters.

All 177 cabins are outside with the same 220-square-foot dimensions, and 123 have verandas. The

The 354-passenger **Radisson Diamond,** *a catamaran with a beam as wide as the QE2 but less than half her length, qualifies as the most unusual cruise ship afloat and is as comfortable as they come. Twice a year it operates between Northern Europe and the Mediterranean, skirting the coasts of France, Portugal, and Spain. Loyalists book this ship no matter where it goes, and that's the emphasis here.*

tan wood trim is matched with shades of green, medium blue, and cream in the patterned curtains, upholstery, bedspreads, and carpets. A queen-size bed (or twins) shares floor space with a two-seat sofa, a chair, a table for dining, and a desk-cum-vanity. For storage the room has two shallow closets, two cabinets, and nine drawers. The minibar includes complimentary bottles of liquor, beer, soft drinks and mineral water. Videos for the VCR are available in the open-shelf library, and the TV brings in CNN, Sky News, and local programs. The blue-gray tiled bathroom has a half-tub and shower.

The supremely designed private balcony has solid bulkhead dividers, slatted wooden wainscoting, and teak decking. Two padded lounge chairs and a round white table provide a relaxing setting.

The Itinerary

The usual eleven-night cruise between Northern Europe and the Mediterranean calls at seven ports in France, Portugal, and Spain, varying from year to year, and includes three sea days. Embarking at **Dover** and sailing through the night, the *Radisson Diamond* anchors off **St. Malo** for a visit to **Mont St. Michel,** a remarkable walled town of narrow streets and an eleventh-century abbey perched high on a rock. The ship cruises around the westernmost tip of France and south into the Bay of Biscay, and the sea days provide a settling-in period.

La Coruna, in northwest Spain, has narrow medieval streets lined with bay-window-fronted houses featuring elaborate brass door knockers. Just down the coast **Vigo** is the port for **Santiago de Compostela's** magnificent twelfth-century cathedral, a principal pilgrimage destination for centuries. Sailing into the Tagus River, **Lisbon,** an old-fashioned capital city built on hills, is best enjoyed with a bus-and-tram day pass. Tour the streets, lined with colorful tile-fronted facades, and the medieval Alfama district, which rises to an elaborate castle worth exploring.

The attractive city of **Cadiz** gives access by road to **Seville**'s great Gothic cathedral, Moorish Alcazar Palace, and residential squares. Passing through the Strait of Gibraltar to **Malaga,** the excursion heads inland to **Granada**'s Alhambra Palace and gardens. **Barcelona** is a great walking city, with medieval streets, Gothic district, Picasso Museum, and Antonio Gaudi's contribution to art nouveau architecture seen in his churches, office buildings, and apartments. Following a final day at sea, the *Radisson Diamond* arrives at **Cannes,** the French Riviera, for disembarkation.

Radisson Seven Seas Cruises' *Radisson Diamond*

Address/Phone: Radisson Seven Seas Cruises, 600 Corporate Drive, Suite 410, Fort Lauderdale, FL 33334; (954) 776–6123 or (800) 333–3333; fax: (954) 722–6763; www.rssc.com

The Ship: *Radisson Diamond,* built in 1992, has a gross tonnage of 20,295, a length of 423 feet, and a draft of 26 feet.

Passengers: 354; age forty and up, largely American, many repeaters

Dress: Suit or tuxedo on a few nights, otherwise jacket and tie, and casual

Officers/Crew: Scandinavian officers; European stewardesses; some Filipino staff in the dining room and deck department

Cabins: 177; all outside and 123 with verandas

Fare: $$$$

What's included: Cruise; air from East Coast, wines at dinner; stocked minibar, tips

What's not included: Port charges, shore excursions, and drinks at the bar

Highlights: Great food at buffets and in beautiful restaurant; the spacious veranda cabins and well-designed outdoor deck space; culturally interesting itinerary

Other itineraries: In addition to the European port-hopping cruise, which operates in spring and fall, *Radisson Diamond* spends May through October in North Europe and the Mediterranean, mid-November to mid-April in the Caribbean and on Panama Canal transits, plus spring and fall transatlantic crossings. The *Song of Flower* makes winter cruises to Southeast Asia and spends summer and fall in Europe. The 320-passenger *Paul Gauguin* cruises from Tahiti, and the 184-passenger *Hanseatic* is in Antarctica; the 490-passenger *Seven Seas Navigator* and the 720-passenger *Seven Seas Mariner* are new and range worldwide.

PETER DEILMANN'S *DEUTSCHLAND*
A National Flagship in the European Tradition

The name of this handsome German flagship, *Deutschland,* simply means Germany. Unlike the multinational crews found aboard most ships today, the *Deutschland's* 260-member crew, and most of the passengers, are largely from the German-speaking countries of Germany, Austria, and Switzerland. The staff's standard of speaking English is as good or even better than on many internationally crewed ships catering to North American passengers.

Within, the *Deutschland* is, without qualification, absolutely beautiful, extremely well designed, and with a public-room layout that suits many different occasions and moods. The decor is richly Edwardian, with art nouveau and art deco flourishes. Public rooms are varied and spacious with never a feeling of crowding, and they run the gamut from light and airy with large windows to one that opens onto side galleries to another that's cozy and enclosed for late-night conversation.

The materials are high quality and carry off the effect better than I have seen on any ship—real marble and faux marble; real wood, wood veneers, and faux burled paneling; some real brass that tarnishes and needs constant polishing and some metal that is brass in color; molding and pilasters that appear to be plaster; excellent Tiffany-style stained glass especially in the ceilings; and very tasteful furnishings.

For quiet reading, playing games, and having afternoon tea, the Lido Terrace, an observation lounge, provides a wonderful light-filled atmosphere with views outside to the surrounding open decks. The furnishings are comfortable white and tan wicker chairs with green and gold patterned cushions.

For a drink before meals, with music provided by a trio, the Lili Marleen Salon, dedicated to Marlene Dietrich, is a cozy space with polished medium-dark paneling, a beamed ceiling with plaster decoration, opaque cut-glass globes, and additional indirect lighting from stately floor lamps. Zum Alten Fritz replicates a dark paneled taverna with its etched glass mirrors and button leather curved banquettes. It offers live music, hot snacks such as bratwurst (frankfurters) and weiss wurst (white veal sausage), and beer by the stein.

The deck space is so good and varied that one needs a very long voyage to enjoy all the outdoor, covered, and enclosed venues furnished with high-quality varnished wooden deck chairs and royal blue cushions. Happily, the ship offers extended cruises.

Dining takes place in a two-sitting main restaurant, the Berlin, in the more private Vierjahreszeiten (Four Seasons) with reservations but no extra charge, and the Lido Gourmet, a buffet offering indoor and outdoor seating, The menus are continental with German specialties, and the preparation is good to excellent.

Some of the courses that we enjoyed were air-dried beef with fresh horseradish; mild French goat cheese with grape seed oil and a baguette; cream of asparagus with baby shrimps; black noodles with lobster and scallops; grilled lemon sole with lime sauce; veal loin with morels and dates in a cream sauce; and white chocolate mousse with basil.

The **Deutschland,** *a thoroughly German ship as the name might imply, offers its passengers an Edwardian atmosphere while roaming the world on non-repeating itineraries. The ship represents a throwback to an earlier era of ocean liner-style cruising, and English-speakers with a penchant for a true seagoing European experience will find that language is no problem at all.*

The lunchtime buffets offer hot and cold meats, a fair variety of salad fixings, lots of cheeses, and excellent desserts. From the grill, one could order freshly prepared shrimp, lamb chops, rib eye steaks, and chicken. At breakfast, the menu caters to European and American tastes. The service in the main dining room is relaxed and professional, and in the Vierjahreszeiten, the dinner sessions are scheduled for up to three hours.

The Kaisersaal is an extraordinarily opulent cabaret lounge furnished in a 1920s bordello style, with comfortable chairs, small table lamps, and a mezzanine with tables for two set next to the railing.

Of the 286 cabins, 224 are outside and 17 outside are singles, and all have white wood-tone paneling, handsomely framed reproduction oil paintings, decent closets, storage, and counter space, color TVs, radios, safes, and stocked refrigerators with charges for their use. Most cabins are moderately sized with less attention paid to elaborate decorative details than in the public rooms.

The prevalence of smoking is as you would find in any European setting. Any American who likes European travel or more specifically travel to Germany will find this ship a most appealing and certainly a most distinctive experience.

The Itinerary

The *Deutschland* explores most of the world's seas, making cruises from Northern Europe in the summer into the Mediterranean and out through Suez to the Indian Ocean in the fall. Some years the ship continues on to Asia and the Pacific or along the African coast, across South Atlantic to the South America, and north via the Amazon basin to New York.

A recent eleven-night **Lisbon** to **Hamburg** cruise had some three dozen Americans booked, and typically Deilmann offered a half-price shore excursion package. Embarking the day prior to sailing north, passengers stay aboard the *Deutschland* for the Lisbon capital visit. The call in northwest Spain gives access to a Roman Catholic pilgrimage site at **Santiago de Compostela,** and the sail up the **Gironde** and **Garonne Rivers** leads to **Bordeaux**'s Medoc wine region. **St. Malo** is for **Mont-St.-Michel,** and across the channel, **Plymouth** was the Pilgrims' port of departure for the New World in 1620. **Jersey** is one of the attractive Channel Islands, and the port of **Dover** is but an hour from **London** or alternatively the ancient Cinque Ports on England's South Coast. The cruise ends at **Hamburg**'s port of **Cuxhaven.**

Peter Deilmann's
Deutschland

Address/Phone: Peter Deilmann Ocean Cruises, 1800 Diagonal Road, Suite 170, Alexandria, VA 22314; (703) 549–1741 or (800) 348–8287; fax: (703) 549–7924; www.deilmann-cruises.com

The Ship: *Deutschland* was completed in 1998. It has a gross tonnage of 22,400, a length of 574 feet, and a draft of 18.4 feet

Passengers: 513, age forty-five and up; German-speaking, plus some Americans on some cruises (inquire when booking)

Dress: Formal, informal, and casual nights

Officers/Crew: German officers; largely German-speaking crew

Cabins: 286, with 224 outside; 17 outside and 50 inside singles

Fare: $$$

What's included: Cruise fare and port charges

What's not included: Airfare, shore excursions, tips, and drinks

Highlights: Splendid art nouveau and Edwardian decor; German-speaking European atmosphere

Other itineraries: The *Deutschland* travels all over the world.

PETER DEILMANN'S *PRUSSIAN PRINCESS*
Cruising the Rhine and Moselle

Peter Deilmann's nine-riverboat fleet cruises primarily in Germany but also in France, Holland, Belgium, Italy, Austria, Hungary, and the Czech Republic. Passengers are German- and English-speaking in varying numbers, so before booking, it is wise to ask about the number of English-speaking passengers expected on the cruise of your choice. The *Prussian Princess*, written *Prinzessin von Preussen* on the bow, is a long, low-slung, three-deck riverboat taking 142 passengers in windowed cabins located on two decks.

Crossing the gangway and boarding A-Deck amidships, the furnished entrance foyer leads into a very dark lounge bar, used for special receptions and for evening performances by the musician/ singer. A tiny lounge on the deck below is well suited to reading and screening travel videos. The more inviting dining room seats all passengers at once, with most tables positioned next to a window; generally, the English-speaking passengers sit together.

The well-prepared and well-presented menu features German and continental cuisine. Lunch and dinner offerings include small-portion samplings of many main courses. Dinner, for example, features an appetizer, a choice of a clear or cream soup, fish, salad, sorbet on

three nights, two main dishes, dessert, cheese from the buffet, coffee, and petits fours. At the top of my list are the cream soups with broccoli, leek and lobster bisque, the lamb, duck, and venison dishes, and desserts such as apple fritters, profiteroles, and tiramisù. The fairly priced wine list naturally emphasizes Moselle and Rhine wines. Lunch offers five served courses, plus salad, cold meats and cheeses from the buffet; the Germans like it that way, whereas Americans tend to want lighter lunches after the first couple of days. On fine days I made a picnic from the buffet and went up on deck.

The seventy average-size cabins come in two sizes: A-Deck doubles have French-door-style windows; the slightly smaller B-Deck twins have large square, sealed windows. The pleasant rooms are decorated with light-wood shelving and contain a closet, a desk, and beds positioned at right angles. Amenities include a telephone and three audio channels, offering popular classics, German music, and local broadcasts. A small bathroom has a shower stall. From the top deck, which stretches nearly the boat's full length, the viewing is excellent. Comforts include ample deck chairs, two covered sections, and an outdoor service of afternoon tea and music on three fine days.

*Peter Deilmann's riverboats ply Germany's waterways, providing the non-German speaker with a convenient way to see the hilltop castles along the Rhine, Romanesque cathedral cities, picture-postcard villages, and vineyards along the slopes of the Moselle. A cruise aboard the **Prussian Princess**, sharing the experience with German passengers on their own turf, can be a rich cultural experience.*

The Itinerary

On my cruise the ship's study leader had near-perfect English, translating all announcements and points of interest in English and German. The bulletin board exhibits maps and handouts with bilingual port information. Except for the entirely German crew show, one feels well catered to. The boat sails through the night on some occasions and ties up on others. Landings are generally quiet locations close to the town centers, ideal for independent sightseeing, an evening ashore, and guided walks. There are shore excursions in most ports, and although the ports vary from year to year, the following are regular calls along the Rhine and Moselle cruise.

The ship sails up the incredibly beautiful **Moselle** through a half dozen locks in October. The vineyards, clinging to the parallel slopes, are turning from green to shades of golden yellow and completely envelop the small towns stretching one or two houses deep along the river. **Cochem** is a compact picture-postcard town, easy to explore on foot; be sure to visit the fairytale nineteenth-century hilltop castle. Farther upriver, a guide took us through the narrow medieval streets of the half-timbered town of **Bernkastel-Kues** and to a wine tasting just across the river. Downstream at **Koblenz,** a commanding fortress and castle overlooks the junction of the Moselle flowing into the Rhine.

The **Rhine** is the world's busiest commercial waterway. Navigation is tricky in the fast-flowing and twisting waters, and the legendary dangerous reputation of the **Lorelei Rock** becomes abundantly clear as we pass. Rebuilt and ruined castles dot the hilltops, shoreline, and midstream islands, where a few once served as tollhouses.

The pretty town of **Rudesheim** has become very touristy, but the city of **Mainz** possesses a life of its own, with a massive 950-year-old Romanesque cathedral, a Gothic church with Marc Chagall stained-glass windows, and a fine museum devoted to Gutenberg and the history of printing. Farther upriver, **Worms** offers another substantial Romanesque cathedral with Gothic additions and a baroque high altar. But **Speyer** may be the favorite stop, a handsome, walkable city with tiny lanes, a massive city gate, and the largest Romanesque cathedral in the world. On the last night the riverboat passed through many locks en route to **Strasbourg** and disembarkation. For a first German cruise, the Rhone and Moselle itinerary is an excellent choice, and the bilingual shipboard operation makes the minority of Americans feel very comfortable.

Peter Deilmann's
Prussian Princess

Address/Phone: Peter Deilmann–EuropAmerica Cruises, 1800 Diagonal Road, Suite 170, Alexandria, VA 22314; (703) 549–1741 or (800) 348–8287; fax: (703) 549–7924; www.deilmann-cruises.com

The Ship: *Prussian Princess,* built in 1991, has a length of 363 feet and a shallow draft.

Passengers: 142; age range fifty-five and up; many German, with a growing number of Americans

Dress: Informal, with jacket and tie on some evenings

Officers/Crew: German

Cabins: 71; average size, all outside with windows; A-Deck rooms with French-door-style windows that open

Fares: $$$

What's included: Cruise and port charges

What's not included: Airfare, excursion, tips, drinks

Highlights: Views of castles, cathedrals, villages, and vineyards; easy access on foot from dock to towns for independent touring; a rich German cultural experience

Other itineraries: In addition to the above Rhine and Moselle cruise, Peter Deilmann's nine riverboats, taking from 58 to 200 passengers, make seven- to fourteen-day cruises of the Rhine, Moselle, Main, Elbe, Danube, Po, and Rhone and the Belgian and Dutch waterways.

KD RIVER CRUISES' *VIKING HEINE*
Danube River Cruising

KD River Cruises got its start early in the steamboat era in 1827, first operating along the Rhine, then expanding to the Elbe, Moselle, Main, Danube, Rhone, and the Seine with eleven riverboats, thirty-six cruise itineraries, and 400 annual departures.

The 104-passenger *Viking Heine* (the former *Heinrich Heine*) is a sleek three-decker with a telescopic wheelhouse and hinged masts to slip under low bridges. On the Upper Deck, boarding level, the forward observation lounge affords terrific views of the river and has a bar, music for dancing, morning and afternoon coffee and cakes, and late-evening snacks. A small reading room is sited next to the reception hall.

The Main Deck houses the indoor swimming pool, sauna, small shop, and the no-smoking restaurant that takes passengers at one sitting at assigned tables. Breakfast is buffet, and lunch, the main meal, runs to five courses, with entrees such as pork ragout, turkey breast, and grilled salmon. The buffet offers salads (for the Americans), cheese and biscuits, and desserts. On a fine day a Sun Deck lunch buffet features German white sausage and potato strudel with sauerkraut. A canopy provides shade, and the fore and aft sections are open.

The fifty-two cabins (including one suite) all have large picture windows, twin beds with one that converts to a sofa and a second that folds away, radio, TV, telephone, minibar, safe, hair dryer, and one's own temperature control. Bathrooms have showers.

The Danube River, one of Europe's great new cruising waterways, is navigable from Germany to the Black Sea and forms the border or passes through eight countries. KD River Cruises operates the **Viking Heine** *on a seven-day itinerary between Budapest, Hungary, and Nuremberg, Germany, including locks along a portion of the Main-Danube Canal, calling at picturesque towns and offering scenic views of castles, cathedrals, and vineyards. KD River Cruises will become* Viking River Cruises *by the end of 2002.*

The Itinerary

For this seven-day itinerary embarking from **Budapest,** the cruise manager will advise passengers, when it's recommended, to take an organized tour and, when it's convenient, to take independent walks. While cruising in daylight, English and German commentary picks out the castles, bridges, monuments, and natural sights; most nights are spent tied up.

The call at **Vienna** allows an afternoon, overnight, and morning to visit the tree-lined Ringstrasse, St. Stephen's Cathedral, and eighteenth-century French-style Schönbrunn Palace, at one time the summer home of the Austrian monarchs, set in a large park with shaped trees and flower beds. From Krems to Melk the boat passes through the narrow and steep **Wachau Valley,** with woods clinging to the slopes on the left and vineyards on the sunny right side. Among the castles and picturesque villages, **Durnstein,** one of the latter, offers a walking tour and wine tasting, and **Melk** is marked by a yellow baroque abbey sitting high on a rock. **Linz,** an industrial city, has a fine old center and main square within walking distance of the landing.

Crossing into **Bavaria, Passau** is located at the junction of three rivers. Here you can take a walking tour and visit Feste Oberhaus, a castle atop a steep hill. **Regensburg**'s city center contains thirteenth- and fourteenth-century houses, a fourteenth-century city hall, and baroque and Gothic churches; Walhalla, the German Hall of Fame built in the nineteenth-century, honors German heroes. Near the end of the upstream cruise, the *Viking Heine* enters the 106-mile **Main-Danube Canal** and the first few of sixteen locks, which raise the riverboat 30 to 50 feet each time. Completed in 1992, the canal connects the Danube's 1,498 navigable miles to the Main River and the Rhine. The cruise ends with a bus transfer to **Nuremberg.**

KD River Cruises' *Viking Heine*

Address/Phone: KD River Cruises of Europe, 2500 Westchester Avenue, Purchase, NY 10577; (914) 696–3600 or (800) 346–6525; fax: (914) 696–0833; www.rivercruises.com

The Ship: *Viking Heine,* built in 1990, has a length of 350 feet and a shallow draft.

Passengers: 104; age range fifty-five and up with about half Germans and half Americans plus some other nationalities

Dress: Jacket and tie for two evenings, otherwise casual

Officers/Crew: Dutch captain and deck crew; Austrian, German, and Swiss hotel staff

Cabins: 51; all similar, outside with big windows, plus one suite

Fare: $$$

What's included: Cruise fare, port charges

What's not included: Airfare, shore excursions, drinks, tips

Highlights: Scenic Danube River cruising and lots to see ashore in towns and cities

Other itineraries: In addition to this seven-night cruise along the Danube, which operates between April and October, KD has two other riverboats making Danube cruises, plus others in the eleven-vessel fleet, eight cruising the Elbe, Main, Moselle, Rhone, and Seine. Together with its new owners, Viking River Cruises, the fleet will number twenty-eight vessels, and cruises will include the rivers of Russia and Ukraine. (Viking River Cruises: 877–66–VIKING; www.vikingrivercruises.com)

ABERCROMBIE & KENT'S *L'ABERCROMBIE*
Barge Canal Cruising in France

The fleet that A & K charters was established by a Francophile Englishman in 1966 and now numbers twenty hotel and charter barges and riverboats. *L'Abercrombie* takes up to twenty-two passengers and a young French and English crew of eight. The barge has two decks, one with a forward plant-filled sun deck, a salon with bar, and a dining room. There are two twin cabins aft, and the rest of the accommodations are on the deck below.

A dinner bell summons passengers at 8:00 P.M. from the foredeck and lounge bar to the adjoining oak-paneled dining room, where one chooses places at four candlelit tables. Both lunch and dinner begin with brief descriptions of the white and red wines and the cheese course. On the first evening on my cruise, the appetizer was whiting in a phyllo pastry with sorrel sauce, followed by grilled lamb with thyme, cheese, and a peach tart. On another occasion we started with a mild gazpacho and continued with tender pork cutlets, ending with a rich chocolate mousse. Lunch is a lighter meal that might include sausage in puff pastry, cold roast beef or pasta, and a variety of salads. Breakfast consists of fresh juices, cereals, bread, croissants, and pastries fetched by the deckhand, who, before you rise, peddles off to the nearest village bakery.

Air-conditioned accommodations are five twin and four double-bed cabins on the lower deck, with opening portholes, and two windowed twins on the upper deck. There's adequate floor space for two to move about, reasonable drawer and closet stowage; and a tiny bathroom with shower. Insulation from outside noise is excellent.

The Itinerary
The itinerary described here is an example of what this type of cruising is like, and some routes, such as this one, change from year to year. In 2001 the similar, twenty-four passenger *Mirabelle* follows much of this route. Ten minutes out of **Paris,** the rakish high-speed train (TGV) hits 168 miles per hour, streaking southeast toward **Burgundy.** Two hours later, the pace drops to the speed of a slow walk aboard a 128-foot hotel barge negotiating the twisting **Canal du Centre,** completed at the end of the eighteenth century. Embarkation for this cruise takes place from the canal towpath that curves above the village of **Santenay,** whose surrounding vineyards supplied us with one of two wines served at the first dinner.

Each night *L'Abercrombie* or *Mirabelle* ties up. Canal barging allows for more flexible independent ac-

Canal and river barging has a romantic aura to it, and there's no better place to partake of the charms, the food, the wine, and the hardly-ever-changing countryside than in the Burgundy Region of France. L'Abercrombie's six-night itinerary is just one of many outstanding choices offered by Abercrombie & Kent along Europe's waterways.

tivities than river cruising does, as one simply steps off the main deck when it is flush with the top of the lock wall. With forty-six locks during the six-day voyage, it is easy to be spontaneous and go biking or walking along the towpath or lark off into the countryside and rejoin the barge later, also allowing evening and before-breakfast strolls. Some locks are automated, and the pilot tugs at a cable to activate the gates and fill or empty the chambers, whereas others are overseen by a lock tender and trusty dog, often living at the site in attractive garden settings. Until recent years the Canal du Centre handled a lot of coal traffic, locally manufactured tiles, and farm goods, but now it is all pleasure barges and boats.

Each day provides a morning or afternoon excursion by bus over country roads with views of Burgundy's rolling farmlands and fields populated by attractive, white Charolais cattle. One day you can visit **Chateau de Couches**, a formidable medieval stronghold purchased by the state after the French Revolution and now, once again, in private hands. After a tour the owner hosts a wine tasting in the castle cellar. On another day, there's a drive to **Autun**, with its Roman theater, temple of Janus, and handsome cathedral of Romanesque origin and later additions. The valley town

of **Cluny** provides a look at the ruins of what at one time was the largest church in Europe, founded by Benedictine monks in the tenth century.

Less culturally oriented outings visit a handmade-chocolate factory and a Saturday market, with stalls selling thirty kinds of olives, dozens of cheeses, live rabbits and poultry, and fruits and vegetables of the nearby countryside. Some passengers opt for hot-air ballooning, lifting off at dawn from an adjacent field and staying aloft for an hour and a half. On the last night the barge ties up at **Paray-le-Monial** within sight of a floodlighted, twelfth-century basilica and Renaissance-style city hall. Barging is a great way to sample the culinary, potable, historical, and scenic delights of La Belle France and the rivers of Europe.

Abercrombie & Kent's
L'Abercrombie

Address/Phone: Abercrombie & Kent International, 1520 Kensington Road, Oak Brook, IL 60523; (630) 954–2944 or (800) 323–7308, brochures only; (800) 757–5884; fax: (630) 954–3324; e-mail: info@ abercrombiekent.com; www.abercrombiekent.com

The Ship: *L'Abercrombie* was first built in 1982 as a commercial barge and has a gross tonnage of 250, a length of 128 feet, and a shallow draft.

Passengers: 22; all ages, mostly Americans; families welcome

Dress: Casual at all times

Officers/Crew: French and British

Cabins: 11; 4 doubles and 7 twins

Fare: $$$$

What's included: Cruise, port charges, excursions (except ballooning), drinks, and wines, TGV first class to/from Paris, transfers

What's not included: Airfare, tips

Highlights: Food, wines, and the lovely Burgundy countryside at a relaxing pace

Other itineraries: Besides this six-night cruise through Burgundy aboard the *L'Abercrombie* or *Mirabelle,* which operates from April into November, there are many other itineraries along the French waterways, the Danube and Po Rivers, and in Holland, Belgium, Ireland, and England, some with themes such as walking, wine, antiques, châteaux, gardens, golf, and tulip time.

PRINCESS CRUISES' *GOLDEN PRINCESS*
Western and Eastern Mediterranean Megaship Cruising

Princess, one of the world's largest cruise lines, is a major provider of European itineraries, and from late May to mid-October, the 109,000-ton *Golden Princess*, a floating resort destination, sails between the Western and Eastern Mediterranean.

The range of public rooms is staggering, yet the scale is more akin to a much smaller ship, with intimate bars such as the clubby Wheelhouse, and Players, a sports bar; the Explorers' Club, with an African and Egyptian theme for dancing; and Skywalkers, a spectacular multilevel observation lounge and nightclub suspended in a cylindrical pod 150 feet above the sea. For entertainment a two-story theater presents big-cast productions, a second lounge hosts comedians, magicians, and soloists, and the three-story atrium is home for a classical string quartet. Gamblers will be hard-pressed to find a larger gaming room at sea than the Atlantis Casino.

In the hands-on shipboard-activities department, there's a nine-hole miniature golf course and a golf simulator, or you can pick up a game of basketball, volleyball, and paddle tennis. Adults and kids will love such virtual-reality experiences as downhill skiing, hang gliding, and motorcycle riding in the Voyages of Discovery room. With almost two acres of open deck, there are four outdoor pools, nine hot tubs, and lots of spaces for relaxing in a deck chair. The spa, high up in its own separate locale, offers all sorts of treatments and has saunas, steam rooms, aerobics classes, and a gym. To prepare for the ports, films and lectures are offered, plus indoor art auctions, games galore, and fashion shows. Kids have a two-deck, indoor-outdoor Fun Zone with a splash pool, hot tub, games, and computers; teenagers have their own disco and deck space with lounge chairs.

The *Golden Princess*'s dining options are best known for variety rather than a gourmet standard. Three main dining rooms, reserved or open seating, are named for the Italian artists Bernini, Canaletto, and Donatello, and the attractively divided spaces give an intimate, if slightly closed in, feel. The Horizon Terrace is open twenty-four hours a day for buffet-style breakfast, lunch, and dinner and between-meal specialties. Reservations are taken for two extra-charge theme restaurants, the Italian Sabatini's Trattoria and the Southwestern Desert Rose. For hunger pangs between meals, the main pool deck has an adjacent hamburger and hot-dog grill and pizzeria, and for an extra charge, ice-cream sundaes and scoops.

For first-time cruisers to the Mediterranean who want everything in the way of shipboard diversions, the giant new 109,000-ton **Golden Princess** *may be the way to go. Summer cruises, hitting the high spots, embark in Barcelona or Istanbul and call at Monte Carlo for the French Riviera, Livorno for Florence and Pisa, Naples for Pompeii and Capri, Venice for romance, Athens for ancient sites, and Kusadasi for the Turkish Coast and Ephesus.*

Of the 1,300 cabins 712 have verandas, but with tiering, passengers above look down on those below. All have refrigerators and TVs with CNN and ESPN. One entire deck is composed exclusively of mini-suites—larger cabins with sitting areas, tub baths, and white-glove butler service to arrange appointments and shore excursions.

The Itinerary

The twelve-day itinerary is well designed, combining highlights of the ancient and modern Mediterranean world with overnight stays in Istanbul, Venice, and Barcelona, permitting full evenings ashore and two full days and four half days at sea to enjoy this ship.

Barcelona is a walkers' paradise for exploring the pedestrian promenade known as the Ramblas, the medieval streets in the Gothic Quarter, and the art nouveau buildings of native son Antonio Gaudi. The overnight stay allows a late evening ashore. Anchoring off **Monte Carlo,** best known for its elegant casino and the palace of **Monaco,** it's a stone's throw to the French Riviera resorts of **Nice, Cannes,** and **Villefranche** and the medieval hill town of **Eze.**

Down the coast in Italy, **Livorno** is the call for the Leaning Tower of Pisa and **Florence** for the Duomo, Ponte Vecchio, and the works of Michelangelo. Mount Vesuvius is clearly visible as the *Golden Princess* sails into the **Bay of Naples,** followed by a visit to **Pompeii.** Pass through the **Strait of Messina,** between Italy's big toe and Sicily; then sail up the Adriatic for an entry by sea into the lagoon at **Venice.** The city of romantic Hollywood films is best be seen on foot and by gondola and vaporetto plying the canals.

Another day at sea brings you around the Peloponese to **Piraeus,** the port for **Athens,** where you can see the Parthenon from the deck of the ship. A couple of hours later you are atop the Acropolis, then below exploring the Plaka, a rabbit warren of narrow streets leading to markets, shops, cafes, and restaurants. Threading through the Greek Islands, the ship comes to the Turkish coastal port of **Kusadasi,** where you have the day to wander the huge bazaar and to drive out to the Greco-Roman city of **Ephesus,** less than an hour away.

As the grand finale, **Istanbul,** one of the world's great harbor cities, should first be seen from the deck of a ship. Arriving via the **Dardenelles** and **Bosphorus,** spiky minarets pierce the skyline that straddles two continents—Europe and Asia. The most famous sights are the Blue Mosque, St. Sophia, Topkapi Palace and its Harem, and the Grand Bazaar and Spice Bazaars.

Princess Cruises'
Golden Princess

Address/Phone: Princess Cruises, 24305 Town Center Drive, Santa Clarita, CA 91355; (661) 753–0000 or (800) 744–6237; fax: (661) 259–3108; www.princesscruises.com

The Ship: *Golden Princess* was built in 2001, has a gross tonnage of 109,000, a length of 951 feet, and a draft of 26 feet.

Passengers: 2,600; age thirty to seventy, mostly Americans, some British

Dress: Suits or tuxedos for the formal nights, jackets for semiformal nights, and slacks and collared shirts for casual nights

Officers/Crew: British and Italian officers; international crew

Cabins: 1,300; 938 outside and 712 with private verandas

Fare: $$$

What's included: Cruise fare, port charges, airfare from East Coast

What's not included: Airfare add-ons from Midwest, West, Canada; excursions; drinks; tips

Highlights: Much to do aboard; alternative restaurants; great itinerary

Other itineraries: In addition to the above twelve-day Mediterranean cruise, operating between June and October, the *Golden Princess* sails on seven-day winter Caribbean cruises from Fort Lauderdale and undertakes transatlantic crossings between seasons. Add-on hotel and land packages are also worth investigating. Alaska is another major destination.

RENAISSANCE CRUISES' R CLASS
Western Mediterranean

Renaissance Cruises' new series of eight identical ships carries up to 684 in a relaxed atmosphere reminiscent of an English hotel, with a variety of lounges and bars attractively wood-paneled and furnished with rich fabrics. The prettiest room is the library, located high up on the ship, offering lots of books and comfy seating areas. The observation lounge is also a sports bar, and a duo plays for late-evening dancing.

There's a choice of four open-seating restaurants for dinner: the 348-seat Club Restaurant, a formal two-tier room with big-view windows on three sides, serving such entrees as crisply roasted raspberry duck and honey-baked tenderloin of pork; the paneled 90-seat Grill (reservations) for steaks, broiled lobster tails, and salmon; the similar-size Italian restaurant (reservations), offering nine entrees; and the Panorama Buffet, for a quick meal. At lunch besides hot entrees, pastas, and salads, a pizzeria and a barbecue, with specials such as barbecue ribs and chicken, are available.

Cabin categories A through D, which constitute 70 percent of the accommodations, have verandas; whereas the categories E, F, and G are outside, and just twenty-five category H cabins are inside. The bathrooms with showers are small. Most of the days are spent in port, so daytime activities are few. In the evenings at sea, however, the casino's blackjack, roulette tables, and slot machines are popular, and the after-dinner shows are lively song-and-dance medleys. For a more thorough ship review, see R Class in the Eastern Mediterranean.

The Itinerary

The cruise operates from Lisbon and Barcelona, and often includes a night in each city. If starting at Portugal's old-fashioned capital city, you will find that **Lisbon** spreads over hills above the Tagus River, and its residential streets are lined with colorful tiled facades. Great museums and waterfront monuments demonstrate Portugal's pioneering maritime feats of exploration, and St. George's Castle is best seen illuminated at night from Rossio Square. Sailing south, the ship stops at **Cadiz,** the attractive

Renaissance Cruises began its second, year-round, moderately priced itinerary in late 1998 along the coast of Spain, Portugal, and Morocco. This highly affordable ten-day cruise embarks in Lisbon and Barcelona.

port for **Seville,** with its great Gothic cathedral, where Christopher Columbus is buried, and whose Giralda Tower was once the minaret of the Great Mosque. The Moorish Alcazar Palace and quiet residential squares are other attractions.

Stopping in **Tangier,** Morocco, you'll get a taste of a city famous for its nightlife, great beach weather lasting into November, the Casbah, and its location just across the Strait from Gibraltar. Down the coast **Casablanca** may be best known for the Hollywood film, but since it wasn't shot here, head for **Rabat,** Morocco's capital and one of its imperial cities. The Casbah, entered through a decorative twelfth-century arch, is noted for its ancient quarter, the Mosque founded in 1050, and the fortifications overlooking the Bou Regreg River.

At **Gibraltar,** one of the last bastions of the British Empire, ride the cable car to the top of the Rock for a view to Africa, and watch out for the Barbary apes, adept pickpocket artists. From coastal **Malaga,** head inland to **Granada's Alhambra,** for the Royal Palace, the Harem, and the audience chamber for the Moorish kings, and the magnificent Arab-style Generalife Gardens, where the kings spent their summers. Up the coast **Almeria**'s Gothic-style cathedral looks like a fortress, because the city needed protection against Barbary pirates, but there are also layers of Carthaginian, Roman, and Arab history.

Sailing out to **Palma de Mallorca,** the principal city in the Balearic Islands, enjoy a delightful combination of a modern tourist center, a popular yachting harbor, and the rabbit warren of streets in the old town. The Gothic cathedral, a medieval masterpiece constructed between the thirteenth and sixteenth centuries, dominates the old city. A trip across the island is a must by coach or by the electric railway through the almond groves and over the mountains to **Port Soller,** a pretty seaside town, bedecked with blue jacaranda trees. **Mahon,** on the less touristy island of **Menorca,** offers good sand beaches, pure white villages, prehistoric ruins, and Christian-era churches dating from the fifth century onward.

The cruise ends at **Barcelona,** a lively walking city, with cafés and restaurants lining the medieval streets, a Gothic district, the Picasso Museum, and fine examples of Antonio Gaudi's own style of art nouveau architecture seen in churches, apartments, and office buildings. An R Class itinerary provides an excellent introduction to the ancient and modern-day Eastern Mediterranean at an affordable package price.

Renaissance Cruises' R Class

Address/Phone: Renaissance Cruises, 350 East Las Olas Boulevard, Suite 800, Fort Lauderdale, FL 33301; (954) 463–0982 or (800) 525–5350; fax: (954) 463–0985; www.renaissancecruises.com

The Ships: R Class ships were completed between 1998 and 2001. The ships have a gross tonnage of 30,200, a length of 593 feet, and a draft of 19.5 feet.

Passengers: 684; mostly Americans, age forty-five and up

Dress: Casual

Officers/Crew: European officers; European and international crew

Cabins: 342; mostly outside 232 with private verandas

Fare: $$

What's included: Cruise only

What's not included: Port charges, shore excursions, drinks, tips, meals on land

Other itineraries: In addition to the above ten-day R Class tour, which is offered year-round, R Class offers an Eastern Mediterranean itinerary between Athens and Istanbul. *R3* and *R4* operate ten-day cruises in French Polynesia from Tahiti.

STAR CLIPPERS' *STAR CLIPPER*
French and Italian Rivieras under Sail

Designed after the mid-nineteenth-century fast clipper ships, the pair are the brainchildren of Swedish yachting enthusiast Mikael Krafft. Completed in Ghent, Belgium, in 1991 and 1992 respectively, the *Star Flyer* and sistership *Star Clipper* are among the largest and tallest sailing ships ever built, with mainmasts topping 226 feet. In price and accommodations they fall somewhere between the Windjammer Barefoot experience and the upscale four Windstar Cruise vessels, skewed to Windstar. As a sailing experience, they are not unlike the historic, former-private yacht *Sea Cloud*.

The *Star Clipper* is generally under sail from late evening to early or mid-morning the next day. Passengers are invited to help with the lines, and some do, while most are content to sit back and look on. The 1,370-horsepower Caterpillar diesel engine kicks in when the wind dies down and is used for maneuvering in tight harbors. The social center is a sheltered deck amidships under a canvas awning, with a sit-up bar and stools around tables. The forward end opens into a lounge, where a grand piano, played by the resident pianist, is tucked under circular skylights cut into the bottom of the suspended swimming pool. Aft of the bar the Edwardian-style library has a clubby atmosphere, with a fireplace and a wall of mahogany-fronted bookcases containing a good selection of popular fiction, travel, and coffee-table books. The furniture, arranged around card tables and in conversational groupings, includes comfy chairs and sofas for a delightful retreat on a damp day.

The open sitting for all meals encourages mixing among the passengers and officers. Breakfast and lunch are served buffet style, with a generous selection of hot and cold items. Dinner, with fish, meat and vegetarian entrees, is served by waiters. The food is of good quality and well prepared, and, at dinner, passengers dress casually but not sloppily.

The moderately sized cabins, some shaped by the ship's hull, have twin beds or a queen and touches that include wood trim, electric lamps mounted in gimbals, and decorative brass counter railings to prevent items from sliding onto the floor. But the *Star Clipper* hardly lists at all; water tanks see to that. Cabins have phones and televisions that screen films, bathrooms are tiny, and there is no room service.

In good weather this cruise is a shared, outdoor experience, with conversation, navigation, and sail handling providing the entertainment. At sea most passengers congregate around the wheelhouse and the two sundeck swimming pools.

Carrying 36,000 square feet of sails from four tall masts and a bowsprit, the barkentine-rigged **Star Clipper** *and* **Star Flyer** *are close equivalents to a true sailing experience, accomplished in considerable comfort and at an affordable price. The French and Italian Rivieras and Mediterranean islands provide a superb cruising playground from May through September, generally undertaken by the* **Star Clipper**. *In summer 2000 the five-masted, square-rigged* **Royal Clipper** *joined the fleet.*

The Itinerary

The helmsman sets a course for the island of **Corsica**, and astern, the twinkling glow of the Italian coast gradually fades into the night. After a day at sea under sail, on the second morning, the steep sandstone cliffs flank the approach to the medieval town of **Bonifacio**, and the *Star Clipper* berths beneath the old town's fortifications. Climb the cliff, and you'll have a splendid view of the ship below.

Then it's a good long sail to the **French Riviera** and a visit to **Monte Carlo**, in the principality of **Monaco**, the domain of the rich and famous with its opulent casino and one of Europe's finest yachting centers. Just east along the coast on the **Italian Riviera, Portofino** is a favorite stop, a miniature seaside village wedged into a narrow valley, overlooked by handsome Italianate villas and the stylish Hotel Splendido. Most passengers go no further than the town's main square for a long leisurely lunch and a bit of shopping.

The port of **Livorno** gives access by bus to the Renaissance city of **Florence** for the Uffizi, a former palace of the Medicis and housing the works of Botticelli, Michelangelo, Titian, and Giotto, the statue of Michelangelo's *David*, the Duomo, and Santa Croce, where Galileo and Michelangelo are buried.

Approaching the island of **Elba**, the captain demonstrates his considerable skill reversing into the tiny basin at **Portoferraio**. From the castle wall, you look down onto the ship, anchored in an idyllic setting and towering over the quayside of red-tiled and pastel-covered houses. Napoleon lived in exile here for about ten months before escaping to France, and his two houses are worth visiting. The ship then sets sails for one last overnight cruise back to **Civitavecchia**.

The *Star Clipper* is a great leveler. There were couples aboard who could buy and sell the ship and others who were working people, and it wasn't easy to tell one from the other. The ships cater to passengers who have done the big ships and who enjoy a working sailing ship, visiting small ports, the informality, and making friends in a relaxed setting.

Star Clippers' *Star Clipper*

Address/Phone: Star Clippers, 4101 Salzebo Street, Coral Gables, FL 33146; (305) 442–0550; reservations: (800) 442–0551; brochures: (800) 442–0550; fax: (305) 442–1611; www.starclippers.com

The Ship: *Star Clipper* was built in 1992, has a gross tonnage of 2,298, a length of 360 feet, and a draft of 18.5 feet.

Passengers: 168; all ages, including some Europeans; English the lingua franca

Dress: Casual at all times

Officers/Crew: European officers; international crew

Cabins: 84; 78 outside and most relatively compact; no verandas

Fare: $$

What's included: Usually cruise only, although cruise-tour rates will include airfare, hotels, some meals, some sightseeing, and transfers

What's not included: For cruise only, airfare, port charges, tips, drinks

Highlights: A terrific outdoor sailing experience; charming ports; relaxed atmosphere

Other itineraries: Besides this seven-night Western Mediterranean cruise, which operates between May and October, the *Star Clipper* offers an alternative Mediterranean cruise, spring and fall transatlantic positioning voyages, and two winter Caribbean itineraries. Sistership *Star Flyer* operates in the Greek islands and along the Turkish coast from May to October, then travels via the Suez Canal to cruise Malaysia and Thailand, returning through the Indian Ocean in April. The 226-passenger *Royal Clipper* also operates in the Western Mediterranean and the Caribbean and undertakes spring and fall transatlantic crossings.

CUNARD LINE'S *CARONIA*
Mediterranean Mosaic

For the first twenty-six years, the *Vistafjord* was well known to older, well-heeled Americans, Germans, and British as a sophisticated ocean liner designed for long sea voyages. Late in 1999 it received a $5 million refit, a name change to *Caronia*, British registry, and a charcoal-gray Cunard hull.

The officers are British and the staff remains mostly European, providing a high level of service that matches the elegant public rooms. The main lounge, with its high ceiling, is an old-fashioned ballroom, ideal for dancing to an orchestra and then enjoying cabaret acts. Forward, the Garden Lounge is the tiered, semi-circular setting for afternoon tea and after-dinner concerts. The former North Cape Bar is now the British-style White Star Bar. Amidships, a proper cinema screens first-run films and hosts special-interest lectures, and Piccadilly nightclub doubles as a daytime reading room, with views over the Veranda Deck pool. Additional rooms are a mahogany-paneled library, a bookshop, and a casino.

The elegant dining room serves some of the best food afloat at one sitting, and the atmosphere is suitably dressy. For an intimate dinner venue, Tivoli, taking reservations for its forty seats, offers an Italian dinner menu. Breakfast and lunch buffets are set up in the cafe and by the pool. A second pool lies deep within the hull in a complex that includes a gym, a sauna, and a massage facility.

Nearly all cabins are outsides and designed for long voyages, with spacious floor plans and good closet and drawer space. All have light wood trim, TVs with VCRs, two-channel radios, phones, safes, minibars, robes, and daily bowls of fresh fruit. Some top-category cabins have verandas, and passengers traveling alone can choose from seventy-three dedicated singles, some outside with tub baths.

The Itinerary

This fifteen-day cruise offers a good balance between eight ports of call, including two days at Venice, and five sea days to enjoy this classic ship. The *Caronia* embarks at **Civitavecchia,** the port for **Rome,** sails south through the **Strait of Messina** between Italy's toe and Sicily, and then sails into the Adriatic to call at the walled city of **Dubrovnik** in **Croatia.** The medieval city is again back on some cruise itineraries, showing off its splendid fifteenth-century palace and seventeenth-century cathedral.

Sailing into **Venice**'s lagoon and past San Marco Square, the *Caronia* remains overnight to allow passengers to visit at leisure one the world's most romantic cities. Explore the narrow lanes and expect to get lost but never for long, buy a day pass and ride the vaporettis along the Grand Canal and out to the Lido, and dine in an outdoor cafe.

The next call is **Katakolon,** the port for **Olympia,** the birthplace of the Olympic Games. Then the ship

The concept of cruising gave birth when nineteenth-century British liners set out on summertime voyages across the North Sea to the Norwegian fjords and south to the Mediterranean. Maintaining that century-old tradition, Cunard's stylish **Caronia** *makes this classic cruise an annual staple.*

sails around the bottom of the **Peloponnesus** to **Piraeus,** the port for **Athens.** Lark out on your own by taking the electric railway up to the city for a climb through the **Agora** to the **Parthenon.** From the **Acropolis,** look down on the **Plaka,** the old section of Athens, where you might go for lunch. Sail east to **Kusadasi** on the Turkish coast. From here take a guided tour of **Ephesus,** once the most important port city in Asia Minor; visit the **House of the Virgin Mary** and browse the street vendors for jewelry, leather, and copper goods back near the ship.

Docking at the island of **Rhodes,** you can again explore on your own the Greek, Roman, Crusader, Turkish, and Italian layers of this marvelous walled city or take a tour to the ancient town of **Lindos** perched high above the sea.

Returning westward, you'll call at **Catania,** located at the foot of **Mount Etna,** a still-active volcano. The seaside city has an eleventh-century Norman cathedral and Roman ruins. Take a tour to the hill town of **Taormina** and have lunch at one of the many outdoor restaurants one level down from the main pedestrian street. During the call at Naples, a hectic cosmopolitan port city set in the shadow of **Mount Vesuvius,** most people leave town for the ruins at **Pompeii,** or take a fast boat to the **Isle of Capri** for the day. Be forewarned, the island's main town is often jammed with tourists, so seek out the quieter residential lanes. Then it's but a short sail back to Civitavecchia and a ninety-minute transfer to Rome.

Cunard Line's *Caronia*

Address/Phone: Cunard Line, 6100 Blue Lagoon Drive, Suite 400, Miami, FL 33126; (305) 563–3000 or (800) 7–CUNARD; fax: (305) 463–3010; www.cunardline.com

The Ship: *Caronia* was completed in 1973 as the *Vistafjord* and has a gross tonnage of 24,492, a length of 627 feet, and a draft of 27 feet.

Passengers: 679, single and double occupancy; ages forty-five and up, Americans, British, Germans, and other Europeans

Dress: Formal, informal, and casual nights

Officers/Crew: British officers; European and Filipino crew

Cabins: 376; 324 outside, 73 singles, and 25 with verandas

Fare: $$$$

What's included: Cruise fare and port charges

What's not included: Airfare, shore excursions, drinks, tips

Highlights: A traditional ocean liner with excellent food and service; Mediterranean ports

Other itineraries: In addition to this fifteen-day Mediterranean cruise, which operates in May, June, July, and August, the *Caronia* also makes cruises to the Black Sea, across the Atlantic, and to South America.

ORIENT LINES' *CROWN ODYSSEY*
The Greek Isles and Italy: From Istanbul to Rome

Orient Lines developed a loyal following with its first ship, the *Marco Polo*, for its unique itineraries, good food and service, and comfortable ambience at a reasonable rate. This success led the company to purchase the *Crown Odyssey*, built in 1988 as Royal Cruise Line's globetrotting flagship. The ship's large cabins, extensive deck space, and classical touches make it a perfect choice for longer sea voyages. Passengers who sail with Orient Lines appreciate the included pre- and post-cruise hotel packages.

Throughout the ship, there is a tremendous feeling of spaciousness and inherent, relaxed comfort. At the top of the ship is the fabulous Top of the Crown, a 360-degree observation lounge with floor-to-ceiling windows.

Most of the ship's public rooms are concentrated on one deck, starting with the Stardust Lounge forward. This one-story show lounge offers fairly good sight lines, but don't expect much high-energy entertainment—most of the passengers wouldn't want such a thing anyway. Farther aft is the ship's true social center, the Monte Carlo Piano Bar. Unfortunately, a glass wall affords the only separation from the casino, and a light ringing from the slot machines can filter in occasionally. However, the room remains surprisingly popular, perhaps due in part to its location next to the two-story atrium.

At the after end is the Yacht Club, offering three casual meals a day. The after end of the room is sectioned off on certain nights to form the ship's alternative restaurant, featuring popular Oriental-themed dinners. The room looks aft through a wall of glass onto the stern and pool area, and a sheltered sitting area outside is a perfect place to start the day.

One deck above is a small bar, again backed by a glass wall, leading to a protected terrace. There is also a small nook on the port side called the Palm Court, filled with cane furniture and lush, green plants. A very comfortable library with both British and American papers, a small Internet cafe, and a proper 210-seat movie theater round out the public spaces.

The ship also offers a wonderful amount of open deck space, including a wide wraparound promenade deck. A beautifully designed section of tiered decks is used for a variety of activities, from reading to shuffleboard. Finally, the ship offers a rarity these days—an attractive and popular indoor pool coupled with the gym and spa.

Cabins are all spacious and cheerful, and the same standard size, except for the suites, and the price differentials only get you a larger window or a bathtub. A variety of bay window suites are also very attractive,

Sailing around the world to a variety of destinations, the comfortable **Crown Odyssey** *offers old-fashioned cruising combined with a strong focus on the destination. An international passenger list adds to a very friendly atmosphere, where passengers are content to enjoy the traditional elements of cruising and dispense with the resort-at-sea extras. On this cruise, you'll enjoy hotel stays in Istanbul and Rome while seeing both the lesser known and the more famous Mediterranean ports.*

with a nice enclosed sitting area framed by a wall of glass. There are sixteen suites with exceptionally roomy balconies.

The ship's main dining room has two wings extending forward, making the large room seem smaller. Extensive use of mirrors and hard surfaces creates more noise than one would like, nonetheless, the food is generally good to very good and is served by efficient and friendly waiters. Every night, the Yacht Club is also open for casual dining, and on some nights more informal dinner is served on the open deck.

The Itinerary

All Orient Lines cruises begin and end with hotel packages, and this cruise starts with two days in **Istanbul.** An included tour will take you to the Blue Mosque and the Grand Bazaar. On your own, visit Topkapi Palace, former home of the Ottoman emperors, or wander along the waterfront. Then board the *Crown Odyssey* and sail through the **Sea of Marmara** to **Kusadasi,** Turkey, for an excursion to the ruins of **Ephesus,** the grandest Greco-Roman complex in Asia Minor.

The next morning you anchor off **Delos,** the uninhabited island where Apollo was said to be born. In the afternoon, a quick sail takes you to charming **Mykonos,** where you can wander the narrow streets designed to fool invaders. A late night departure allows you to watch the sunset over the harbor.

Imagine waking up the next morning inside a huge volcanic caldera, with magnificent cliffs rising straight from the ocean. This is **Santorini,** with beautiful villages perched precariously on the edge of the cliff. Excursions are offered to the ruins of **Akrotiri** and to a local winery.

Refreshed, you will spend the morning in the small island nation of **Malta.** The ship docks in downtown **Valletta,** a fascinating city known for its unique architecture and charm. The island clearly retains its own flavor, isolated in the middle of the sea.

The next day brings Italy's fabled **Amalfi Coast,** and the *Crown Odyssey* anchors off exclusive **Sorrento,** where **Mount Vesuvius** looms in the distance. You can also take excursions by bus to **Pompeii** or by boat to **Capri,** or easily travel on your own by train, for a few dollars, to cosmopolitan **Naples.**

Your disembarkation port will be **Civitavecchia,** to begin your two-day excursion in **Rome.** After the quick transfer to your hotel, an included tour that afternoon takes you to the Coliseum and St. Peter's Cathedral.

Orient Lines' *Crown Odyssey*

Address/Phone: 1510 S.E. 17th St., Suite 400, Fort Lauderdale, FL 33316; (954) 527–6660 or (800) 333–7300; fax: (954) 527–6657; e-mail: info@ orientlines.com; www.orientlines.com

The Ship: *Crown Odyssey* was built in 1988 for Royal Cruise Line. It has a gross tonnage of 34,250, a length of 614 feet, and a draft of 24 feet.

Passengers: 1,052, with up to half of the passengers from abroad, although almost all will be English speaking

Dress: In the Mediterranean, the ship is more casual, with a jacket and tie needed only twice. The rest of the year, the ship is decidedly more formal.

Officers/Crew: International officers; Filipino crew

Cabins: 526, of which 412 are outside and 16 have verandas

Fare: $$$

What's included: Airfare, pre- and post-cruise hotel package with tours, transfers

What's not included: Port charges, tips, shore excursions

Highlights: A longer, more in-depth look at some Mediterranean highlights and lesser-known ports, with included hotel stays on a very comfortable, happy ship with similarly interested passengers

Other itineraries: In addition to this twelve-day cruise tour in the Mediterranean that operates in the summer, the *Crown Odyssey* sails through Suez to the Indian Ocean, Southeast Asia, and Australasia.

RENAISSANCE CRUISES' R CLASS

Eastern Mediterranean: Year-Round

Renaissance Cruises, at one time known for its far-flung fleet of eight boutique, 114-berth passenger ships, has now launched a new series of eight, in service or on order, carrying up to 684 passengers. *R1*, the first to enter service in mid-1998, was joined later in the year by *R2* for a year-round Western Mediterranean/Iberian route. The eight identical ships offer a sophisticated English hotel-style atmosphere, drawing mostly American passengers age fifty and up.

The attractive variety of lounges and bars are handsomely wood-paneled (a medium to dark veneer), with furniture fabrics in reds and blues with light accents, oriental-style carpets, pretty wall lamps, and marble mantel fireplaces. The library instantly became my favorite room, located high up and offering a generous open-shelf selection of fiction, nonfiction, travel guides, and reference books. Three comfy seating areas include one with a dome ceiling painted to resemble a greenhouse and depicting birds in flight. Two IBM computers are tucked away in a quiet corner. The partitioned observation lounge-cum-sports bar provides sweeping views ahead, a dozen TV screens, and a duo for late-evening dancing.

With a choice of four open-seating restaurants at dinner, unusual for a ship of this size, dining is a sheer delight. Apollo, the well-reputed caterer that also serves Celebrity Cruises, provides a mostly European service staff, well trained and attentive.

The largest dining venue is the 348-seat Club Restaurant, a formal two-tier room with tables and banquettes accommodating two to eight, big-view windows on three sides, and a pianist playing adjacent to a dance floor. I enjoyed such entrees as crisply roasted raspberry duck and honey-baked tenderloin of pork and, for dessert, cherry strudel with cinnamon sauce. The handsome wood-paneled Grill (seating ninety by reservation) provides such entrees as moist Norwegian salmon one night and tender broiled lobster tails the other. Next door, the similar-size, pale yellow and gold Italian restaurant offers nine entrees. Two favorites are fusilli with grilled chicken, broccoli, roasted pine nuts, sundried tomatoes, and Montrachet cheese; and sage veal medallions, with prosciutto and grilled vegetable polenta with a Marsala wine sauce, followed by a dessert of lemon-mascarpone-brûleé tart with pecan flavor.

The Panorama Buffet, a sensible choice for a quick meal when returning after a long tour, comes more alive during the day with a cheerful, indoor, potted-palm atmosphere and tables outdoors overlooking the stern and under cover near the lido pool. At lunch besides hot entrees, pastas, and salads, a pizzeria and a barbecue, with hamburgers, hot dogs, and specials such as barbecue ribs and chicken, are available.

Cabin categories A through D, nearly 70 percent of the accommodations, have private verandas, whereas categories E, F, and G have ocean views, and just

Renaissance Cruises has charted new directions by operating year-round, moderately priced, destination-oriented itineraries with ships that offer multiple dining options and a casual country-club onboard atmosphere. This ten-day cruise leaves Istanbul for ports in Turkey, Greece, and Cyprus.

twenty-five in category H cabins are inside without windows or portholes. A typical cheerfully decorated veranda cabin has a king-size bed, a two-seat sofa adjacent to the sliding glass door, and a TV that provides nine daily films plus CNN, CNBC, and Euronews broadcasts. The bathrooms with showers are small. The private veranda, furnished with two white plastic chairs and a small table, is ideal for breakfast and serves as a quiet retreat at the end of a long day.

Daytime activities at sea are routine trivia quizzes, jackpot bingo, shuffleboard, and golf chipping tournaments, a fashion show, a jewelry seminar, and the casino's blackjack and roulette tables and slot machines. The after-dinner shows are typical popular song-and-dance medleys and fast-paced acts by a pair of clever puppeteers working dozens of their own homemade puppets.

The Itinerary

The ten-day cruise embarks in **Istanbul** and includes two sea days, relaxing respites between intervening daily ports. November is the best month for avoiding crowds yet having a chance at decent weather.

During the call at **Kusadasi,** one all-day tour visits the great Roman city of **Ephesus,** which once boasted a population of 300,000. See the fourth-century B.C. temples of Apollo at **Didyma** and Athena at **Priene,** and enjoy an excellent lunch of Turkish appetizers and grilled fish. Following an overnight sail to **Rhodes,** one can tour the medieval and Crusader city on foot and enjoy cafe life down by the old harbor. During the call at **Limassol** on **Cyprus,** see the fine mosaic-tile floors at **Paphos,** quaint villages in the **Troodos Mountains,** or the Greek side of the divided city (with Turkey) of **Nicosia.** Here on excellent archaeological museum displays a votive collection of 2,000 terra-cotta figures.

Sailing eastward to **Israel,** the *R1* docks at **Haifa** for **Nazareth** and **Galilee,** and at **Ashdod** for the Christian sites in **Bethlehem** and **Jerusalem** and the latter's Jewish and Arab sections. On the second day, choose between **Masada** and the **Dead Sea,** including a salty swim, or modern, secular **Tel Aviv** and the partly restored ancient port of **Jaffa.** Calls at Israeli ports were suspended at the time of writing, and Antalya in southern Turkey was substituted.

After a day at sea, **Heraklion** on the island of Crete is but a few miles from **Knossos,** the palace of King Minos and best known as the labyrinth because of the many rooms and complex passages. The cruise ends at **Piraeus,** a port for **Athens,** providing an excellent finale to the ancient and modern-day Eastern Mediterranean at an affordable price.

Renaissance Cruises' R Class

Address/Phone: Renaissance Cruises, 350 Las Olas Boulevard, Suite 800, Fort Lauderdale, FL 33301; (954) 463–0982 or (800) 525–5350; fax: (954) 463–0985; www.renaissancecruises.com

The Ships: R Class ships were completed between 1998 and 2001. The ships have a gross tonnage of 30,200, a length of 593 feet, and a draft of 19.5 feet.

Passengers: 684; mostly Americans who tend to be forty-five and up

Dress: Casual

Officers/Crew: European officers; European and international crew

Cabins: 342; mostly outside, 232 with private verandas

Fare: $$

What's included: Cruise only

What's not included: Port charges, shore excursions, drinks, tips

Other itineraries: In addition to the above ten-day R Class Eastern Mediterranean cruise, which is offered year-round, there are shorter itineraries in this region, and R Class offers a ten-day itinerary between Lisbon and Barcelona. *R3* and *R4* operate in French Polynesia on ten-day cruises from Tahiti.

ROYAL OLYMPIA'S *OLYMPIA VOYAGER*
Three Continents in One Week

The *Olympia Voyager* is a true thoroughbred and is a completely new start for Royal Olympia, which otherwise operates a fleet of older liners. Owned by a Greek company and staffed with mostly Greek crew, this is one of the few ships left that has a national identity. Along with her sistership, the *Olympia Explorer,* the *Olympia Voyager* catapults Royal Olympia to an up-and-coming line with two spectacular new ships.

While most choose the cruise solely for its unique itinerary, the ship successfully blends modern technology with fresh but classically influenced interiors, and her relatively small size (840 passengers) is perfect for those who don't need—or want—the resort-at-sea atmosphere found on larger ships. All in all, the ship offers a culturally rich experience that is crowned by a very good onboard lecture program.

Executed by the same designers who did the Celebrity's ships, the interiors seem upscale but not stuffy. There is extensive use of a cherry wood paneling and illuminated glass throughout. For such a small ship, there is a surprisingly spacious feel with a good variety of spaces. Starting at the top, the Anemnos disco doubles as an observation lounge, offering 270-degree views. With the large dance floor crowned by a silver dome, the room feels a bit too much like the nightclub even when at sea. Nonetheless, it still works

well, even for afternoon tea, and it's a wonderful place to sit on the last day while cruising between the Greek islands en route to Mykonos.

The ship's social hub is the Piano Bar, done in a healthy flesh color on one side of the room and a solid blue on the other. The Alexander the Great Lounge is a simple one-story showroom used for lectures and evening entertainment, and directly aft is the twenty-person Voyager Room, a plush smoking room with large, soft couches. There is also a library, small casino, and spa and gym area. The ship's only drawback is a lack of good deck space; promenade space is virtually nonexistent.

The Dining Room, serving good to average food (with Greek night offering some excellent national specialties), is situated aft and cleverly divided into three areas, allowing an intimate feeling no matter where you are seated. With blue and rust colored chairs set against a rich blue carpet, this is a very inviting room. The buffet, one deck above, is one of the more attractive lido areas afloat and serves a good selection for breakfast and lunch. A pizza parlor by the swimming pool offers excellent varieties of pies from early afternoon to well into the evening.

Standard cabins are only 140 square feet, but well laid out with TVs, safes, and minibars. There are only twelve veranda cabins on board, although the bal-

Feeling more like a speedboat than a cruise ship, the sleek and stylish **Olympia Voyager** *zips around the Mediterranean in the best one-week sampler itinerary available. Because of her remarkable speed (30 knots), the ship visits three continents in one week, and highlights include stops in Egypt, Israel (subject to confirmation), and Turkey.*

conies are unusually deep and can easily accommodate a cocktail party. Of particular note are the ship's sixteen bay window suites, which have floor-to-ceiling windowed alcoves projecting out from the hull of the ship. Cabins all the way aft on Decks 2 and 3 can experience some vibration and noise at top speed.

While you shouldn't expect luxury service, it is usually cheerful and efficient. Zipping around the corners of the Mediterranean at 28 to 30 knots is exciting. Passengers who come for a port-intensive introduction to the Mediterranean—and who want some insight into the area they are traveling—will be very satisfied with this new ship.

The Itinerary

The itinerary is really the ship's selling point, covering a large variety of ports with several different cultures in only a week. The ship sails from **Piraeus,** Greece, at 9:00 P.M., allowing passengers the opportunity to visit the **Parthenon** in **Athens.** The next morning passengers awake to the spectacular sight of **Santorini,** with its villages perched on the top of a mighty precipice.

Leaving Santorini in the afternoon, the ship puts its speed to good use, and the next morning you awake to find yourself on the other side of the Mediterranean in **Alexandria,** Egypt. While most passengers take all-day excursions to the **Pyramids,** there is the option of spending the time in Alexandria, a port city with a long history.

The next morning offers the chance to explore another fabled Mediterranean capital when you dock in **Ashdod,** Israel. (At the time of writing, the call at Ashdod had been replaced by two days in **Egypt.**) Many passengers visit **Jerusalem** and **Bethlehem,** but an excursion to the **Dead Sea** and **Masada** is also popular.

The *Olympia Voyager* calls next at the island of **Rhodes,** with an afternoon visit to the multilayered historic walled city, before sailing to **Istanbul** the next day. From Hagia Sophia and the Blue Mosque to the ferries running up the **Bosphorus** into the Black Sea, the city abounds with an exotic energy.

The last day of the cruise starts with a morning visit to **Kusadasi,** Turkey, for an excursion to the remarkable ruins of **Ephesus** and the house of the Virgin Mary. After a relaxing afternoon at sea, the ship anchors off **Mykonos** in the early evening, allowing passengers to dine ashore before arriving in **Piraeus** the next morning.

Royal Olympia's
Olympia Voyager

Address/Phone: Royal Olympia Cruises, 805 Third Avenue, New York, NY 10022 (212) 688–7555 or (800) 872–6400; fax: (888) 662–6237; www.royalolympiacruises.com

The Ship: *Olympia Voyager* began sailing in June 2000 and is comfortably sized at 25,000 tons, 590 feet long, and 24 feet in draft.

Passengers: 836; 70 percent Americans, the rest European, age forty and up

Dress: Casual most nights; a jacket is requested on two nights

Officers/Crew: Greek officers; international (but predominantly Greek) crew

Cabins: 418, of which 12 have balconies and 16 are bay window suites

Fare: $$$

What's included: Cruise fare

What's not included: Airfare, port charges, tips, drinks, shore excursions

Highlights: A superb Mediterranean itinerary on a sleek new ship with good cultural emphasis on the destinations

Other itineraries: In addition to this one-week, three-continents cruise that operates between May and November, the sistership *Olympia Explorer* sails out of Venice or Athens on a seven-day Grand Aegean and Adriatic itinerary. In the winter, *Olympia Voyager* visits the Orinoco and Amazon Rivers.

WINDSTAR CRUISES' *WIND SPIRIT*
Greek Islands and Coastal Turkey

Launched in 1986, Windstar Cruises combines the best of nineteenth-century clipper-ship design with the best of modern yacht engineering aboard its fleet of four- and five-masted sailing ships. While the *Wind Spirit*'s proud masts and yards of white sails cut an ever-so-attractive profile, the sails unfurl at the touch of a button. Windstar cruising is a top-of-the-line, ultracomfortable experience, and a no-jackets-needed policy is appreciated by the stylish, formality-eschewing guests, mostly professional couples in their thirties to sixties.

Onboard, stained teak, brass details, and lots of navy-blue fabrics and carpeting and caramel-colored leathers lend a traditional nautical ambience. Passengers can visit the bridge at any time to watch the computerized sails at work. Intentionally, there are few organized activities offered, and the pool deck, with its hot tub, chaise longues and open-air bar, is conducive to conversing, sunbathing, or just peaceful repose. The video library and CD collection are popular pastimes for in-cabin entertainment.

In the vaguely nautical-looking Lounge, passengers congregate for port talks, pre- and post-dinner drinks, and dancing and listening to the pianist and vocalist. Local entertainment may come aboard at a port of call, and a modest casino offers slots, blackjack, and Caribbean stud poker. In addition, a tiny gym is housed in a cabin-sized room, with an adjacent coed sauna.

The food is inventive and imaginative, as reflected by an appetizer such as a corn risotto with wild mushrooms and basil, perhaps followed by an artfully presented potato-crusted fish with braised leeks and apple-smoked bacon, or a salmon tournedos with an herb crust served with stewed tomatoes and garlicky broccoli rabe. Irresistible desserts like banana pie with raspberry sauce and French profiteroles with hot-fudge sauce are beyond tempting. The once-a-week evening pool-deck barbecue is a grand party under the stars. There are two open-seating dining venues: The Restaurant, accented with teakwood trim and wood-paneling and pillars wrapped in hemp, is used for dinner only; and The Veranda, a sunny, window-lined room with additional tables under umbrellas, serves breakfast and lunch.

All twin-portholed cabins are similar wood-tone outsides measuring 188 square feet and equipped with a VCR and a TV showing CNN and lots of movies, a CD player, a minibar, bathrobes, fresh fruit, and a compact closet. Roomy teakwood-decked bathrooms are well laid-out and come with hair dryer and circular shower stalls.

The Itinerary
The weekly departures alternate between the Athenian port of **Piraeus** and **Istanbul.** When sailing from Greece, the first call is **Mykonos,** where, as in most ports, there is no need to take an organized excursion.

Windstar Cruises operates some of the most romantic and cozy, yet roomy, small ships on the high seas. These engine-powered sailing ships look chic and offer just the right balance of creature comforts and first-class cuisine, along with a casual, unregimented lifestyle that well suits exploring the Greek Isles and Turkish coast.

Hop the shuttle provided by the ship and walk the town from end to end, enjoying the classic white-washed, blue-domed chapels and maze of streets; then choose a seaside restaurant for a Greek salad and plate of calamari.

The approach to **Santorini**'s cliff rim is nothing short of spectacular, and to reach the town a thousand feet up, hire a donkey, take the cable car, or use the zigzagging stairs. Besides the bird's-eye views, browse the cobbled streets and sample the fresh fish and Santorini white wines. Sailing eastward to **Rhodes,** the medieval city is a short walk from the ship, and within the walls are bustling squares, cobblestone side streets leading to small shops and some wonderful restaurants, perhaps for dinner, as the ship stays until nearly midnight. One excursion visits historic **Lindos,** perched high on a steep cliff above the sea.

Bodrum, a Turkish yachting and holiday port, has a Crusader past with fortified towers dominating the town and lots of resort-style shops and fish restaurants, where you choose the fish displayed whole for cooking. Weather conditions permitting, passengers may be able to go kayaking, sailing, windsurfing, and swimming from the water-sports platform lowered at the stern. Then up the coast at **Kusadasi,** first-timers should take the tour to **Ephesus,** to stand before the towering Library of Celsus and climb the steps of the great theater—but be prepared for hordes of other tourists. The pièce de résistance is the arrival in **Istanbul,** a breathtaking finale, with minarets rising up all around, with Topaki Palace and the Galata Tower adding considerable character to the skyline.

Windstar Cruises' *Wind Spirit*

Address/Phone: Windstar Cruises, 300 Elliott Avenue West, Seattle, WA 98119; (206) 281–3535 or (800) 258–7245; brochures: (800) 626–9900; fax: (206) 286–3229; www.windstarcruises.com

The Ship: *Wind Spirit* was built in 1988, has a gross tonnage of 5,350, a length of 440 feet, and a draft of 13 feet.

Passengers: 148; mostly American, thirty and up

Dress: Casual at all times

Officers/Crew: British officers; Filipino and Indonesian crew

Cabins: 74; all similar cabins, all outside, and no verandas

Fare: $$$$

What's included: Cruise fare, port charges, water sports, basic tips

What's not included: Airfare, drinks, shore excursions, extra tips

Highlights: Cuisine, ship itself, intimate atmosphere, service; Mediterranean itinerary

Other itineraries: In addition to these seven-night Eastern Mediterranean cruises, which operate between May and October, the four-ship fleet offers other Mediterranean itineraries, transatlantic positioning voyages, Costa Rican coastal cruises, several Caribbean programs, and a new ten-day program in New Zealand, plus long positioning voyages.

SWAN HELLENIC'S *MINERVA*
Eastern Mediterranean and Red Sea

Swan Hellenic, a British firm established in 1955 by two brothers named Swan, draws the upper end of the British market, plus Anglophile Americans who are in the know. Owned by the Peninsular and Oriental Steam Navigation Company of London, Swan Hellenic operates the chartered 12,500-ton *Minerva,* a purpose-built ship completed in April 1996. Stepping aboard is entering a seagoing British club—paneled walls, leather chairs, original paintings, prints, antique maps and passenger-donated photographs, and a wonderful library in which to disappear for delving into travel guides, references, and novels.

The main lounge, used for the daytime lecture program, doubles as a social setting in the evening for after-dinner coffee and for dancing to a four-piece band. Just aft, the Wheeler Bar employs a resident pianist, and one deck up, the cheerful aquamarine-and-green Orpheus Bar is a potted-palm alternative. Meeting fellow passengers is facilitated by open-seating dining, and men wear jacket and tie on nights at sea. The less formal Bridge Café provides buffet breakfast, lunch, and dinner indoors and outside around the pool. The food is good continental fare. Outside, the Promenade Deck is great for walking, but although ample space exists for lounging, there is limited shade from the sun. The 170 twin-bedded cabins (136 outside) have small writing desks, chairs, TVs, adequate closet and drawer space, and bathrooms with showers and, in the higher categories, tubs.

The Itinerary

For this cruise Swan carries Middle East historians, archaeologists, and Egyptologists, plus an expert in the region's political complexities, most hailing from British universities. The outstanding enrichment program goes beyond the forty-five-minute talks as the lecturers join in at meals and ashore. On my cruise a former archbishop of Canterbury enchanted us with Byzantine history in a Greco-Roman amphitheater and later conducted an unforgettable worship service to commemorate Veteran's Day (Remembrance Day in England) while anchored in Egypt's Great Bitter Lake, the central portion of the Suez Canal.

The ports of call vary every year and are likely to include Turkish coastal ports at the start, but the core of the cruise begins when the ship sails through the Eastern Mediterranean to Syria. From **Latakia,** where the inhabitants of ancient Ugarit developed an alphabet of thirty letters that eventually became ours, travel inland to **Aleppo,** whose central bazaar has 6 miles of covered passages. In rows of tiny shops, blacksmiths work

The Arab world has some of the finest ancient Greek, Roman, and Crusader sites found anywhere, little known to most North Americans, who generally think of Greece and Turkey. Swan Hellenic assembles twice-annual itineraries for its 344-passenger **Minerva** *that call at ports in Syria, Egypt, and Jordan and pass through the Suez Canal. Most passengers on these culturally rich cruises will be British.*

at open hearths, bakers sweat in front of hot ovens, and jewelers beat gold into necklaces and bracelets. Many Aleppo women have their faces hidden behind thick black veils, and forty-five-year-old Chevrolets, Fords, DeSotos, and Plymouths roam the streets. Then in **Damascus** the Great Mosque, built on the site of a church in the eighth century and retaining the Christian baptismal font, is located adjacent to the Roman Temple of Jupiter. The visible overlays of history help one appreciate Damascus's claim as the world's oldest continuously inhabited large city. The all-day excursions from the ship include Middle Eastern cooking for a taste of hummus (mashed chickpeas with sesame, oil, garlic, and lemon), kebab in yogurt, lamb with rice, pine nuts, and almonds, chicken in a lemon sauce, and fresh pita bread.

After sailing south the ship ties up at **Port Said.** Disembark for the drive to **Cairo** and its museum, housing some of the world's most beautifully detailed objects, including the treasures of Tutankhamun, whose tomb you see later in the cruise. Then visit the **Great Pyramids** rising from the desert. From Port Said the *Minerva* sails in convoy into the **Suez Canal**—normally a twelve-hour transit through the desert—out into the Red Sea to call at the Egyptian port of **Safaga.** The drive to the **Nile Valley** takes three hours. During a two-day visit walk the grand Avenue of Sphinxes to the Temple of **Karnak** and cross to the west bank by ferry to the Valley of the Tombs of the Kings and Queens. A descent into the chambers of Rameses I and IV reveals intricate and colorful hieroglyphs that depict ancient Egyptians' explanation of the cycle of night and day.

Sailing around the tip of the **Sinai Peninsula** into the Gulf of Aqaba, the *Minerva* docks at the Jordanian port of **Aqaba** for a two-day excursion to **Amman,** the capital, and to **Jerash,** a superb limestone-and-marble Roman provincial city with a colonnaded shopping street and Temple of Artemis, shifted, but not toppled, by an eighth-century earthquake. To reach the rock tombs at **Petra,** take a horseback ride through a narrow canyon, where, at the far end, you face a massive stone temple, entirely carved out of natural rock. In a shallow valley a ring of burial chambers built by the Nabateans about the time of Christ sits high up the cliff face. This exotic, late-fall cruise ends with a Swan Hellenic charter flight back to **London,** and the itinerary with variations operates in reverse in spring.

Swan Hellenic's *Minerva*

Address/Phone: Swan Hellenic Cruises, Kartagener Associates Inc., 631 Commack Road, Suite 1A, Commack, NY 11725; (877) 219–4239; fax: (631) 858–1279; www.swanhellenic.com

The Ship: *Minerva* was built in 1996 from an unfinished Ukrainian hull and has a gross tonnage of 12,500, a length of 436 feet, and draft of 19.6 feet.

Passengers: 344. Age is forty and up and largely British; most Americans book with a museum or an alumni group

Dress: Jacket and tie are expected on evenings at sea.

Officers/Crew: British captain and European officers; mostly Filipino crew

Cabins: 170; mostly average size and 12 with verandas

Fare: $$$$

What's included: Cruise and port charges, program of shore excursions for every port, all tips aboard and to guides ashore, and charter flights between London and the ship

What's not included: Airfare between the United States and London and optional shore excursions, drinks

Highlights: Varied in-depth itineraries; excellent lecturers and cultural enrichment program aboard and ashore; terrific organization; ports of outstanding interest

Other itineraries: In addition to the above cruise between the Eastern Mediterranean and Red Sea, which is offered in late fall and early spring, the *Minerva* makes year-round nonrepeating eight- to twenty-five-day cruises in the Mediterranean, Iberia, around Britain, to Norway and the Baltic, and into the Indian Ocean and Southeast Asia.

AFRICA, THE MIDDLE EAST, AND THE INDIAN OCEAN

ST HELENA LINE'S RMS *ST. HELENA*
Into the Remote South Atlantic via Mail Ship

In 1978 Curnow Shipping of Falmouth, Cornwall, began operating a passenger, mail, and cargo service under a contract with the British Government between Britain, the Canary Islands, Ascension, St. Helena, and Cape Town to replace the one hundred years of liner service operated by the Union-Castle Line. Now Andrew Weir Shipping holds the five-year contract.

Purpose-built in a Scottish shipyard in 1990 to serve the islands, the present RMS, as she is affectionately known, undertakes four round-trip sailings a year from Cardiff, Wales, to the island and makes additional sailings north from Cape Town, offering the comfortable facilities of a small liner for 128 passengers and a British and St. Helenian crew of sixty-five.

The homey public rooms include a two-section forward observation lounge with a bar, a video for screening films, and a reading area. Aft the Sun Lounge looks onto the open lido with outdoor pool, and a light breakfast and lunch are served here daily. The dining room, on a lower deck, operates with two reserved sittings at dinner, and the food is good British fare, such as tasty soups, lunchtime curries, dinner roasts, and well-prepared fish. The plainly furnished cabins are outside, with windows or portholes, twin beds, uppers and lowers, and private shower and toilet. Budget accommo-

dations, reserved for the "Saints"—a people of mixed British, South Asian, East Indian, and Madagascar origin—are sometimes available for nonisland passengers.

The Itinerary
On our July voyage we embarked at **Cardiff Docks** in South Wales for the two-week voyage to St. Helena, and following a week on the island, onward passage to Cape Town, South Africa. Among the passengers were the Saints, who make up about half of the complement—students returning from university, persons on leave from jobs abroad, and others planning to resettle in their island home. The visitors came from Britain, Germany, France, South Africa, and the United States. Stored below decks were ninety-three bags of mail and parcels, refrigerated and frozen food, medical equipment and drugs, planks of a West African wood resistant to white ants, educational textbooks, nine automobiles, and one fifth of a ton of stamps, one of the island's few sources of income.

During the cycle of gradually warming days, we established a daytime routine of reading and socializing on deck, visiting the bridge, and taking a swim or playing deck tennis with the officers atop the forward cargo hatch. In the evening the purser had an uncanny

*The island of St. Helena, a British South Atlantic territory located 1,200 miles off the coast of Africa, may be the world's most significant place with no airport. For the mountainous island's 5,500 inhabitants, the 6,767-ton Royal Mail Ship **St. Helena** provides the sole link to the outside world. For visitors the voyage is one of the last true ocean-liner experiences, plus offering the added bonus of a full week on the island and passage onto Cape Town, South Africa.*

knack of getting everyone involved in creative activities: frog racing, quizzes, and pantomime, all old-fashioned shipboard fun. Such is the atmosphere aboard a purposeful ocean liner.

After a six-hour call at **Tenerife,** the Canary Islands, the RMS leaves the main shipping lanes for the remote South Atlantic. The sea remains placid and quite empty, erupting occasionally when flying fish and porpoises break the surface. A dozen days after leaving Cardiff, **Ascension** comes into view, a desolate and forbidding volcanic island rising 2,800 feet above sea level from the mid-Atlantic ridge. The ship anchors to take on passengers while the purser gives a tour ashore, weather permitting.

Two days later, **St. Helena** spreads across the horizon beneath a low cloud clinging to the mountain peaks. Brown at the edges and green in the center, the island's steep cliffs provide a natural fortress. The RMS anchors off Jamestown, a pastel-colored nineteenth-century Georgian town, sandwiched into a deep valley that slices inland to the island's incredibly beautiful central highlands.

Through passengers get the bonus of a week on the island while the RMS discharges her cargo and makes a passenger run to Ascension and back. Most visitors stay at two small hotels in Jamestown, whereas others choose self-catering cottages up in the hills, which means hiring a car and negotiating twisting, one-lane tracks and blind hairpin curves for touring and grocery shopping.

Napoleon spent six years here from 1815 until his death in 1821, and Longwood, his permanent residence and gardens, is open to visitors; nearby, Deadwood Plain is home to the island's indigenous wirebird. Transit passengers may be invited for a tour of Plantation House, a handsome 1791-built mansion and grounds that is home to a giant Seychellois tortoise named Jonathan, who is reputed to be nearing his 170th birthday. There are miles of walking trails around the coast and down to secluded bays, with rewarding mountain vistas and seascapes of pounding surf. Jamestown offers a small museum, a pretty Anglican church, a few shops, and a couple of restaurants, but the main attraction is main street, the island's social center, where everyone gathers to talk.

After a week the RMS returns and embarks passengers for **Cape Town,** a five-day voyage; then, just short of four weeks after departing Cardiff, the little ship sails into Table Bay as dawn breaks behind Table Mountain. Loading fresh food, supplies, cement, and coal takes three days; then the ship returns northward.

St. Helena Line's
RMS *St. Helena*

Address/Phone: St. Helena Line, Andrew Weir Shipping Ltd., Dexter House, 2 Royal Mint Court, London EC3N 4XX, England; (011) 44 207 265 0808; fax: (011) 44 207 816 4992; www.aws.co.uk

The ship: RMS *St. Helena* was built in 1990, has a gross tonnage of 6,767, a length of 344 feet, and a draft of 19.6 feet.

Passengers: 128 in all berths. Passengers of every age travel in the ship, with St. Helenians, British, and South Africans predominating, plus Europeans and some Americans.

Dress: Jacket at dinnertime only

Officers/crew: British and St. Helenian officers; St. Helenian crew

Cabins: 49; mostly outside with two to four berths, plus a few inside without facilities sold at subsidized fares for St. Helenians

Fare: $$

What's included: Sea fare only unless you purchase an air-sea package

What's not included: Shore excursions, tips, drinks, and the hotel or cottage stay on the island, which must be arranged in advance through the line or done independently by fax

Other itineraries: In addition to the one-month southbound voyage described here, the RMS *St. Helena* makes similar northbound trips, also calling at Banjul, The Gambia, and round-trip voyages that sail from Cape Town to St. Helena, where passengers go ashore for the week, while the ship sails to Ascension and returns via St. Helena to embark passengers for Cape Town. Once a year, the ship also makes a two-week round-trip voyage to the even more remote island of Tristan da Cunha, located about halfway between South Africa and South America. This one sells out well in advance.

CUNARD LINE'S *QUEEN ELIZABETH 2*
An Ocean Liner Voyage: England to South Africa

Cunard initiated regular liner services over a century and a half ago, and the *QE2* carries on the grand tradition. A long liner voyage is a highly social experience, and the *QE2* offers many venues, with no less than ten bars and lounges from which to choose. I like the Chart Room, sitting along the enclosed promenade to people watch during the day or, more privately, inside at night. A harpist or a pianist, using the *Queen Mary*'s old grand piano, is there to add to the atmosphere. The Yacht Club, located all the way aft, has music before dinner, too, and at night it is the place to meet the officers and staff. Being a British ship, the Golden Lion Pub stocks more types of British, European, and North American beers than most people know exist.

Formal afternoon tea, accompanied by music, is served in the elegant Queens Room, which later becomes a ballroom for dancing to a full orchestra. The library has a staff of two professionals, who maintain watch over the reading room and the library shop, which sells shipping books, videos, postcards, and posters.

Cunard Line represents history at sea, 160 years of it, and a circular mural in the Midships Lobby evokes that sense of embarking and being at sea. Artists Stephen Card and Hanley Crossley have painted the Cunard fleet in all sorts of settings on "G" Stairway, and a wonderfully cluttered case of memorabilia displays menus, brochures, silver souvenir spoons, and ashtrays. A favorite pastime is studying the montage of unlabeled celebrity photos, and guessing who's who.

The *QE2* has a proper big-screen movie theater with a cozy balcony, a grand space that also hosts lectures by a well-known author, a South African political analyst, or a maritime historian. On Sunday morning the captain leads an interdenominational church service. For active passengers, the *QE2* Spa and an indoor pool allows you to continue your exercise if the weather outside is not cooperating, while you sail from a late English autumn to a South African summer. You can hit a golf ball, play Ping-Pong, jog into head winds, and be pushed along by tail winds on the Boat Deck.

Cabins come in every imaginable configuration, but for the most evocative accommodations afloat, book one of the wood-paneled rooms on One Deck, with a large elliptical window, satin walls, walk-in closet, and commodious bathroom with tub. Veranda suites have their own private deck, and passengers traveling alone can choose from 150 dedicated inside and outside single cabins.

*One of the world's great sea routes, between England and South Africa, has been revived with the **Queen Elizabeth 2** undertaking the historic Union-Castle Line mail route on a round-trip voyage between Southampton, England, and Cape Town, South Africa. The fifteen-day voyages include two to four ports of call and ten days at sea to experience life aboard the best-known liner in the world.*

The cabin determines your assigned restaurant, and the top categories include the two-level Queens Grill or the more intimate Britannia and Princess grills. The grand Caronia Restaurant has portraits of the royal family flanking the entrance, and its foyer displays a huge lighted model of the four-funneled 1907 *Mauretania.* This name also applies to the ship's fifth restaurant. The Lido Restaurant serves all three meals, and the Pavilion, one deck down, satisfies diners who want to stay by the pool and pair of whirlpools.

The Itinerary

The *QE2*'s line voyage to and from South Africa attracts a lot of interest because there are many people living at either end of this historic sea route who remember the Union-Castle mail-ship days.

Sailing from the Queen Elizabeth II Terminal in **Southampton,** the ship spends the first two days in the chilly seas heading south through the Bay of Biscay to **Funchal,** the lovely port on the island of **Madeira.** Belonging to Portugal, the island is well worth a half-day tour to explore the rugged coastline, vineyards, and villages, followed by a formal afternoon tea on the terrace of Reid's, one of the great hotels of the world. Enjoy the harbor view and a walk through the gardens.

Two more sea days bring the *QE2* into much warmer weather and to the **Cape Verde Islands,** also Portuguese but with an African flavor and not often visited by cruise ships. The Crossing the Line (**Equator**) ceremony will be the major event of the three-day passage to the island of **St. Helena,** the world's most remote significant place without an airport. Only the Royal Mail Ship *St. Helena* calls here on a regular basis, supplying the island with everything it requires and taking the "Saints" to work aboard and returning them home. The visit will include a tour through the verdant hills out to Napoleon's final place of exile, or you can take a walk through a perfectly preserved Georgian town, Jamestown, where you land.

Embarking for **Cape Town,** three more days are spent at sea, and, on the fourth morning, the *QE2* sails into Table Bay beneath Table Mountain, a beautiful harbor meant to be first seen from the deck of a ship. The *QE2* is your hotel for one more day before disembarking and taking on new passengers for the northward return trip via **St. Helena, Ascension, Tenerife, Lisbon,** and finally **Southampton.** In 2002 the southbound ports are Funchal, Dakar, and Ascension. The northbound ports are Walvis Bay, St. Helena, Tenerife, and Lisbon.

Cunard Line's
Queen Elizabeth 2

Address/Phone: Cunard Line, 6100 Blue Lagoon Drive, Suite 400, Miami, FL 33126; (305) 563–3000 or (800) 7–CUNARD; fax: (305) 463–3010; www.cunardline.com

The Ship: *Queen Elizabeth 2* was built in 1969, has a gross tonnage of 70,327, a length of 963 feet, and a deep draft of 33 feet.

Passengers: 1,740, double occupancy; Americans, British, and Europeans, age fifty and up

Dress: Formal attire on many nights at sea; also theme, semiformal, and casual nights

Officers/Crew: British officers; international staff

Cabins: 925; sold in twenty-one wide-ranging categories, 689 outside, 150 singles, and 30 with verandas. Cabin determines restaurant allocation.

Fare: $$$

What's included: Cruise fare and port charges

What's not included: Airfare, shore excursions, drinks, and tips

Highlights: A great ocean voyage on the world's best-known ship

Other itineraries: In addition to the two fifteen-day England–South Africa voyages, which operate in from late October to December, the *QE2* makes traditional six-night Atlantic crossings, cruises from New York to New England, Canada, and the Caribbean, and from England to Northern Europe, Iberia, the Mediterranean, and around the world.

SILVERSEA CRUISES' *SILVER WIND*

East and South Africa Sea Safari

Silversea Cruises, one of the industry's highest rated companies, is also one of the few lines that still provides an almost all-inclusive package aboard its 388-passenger *Silver Shadow* and *Silver Whisper* and the 296-passenger *Silver Cloud* and *Silver Wind,* the latter the ship for this exotic voyage. Built in an Italian yard and flying the Italian flag, the *Silver Wind*'s public rooms, stacked aft with cabins forward, are of a distinctive Italian design. In the windowed main restaurant, Murano-glass capitals decorate the columns, convex illuminated ceiling panels offer soft lighting, and a raised, concave central dome is flanked by metal filigree. Seating is open, and the menu is continental and Italian, catering well to the American and European passenger list.

The tiered Venetian Show Lounge's fanciful artistic lighting contrasts nicely with the rich blue-and-red upholstery on the banquettes and facing chairs. High-level side wings end with steps down to the orchestra level, where ramps lead out into the main bar, the ship's social center. Entertainment in the theater consists of small groups, not lavish shows, and a special lecture program provided by *National Geographic* magazine, while the bar hosts a band for dancing and a pianist for listening.

Alternative dining takes place in the indoor-outdoor Terrace Café for breakfast, lunch, and a reservation-only Italian dinner. The Panorama Lounge, high up and aft, is set up for early-morning breakfast and later becomes a quiet venue for afternoon tea, predinner cocktails, or just a quiet read. Service is European sophistication throughout. Ample deck chairs surround a good-size pool and two whirlpools; and one deck above, a wraparound mezzanine sees joggers, walkers, and additional deck furniture.

The 295-square-foot Veranda Suites number 102 of the 148 cabins, and only the thirty-eight Vista Suites lack the outdoor teak deck. The decor is plush, with light woods trimming the furniture and walls. The bedroom is divided from the sitting area by an archway with a drop curtain, and the marble bathroom combines a tub and shower. The lounge, positioned next to the veranda-deck door, has a sofa and two armchairs for in-suite entertaining and dining. Additional amenities are a minibar, a stocked refrigerator, and a TV/VCR.

The Itinerary

With Table Mountain as a backdrop, the *Silver Wind* sets sail from **Cape Town** for a day at sea and a call at **Port Elizabeth,** the eastern end of the famous **Garden Route,** a scenic stretch of South Africa's fabulous coastline. Seaside **Durban** is a blend of the modern South Africa, combining African, Asian, and European culture, and **Richard's Bay** gives access to **Umfolozi** and **Hluhluwe** game reserves, home to the white rhino and to

Cape Town to Mombasa, an old colonial sea route, is a step back in time when this side of Africa had a strong British and French influence and, to some extent, still does. Silversea offers one, or sometimes two, annual cruises, stopping along the coast and taking in Madagascar and the Comoro Islands on the way north.

KwaZulu, the region for southern Africa's legendary warrior people.

Northward through the Mozambique Channel, enrichment lectures prepare you for visiting **Madagascar,** where, at **Nosy Be,** a monkeylike mammal called a lemur lives and fishing is the dominant trade. The call also includes a beach barbecue. The much smaller **Comoro Islands,** with Mayotte still under French control, recall the South Pacific as the ship enters a protected lagoon set against a backdrop of lush forests and volcanic peaks. Sailing the *Silver Wind* northwestward, **Zanzibar** conjures up intrigue, explorers, and the former slave trade, and, on this fragrant spice island, the scent is cloves. The old Arab quarter is a rabbit warren of narrow streets lined with residences fronted by carved wooden doors and brass knobs. On the last morning the *Silver Wind* sails into **Mombasa,** a trading port for more than one thousand years, dominated by the Portuguese-built Fort Jesus. Since you came this far, consider taking one of the **Kenya** safari packages or one in South Africa before the cruise.

Silversea Cruises' *Silver Wind*

Address/Phone: Silversea Cruises, 110 East Broward Boulevard, Fort Lauderdale, FL 33301; (954) 522–4477 or (800) 774–9996; fax: (954) 522–4499; www.silversea.com

The Ship: *Silver Wind,* completed in 1995, has a gross tonnage of 16,800, a length of 514 feet, and a draft of 17 feet.

Passengers: 296; largely Americans age forty-five and up, but also some Europeans and others

Dress: Formal, informal, and casual nights

Officers/Crew: Italian officers, mostly European crew

Cabins: 148 outside suites, all but 38 with verandas

Fares: $$$$$

What's included: Air-sea program, port charges, hotel stay, transfers, all drinks, and wines at lunch and dinner, gratuities, usually a special excursion

What's not included: Excursions, pre- and post-cruise land packages

Highlights: Stylish atmosphere and top-of-the-line food and services

Other itineraries: In addition to this sixteen-day South and East African cruise, which usually operates in March and November–December, several land safari packages are available. Silversea also cruises to Europe, Asia, Australia, and North and South America. This itinerary may also operate in the southbound direction and may substitute other calls such as Mauritius and Reunion.

LINDBLAD EXPEDITIONS' *HAPI I*

Egypt's Nile Valley

Lindblad Expeditions, the creation of Sven-Olof Lindblad, is the top American expedition-style cruise company, and the Egyptian program is just one of its many offerings. Any trip to Egypt should include Cairo, Aswan, Abu Simbel, and Luxor, and in this case the cruise portion is a full seven days, longer than most.

The *Hapi I* is a well-maintained, air-conditioned, four-deck riverboat with lots of outside deck space, both levels partially covered with awnings, for reading, sunbathing, socializing, and taking in riverbank sights. The Sun Deck has a bathtub-size pool, and the Bridge Deck below has a shaded outdoor setup for lunch as weather permits. Forward, the main lounge has a bar, and an adjacent room just aft of the bridge contains a small library and the VCR.

The dining room has four round eight-person tables, and the four waiters and maître d' are attentive and responsive. Breakfast and lunch are buffet, and dinner is quite elegant, with candles and linen. The food is ample but not particularly memorable, though some attempts are made to include Middle Eastern dishes. The beer is excellent, and the local wine is light and palatable—both are on the house at mealtimes—while the coffee is unexpectedly good.

The cabins (238 square feet) have more than adequate storage, and those on the upper deck have windows that open. Bathrooms are commodious, with generous counter space and shower stalls. The 280-square-foot junior suites on the lower deck have, in addition, an alcove with two armchairs.

Onboard activities consist of good lectures, outdated videos, and, on our cruise, a lecture by the Director of Antiquities for Luxor and the Valleys (Kings, and Queens, Nobles). Aboard ship, in the coaches, and at the sites, security was both conspicuous and unobtrusive.

The Itinerary

This itinerary, longer than most, sails downriver to Dendera and gives extra time in both Aswan and Luxor. Groups larger than twenty have two guides, and ours were first-class, with strong academic credentials, excellent language skills, a fine sense of timing (to avoid the largest crowds), and a sensitive understanding of what the group is up for.

One of the great features of this itinerary is over nighting at Abu Simbel, which allows leisurely dusk and dawn visits to the Temple of Rameses II, four 65-foot statues flanking the entrance where, inside, vivid reliefs

Without the River Nile there would be no Egypt, and no journey to Egypt would be even remotely complete without a Nile cruise. Upward of 250 riverboats crowd the Upper Nile, but Lindblad Expeditions does one of the best jobs insulating its passengers from the crowds, and its chartered **Hapi I** *is as fine a riverboat as there is.*

depict Rameses' battle triumphs. Adjacent is the equally impressive Temple of Nefertari, Rameses' favorite wife.

Boarding the *Hapi I* at **Aswan,** the boat becomes a hotel when moored at the riverbank, with plenty of time for browsing ashore and shopping at both Aswan and Luxor. En route from Aswan to Luxor, the small temple at **Esna,** located in the middle of a lively town, is 30 feet below grade and is threatened by the rising water table, one of the many, and this time negative, consequences of the **Aswan Dam.** Unfortunately, it can't be moved; every inch of its twenty-four columns are covered with wonderful inscriptions and topped by unique capitals, on which several stone frogs are perched, peering over the edges.

Kom Ombo's unique features are double portals and double sanctuaries containing mummified crocodiles and a painted ceiling panel with the wings of Horus in a fine state of preservation. Farther downstream at **Edfu,** horse-drawn carriages clip-clop out to the Temple of Horus, the falcon god, with remarkable storytelling reverse reliefs. An outside passageway is decorated with two guardian Horuses at the entry.

At **Luxor,** visits are made to the **Temple of Karnak,** with its great hypostyle hall, a forest of 134 columns that rise 70 feet, and to the excellent Luxor Museum for statuary found in the area and the mural from the Temple of Aton. On the Nile's West Bank opposite Luxor, the tombs in the Valleys are constantly being opened and closed, but you will see the Colossus of Memnon and the Rameseum. In the **Valley of the Kings,** our group saw the burial chambers for Rameses III and VI, the latter with vividly painted scenes in a remarkable state of preservation. Our energetic guides got their groups to the ticket kiosk early enough to get the very limited number of first-come, first-served tickets for the tomb of **Tutankhamun.** The dramatic story of its discovery lost nothing in the retelling at the site.

The **Temple of Dendera,** up the map and down the Nile north of Luxor, is isolated at the edge of the desert, and the Roman era structure, unique because of its intact roof and excellent overall condition, has a depiction of Cleopatra—and even graffiti left behind by a 1799 Napoleonic expedition. If one comes reasonably well informed, interest is not likely to flag, especially when the guides are as good as these two were.

Lindblad Expeditions' *Hapi I*

Address/Phone: Lindblad Expeditions, 720 Fifth Avenue, Sixth Floor, New York, NY 10019; (212) 765-7740 or (800) 397-3348; fax: (212) 265-3770; e-mail: travel@expeditions.com; www.expeditions.com

The Ship: *Hapi I,* built in 1989, has a gross tonnage of 650, a length of 188 feet, and a shallow draft.

Passengers: 30; mostly Americans, fifty and up

Dress: Casual at all times

Officers/Crew: Egyptian

Cabins: 15 roomy cabins, including 3 junior suites

Fare: $$$$

What's included: A complete package, including airfare within Egypt, hotels, most meals on land, transfers, excursions, beer and wine at meals, and hotel and transfer tips

What's not included: International airfare, bar drinks, tips for the guides and boat crew

Highlights: Seeing some of the greatest sights in the Ancient World, with terrific guides, and accomplished in considerable comfort

Other itineraries: Besides this seven-day Nile cruise plus land package, operating between late September and the end of March, Lindblad Expeditions offers trips and cruises all over the world, including Galápagos and the Pacific Northwest.

MAUPINTOUR FLOTEL NILE CRUISES'
NILE ROMANCE
Egypt and Nile River Cruise

Maupintour has been operating worldwide tours since 1951, and this experience gives one reassurance when traveling beyond the western world, in this case, Egypt. The 150-passenger *Nile Romance* is used for the ten-day program, and although Maupintour participants will travel as a separate group with their own Egyptologist while in Cairo and on excursions from the riverboat, they join others on the cruise.

The lounge and dining room are characterized by an ornate mahogany ceiling that one might expect to find in northern climes. The sundeck offers ample space for sunbathing and using the pool and Jacuzzi or sitting comfortably under cover to read and play cards. Oleander tubs are placed at the pool's four corners, flowers hang from the awnings, and window boxes range the length of the deck.

The food is generous servings of eastern Mediterranean-style dishes, served at one sitting and notable for the fine breads, but meat dishes are generally tough. Because of taxes, European wines are very ex-

pensive, and the most economical and acceptable is the Omar Khayyam red. Cabins have twin beds, an L-shaped sofa, a large window, a writing desk, a TV, and a minibar for storing bottled water.

The Itineraries

Ten-day Cruise Tour: This trip really comprises only seven days of touring, as Day One is spent leaving the United States and Day Two is spent getting across Europe to **Cairo** and the hotel, happily with guaranteed rooms facing the Nile. Day Three includes a guided visit to the **Egyptian Museum,** where some of the finest pharaonic artifacts are on display such as the gold mask, toys, jewelry, and splendid throne from the tomb of "Boy King" Tutankhamun, which is seen later during the cruise. You see modern Arab Cairo on visits to the Khan el Khalili bazaar and the Mohammed Ali Mosque in the Citadel in the Old City. The next day is spent just outside Cairo at the three **Great Pyramids** and the **Sphinx,** including the de rigueur camel ride,

With more than 250 riverboats cruising the Nile, the choice is daunting, but going with the good name of Maupintour will provide top Egyptologist guides and excellent organization for what is otherwise, if often, a chaotic independent travel experience. You can choose from a ten-day cruise and tour that will include four days on the Nile and visits to Abu Simbel and Cairo, or a seventeen-day combination for a six-day Nile cruise that adds Dendera and a coach trip through the Nile Delta to Alexandria.

then on a drive to **Memphis,** ancient Egypt's first capital, to see Djoser's **Step Pyramid,** the world's oldest free-standing stone structure, and the thirty-chamber mastaba (tomb) of Mereruka.

On Day Five you fly south to **Luxor** and visit the **Temple at Karnak** and walk the 2-mile Avenue of Ram-headed Sphinxes to the Luxor Temple, remarkably preserved by centuries of sand into the nineteenth-century. Then it's time to embark in the riverboat *Nile Romance* for lunch, a quiet afternoon, and a Sound and Light show in the evening.

Early the next morning, you cross the Nile to the Colossi of Memnon, the colonnaded temple of **Queen Hatshepsut** and **Tutankhamun** tombs, where you hear the dramatic story of discovery. The afternoon is spent cruising up the Nile, which is south on the map. Day Seven brings the **Temple of Horus,** the falcon god, at **Edfu,** and, at **Kom Ombo,** the two shrines to Horus, here the related hawk god, and Sobek, the crocodile god. Day Eight begins with a morning cruise to **Aswan,** where you see the **High Dam,** the world's largest landfill dam, and below it the **Temple of Philae,** reconstructed on an island in the Nile, and a quarry wherein lies an unfinished granite obelisk.

On the last full day in Egypt, you disembark and fly south to **Abu Simbel,** the temple complex carved from solid rock, which is dedicated to Pharaoh Ramses II and Nefertari, his wife. Beginning in 1965 the monument was moved in pieces 200 feet above the waters of the Nile rising behind the new Aswan High Dam. Fly to **Cairo** for a final overnight and then, on Day Ten, fly home.

Seventeen-day Cruise Tour: This longer itinerary uses the 236-foot, 116-passenger riverboat *Oberoi Philae,* built in 1996, with most of the same amenities as the *Nile Romance* plus cabins with private verandas and TVs. The additional days add the Sound and Light Show at the **Pyramids** because the land portion of this tour stays nearby at the Mena House Oberoi Hotel, and they allow more time in **Cairo** plus a two-day visit to **Alexandria,** traveling by bus, to see the Royal Jewelry Museum, the Greco-Roman Museum, and Sultan Bey's Fort, built on the former site of the world's first lighthouse, the Tower of Pharos. The Nile cruise lasts six days to add the Temple of Hathor at **Dendera** and a night at **Aswan** with a felucca cruise around **Elephantine Island** to the botanical garden and the Aga Khan Mausoleum.

Maupintour Flotel Nile Cruises' *Nile Romance*

Address/Phone: Maupintour, P.O. Box 807, Lawrence, KS 66044; (800) 255–4266; www.maupintour.com

The Ship: *Nile Romance,* operated by Flotel Nile Cruises, was built in 1989, has a length of 239 feet, and a shallow draft.

Passengers: 150; Americans and Europeans, age forty and up

Dress: Casual

Officers/Crew: Egyptian

Cabins: 75; all outside, twin-bedded

Fare: $$$

What's included: Cruise fare, port charges, excursions, most meals on land, cruise tipping, flights within Egypt; international air add-ons available

What's not included: Airfare, drinks, some meals on land, tips to Egyptologist guide

Highlights: Sites of Ancient Egypt, excellent Egyptologist

Other itineraries: Maupintour also uses Oberoi Hotel's Oberoi Philae on a seventeen-day cruise tour and operates tours and cruise tours to most parts of the world.

ORIENT LINES' *CROWN ODYSSEY*
Passage to India

Orient Lines, originally a British-owned company, is now part of Star Cruises, Malaysia, which also owns Norwegian Cruise Line. The *Crown Odyssey* was built in 1988 as the flagship for the now defunct Royal Cruise Line, then passed to Norwegian Cruise Line. The 617-foot ship accommodates 1,052 passengers, Scandinavian officers, and a largely Filipino crew of 470. She joined the *Marco Polo* in May 2000 and assumes some of its itineraries, including those bound east of Suez for India, Southeast Asia, Australia, and New Zealand. Passengers generally come from the United States, Britain, and Australia and are sociable, well-traveled types.

Decor in the public rooms runs to art deco touches, with considerable use of brass, chrome, and glass. On the highest deck, the delightful Top of the Crown observation lounge offers sweeping views in three directions. While quiet during the day, it is a popular bar at sundown and transforms into a disco at night. The main deck of the public rooms includes a semicircular show lounge, an adjacent small bar, a second lounge attached to the large casino and shops, and the aft-facing Yacht Club, a disappointingly plain room, which transforms into a soothing setting at night for Mediterranean and Asian meals by reservation. Afternoon tea is served in the tiny Palm Court, and the comfortable library offers a good selection of books.

The fine enrichment program includes lectures on topics such as Eastern religions and art and postcolonial politics, plus folkloric groups and standard entertainment. The ship has one of the best and most spacious indoor pools on any ship, two flanking whirlpools, a sauna, a gym, and a beauty salon. Outdoor spaces include a forward observation deck, two pools, two whirlpools with views over the stern, and good open and covered deck space for chairs.

The two-seating dining room is large and noisy, like that aboard the *Marco Polo,* with a stained-glass ceiling that reverberates the sound. The food does not yet quite match the quality and creativity found aboard its running mate.

Three-quarters of the 513 cabins are outside, and half have tubs, popular with an older clientele on long voyages. All cabins have three-channel radios, direct-dial phones, TVs, and room service for breakfast. Closet and drawer space is ample, and soundproofing between cabins is good. Seventy-four suites have sitting areas and floor-to-ceiling windows, and sixteen penthouse suites have private balconies, VCRs, and whirlpool tubs. The *Crown Odyssey* provides a highly

*Here's an exotic eleven-day voyage across the Indian Ocean from Singapore to India via Malaysia, Thailand, and Sri Lanka, bracketed by a seven-day land package that adds depth to the travel experience. Orient Lines' **Crown Odyssey** is a great-value, mid-size liner attracting an English-speaking union of Americans, British, and Australians who come for the creative itineraries and easy social ambience. This itinerary will also operate in the reverse direction from India in November 2001.*

suitable running mate to the popular *Marco Polo,* and passengers who remember her early days will find her once again in good form for a longer voyage such as this one.

The Itinerary

When the *Crown Odyssey* sails westbound to India, the cruise begins with a two-night hotel stay in **Singapore,** a modern, well-run city state, which provides an easy entry into Asia. The highlights include a restored nineteenth-century Chinatown, outdoor dining along the Singapore River, a colonial downtown with a lively, Victorian food court frequented by local office workers, sophisticated shopping along Orchard Road, an outstanding botanical garden, a night safari to see the nocturnal zoo animals, and World War II Changi Prison Museum.

Leaving Singapore, the *Crown Odyssey* first sails up the coast to the port for **Kuala Lumpur,** Malaysia's burgeoning capital city, which boasts the world's two tallest office towers. The island of **Penang** is largely Chinese, with an old-fashioned commercial center, Buddhist temples—including one featuring resident cobras—and good beaches, the latter also part of the scene in **Phuket,** Thailand.

This is a ship to enjoy while crossing the Indian Ocean to **Colombo,** the Sri Lankan capital where elephants still work in the forests near **Kandy,** a mountain resort dedicated to Buddha. Sailing around to **Cochin** in southern India, the call reveals amazing layers of civilizations brought by the Chinese, Jews, Arabs, Europeans, and Indians. Quite unforgettable are the rhythmic sights of fishermen casting huge nets from shore the way the Chinese taught them a thousand years ago.

The cruise portion ends at **Mumbai (Bombay),** a teeming European-built, but now thoroughly Indian, port city marked by the ceremonial Gateway of India, Victorian Crawford Market, and Gandhi's residence. The flight north to **Agra** includes a two-night stay to see the white marble **Taj Mahal** and abandoned Mogul city of **Fatehpur Sikri;** then you travel by bus to the Indian capital at **New Delhi** to see its Red Fort and Viceroy's Palace.

The combination of the *Crown Odyssey*'s special atmosphere, the genuinely interested passengers, and creative land extensions make this one of the best-value travel experiences offered by any line. The ship is well worth considering for other cruising regions.

Orient Lines' *Crown Odyssey*

Address/Phone: 1510 S.E. 17th Street, Suite 400, Fort Lauderdale, FL 33316; (954) 527–6660 or (800) 333–7300; fax: (954) 527–6657; e-mail: info@ orientlines.com; www.orientlines.com

The Ship: *Crown Odyssey* was built in 1988 for Royal Cruise Line. It has a gross tonnage of 34,250, a length of 614 feet, and a draft of 24 feet.

Passengers: 1,052, with up to half of the passengers from abroad, although almost all will be English-speaking

Dress: On this longer itinerary, the ship is decidedly more formal than in the Mediterranean.

Officers/Crew: International officers; Filipino crew

Cabins: 526; 412 are outside and 16 have verandas

Fare: $$$

What's included: Airfare, pre- and post-cruise hotel package with tours, transfers

What's not included: Port charges, tips, shore excursions

Highlights: A longer, more in-depth look at Indian Ocean and Southeast Asian highlights, with included hotel stays on a very comfortable, happy ship with similarly interested passengers.

Other itineraries: In addition to this eleven-day cruise plus land tour in the Indian Ocean that operates variously both late and in the year and early in the next, the *Crown Odyssey* sails in Southeast Asia and Australasia and in the Mediterranean in summer.

SOUTHEAST ASIA
AND THE FAR EAST

STAR CLIPPERS' *STAR FLYER*
Thailand and Malaysia: Gems of the Andaman Sea

The company's owner, Mikael Krafft, built the ship and its identical sister, the *Star Clipper*, in the early 1990s, seeking to re-create the classic clipper ship of the nineteenth century. That said, the *Star Flyer* is actually quite modern, with a diesel engine, an antirolling system, a bow thruster, Dacron sails, and electronic winches, relying only partly on sails for its power. But to an untrained eye, the ship feels like a tall ship, and that's what matters.

The public rooms are comfortable, almost elegant, with a wood-paneled library and piano lounge and a cozy nautical-theme restaurant. Nightly home-style entertainment takes place on deck (sheltered by a sail-like tarp) by the Tropical Bar, the main hub of activity before and after dinner. One night you'll enjoy a very entertaining crew talent show, and another a Thai dance show by local performers. A pianist plays jazzy tunes in the Piano Bar each night.

Overall, the food gets a solid "good" rating, with breakfast and lunch buffets being the best offerings. All meals are open seating and served in the restaurant at banquettes and tables of four, six, and eight, and the dress code is always casual but tasteful. Catering to the large European clientele, buffets include a good se-lection of cheeses, like Brie and smoked Gouda, several types of salad, cold cuts, and fish. Dinner, which is sometimes sit-down and sometimes buffet, can be somewhat chaotic and rushed. Waiters and bartenders dress in costume for the week's Thai and Indian theme meals, which include lobster and shrimp with rice pilaf, beef curry, and Nasi Goreng (rice with spicy peanut sauce). A Thai chef prepares delicious made-to-order native dishes several days a week, like Tom Yam Goong (spicy soup with shrimp) and Pad See Thai (fried noodles with veggies and choice of meat).

Cabins are roomy for a ship of this size and are de-signed with a pleasant nautical motif—blue fabrics and carpeting, portholes, brass-tone lighting fixtures, and a dark-wood trim framing the off-white furniture and walls. The majority have twin beds convertible into doubles. Storage space is more than adequate for a ca-sual cruise in a warm climate. Cabins have TVs (except the four inside cabins) that show movies and news, a telephone, a hair dryer, and a safe. Standard bath-rooms are small, with narrow showers. The eight deluxe cabins, which open onto the main deck (and can get noisy), have minibars and whirlpool bathtubs.

The Star Flyer's long hull, needle-sharp bowsprit, four towering masts, and 36,000 square feet of sails recall a romantic, swashbuckling era of ship travel. The ship spends November through April in the Far East, alternating between two seven-night itineraries along the western coast of Thailand and Malaysia, visiting remote islands and waterways with exotic-sounding names you'll struggle to pronounce.

The Itinerary

Adventurous and comfortable, the 170-passenger *Star Flyer* offers a carefree lifestyle. You can climb the masts and help pull in the sails, crawl into the bow netting, lounge by one of the two small pools, or chat with the captain. Passengers, an eclectic international mix, feel pampered, as they would on a friend's yacht. If you're looking for action, shopping, culture, and organized tours, you won't find it here. At most only a handful of shore excursions are offered, such as a tour on pretty **Penang Island** to a butterfly farm, Snake Temple, a batik factory, and Chinatown; and in **Phang Nga Bay** a scenic motorboat trip to a Muslim village built on stilts and through an amazing sea of rock formations to the touristy James Bond island where the movie *Man with the Golden Gun* was filmed. For the most part the *Star Flyer*'s itineraries are passive, like moving through a nature documentary in a landscape that is haunting and mysterious; and the sea is marked by craggy rock formations rising 1,000 feet seemingly out of nowhere.

Sailing from one far-flung island cluster to another, the ship anchors offshore, and passengers shuttle back and forth by tender. Activities in port revolve around beaches and water sports, all complimentary. Snorkeling equipment is issued for the week, and for water-skiing and banana-boat rides, the young sports staff operates four Zodiacs that are carried along with the ship. Other activities include a beach barbecue on a nearly deserted island paradise with silky white-sand beaches and tender rides to get great shots of the ship under sail against the rocky landscape. The captain, at story time, gives a daily talk about the history of sailing. But, for the most part, socializing among passengers and with the crew is the main onboard activity.

Star Clippers' *Star Flyer*

Address/Phone: Star Clippers, 4101 Salzebo Street, Coral Gables, FL 33146; (305) 442–0550; reservations: (800) 442–0551; brochures: (800) 442–0556; fax: (305) 442–1611; www.starclippers.com

The Ship: *Star Flyer* was built in 1991, has a gross tonnage of 2,298, a length of 360 feet, and a draft of 18.5 feet.

Passengers: 168; all ages, including Americans and Europeans; English the lingua franca

Dress: Casual at all times

Officers/Crew: European officers; international crew

Cabins: 84; 78 outside and most relatively compact; no verandas

Fare: $$

What's included: Usually cruise only, although cruise-tour rates will include air, hotels, some meals, some sightseeing, and transfers

What's not included: For cruise only, airfare, port charges, shore excursions, tips, drinks

Highlights: The ship is very much a destination and makes one feel adventurous, recalling the sailing-ship past. An exotic itinerary for an exotic ship, cruising among friends.

Other itineraries: Besides these seven-night alternating itineraries from Phuket, Thailand, along the west coast of Thailand and Malaysia, which are offered between November and March, the *Star Flyer* returns through the Indian Ocean to cruise the Greek islands and the Turkish coast from May to October. Between May and September the *Royal Clipper* and *Star Clipper* offer alternative Western Mediterranean cruises, spring and fall transatlantic positioning voyages, and two winter Caribbean itineraries.

RADISSON SEVEN SEAS' *SONG OF FLOWER*
Vietnam's Coastal Cities

Radisson Seven Seas owns or markets several high-end small to medium-size ships, and the 180-passenger *Song of Flower* is one of the best values for serious destinations. The 8,282-ton ship was converted from a roll-on roll-off cargo ship to a cruise ship in 1986, and she was first operated by Exploration Cruise Lines as the *Explorer Starship*. Since 1990 she has only gotten better and attracts a well-traveled and well-educated clientele who are genuinely interested in where they are going.

Being small, the ship has a limited range of public rooms, but all are attractively decorated with high-quality furnishings. The observation lounge, above the bridge, is the venue for afternoon tea and a quiet read; the main lounge has gently tiered seating for lectures, small shows, and a five-piece band; and a substantial library has a collection of fiction, nonfiction, and reference books and videos.

The main restaurant, on a lower deck with an open-seating policy, is supplemented by a Northern Italian reservations-only, thirty-seat trattoria. In both restaurants, the food and service by European and Filipino stewards is uniformly excellent, and all beverages, including table wines, are included in the fares. Lunchtime deck buffets provide varied themes such as sushi, Italian, Oriental, and Mexican, with some dishes prepared to order, including omelets at breakfast. The lido, flanked by the twin funnels, is marred by noise when the ship is underway.

The cabins are all outside, with windows or portholes, and include complimentary stocked minibars and refrigerators, locked drawers, televisions with VCRs, terrycloth robes, direct-dial telephones, and private bathrooms with showers and half baths or full tubs. B-category has private verandas, and A cabins are suites. Passengers also get laundry and dry cleaning service and complimentary twenty-four-hour room service.

Deck space is roomy around the after pool, with additional deck chairs on the horseshoe mezzanine above. There is limited walking along the narrow side decks, a small forward observation deck, and an open bridge policy during daylight hours at sea.

The Itinerary

Depending on the cruise, the ship on a northbound cruise may embark in **Thailand**, **Singapore**, or **Indonesia**, with normally a day or two at sea for passengers to become acquainted with the ship and partake of the excellent lecture enrichment program.

Vietnam is a relatively new cruising destination and a good one, as the country is linear and most sites are located near the coast. The Song of Flower, with its very popular following, makes several coastal cruises each year, with Hong Kong usually one end point and Singapore or Bangkok the other.

Sailing out of the **South China Sea** into the broad **Mekong Delta,** the ship passes the former French resort at **Vung Tau** and begins to gingerly pick its way through a steady stream of wooden fishing and cargo boats to follow the arcing **Saigon River** channel. **Saigon** remains the favored designation for what is now officially known as **Ho Chi Minh City.** Docking alongside the central district for two days allows passengers to tour the city and surrounding countryside.

Visits are made to the former South Vietnamese presidential palace, and from the balcony you will readily recall television footage of North Vietnamese tanks crashing through the gates on April 30, 1975. The former American Embassy, where the last helicopter took off amid the chaos of evacuation, has been pulled down. From the nineteenth-century French colonial days, the legacies are Notre Dame Cathedral, the General Post Office, and the former City Hall, the latter two exhibiting high Victorian style.

At the National Museum, a repository of Vietnamese and Chinese art, the uniquely Vietnamese water puppet show has unseen performers maneuvering colorful wooden representations of fish, serpents, frogs, and humans around a pond that serves as the stage. You get to mingle with the local population at the **Cholon** produce market in Chinatown and on the streets outside the stylishly restored Continental and Rex Hotels, the latter's roof garden a popular nightspot. Then extend the day by dining out. Except at the most expensive restaurants, a full Vietnamese dinner should cost less than $25.

Following a night aboard ship, it's a two-hour drive to the Cu Chi Tunnels, a maze of underground passages and chambers started after World War II, ultimately stretching from the southern end of the **Ho Chi Minh Trail** to the Saigon River. From well-concealed entrances, the Viet Cong sniped at the enemy and quickly retreated, and when the going got tough they could remain underground for weeks at a time. Several hundred feet of tunnels at three levels have been enlarged to allow tourists to explore, though this site is not recommended for the claustrophobic.

Generally, there's a sea day en route to **Danang,** then a three-hour drive north along Route 1, crossing the **Cloud Pass** and descending to hug the scenic coastline into **Hue.** The city is now a peaceful place of wide tree-lined boulevards paralleling the **Perfume River** and set against a backdrop of mountains bordering Laos. Visits include nineteenth-century imperial tombs and pleasure gardens, the partly restored remains of the once grand imperial palace that was vir-

tually leveled during the Tet Offensive, and a commanding seventeenth-century pagoda overlooking the Perfume River.

The *Song of Flower* docks at **Haiphong Harbor.** The drive inland passes through a timeless landscape of rice paddies, with bent-over figures weeding, working simple irrigation devices, and tending their water buffalo. **Hanoi,** a low-rise city that was planned around Chinese-style lakes dotted with temples and French-designed parks, boulevards, ocher-colored rowhouses and public buildings, presents a far slower pace than Saigon, and the streets, thick with bicycles and motorbikes, make walking less intimidating.

A somber mausoleum, guarded by smartly uniformed soldiers enforcing a strict code of behavior (proper dress, no talking, and hands at one's side) holds the embalmed and spotlighted body of **Ho Chi Minh,** the country's much-loved patriot who died in 1969. Uncle Ho, as he is affectionately known, refused to live in the nearby flamboyant French-built palace and instead occupied a small wooden lakeside bungalow that you can visit.

The Temple of Literature, founded in the eleventh century, features Confucian pavilions and a collection of stellae, or tablets, resting atop stone frogs. Lunch may be served at the handsomely restored, 1911 Metropole Hotel before you explore on foot the Quarter of 36 Streets, each block specializing in some commodity such as paper goods, silver, silk, flowers, porcelain, or hardware.

For a final call, the *Song of Flower* anchors in **Halong Bay,** a national park made up of 3,000 towering limestone islets, where you board sailing junks for a morning cruise through a fantastic natural wonder, similar to the conical peaks that dot the River Li at Guilin in China, and peppered with grottoes accessible by small boat.

Finally the ship sails into **Hong Kong** harbor between Victoria Peak on Hong Kong Island and the **Kowloon Peninsula,** docking at the Ocean Terminal with two days ahead to enjoy the former British colony.

Normally, Radisson Seven Seas uses The Regent in Hong Kong, rated as one of the world's finest hotels, occupying an outstanding location directly over the harbor and facing the Hong Kong skyline. Hong Kong island touring includes the incline railway for the view from Victoria Peak, a bus to the seaside at Repulse Bay, and a sampan cruise through Aberdeen's typhoon shelter. On the **Kowloon** side, there are visits to a Taoist temple, the jade and bird market, and Nathan and Canton Road shops.

Radisson Seven Seas' *Song of Flower*

Address/Phone: Radisson Seven Seas Cruises, 600 Corporate Drive, Suite 410, Fort Lauderdale, FL 33334; (954) 776–6123 or (800) 333–3333; fax: (954) 722–6763; www.rssc.com

The Ship: *Song of Flower* was built in 1974 and converted into the cruise ship *Explorer Starship* in 1986. She has a gross tonnage of 8,282, a length of 407 feet, and a draft of 16 feet.

Passengers: 180; age forty-five and up; mostly Americans, some Europeans and Australians

Dress: Informal and casual

Officers/Crew: Norwegian officers; Filipino crew

Cabins: 100; roomy and all outside, 10 with verandas

Fare: $$$$

What's included: Cruise fare, selected shore excursions, wines, liquor and soft drinks, tips, hotel nights, some sightseeing, transfers, pre- and post cruise; sometimes airfare from the West Coast

What's not included: Port charges; add-on air from Midwest, East Coast

Highlights: Excellent itinerary, organization, lecturers, onboard atmosphere

Other itineraries: In addition to this eleven-night Vietnam cruise that normally operates in January and February, the *Song of Flower* makes cruises elsewhere in Southeast Asia, into the Indian Ocean, and in the Mediterranean and Northern Europe. Radisson Seven Seas also operates the *Hanseatic,* the 320-passenger *Paul Gauguin,* the 350-passenger catamaran *Radisson Diamond,* the 490-passenger *Seven Seas Navigator,* and the 720-passenger *Seven Seas Mariner.*

SEABOURN CRUISE LINE'S *SEABOURN SPIRIT*
Coastal Vietnam Sojourn

The *Seabourn Spirit,* one of three roughly 10,000-gross-register-ton, 200-passenger sisters, provides the ultimate in quiet, luxurious shipboard living, albeit at a high price. Passengers are well-traveled couples or friends traveling together, and few will be making a first cruise. Socializing is a major part of life aboard. Decorated in an understated Scandinavian style, the Club, a glass-partitioned complex, includes a lounge, a cocktail bar, and a casino. Drinks with music take place here before and after dinner, plus dancing and a cabaret show. During the days at sea, in the Amundsen Lounge, guest lecturers will give talks relating to East Asian history, relations with the United States, and economic issues.

With open seating for all meals, one has the choice of sitting alone or sharing a table. The menus are designed to encourage sampling five or six courses, and big eaters can order larger portions. The cold soups, rack of veal, saddle of venison, and broiled salmon were particularly memorable entrees, and, overall, the food and service is some of the best afloat. Poured wines are complimentary, as are all drinks. The Veranda Café offers both indoor seating and a single line of tables under a canvas awning at stern, and breakfast time is a particularly friendly hour to meet other passengers.

A chef takes special orders for eggs Benedict, Belgian waffles, and blueberry pancakes. Lunch is also served here and even more informally at the Sky Bar above the pool. Other than on hosted evenings, the Veranda Café serves dinner by reservation, with an Italian or Oriental theme.

Most passengers occupy similar 277-square-foot, one-room suites with a large sitting area next to a picture window. Thirty-six suites have been refitted with French balconies, in place of the large windows. Amenities are minibar bar and refrigerator, TV/VCR, radio, walk-in closet with a safe, and marble bathroom with double sinks and a tub.

On a warm-weather cruise, the lido provides protection from the sun and two popular Jacuzzis for cooling off after a steamy day ashore, plus an awkwardly sited outdoor pool. The spa offers an exercise room, two saunas, steam rooms, and a masseuse.

The Itinerary

On this cruise, the *Seabourn Spirit* embarks in **Bangkok.** Sailing south into the Gulf of Thailand, the ship's first call is at the island of **Ko Kood,** followed by a full day at sea. Sailing out of the South China Sea into the broad Mekong Delta, the ship follows the

Vietnam makes an ideal cruising destination because most cities, sites, and scenic attractions are located along the coast, and land and air travel within the country is not yet well developed. Several upscale ships make a few coastal cruises each year, with Hong Kong usually one end point and Singapore or Bangkok the other. The ten-day cruise described here is aboard the **Seabourn Spirit.**

Saigon River channel to **Saigon,** now officially **Ho Chi Minh City.**

During the overnight stay docked next to the city center, visits include the former South Vietnamese presidential palace. Legacies from nineteenth-century French colonial days are Notre Dame Cathedral, the General Post Office, and the former City Hall. At the National Museum, a repository of Vietnamese and Chinese art, the Vietnamese water puppet show has unseen performers who maneuver colorful wooden representations of fish, serpents, frogs, and humans.

A two-hour drive takes you to the Cu Chi Tunnels, a maze of underground passages and chambers started after World War II; from their well-concealed entrances, the Viet Cong sniped at the enemy and quickly retreated underground, where they could remain for weeks at a time. Several hundred feet of tunnels at three levels have been enlarged to allow tourists to explore, though it's not recommended for the claustrophobic.

Following two nights and a day at sea, the ship calls at **Danang.** From here a three-hour scenic drive north along Route 1 crosses the Cloud Pass and descends to hug the low coastline into **Hue.** The city, located along the Perfume River, offers a glimpse at what formerly was a grand imperial palace virtually leveled during the 1968 Tet Offensive.

For the visit to **Hanoi,** this cruise calls at **Hongai,** but other cruises may use **Haiphong Harbor.** Regardless, the drive inland passes through a timeless landscape of rice paddies. Hanoi, a low-rise city built around Chinese-style lakes, presents a far slower pace than Saigon. A somber mausoleum, guarded by smartly uniformed soldiers, holds the embalmed body of Ho Chi Minh, the country's much-loved patriot who died in 1969. There may be time to explore the Quarter of 36 Streets, each block specializing in some commodity such as paper goods, silver, silk, flowers, or hardware.

Entering **Halong Bay,** a national park made up of 3,000 towering limestone islets, you cruise through a fantastic natural wonder, similar to the conical peaks that dot the River Li at Guilin in China. After a final day at sea, the ship sails into **Hong Kong** harbor. Most visitors stay a few days to ride the incline railway for the view from Victoria Peak, or cross the island to seaside Repulse Bay and Aberdeen's typhoon shelter. On the **Kowloon** side there are visits to a Taoist temple, the jade and bird market, and Nathan and Canton Road shops.

Seabourn Cruise Line's
Seabourn Spirit

Address/Phone: Seabourn Cruise Line, 610 Blue Lagoon Drive, Suite 400, Miami, FL 33126; (305) 563–3000 or (800) 929–9391; fax: (305) 463–3010; www.seabourn.com

The Ship: *Seabourn Spirit* was built in 1989 and has a gross tonnage of 9,975, a length of 440 feet, and a draft of 17 feet.

Passengers: 204; mostly Americans, age fifty and up

Dress: Formal, informal, and casual nights

Officers/Crew: Norwegian officers; mostly European crew, plus some Filipinos

Cabins: 102; all outside suites, the majority identical except for location; six with verandas. Thirty-six French balconies (window-type double doors set before a railing) have been added to some suites in the place of sealed windows.

Fare: $$$$$

What's included: Cruise, port charges, three nights in Bangkok, wine and drinks, tips

What's not included: Airfare, transfers, shore excursions

Highlights: A luxurious and enriching way to visit Vietnam

Other itineraries: In addition to this thirteen-day cruise tour between Bangkok and Singapore, operating in January and February 2000, there are similar cruises with Vietnam the primary focus between January and March 2000 and December 2000 and January 2001. Seabourn offers global itineraries, including *Seabourn Legend* in South America.

VICTORIA CRUISES' *VICTORIA I*
Cruising the Yangtze

In 1994 Victoria Cruises, a Sino-American joint venture, brought international standards to Yangtze River travel when the 154-passenger *Victoria I* entered service, followed by *Victoria II, III,* and *V,* and four additional ships. First-time visitors to China will want to visit several destinations such as Beijing, Shanghai, Suzhou, Xian, and Guilin, so Victoria Cruises concentrates on the Yangtze's most scenic portion, the 870 miles between Wuhan and Chongqing, a trip of four nights downstream and five nights upstream.

The riverboats are roomy and comfortable. The entrance foyer, with a second deck mezzanine, serves as a shipboard junction. On the way up to the observation lounge, you pass an artist in residence demonstrating the art of Chinese painting. The large lounge and bar doubles as a party room and venue for cabaret-style entertainment. During the day informative lectures on Chinese history and traditions take place here and on the open decks. There is also a small reference library, a conference room, and a business center.

Tour groups and independent travelers are assigned a choice of tables at a single seating. Breakfast is a buffet with both Chinese and Western food, whereas the buffet lunches and served dinners consist mainly of Chinese dishes, marked by excellent ingredients but, with a few exceptions, rather bland fare. Beer, soft drinks, and bottled water are included at meals, and the Chinese staff provides willing service in the restaurant and bar and at the reception desk.

The inviting standard-category cabins (seventy of the seventy-seven rooms) have twin beds set before a huge picture window with sliding panels. Amenities also include a writing desk, a closed-circuit TV, adequate storage space, and a small bathroom with shower. The outdoor space is generous. My favorite spot is the forward observation deck below the bridge. The open top deck also has a Jacuzzi.

The Itinerary

The **Yangtze** is south China's principal highway, and tugs, barges, cargo ships, ferries, passenger steamers, and cruise boats maneuver along the constantly shifting channel. This cruise shows the many aspects of this complex country.

At the smoky industrial town of **Yichang,** the boat passes through the Gezhouba Dam, China's largest, rising 65 feet in a single lock. This dam is nothing compared to the 600-foot-high **Three Gorges Dam** now under construction just upriver at **Sandouping,** which, when completed, will flood many historical sites. If everything goes as planned, by 2009 a reservoir will stretch back 370 miles, submerging 1,500 towns and villages and 72,000 acres of agricultural land, forcing

The major attraction of a Yangtze River cruise may be the legendary passage through the misty Three Gorges, but the river journey offers additional, poignant insights into timeless rural traditions, small-town life, and the frenzied industrial development of present-day China. There are several riverboat companies that achieve acceptable western standards, and Victoria Cruises is one of them.

the resettlement of 1.3 million people. The project is expected to supply 15 percent of China's electricity, control flooding, facilitate navigation by eliminating rapids, and boost national pride.

During the stop at **Wushan,** make your way up a lively main street of shops and food stalls to high ground overlooking the junction of the Yangtze and **Daning** Rivers. At the far end of town, you board longboats that sputter up through the Daning River rapids into the **Three Little Gorges,** and when the strong currents threaten to stop progress, two men pole mightily to maintain headway.

The main event, the passage through the **Three Gorges,** extends over two days. The 47-mile **Xiling Gorge** at one time was considered the most dangerous of all. Numerous steamers came to grief in the rock-strewn rapids before a safe channel was blasted through in the 1950s. A temple, built 1,500 years ago, is silhouetted against the sky. The 35-mile **Wu Gorge's** sheer cliffs rise to green-clad limestone peaks often enshrouded in swirling mists, and the highest, Goddess Peak, resembles a woman kneeling in front of a pillar. **Qutang Gorge** is dramatically flanked by 4,000-foot mountains that squeeze the river into a narrow canyon, inhibiting two-way traffic.

Beyond the attractive walled city of **Fengjie,** where stone steps lead up from the river landings to Ming Dynasty gates, hundreds of coolies load coal into baskets and with rapid steps file down to ships at the water's edge. At **Fengdu,** known as the City of Ghosts, a temple complex, which dates back to the Han Dynasty (206 B.C. to A.D. 220), has undergone extensive reconstruction. Disembarking at **Chongqing,** passengers will see that the city is usually enveloped in fog, a natural phenomenon exacerbated by industrial pollution.

Victoria Cruises' *Victoria I*

Address/Phone: Victoria Cruises, 57–08 39th Avenue, Woodside, NY 11377; (212) 818–1680 or (800) 348–8084; fax: (212) 818–9889; e-mail: info@victoriacruises.com; www.victoriacruises.com

The Ship: *Victoria I* was built in 1994. It has a gross tonnage of 3,424, a length of 287 feet, and a draft of 8.5 feet.

Passengers: 154; age forty and up; mostly Americans on China tours; many Chinese Americans, Asian Chinese, and some Europeans

Dress: Casual

Officers/Crew: Chinese officers and crew; American cruise and enrichment staff

Cabins: 70; moderate size, plus seven suites

Fare: $$

What's included: For independent travelers, port charges and beer, soft drinks, and bottled water with meals

What's not included: Airfare, tips, drinks not served at meals, and shore excursions (highly recommended inexpensive package available)

Highlights: The Three Gorges, plus a terrific insight into rural and industrial China

Other itineraries: In addition to the cruise between Wuhan and Chongqing, offered between March and early December, the company operates on the lower Yangtze between Shanghai and Wuhan, stopping at Yangzhou, Nanjing, Huangshan (Yellow Mountain), and Lushan. Passengers may remain for the entire ten-day trip up to Chongqing or eight days downstream. The best months to travel are May–June and September–October; July and August are unpleasantly hot and humid; fog descends on the river in winter. Tour operators that include the Yangtze in their programs are: General Tours/TBI tours (800–223–0266), Maupintour (800–255–4266), Travcoa (800–992–2003), and Uniworld (800–733–7820).

'EGAL CHINA CRUISES' *PRINCESS ELAINE*
Yangtze River: The Gorges and Much More

Regal China Cruises, established in 1993, operates three large riverboats completed in Germany, the only ones cruising the Yangtze that were constructed outside China. Although they have a high quality of design and workmanship, their length makes them less nimble than those built specially for Yangtze River cruising.

The 258-passenger *Princess Elaine* and her two sisters are fast, four-deck, well-equipped riverboats that bring European standards to the Yangtze. Two forward lounges afford views ahead: the Lotus Bar and the smaller Misty Lounge, which also serves as a tea and games room and a library. The Jade Ballroom is the venue for Chinese opera, dance and acrobatic shows, as well as live music, dancing, ka_____ _____ _____ctures. Passengers are norma_____ either the large Golden Pavilic_____'s Dining Room, both serving _____ buffet style at one or two s_____ _____ on the passenger count.

The 134 cabins, arranged over all four passenger decks, have large windows, private shower and toilet, refrigerators, TVs, in-house telephones, and twenty-four-hour room service. The 114 double rooms have twin beds separated by a night table, plus a tiny sitting area by the window, whereas the ten suites have separate bedrooms and lounges and windows for both. The ten singles are narrow rooms with a small entrance foyer. Many face onto a side promenade, but the doors open onto the central corridor.

The Yangzte River, the main highway leading deeply into Central China, is a busy navigable waterway used by freight barges, scheduled passenger riverboats, and comfortable cruisers offering high western standards such as the Regal China Cruises' fleet. Most travelers want to see the famous Three Gorges, but they also get a close–up look at rural, industrial, and legendary China, not normally found on land tours.

In addition to the viewing there are lots of daytime activities—a mix of East and West. The English-speaking cruise director organizes lectures, talks on deck, and sessions devoted to the Chinese language, the art of calligraphy, mah-Jongg, and tai chi. The health club offers a sauna and gym and Chinese medicine such as acupuncture, acupressure, and massage. A business center is equipped with copying services, satellite communications, phone, and fax machines. Additional services are a gift shop, a post office, and a physician with training in both Chinese and Western medicine.

The Itinerary
For the Yangtze River itinerary, see Victoria Cruises.

Regal China Cruises'
Princess Elaine

Address/Phone: Regal China Cruises, 57 West 38th Street, New York, NY 10018; (212) 768–3388 or (800) 808–3388; fax: (212) 768–4939; e-mail: rccny@aol.com

The Ships: *Princess Elaine* and identical sisters *Princess Jeannie* and *Princess Sheena* have a gross tonnage of 5,963, a length of 424 feet, and a shallow draft.

Passengers: 258; age forty and up; some ethnic Chinese aboard as well as Americans and Europeans, mostly as part of a China tour

Dress: Casual at all times

Officers/Crew: Chinese officers and crew; Western cruise staff

Cabins: 114 doubles, 10 suites, and 10 singles; all outside with windows, refrigerator, TV, telephone, and private showers; bathtubs and bidets in the suites

Fare: $$

What's included: For independent travelers, cruise and port charges, drinks with meals

What's not included: Airfare, excursions (moderately priced package), bar drinks, tips

Highlights: The Three Gorges, plus a terrific insight into rural and industrial China

Other itineraries: In addition to the above cruise, four days downstream and six days upstream, between Chongqing and Wuhan, which operates from March to November, Regal also runs a short three-day winter itinerary from Yichang that includes the Three Gorges, the Daning River, Fengjie, and the construction site for the huge dam. Several of the tour operators that include the Yangtze in their programs are: Abercrombie & Kent (800–323–7308), China Travel Service (800 332–2831), Pacific Holidays (800–355–8025).

POLAR REGIONS

CLIPPER CRUISE LINE'S *CLIPPER ADVENTURER*
Greenland and the Canadian Arctic

Clipper Cruise Line, based in St. Louis, got its start in 1983 with the first of three U.S.-flag coastal ships, two of which the company still operates—the 102-passenger *Nantucket Clipper* and 138-passenger *Yorktown Clipper*. In 1998 the line introduced the 122-passenger *Clipper Adventurer,* not the company's first venture into expedition cruising, but the first such ship the company owned. Built in 1975 for the Murmansk Shipping Company, the 4,500-ton, 330-foot passenger vessel first traded as the *Alla Tarasova* in the remote seas north of Russia. After undergoing $14.8 million of work in a Danish shipyard, the rugged little liner was transformed into a graceful, stabilized beauty within and without.

Her public rooms are paneled with mahogany-wood grain, and the furnishings are upholstered in bold-colored fabrics of deep blue, red, and aquamarine and patterned with stripes, checks, and flecks. The forward lounge and bar, with a pronounced upward sheer, comfortably seats all passengers in chairs and curved banquettes for talks, films, light buffets, and socializing. Amidships, the Clipper Club, with a second bar, card tables, and settees, leads aft to an attractive open-seating restaurant with deep windows on three sides to bring in natural light. From the Promenade

Deck a central staircase leads up to the library, a warm and quiet retreat for readers, puzzle addicts, and board-game players. The captain's twenty-four-hour open-bridge policy is a big draw, and from the bridge wings, it's a few steps down to the forward observation deck or aft for a brisk walk along the broad Boat Deck.

Clipper's chefs, trained at the Culinary Institute of America, produce fine meals. The menu runs to North Atlantic salmon, sea bass, lobster tails, roasted duckling, pork tenderloin, prime ribs, tasty wild mushroom and roasted pepper soups, ever-changing salads, and freshly baked cakes and pies, accompanied by a fairly priced wine list.

Seven categories of outside cabins, with portholes or windows, have parallel or L-shaped twin beds (but no queens), four closets, wood wainscoting, decent floor space, and bathrooms with showers. Cabins on the Promenade Deck look onto the side-enclosed promenade and through a second set of glass to the sea.

The Itinerary
The actual landings in **Greenland,** the sub-Arctic, and **Arctic** change from year to year. The weather is always a factor, but the description here will give you a flavor of what it is like to explore these remote regions.

*The **Clipper Adventurer** is one of the best expedition-style vessels to come along in years, an ideal vehicle to cruise the northern polar regions. The remoteness, the considerable beauty, and the chance to see wildlife close up are major attractions.*

Depending on the itineraries the expedition staff usually hails from the United States, Canada, and Britain, and they accompany passengers on Zodiac runs ashore, give talks, and mingle at meals. Most passengers will be American, and they will on average be younger than those aboard Clipper's two coastal ships. Children who are comfortable in adult company will enjoy wildlife spotting.

From the air, Greenland, the world's largest island, appears as a dark, forbidding landscape of stony mountains incised by deep blue fjords. Soon after sailing, you may be donning rubber boots for a wet landing by Zodiac to visit the ruins of the settlement that Erik the Red established in A.D. 983, now a sheep farm. At **Nuuk,** Greenland's bleak capital, the unusual museum displays four well-preserved 500-year-old mummies.

During our choppy passage across **Davis Strait,** the ship came upon a large pod of spouting fin whales. Later at dinner, anchored in a fjord off **Baffin Island,** a polar bear and her two cubs came down to the water's edge.

On outings ashore passengers divide into groups according to the length of the hikes, and in polar bear country, the guides carry powerful shotguns and radios. Arctic white and yellow poppies, blue harebells, mosses, and 1-inch-high polar forests of birch, juniper, and willow form the colorful and often spongy tundra underfoot. The sightings of moose and caribou are often distant, but the physical beauty of the wild, untouched landscape, in temperatures that range from the mid 40s to the mid 60s, proves most satisfying. The Zodiac trips bring you close to polar bears, to islands inhabited with lounging walrus or ring-neck seals, and steep cliff faces. Visits to isolated Inuit villages give insights into traditions of bone and soapstone carving, gymnastics, and the unusual sight and sound of throat singing.

Passengers sign up to be awakened for the pulsating display of Northern Lights, and we slowed to pass through thick lines of pack ice or changed course to avoid the wonderful shapes and colors of icebergs drifting south. The *Clipper Adventurer* is ice-strengthened, so there is no danger of becoming stranded. In the cozy surroundings of life onboard, the expedition staff pools years of experience and enthusiasm to give about a dozen well-attended talks, some slide illustrated, and lively predinner recaps of the days' events and what lies ahead.

Clipper Cruise Line's
Clipper Adventurer

Address/phone: Clipper Cruise Line, 7711 Bonhomme Avenue, St. Louis, MO 63105; (800) 325-0010 or (314) 727-2929; fax; (314) 727-6576; e-mail: SmallShip@aol.com; www.clippercruise.com

The Ship: *Clipper Adventurer,* built in 1975 as the Russian-flag *Alla Tarasova* and rebuilt in 1998, has a gross tonnage of 4,575, a length of 330 feet, and a draft of 16 feet.

Passengers: 122; age fifty and up, nearly all American

Dress: Casual at all times

Officers/Crew: Scandinavian and Filipino officers; American bar staff; Filipino wait staff, deckhands, and cabin stewardesses

Cabins: 61; all outside, average size

Fare: $$$$

What's included: Cruise, port charges, all excursions, connecting charter flights between Ottawa or other Canadian gateway and the ship, hotel nights near airport, if required

What's not included: Drinks, tips

Highlights: Visiting remote islands, seeing wildlife, hiking the tundra; a well-run ship

Other itineraries: In addition to this Canadian and Greenland summer itinerary, the *Clipper Adventurer* offers late spring and summer trips in the Mediterranean, Iberia, Northern Europe, and Iceland; in the fall south along the U.S. East Coast to South America and the Amazon and winter in Antarctica and the Falklands; *Yorktown Clipper's* California Rivers and the *Nantucket Clipper* on the East Coast.

RADISSON SEVEN SEAS CRUISES' *HANSEATIC*
Cruising to Antarctica

Radisson Seven Seas charters the upscale, German-owned, 188-passenger *Hanseatic* for Antarctica cruises, embarking at Ushuaia in southern Argentina.

Public rooms include a forward observation lounge/bar with excellent sight lines and a small adjoining library with a reference-book section. A pianist plays in the evening, and tempting, hot hors d'oeuvres appear about 11:00 P.M. The main stern lounge comfortably seats everyone for social gatherings, afternoon tea and pastries accompanied by a four-piece band, recaps of the day's activities before dinner, and light cabaret on selected nights. The open bridge becomes a popular gathering place to chat with the officer of the watch and to study the charts. Additional amenities include a fitness room, a massage facility, a sauna, a beauty salon, a tiny outdoor pool, a glass-enclosed Jacuzzi, and a boutique for clothing, souvenirs, and sundries.

The roomy windowed restaurant, with open single seating, offers a distinctly European menu featuring excellent cream soups, good seafood, varied salads, and nightly game dishes, as well as a light menu. Breakfast and lunch have buffet and menu selections, whereas dinner is from a menu only. The informal breakfast and lunch buffet, two decks above, is an alternative, and it becomes a reservations-only Oriental restaurant at night.

The ninety similar outside double cabins (with windows or portholes), which measure 236 square feet, have a sitting area, a TV/VCR, a radio, a complimentary nonalcoholic minibar, a hair dryer, and a tub bath. Four one-room suites offer butler service.

The Itinerary
In Darwin Hall the naturalist staff, combining years of experience working in Antarctica and engaged in research, give enrichment lectures, which are also broadcast on cabin TVs.

Embarking at **Ushuaia**, we had two choppy nights and a day at sea, then made landfall off the **Falklands**. Wearing rubber boots and parkas provided by the ship, we made our first wet Zodiac (inflatable craft) landing at a combination private sheep farm and nature preserve to visit a cliffside rookery of nesting rockhopper penguins, black-browed albatross, and blue-eyed cormorants. On approach the sounds were more akin to a barnyard of domestic animals than a colony of birds, and with it came the strong odor of guano. Especially fun to watch are the 2-foot-tall penguins as they literally hop their way up the steep path from the beach.

A school of playful dolphins accompanied our second landing, followed by an optional 3-mile walk through a hillside colony of burrowing Magellanic pen-

When you open a reference book on Antarctica, the very first paragraph indicates that the white continent qualifies as the coldest, driest, windiest, and iciest landmass in the world, and the surrounding Southern Ocean ships up into the stormiest seas. Antarctica sounds like a prime destination for the masochist; yet once you step ashore from the expedition ship **Hanseatic,** *a completely different set of superlatives will come to mind.*

guins and across sloping fields of a working farm to the main house for a proper English tea. A visit to **Port Stanley** provided a sleepy bit of old England transferred to the South Atlantic, an eccentric museum packed with historic and natural-history exhibits, a safe harbor refuge for battered sailing ships, and a hand-made-woolen sweater shop looked after by local women with an English accent all their own.

During the crossing of the **Drake Passage,** it may be rough, even tempestuous, so come prepared for this and possible changes of itinerary because of high winds. The daytime temperatures rise above freezing and often into the 40s and 50s.

Volcanic **Paulet Island** is home to some 200,000 Adélie penguins, and **Half Moon Island** provides a rocky setting for several colonies of chinstrap penguins, Weddell seals, and fur seals in the shadow of 4,000- to 6,000-foot glacier-covered mountains. In the drowned caldera of **Deception Island,** you'll find the eerie ruins of a whaling station and a British research base, quickly abandoned in 1969 at the onset of a volcanic eruption. Steam and the smell of sulfur rose through the black sand.

On my cruise we circled a towering conical iceberg estimated to be 250 feet high and later sailed between two tabular bergs measuring thousands of feet in length and generating their own strong winds. Near a tiny Argentinian base, Zodiacs took us into **Paradise Bay,** ringed by ragged glaciers, pockmarked with blue ice grottoes, that occasionally calved with a sharp crack. Two more landings added the sight and far worse smell of a colony of molting young elephant seals, one estimated to weigh 4,000 pounds; a gentoo penguin rookery; and a Russian research station, where we off-loaded three tons of equipment and embarked two German scientists.

Northbound, the dreaded **Drake Passage** lived up to its well-deserved reputation, but by late morning the storm abated, and the visit to **Cape Horn** was so tranquil that one almost forgot the night before. Reentering the **Beagle Channel,** the *Hanseatic* docks at **Ushuaia.** Some passengers fly directly home, and others stop over in **Buenos Aires** to enjoy its turn-of-the-century architecture, street life, restaurants and cafes, and stylish residents.

Radisson Seven Seas Cruises's *Hanseatic*

Address/Phone: Radisson Seven Seas Cruises, 600 Corporate Drive, Suite 410, Fort Lauderdale, FL 3334; (954) 776–6123 or (800) 333–3333; fax: (954) 722–6763; www.rssc.com

The Ship: *Hanseatic* was completed in 1993, has a gross tonnage of 8,378, a length of 403 feet, and a draft of 15.5 feet.

Passengers: 184; ages forty-five and up, mostly Americans

Dress: Jacket and tie for some evenings, otherwise casual

Officers/Crew: German officers; German and Northern European hotel staff; Filipino deck crew

Cabins: 92; doubles and twins, all outside, with sitting areas; suites on the Bridge Deck

Fare: $$$$

What's included: Cruise, port charges, shore excursions, tips

What's not included: Airfares, drinks

Highlights: Variety of wildlife, shapes and color of icebergs, landscape, a true adventure

Other itineraries: In addition to this Antarctic cruise, Radisson Seven Seas also markets the *Paul Gauguin* and operates the *Song of Flower,* the *Radisson Diamond,* the *Seven Seas Navigator,* and the *Seven Seas Mariner.*

CLIPPER CRUISE LINE'S *CLIPPER ADVENTURER*
Cruising the White Continent

St. Louis-based Clipper Cruise Line, in business since 1983, operates four small ships, one of which is the 122-passenger *Clipper Adventurer*, introduced in 1988. Rebuilt from the Russian-flag *Alla Tarasova,* the ship operates in the style of a seagoing club.

The public rooms, paneled with mahogany-wood grain, include a forward lounge and bar, seating all passengers for talks, films, and light breakfast and lunch buffets. The Clipper Club, a second bar with card tables and settees, leads aft to an open-seating restaurant with wraparound windows. The menus feature grilled salmon, sea bass, roasted duckling, prime ribs, tasty wild mushroom and roasted pepper soups, fresh salads, and freshly baked cakes and pies. The library, one deck above, is a warm and quiet retreat for readers, puzzle addicts, and board-game players. With an open-bridge policy, the ship provides passengers with another popular social center.

The all outside cabins (portholes or windows) fall into seven categories and have parallel or L-shaped twin beds, good closet space, and bathrooms with showers. Promenade Deck cabins look through two sets of glass to the sea.

The Itinerary

Following two days experiencing the cafe, restaurant, and street life of **Buenos Aires,** embarkation takes place at the southern Argentinean port of **Ushuaia.** Orientation talks are scheduled during the two nights and a day en route to the **Falklands,** the British islands invaded by Argentina in 1982.

The first wet Zodiac landing visits a cliffside rookery of nesting rockhopper penguins, black-browed albatross, and blue-eyed cormorants. Seated on a nearby rock, I watched a well-ordered line of 2-foot-high penguins literally hop their way up the steep path from the beach, bellies full of fish and krill (shrimplike crustacean) for regurgitating into the mouths of their fluffy chicks. A second landing provided a gentle 3-mile walk through an active hillside colony of burrowing Magellanic penguins, who pop up to have a look as we pass. **Port Stanley,** the island capital, is a sleepy bit of old England transferred to the South Atlantic. Here you can visit with the world's most southerly Anglican cathedral and an eccentric museum packed with historic and natural-history exhibits overseen by a delightful curator.

*The Antarctic continent is the most pristine and least populated place on earth, and an international treaty signed in 1959 aims to keep it that way. Antarctica's wildlife is the tamest and least fearful of humanity, and its scenery, seen through the clearest air, presents a breathtaking combination of majestic mountains draped by massive glaciers and rugged islands spread across a seascape peppered with icebergs longer than a football field. Add the Falkland Islands, and the nimble **Clipper Adventurer** will take you on an adventure cruise in a thoroughly professional manner.*

During the forty-eight-hour crossing of the **Drake Passage,** which can be extremely rough, the naturalists might spot Wilson's storm petrels, Antarctic terns, and the huge wandering albatross, which boasts a wingspan of up to 9 feet. Landings on the Antarctic Peninsula may vary from cruise to cruise because of high winds and weather, but you see Adélie penguins in several locations and, on **Half Moon Island,** colonies of chinstrap penguins, Weddell seals, and fur seals. Stay ashore as long as you can to enjoy their antics. The Antarctic summer comes with almost twenty-four hours of daylight and temperatures that may rise into the 50s.

Cruising into the drowned caldera of **Deception Island,** the *Clipper Adventurer* drops anchor for a walk among the eerie ruins of a whaling station and British research base, quickly abandoned just prior to a volcanic eruption in 1969. Steam and the smell of sulfur percolate through the black sand. Continuing south, towering icebergs with fantastic shapes and shades of blue and green often generate their own strong winds even when it otherwise seems calm. Other landings add the sight and smell of molting young elephant seals, weighing up to 4,000 pounds, a gentoo penguin rookery, and a Russian research station. Northbound, hold on for a second crossing of the **Drake Passage,** understandably feared by the legendary Cape Horners battling monstrous seas for days on end, until the ship reaches lee of **Tierra del Fuego,** finally docking at **Ushuaia.**

Clipper Cruise Line's *Clipper Adventurer*

Address/Phone: Clipper Cruise Line, 7711 Bonhomme Avenue, St. Louis, MO 63105; (314) 727–2929 or (800) 325–0010; fax: (314) 727–6576; e-mail: SmallShip@aol.com; www.clippercruise.com

The Ship: *Clipper Adventurer,* built in 1975 as the Russian-flag *Alla Tarasova* and rebuilt in 1998, has a gross tonnage of 4,575, a length of 330 feet, and a draft of 16 feet.

Passengers: 122; age fifty and up, nearly all American

Dress: Casual at all times

Officers/Crew: Scandinavian; Filipino officers; American bar staff; Filipino wait staff, deckhands, and cabin stewardesses

Cabins: 61; all outside, average size

Fare: $$$$

What's included: Cruise, port charges, all shore excursions, connecting flights between Buenos Aires and the ship, hotel night in Buenos Aires

What's not included: Airfare between the United States and Buenos Aires, drinks, tips

Highlights: Incredible beauty of Antarctica, icebergs, many types of penguins, remote research stations, British colony of the Falklands, excellent enrichment program

Other itineraries: In addition to this Antarctica and the Falklands winter itinerary, one cruise also including South Georgia, the *Clipper Adventurer* offers late spring and summer trips in the Mediterranean, Northern Europe, Iceland, Greenland, and Arctic Canada; and in fall south along the U.S. East Coast to South America and the Amazon. The *Yorktown Clipper* cruises California's rivers and the *Nantucket Clipper* cruisses the East Coast.

LINDBLAD EXPEDITIONS' *ENDEAVOUR*
Antarctica, Falklands, and South Georgia

Originally built for the North Sea fishing industry, the *Endeavour* is an extremely well-built and well-maintained expedition ship that was very recently refitted. The Scandinavian officers and Filipino crew provide a disciplined yet happy ship, and they mix well with the older, well-traveled, and mostly American passengers. The ship has an open-bridge policy, a very popular feature. With a hull hardened for ice and a deep 21-foot draft, she can take the pounding seas of the South Atlantic and upon occasion has seen the worst weather that nature can produce.

On the Bridge Deck, a small, large-windowed library offers comfortable seating and lots of books on history, ecology, geography, and fauna and flora, plus twenty-four-hour coffee- and tea-making facilities. Aft is a cluster that includes a small gym with treadmills, bikes, a sauna, and an e-mail station. The Veranda Deck below houses the spacious lounge and bar where evening recaps take place, plus the lecture program—up to three on a sea day—that often includes slides and videos screened on TV monitors.

One naturalist is a diver who will show footage taken that same day of undersea marine life such as shrimp, octopus, dolphins, and acrobatic seals. A professionally produced ninety-minute trip video, with music and commentary, is available for purchase at the end of the cruise.

Forward on the Upper Deck, the restaurant has an open-seating policy, with tables for two to eight, buffet-style meals for breakfast and lunch, and table service from a menu for dinner. The food gets good marks for variety, preparation, and presentation.

The cabins are comfortable, all outside with windows or portholes, and most have beds placed athwartships to minimize rolling. The cabin radio airs announcements and music, and the closet and drawer space is adequate for a casual cruise. There is a lock drawer. As on Lindblad's other ships, there are no cabin keys.

Viewing is excellent from the forward observation deck, the bow, the bridge wings, and the port and starboard sides and aft. Some of the deck space is sheltered.

The Itinerary

This twenty-four-day cruise-tour begins in **Santiago,** Chile, with a night's hotel stay and sightseeing, then a flight south to **Punta Arenas** for boarding the ship. Depending on the weather, the *Endeavour* may or may not stop at Cape Horn before making the two-day **Drake Passage** to the **Antarctic Peninsula.**

The ship first sails into **Deception Island**'s water-filled extinct volcano, with whaling station ruins to explore. At **Paradise Island,** two-person kayaks provide some close-up penguin and iceberg inspections. **Palmer**

The most extensive cruises that take in Antarctica also include the Falkland Islands and remote South Georgia, giving travelers who have the time, money, and interest an in-depth look at the bird and animal life in the Southern Ocean, plus the Ernest Shackleton connections. The Endeavour (formerly Caledonian Star) is a fine ship for these waters.

Station is a U.S. research center that welcomes only a very few ships each year, and the scientists offer a tour to show how the base operates and to give you a look at the marine life under study in tanks. The ship also visits **Port Lockroy,** a landlocked harbor and location for a British station, for a tour and to pick up mail.

In the **Weddell Sea,** the *Endeavour* may experience pack ice, with slabs large enough to climb over, while the captain keeps watch to see that the ship does not get caught should the ice shift with a change of wind direction.

Ernest Shackleton and his crew made their longest stay on **Elephant Island** before he and a handful of men set out in a very small boat for **South Georgia.** The *Endeavour* will make up to eleven landings here at such places as **King Haakon Bay** on the west coast, where Shackleton landed, and **Peggotty Camp,** where he began his march across island to rescue his stranded crew. At **St. Andrews Bay,** on the lee side of the island, passengers may have a beach reception committee of literally thousands of king penguins, plus a herd of elephant seals that deserve a wide berth.

Grytviken is an abandoned whaling station, and the naturalists offer a two-mile hike over mountain. The settlement has a museum of South Georgia island history, remnants of the whaling activities, and the cemetery where Shackleton is buried.

Between here and the Falklands, Shag Rocks, cone-shaped protrusions rising from the sea, swarm with bird life, and here on one cruise eight right whales were sighted. On the Falklands, Port Stanley is a charming British town deep in the South Atlantic, while nearby Carcass Island offers a scenic 2.5-mile trek, at the end of which a farming family serves afternoon tea.

This is the ultimate in a South Atlantic cruise, and the passengers who come aboard are in for the best that Lindblad has to offer—the fine ship, its personnel and the expedition leader, and naturalists who share their knowledge and enthusiasm at informal presentations, meals, in Zodiacs, and ashore.

Lindblad Expeditions' *Endeavour*

Address/Phone: Lindblad Expeditions, 720 Fifth Avenue, Sixth Floor, New York, NY 10019; (212) 765–7740 or (800) 397-3348; fax: (212) 265-3370; e-mail: explore@expeditions.com; www.expeditions.com

The Ship: *Endeavour* was originally built in 1966 for the fishing industry. It was rebuilt as a cruise ship and renamed *North Star* and *Caledonian Star* before taking on the present name. The gross tonnage is 3,132, the length is 295 feet, and the draft is 21 feet.

Passengers: 113, mostly Americans, age fifty-five and up

Dress: Casual

Officers/Crew: Scandinavian officers; Filipino crew

Cabins: 61; all outside, twin beds, no verandas

Fare: $$$$

What's included: Cruise, port charges, shore excursions

What's not included: Airfare, tips, drinks

Highlights: In-depth tour of Antarctica, the Falklands, and South Georgia; Shackleton connections, naturalist staff, ambience on board

Other itineraries: Apart from this twenty-four-day cruise to Antarctica, the Falklands, and South Georgia, the *Endeavour* sails along the South America coast and in Northern Europe and the Mediterranean. The *Polaris* cruises within the Galápagos and the *Sea Lion* and *Sea Bird* cruise to Alaska, along the Columbia and Snake Rivers, along California rivers, and in the Sea of Cortez.

CIRCUMNAVIGATIONS

CUNARD LINE'S *QUEEN ELIZABETH 2*
Around the World in 106 Days

Cunard initiated annual world cruises in the 1920s, and the *QE2* has carried on the grand tradition for more than two decades. Her speed, up to 28.5 knots, means she can include more ports and stay longer than any other ship. Designed as an ocean liner, she takes the seas as well as any ship afloat, an important consideration when facing every season and type of weather.

A world cruise is a highly social experience, and the *QE2* offers so many venues for a good time. Looking to join friends for a drink before lunch or dinner? Well, there are no less than ten watering holes from which to choose. My favorite is the Chart Room, a nicely divided room where you can choose between a seat along the enclosed promenade to people watch or, more privately, away from the foot traffic. Either way, a harpist or a pianist using the *Queen Mary*'s old grand piano is there to add to the atmosphere. The Yacht Club, located all the way aft, has music before dinner, too, and is the gathering spot to meet the officers and staff when they come off duty at night. For something more informal the Golden Lion pub stocks more types of British, European, and North American beers than most people know exist.

Formal afternoon tea, including those crustless sandwiches and pastries, is served in the elegant Queens Room, which later is transformed into a proper ballroom for dancing to a full orchestra. Those old photographs showing couples bundled in steamer rugs sipping bouillon and afternoon tea come to life high up on the Sun Deck, in the shadow of the tall funnel that sports the famous Cunard Red. The library is the most elaborate for any ship, with two professional librarians in charge of the reading room, and a library shop that sells shipping books, videos, postcards, and posters.

Cunard Line represents history at sea, 160 years of it. Upon boarding, a circular mural in the Midships Lobby evokes that sense of embarking and being at sea. Artists Stephen Card and Hanley Crossley have painted the Cunard fleet in all sorts of settings on "G" Stairway, and a wonderfully cluttered case of memorabilia displays menus, brochures, souvenir spoons, and ashtrays. Passengers enjoy studying the montage of unlabeled celebrity photos and guessing who's who with others.

The *QE2* has a proper big-screen movie theater with a cozy balcony, a grand space that also hosts lectures by a well-known author, a financial analyst, or an astute Washington correspondent. On Sunday

The ultimate voyage, a circumnavigation of the globe, is an annual Queen Elizabeth 2 tradition. Sign on for the full 106 days from New York or Florida in early January or book a segment—San Francisco to Sydney or Singapore to Cape Town—to experience something of what it is like to sail on the best-known liner in the world.

morning the captain leads an interdenominational service. For active passengers the *QE2* Spa is as good as any afloat, and an indoor pool invites you to continue your exercise if the weather is not conducive to taking an open-air dip. You can hit a golf ball, play Ping-Pong, jog into head winds, and be pushed by tail winds on the Boat Deck.

Cabins come in every imaginable configuration, but if you want the most evocative accommodations afloat, choose one of the wood-paneled rooms on One Deck, which have a large elliptical window, satin walls, a walk-in closet, and a corner in which to place your standing steamer trunk. Higher up are balcony suites reached by a private entrance, and single passengers will find a selection of 105 dedicated inside and outside single cabins.

Your cabin choice determines your restaurant. Starting at the top of the ship, the two-level Queens Grill allows ordering off the menu, as do the more intimate side-facing Britannia and Princess Grills. An extra-high ceiling is a feature of the mahogany-paneled Caronia Restaurant, whose entrance is flanked by portraits of the royal family and a huge model of the 1907 Cunard speedster *Mauretania*. That great name is also the name of the ship's fifth restaurant, but the dining options do not stop there. The Lido Restaurant serves all three meals, and the Pavilion, one deck down, satisfies diners who want to stay by the pool and pair of whirlpools.

The Itinerary

Each year some first-time ports are added, but the normal route out from New York and Florida is via **Panama** and across the **Pacific;** then the ship could swing up to **Japan** or, in the case of the year 2002, drop down to **Australia.** From the **Far East** the ship may go via **Suez** and the **Mediterranean** or via **South Africa** (year 2002), then north to **England** and back across the **Atlantic.** The more than three dozen ports are often separated by one to four sea days.

A program of shore excursions is certainly helpful when visiting some of the spectacular sights in **Hawaii, Bali,** and **Cape Town,** or in intimidating ports such as **Manila, Cochin,** or **Mumbai,** but you might be quite happy going on your own in **Hong Kong, Sydney,** or **Singapore.**

Cunard Line's
Queen Elizabeth 2

Address/Phone: Cunard Line, 6100 Blue Lagoon Drive, Suite 400, Miami, FL 33126; (800) 7–CUNARD; fax: (305) 463–3010; www.cunardline.com

The Ship: *Queen Elizabeth 2* was built in 1969, has a gross tonnage of 70,327, a length of 963 feet, and a deep draft of 33 feet.

Passengers: 1,740; American, British, and Europeans, age fifty and up

Dress: Formal attire on many nights at sea, also theme, semiformal, and casual nights

Officers/Crew: British officers; international staff

Cabins: 925, sold in twenty-one wide-ranging categories; 689 outside, 150 single, and 30 with verandas. Cabin determines restaurant allocation.

Fare: $$$$

What's included: For full world-cruise passengers—first-class airfare, port charges, one precruise hotel night

What's not included: Shore excursions, drinks, tips

Highlights: The ultimate ocean voyage on the world's best-known ship

Other itineraries: In addition to the world cruise, which operates between early January to just after the middle of April, the QE2 makes six-night Atlantic crossings between New York, occasionally other U.S. ports, and Southampton, and cruises from New York to New England, Canada, and the Caribbean, and from Southampton to the British Isles, Northern Europe, Iberia, Mediterranean, and South Africa.

HOLLAND AMERICA LINE'S
ROTTERDAM AND *AMSTERDAM*
Circumnavigating the Globe

Holland America Line began operating ships in 1873 with the first *Rotterdam,* and the 1997-built ship of this name represents a larger and faster ship than those of the successful series that began with the *Statendam* in 1992. While there are some attempts at providing a continuum of features from the *Rotterdam V,* this *Rotterdam VI* is a completely new ship designed for today's market, with many more amenities and a faster service speed (25 knots) to allow for more calls and additional time in port.

Like the *Statendam*-class ships, there is an enormous range, size, and style of public rooms. The Crow's Nest on this ship is a lounge, not a disco in disguise, with three distinct sections for use as a reading-cum-dozing room during the day, a quiet bar before dinner, and a spot to dance the night away on a lighted, cracked-glass dance floor. As you walk aft, the door opens onto the vast lido deck, protected in bad weather by a roll-back roof, with a pool, a wading pool, and two octagon-shaped whirlpools. The covered, outdoor seating provides an extension to the 400-seat air-conditioned Lido Restaurant.

Most of the indoor public spaces are along the entire length of Upper Promenade and Promenade Decks. Four big production shows use the 557-seat Queens Lounge, a bi-level theater. Aft of the balcony level, one enters the three-story atrium, dominated by an elaborate replica of a seventeenth-century Flemish clock. To the side the Ocean Bar is often the social center, with a band, a dance floor, and a sit-up bar.

The Explorer's Lounge has a marble, floral-patterned dance floor, a bright red piano, and a new painting depicting the old Amsterdam waterfront. High-quality fabrics here and throughout the ship turn the eye with attractive, bold designs and colors. Also on this deck are the casino, small library, and card, puzzle, and conference rooms. For maritime buffs the six *Rotterdams* are featured in outstanding original oil paintings by Bermuda artist Stephen Card, one per landing on the forward staircase.

Promenade Deck features a 165-seat cinema and it houses the Odyssey Restaurant, an alternative Italian restaurant, formal and old-fashioned, which seats eighty-eight by reservation only. The menu makes a distinctive change from the international-style menu found in the spectacular two-level La Fontaine Dining Room, which seats 747.

The **Rotterdam** *carries one of Holland America's most famous names and is well known for making around-the-world cruises. The previous* **Rotterdam** *made twenty-nine, so the current one comes with an experienced pedigree, including many staff who know how to please on a long voyage that begins in early January and ends near the end of April. Of course, not everyone can make the complete circuit, and segments such as Los Angeles to Sydney or Singapore to New York are available. For 2002, sistership* **Amsterdam** *makes her inaugural world cruise.*

Private dining takes place in the attached Queen's Room and King's Room, the latter where the captain and hotel manager host all passengers during a world cruise. On deck there are two pools, practice tennis courts, a wide wraparound promenade, and several quiet recesses. The spa has a beauty salon, sauna, a steam room, a massage facility, and equipment that includes stationary bicycles, rowing machines, trotters, and leg and arm extenders—all with a great view over the almost invisible bow.

The 658 cabins are 80 percent outside and include an entire concierge deck with four penthouses (1,126 square feet) and thirty-six veranda suites (565 square feet), with a private reception lounge and writing room tucked in. The Verandah Deck comprises 121 veranda minisuites—long, narrow rooms with twin or queen beds, sofa, chair, stool, coffee table, vanity-cum-desk, minibar, fridge, and TV/VCR. The standard staterooms occupy three complete lower decks; those on Lower Promenade face the open deck, and some, marked on the plans, have partially obstructed views.

This new *Rotterdam,* loaded with artworks, is a cut above the popular and successful *Statendam*-class in spaciousness, improved layout, and speed.

The Itinerary

Every year the world cruise offers a fresh itinerary, and in the year 2002 the *Amsterdam* will be sailing westward on a creative one-hundred-day itinerary. Officially, the cruise begins in **Los Angeles,** but passengers may board in **Fort Lauderdale** sixteen days earlier for the trans-canal segment including eight ports of call in the **Southern Caribbean** and on the west coast of **Central America** and **Mexico.**

From Los Angeles, the ship sails via **Hawaii (Honolulu** and **Kona)** and the **South Pacific** to five ports in **New Zealand,** four ports via the bottom of **Australia** to **Indonesia,** the **Philippines,** and **Hong Kong.** Southeast Asian ports include **Da Nang, Sihanoukville, Singapore, Port Klang (Kuala Lumpur),** and **Phuket,** then across the Indian Ocean to **Mumbai (Bombay)** and into the Persian Gulf to **Dubai** and **Muscat.** Red Sea ports are **Jeddah (Saudi Arabia)** and **Sharm el Sheik (Sinai)** and following the daylight **Suez** transit, **Alexandria** for **Cairo, Israel, Santorini, Naples, Civitavecchia (Rome), Ajaccio, Barcelona, Cadiz,** and via **Funchal** to **New York** and **Fort Lauderdale.**

Holland America Line's
Rotterdam and *Amsterdam*

Address/Phone: Holland America Line, 300 Elliott Avenue West, Seattle, WA 98119; (800) 426–0327, fax: (206) 281–7110; www.hollandamerica.com

The Ship: *Rotterdam* was completed in 1997 and has a gross tonnage of 59,652. *Amsterdam* was completed in 2000 and has a gross tonnage of 61,000. Both have a length of 778 feet and a draft of 25 feet.

Passengers: *Rotterdam* 1,320; *Amsterdam* 1,380; mostly Americans, age sixty and up

Dress: Formal, informal, casual, and theme nights

Officers/Crew: Dutch officers; Indonesian and Filipino crew

Cabins: *Rotterdam* 660; 542 outside and 160 with verandas. *Amsterdam* 690, 557 outside and 172 with verandas

Fare: $$$

What's included: Cruise only, tips included but most will add to this

What's not included: Airfare, port charges, drinks, shore excursions

Highlights: Classy, beautifully decorated ships and a most unusual itinerary

Other itineraries: In addition to the world cruise, operating between early January and late April, Holland America's large fleet covers the globe, including Alaska, the Panama Canal, and South America.

P&O CRUISES' *ORIANA*

Sailing around the World: British Style

The official name of the line is a mouthful—The Peninsular and Oriental Steam Navigation Company—but people in the know simply say "P&O." The company dates back to 1837, three years before Samuel Cunard launched his transatlantic mail and passenger service. P&O expanded with the British Empire, east via Suez to India, to colonies in Asia, Australia, and New Zealand. London-based P&O is the parent company of Princess Cruises.

The 69,000-ton *Oriana* entered service in 1995, maintaining the tradition of offering a wide range of public rooms (seventeen) to satisfy all tastes and lifestyles. If your preference is for after-dinner coffee and a liqueur in genteel surroundings, the living room atmosphere of Anderson's, one of P&O's founding fathers, will suit. Evening classical concerts take place in the chandeliered Curzon Room, while extravaganzas debut in the Theater Royal and nightclub acts come alive in the Pacific Lounge. Monte Carlo is the casino, small by American standards, and Harlequins is the disco. For a pint of ale, Lord's Tavern has a cricketing theme; for readers and dozers the Thackery Room has comfortable wing chairs, and the library has lots of books. Crichton's is the largest card room at sea, and bridge instruction and dance classes are always offered.

My favorite room has always been P&O's Crows Nest. On the *Oriana* it is a superb spacious forward observation bar/lounge, with a trio playing and singing before and after dinner. The centerpiece is a 6-foot builders' model of the *Ranpura*, one of P&O's 1920s liners built for the colonial run to Bombay. P&O owns an outstanding art collection, and oil paintings, water colors, needlepoint tapestries, and historic documents are to be found throughout the ship.

British food has its own reputation, but it has come a long way in the last decade, and the *Oriana*'s menus and presentation are no exception. The great British breakfast has never been criticized except for offering too much to eat so early in the day. Don't count on lots of pasta dishes, as on Princess ships, or even dinner salads, as the British eat rabbit food at lunch. The cream soups are excellent, and so is the roast beef and lamb, as one might expect. Desserts are delicious, and the daily lunchtime curry is a great favorite. On formal nights nearly every British male dons a dinner jacket, and the women appear in all manner of ball gowns. Officers are British and host tables at dinner, whereas the well-trained service staff is mostly Indian, many from Goa. Besides two main restaurants, breakfast and

The World Cruise is an annual staple for the stately Oriana, and no one does it any better than P&O, the oldest shipping company on the high seas. This global voyage is a kind of English-speaking union catering to British, Australians, New Zealanders, and North Americans, but it still helps to be an Anglophile to appreciate the decidedly English atmosphere. Embarkation for most Americans is Southampton for 2002, with disembarkation in San Francisco, but the complete three-month global route starts and finishes up in England.

lunch are also available in the Conservatory, which has both indoor and outdoor seating.

With the company's long history of taking families to jobs and new lives overseas, the children's facilities are outstanding. An entire area, devoted to various age levels, includes a large indoor and outdoor play-room, a games arcade, a cinema, a paddle pool, a swimming pool, a Jacuzzi, and even a night nursery for late-night parents.

A wide range of cabin types features 114 dedicated single cabins—a rarity in the modern cruise industry but a P&O tradition—that are available on six passenger decks. For example, a B-category double has a balcony, a sitting area, lots of storage space, a generous-size bathroom with tub, plus amenities such as TV and refrigerator. Economical four-berth cabins are booked by families.

The *Oriana* offers acres of open-deck space plus golf, cricket, and football (read soccer) nets, deck tennis, deck quoits, shuffleboard, and two adult pools and Jacuzzis. On every voyage the British officers take on the passengers at a cricket match. The wide promenade offers deck chairs, with lifeboats above giving shade and a view of a steady stream of humanity doing counterclockwise constitutionals before and after breakfast.

The Itinerary

Round-the-world cruises alter itineraries every year to keep loyalists happy, and, on this ship, ports often take second place to life onboard. Every cruise carries a port lecturer, an entertaining type with a British sense of humor. Some passengers take the entire voyage, three months plus, although most book segments of a couple of weeks to a month or more.

The *Oriana* invariably leaves **Southampton,** England, in early January, and in 2002 sails eastward via the **Mediterranean** to **Egypt** and the **Suez Canal, Oman, India, Southeast Asia,** and **Hong Kong,** then south via the **Philippines** and **Indonesia** to ports in **Australia,** where many disembark to stay with friends and relations, and others, especially Australians, board for the voyage to Europe to visit their roots.

The trans-Pacific portion sails via **New Zealand, Tonga, American Samoa,** and **Hawaii** to **San Francisco,** then via **Acapulco,** the **Panama Canal,** and three **Caribbean** ports to **Madeira** and **Southampton,** arriving back in early April, having called at thirty ports.

P&O Cruises' *Oriana*

Phone: P&O Cruises, (011) 44 171 800 2556 or (800) 340–7674; www.pocruises.com. Also Golden Bear Travel (800) 551–1000.

The Ship: *Oriana* was built in 1995, has a gross tonnage of 69,153, a length of 853 feet, and a draft of 25.9 feet.

Passengers: 1,828; all ages, but older on longer cruises; a mix of British, Australians, Americans, and some Europeans

Dress: Formal and informal nights onboard; casual in port

Officers/Crew: British officers; mostly Indian hotel staff; Pakistani deck and engine crew

Cabins: 914, with a wide range of configurations; 114 singles, 110 four-berth, 118 verandas

Fare: $$$

What is included: Cruise only unless part of a package

What's not included: Airfare, port charges, shore excursions, drinks, and tips

Highlights: Very British atmosphere, lots of activities, and a beautifully operated ship

Other itineraries: In addition to the annual world cruise, the *Oriana* offers spring-to-early winter nonrepeating cruises of from nine days to three weeks from Southampton, England, to northern European ports, the Atlantic islands, and the Mediterranean. P&O operates the *Arcadia,* formerly Princess Cruises' *Star Princess;* the traditional *Victoria,* formerly the *Kungsholm,* which will leave the fleet in late 2002; and the *Aurora,* this latter also making a world cruise westbound from England via Panama, San Francisco, the Pacific, Australia, Southeast Asia, South Africa, South America, and back to England from early January to early April 2002.

APPENDIX

SHIPS BY SIZE

Small Ships take up to 400 passengers, double occupancy, and include all the expedition-style vessels, riverboats (except the two largest Mississippi sternwheelers), and coastal cruise vessels and most of the super luxurious boutique ships:

Midsize Ships, taking from 400 to 1,000 passengers, are relatively few in number and include some of the ferry liners (total passenger capacity) and a few of the top luxury ships:

Large Ships carrying more than 1,000 passengers include most of the megaships that also appear in the City at Sea category, those that will appeal to families, and several of the largest Scandinavian ferry liners. The largest, including more on order, exceed 2,500 passengers when all berths are occupied, and a few even top 3,000 (not including crews numbering 1,000).

TYPES OF CRUISES

Expedition-style Cruises

Some of the best destination-oriented cruises take place aboard small expedition vessels offering what are often called soft adventure or naturalist cruises. These explore remote and exotic parts of the globe such as the Arctic, Antarctica, the Upper Amazon, and Australia's Great Barrier Reef. Some incorporate a distinctive interest in the local culture, and often the lines invite experts in natural history, ecology, anthropology, and wildlife to give enrichment talks aboard ship and to accompany passengers ashore.

Cultural Enrichment Cruises

While a number of expedition-style cruises carrying a lecture staff have some cultural orientation, the list here includes those that emphasize the region through which they are sailing, with onboard experts in the fields of history, politics, and archaeology.

Cruising under Sail

Sailing ships often draw people who would not otherwise take a standard big ship cruise. These ships also operate with diesel engines when winds are not favorable and for maneuvering in port.

Super Luxury

Some high-end ships offer all-suite accommodations and the very best food and service afloat. Most are relatively small and take 300 passengers or fewer, but there are exceptions in the midsize category and aboard the Queen Elizabeth 2 when booking grill-class accommodations.

Cruising with Children

Families traveling with children can enjoy a wide variety of activities, including separate supervised areas catering to several age levels. Most lines provide baby-sitting services, and some British ships have matrons to look after very small children and an early sitting for supper. Overnight ferry cruises are fun for children, offering informal dining and playrooms and games arcades aboard Scandinavian ships. A few soft adventure–type cruises are included for their orientation toward water activities.

Honeymooners and Romantics

Many lines have honeymoon packages, and the captains of the *Grand Princess* and the *Golden Princess* can perform civil marriage ceremonies. The hopelessly romantic will also enjoy the sail cruisers.

Cruising with Foreigners

Sailing with different nationalities can be an enriching experience, especially in European waters. On a few ships, Americans may be in the minority, but all languages will be equally catered for. Some ships, as indicated, may carry mostly British or German-speaking passengers, and a few may be English-speaking unions (ESU) of Americans, British, Australians, New Zealanders, and South Africans.

Cities at Sea

The largest ships afloat are virtual urban centers with many activities, varied entertainment, large casinos, shopping malls, acres of deck space, several outdoor pools and whirlpools, elaborate health and fitness spas, and multiple dining options.

No Mal de Mer

Seasickness does affect some passengers and is a worry for others, so we are listing those ships navigating rivers and inshore waters that are less likely to cause any upset stomachs. Those marked * also offer some itineraries with short open sea stretches.

INDEX

PHOTO CREDITS

Many thanks to the following people and cruise lines for providing photos: pp. 1, 20 top, and 100: Cruise West; pp. 2, 65–67, 202, and 237: Cunard Line; p. 5: Regal Cruises; pp. 6–7: Scotia Prince Cruises; pp. 9–10, 95, 105–6, 129, 146–48, 235, 238, and 240: Holland America Line; pp. 12, 62, 74–75, 180, and 242: Princess Cruises; pp. 14–15: Norwegian Cruise Line; pp. 16–17, 152–54, 170–71, 216–17, 218 right, 225, and 228–29: Radisson Seven Seas Cruises; p. 19: Andrew Kilk; pp. 21–22 and 96–97: Alaska's Glacier Bay Tours & Cruises; p. 26: BC Ferries; pp. 28, 29 top, 34 bottom, 35, and 39: American Canadian Caribbean Line; pp. 32, 33 left, and 230: Clipper Cruise Line; pp. 37–38, 41–44, and 52: Delta Queen Steamboat Co.; pp. 45–46: RiverBarge Excursion Lines; pp. 47–48, 226–27, and 231 right: © Wolfgang Kaehler/Clipper Cruise Line; pp. 49 and 206: Lindblad Expeditions; pp. 50 top and 232–33: Ralph Lee Hopkins/Lindblad Expeditions; pp. 53–55: St. Lawrence Cruise Lines; pp. 56 and 57 bottom: Ontario Waterway Cruises; p. 59: Michael and Melodie Foster; pp. 60 and 80–81: Celebrity Cruises; p. 70 top: © GTP Miami/Star Clippers; pp. 69, 70 bottom, and 214: © Harvey Lloyd/ Star Clippers; pp. 71 and 87–88: Windstar Cruises/Harvey Lloyd; p. 72: © 2001 The Walt Disney Company; p. 73: © 2000 The Walt Disney Company; pp. 76–79: Andy Newman/Carnival Cruise Lines; pp. 82–83, 98–99, 130, and 132: Royal Caribbean International; pp. 84–86: Sea Cloud Cruises; pp.91–92: Windjammer Barefoot Cruises; pp. 93–94: W. Bradford Hatry; p. 101: Suellyn P. Scull; pp. 102 and 156–57: Crystal Cruises; p. 104: Andy Newman/Holland American Line; pp. 107–9 and 178–79: Abercrombie & Kent; pp. 112–14: © Len Kaufman/Royal Olympic Cruises; pp. 115–16: Canodros; p. 117 top: © Ralph Hammelbacher/Lindblad Expeditions; p. 117 bottom: Kevin Shaffer/Lindblad Expeditions; pp. 119–20 and 219–20: Seabourn Cruise Line; pp. 121, 123, 140, 142, 199, and 210: Orient Lines; pp. 124, 138, 204, and 205 right: Silversea Cruises; pp. 126–27: Cruceros Australis; pp. 129 and 143–45: American Hawaii Cruises; pp. 149–51, 182–83, and 190: Renaissance Cruises; p. 155: Silja Line; pp. 158 and 159 bottom: Hebridean Island Cruises; pp. 160: Charles Tate/P&O Scottish Ferries; pp. 162, 166, and 167 top: Norwegian Coastal Voyage Inc.; p. 164: W. J. Mayes; p.167 bottom: Nick Nicholson/Norwegian Coastal Voyage Inc.; pp. 169 and 197: Swan Hellenic; pp. 172–73 and 175: Peter Deilmann Cruises; p. 174: W. Walter Hayum/Peter Deilmann Cruises; p. 175: Peter Deilmann Cruises; p. 176: KD River Cruises of Europe; p. 192: Royal Olympia Cruises; p. 194 top: Tim Thompson/Windstar Cruises; p. 194 bottom: Windstar Cruises/Gerald Brimacombe; p. 195: Nick Nicholson/Windstar Cruises; pp. 213 and 221–22: Victoria Cruises; pp. 223–24: Regal China Cruises; p. 239: © 2000 Michael Verdure/Holland America Line; p. 241: P&O Cruises; and images by Photodisk.

The following photos are by the author: pp. v, 20 bottom, 23–26, 27 bottom, 29 bottom, 30, 31 bottom right, 34 top, 36, 64, 68, 89, 110–11, 122, 125, 131, 133–36, 139, 141, 159 top, 161, 168, 181, 184, 185 bottom, 186+89, 191, 193, 196, 201–2, 203, 205 left, 208–9, 211, 215 top, 218 left, 231 left, and 236.

ABOUT THE AUTHOR

Theodore W. Scull has spent three and a half years at sea on ocean liners, expeditions vessels, sailing ships, riverboats, and overnight ferries from Alaska to Zanzibar. He is contributing (cruise) editor for *Travel Holiday*; writes for nearly every issue of *Cruise Travel*; and edits a regular column—"Cruise Ship Review"—for *Ships Monthly* in England. He has written for Internet sites, including Expedia.com and Cruisemates.com. He has also written five other books on travel and transportation. He and his wife, Suellyn, are longtime residents of Manhattan.

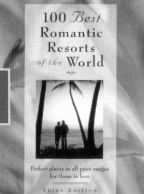

100 BEST

So many choices . . . so little time.

Let our guides introduce
you to the very finest in travel
experiences and accommodations,
and decide for yourself which best
suits your needs and interests.

Travel doesn't get any better than this!